Old roots in new
lands

DATE DUE

OLD ROOTS IN
NEW LANDS

Recent Titles in
CONTRIBUTIONS IN AFRO-AMERICAN AND AFRICAN STUDIES
SERIES ADVISER: Hollis R. Lynch

Ebony Kinship: Africa, Africans, and the Afro-American
Robert G. Weisbord

Slavery and Race Relations in Latin America
Robert Brent Toplin, editor

No Crystal Stair: Black Life and the *Messenger,* 1917-1928
Theodore Kornweibel, Jr.

"Good Time Coming?": Black Nevadans in the Nineteenth Century
Elmer R. Rusco

Race First: Ideological and Organizational Struggles of Marcus Garvey and the Universal Negro Improvement Association
Tony Martin

Silence to the Drums: A Survey of the Literature of the Harlem Renaissance
Margaret Perry

Internal Combustion: The Races in Detroit, 1915-1926
David Allan Levine

Henry Sylvester Williams and the Origins of the Pan African Movement, 1869-1911
Owen Charles Mathurin

Periodic Markets, Urbanization, and Regional Planning: A Case Study from Western Kenya
Robert A. Obudho and Peter P. Waller

Frederick Douglass on Women's Rights
Philip S. Foner, editor

Travail and Triumph: Black Life and Culture in the South Since the Civil War
Arnold H. Taylor

Red Over Black: Black Slavery Among the Cherokee Indians
R. Halliburton, Jr.

New Rulers in the Ghetto: The Community Development Corporation and Urban Poverty
Harry Edward Berndt

The FLN in Algeria: Party Development in a Revolutionary Society
Henry F. Jackson

OLD ROOTS IN
NEW LANDS
————HISTORICAL AND ANTHROPOLOGICAL PERSPECTIVES ON BLACK EXPERIENCES IN THE AMERICAS——

edited by ANN M. PESCATELLO

CONTRIBUTIONS IN AFRO-AMERICAN AND AFRICAN STUDIES, NUMBER 31

 GREENWOOD PRESS
Westport, Connecticut . London, England

Library of Congress Cataloging in Publication Data
Main entry under title:

Old roots in new lands.

(Contributions in Afro-American and African studies ; no. 31)
Bibliography: p.
Includes index.
1. Blacks—Caribbean area—Addresses, essays, lectures. 2. Blacks—South American—
Addresses, essays, lectures. I. Pescatello, Ann M. II. Series.
F2191.B55042   972.9'004'96   76-50409
ISBN 0-8371-9476-8

Library of Congress Catalog Card Number: 76-50409
ISBN: 0-8371-9476-8

First published in 1977

Greenwood Press, Inc.
51 Riverside Avenue, Westport, Connecticut 06880

Printed in the United States of America

Contents

FOR BLACK PEOPLE—

Who Have Been Able to Endure the World of the Whites

Maps and Illustrations

Tables

Contributors

ROGER ABRAHAMS is one of the world's leading folkorists. He is the author of innumerable reviews and articles, and has written and edited several volumes, including *Deep Down in the Jungle, Anglo-American Folksong Style* (with George Foss), and *Deep the Water, Shallow the Shore.* Formerly the director of Afro-American Studies at the University of Texas, Austin, he is presently the chairman of the Department of English at that university.

MICHAEL CRATON is a leading expert on cultures and societies of the British Caribbean (West Indies). He is the author of several articles and reviews, and has also authored or co-authored several books, among them *History of the Bahamas, A Jamaican Plantation* (with James Walvin), *Sinews of Empire, A Short History of British Slavery,* and *Searching for the Invisible Man.* He is professor of History, University of Waterloo, Ontario, Canada.

MARY W. HELMS' major research interst has been in the cultures and societies of the Spanish-speaking Caribbean areas, particularly Central America. She is the author of several articles and two books that focus on these interests. Among the books are *Asang: Adaptation to Culture Contact in a Miskito Community* and *Middle America: A Culture History of Heartland and Frontiers.* She is lecturer in Anthropology at Northwestern University, Chicago.

MARY C. KARASCH is a student of Brazilian history and Afro-Latin American subcultures within Latin America. She is the author of several articles on this subject and of a forthcoming book, *Slave Life in Rio de Janeiro, 1808-1850.* She is associate professor of History at Oakland University, Michigan.

DOUGLASS MIDGETT has undertaken most of his research work in the British Caribbean cultures. He is the author of several articles dealing with biculturalism, identity, and bilingualism. His forthcoming book, *Struggling Man,* is concerned with the migration of West Indian males to Great Britain. He is assistant professor of Anthropology at the University of Iowa.

MICHAEL D. OLIEN has particular interest in methodological problems of ethnohistory and in the cultural ecology of Afro-American and especially Central American societies. He is the author of several articles on these subjects and has written several books such as *The The Negro in Costa Rica: The Role of an Ethnic Minority in a Developing Society* and *Latin Americans: Contemporary Peoples and Their Cultural Traditions.* He is associate professor of Anthropology, University of Georgia.

ANN M. PESCATELLO is concerned with social groups and cultural anthropology as it relates to areas of Latin America, Africa, and Asia in the Iberian Empire. She is the author of several major articles, the editor of and contributor to *Female and Male in Latin America. Essays* and *The African in Latin America,* and the author of *Power and Pawn. Females in Iberian Families, Cultures, and Societies.* She is director of the Council of Intercultural and Comparative Studies and senior research associate, University of California, Berkeley.

E. EDWARD PIERCE has undertaken most of his research work in the Guianas which are on the South American mainland but rim the Caribbean. He is the author of several articles that focus on personal networks and ethnographic surveys in Afro-Creole social organization and is completing a book on social organization in Paramaribo, Surinam. He is assistant professor of Anthropology, State University College of New York.

NORMAN E. WHITTEN, Jr. is one of today's foremost scholars on Afro-Hispanic studies, on social organization in Afro-American societies and cultures, and on personal networks studies. He is the author of numerous articles and the author and editor of several books, among them *Class, Kinship, and Power in an Ecuadorian Town: The Negroes of San Lorenzo, Black Frontiersmen: A South American Case, Sacha Runa: Ethnicity and Adaptation of Ecuadorian Jungle Quicha* (with Dorothea Whitten), and *Afro-American Anthropology: Contemporary Perspectives* (edited with John Szwed. He is professor of Anthropology, University of Illinois.

Preface

An exhaustive study of the Afro-American experience would be so massive an undertaking that it could not be accommodated within the structure of a single book. Even if time frames, geographic areas, and topics were limited, the printed results would still reflect an arbitrary and selective commentary. This difficulty is in part a function of the complex nature of the African heritage and the black experience during slavery, and of the enormous varieties in the experiences of slave and free after abolition in the Americas.

It would seem that all of this variety and complexity would have generated shelves of publications on the subject. While there are numerous volumes on the blacks in North America, few deal with Afro-American experiences in Latin America and the Caribbean. This scholarly imbalance is unfortunate, for the black experience in the United States has not been nearly so important in the total development of the Americas as that in Latin America and the Caribbean. (See Tables 1 and 2 in the first essay.)

The contributors to this volume have examined some perceptions and praxis derivative from the African diaspora. There are conflicting views on the results of that diaspora from Africa. A major theory, which some scholars still support, is that the Afro-American has no past.[1] That view, first challenged decades ago by Melville Herskovits, has been steadfastly attacked.[2] A growing number of sophisticated studies is supporting the Herskovits theory and demonstrating conclusively that Afro-Americans are African as well as European in their cultural heritages and forms.[3]

This reaffirmation of Herskovits's theory is important not merely for its content, but also for the new directions it takes in conceptualization and methodology. In seeking to disprove the myth that Africans in the New World had no past, Herskovits was concerned with surface phenomena, identifying survivals and retentions of the African past. His ethnography focused on what were specifically Africanisms rather than the totality of their cultural milieus. The approach used in the new studies is more sophisticated than Herskovits's because it has built on decades of research and technique developments which his work generated. In essence, the neo-Herskovitsian studies have centered on what Sidney Mintz calls "a 'grammar' of African cultures, . . . renewed attention to the dynamics of change . . . identifying more fundamental stylistic and cognitive features of that past, and at systematizing methodologies for further work."[4]

The essays presented here reflect our commitment to the theory that Afro-Americans do have a substantive and rich African heritage and that African styles and forms have persisted. Our commitment to that theory is qualified by the varied and often unpleasant circumstances of the black experience in the Americas. Nonetheless, each essay defines fundamental stylistic and cognitive features, whether in labor devices, modes of resistance, family organization, performance practices, or the like.

The overriding theme of this work is the complex of similarities and differences in the Afro-American experience and the variety and richness of the Afro-American's historical past and present. In the still amorphous area of African diaspora studies for the Caribbean and Latin America, topics and time frames are arbitrary. Our topical format has been to document and to analyze several kinds of black experiences and their impact on selected Latin American and Caribbean societies, cultures, and subcultures. Some of these were chosen because of their preestablished importance in the schema of Afro-American studies. Others were chosen because little, if any, published material is available on their socio-environmental contexts for black experiences. The time frame was arbitrarily "limited" to the nineteenth and twentieth centuries.

The essays in this volume fulfill several purposes. First, they demonstrate the increasingly varied and sophisticated methodology available to students of historical and contemporary ethnic studies. In addition, they highlight the crossover value of research conducted in different disciplines in different time frames. Also, they draw attention to previously neglected geographical areas and social dimensions, thus expanding our supply of examples and enriching our comparative perspective. Finally, these essays suggest both the possibilities for generalization and the dangers involved in such attempts.

Just what is an Afro-American? For the purposes of this work, Roger Abrahams' concept of the Afro-American has been adopted: that is, one who is part of an Afro-American culture, which is a unique configuration of cultural traits. An Afro-American community is a community that defines itself as Afro-American regardless of whether there is mixed blood. The more specific terms Afro-Hispanic, Afro-Brazilian, and Afro-Caribbean carry the above concepts into the context of geographically or linguistically defined areas.

The first essay presents an overview of five centuries of Afro-American history and sets the historical perspective for the essays that follow. It emphasizes four elements: the African heritage of slavery, the Atlantic slave trade, the variegated life and labor of Afro-Americans within the south Atlantic system, and the persistence of old patterns and the reinforcement of new ones.

The next two studies deal with Brazil in the nineteenth century. From 1800 to 1870 an estimated 1.35 million Africans were introduced into Brazil both legally and illegally. Focusing on the southern half of that country, specifically Rio de Janeiro, Mary Karasch analyzes various newly recruited Afro-American groups in that capital city. Karasch discusses their adaptation to their new roles in slavery, their resistance to the institution, and how their experiences as slaves in Rio conditioned them for their new existence as free persons.

Ann Pescatello examines the range of nineteenth-century modes of re-actions to slavery in Brazil, particularly in the northern half of the country. The various ways by which slaves dealt with their condition of servitude are put into the historical context of Brazilian slavery. Types of resistance, their location, and the timing of their occurrence provide a basis for conclusions on the nature of race relations in contemporary Brazil.

From Brazil, which is perhaps the most analyzed geographic area of black experience in South America we move up the eastern coast of Latin America to one of the least analyzed areas, Surinam (formerly Dutch Guiana). In his essay, Edward Pierce studies the densely populated coastal settlements, using some critical characteristics of Afro-American populations to analyze the experience of the Nengre, or lower status Creoles, of coastal Surinam. In order to clarify dimensions of dynamics and change, Pierce focuses on family organization within the framework of an ethnohistorical analysis.

The following two essays center on Central America, an important region in the Caribbean that is often neglected in the scholarship on the blacks. Michael Olien examines a society known for its "white-ness"—Costa Rica—and the adaptation of West Indians to that society. As a case in point, Olien has chosen Limón province which encom-passes the entire eastern coastline in Costa Rica, from Nicaragua to Panama, and which also includes most of the eastern lowland hinter-land. One of Olien's conclusions is that the blacks in Costa Rica under-went a different adaptation process from that experienced by blacks in other parts of Latin America. Blacks in Costa Rica adapted first to North American culture; their integration into Costa Rican society began only after the United Fruit Company abandoned the eastern lowlands in 1942.

Mary Helms discusses the Miskito of coastal Central America, par-ticularly the areas of eastern Nicaragua and eastern Honduras, and gives particular attention to the problem of culture identity and culture patterns. Her Miskito peoples are in sharp contrast to the black Caribs of Belize (British Honduras) and Honduras and to the West Indians of Costa Rica. Her findings reveal an ethnic community which began as a mix of African and Amerindian and which, through culture contact, has lost almost all of its African identity.

Following these three essays on racial identity in the peripheral Caribbean is Roger Abrahams' work on the range of black folk cul-ture, and retentions and adaptations in it. He states that, although these retentions and adaptations are selective, they are crucial to an understanding of institutions which the blacks adopted in their New World environments and thus elucidate their total experiences under slavery. Abrahams maintains that the focus and uses of the tea cere-mony in the West Indies (former British Caribbean) were changed along with some aspects of the pattern of performance. These changes, he contends, were in accord with the ethical and aesthetic demands of a conceptual system shared by Africans and Afro-Americans.

One of the major avenues of Afro-American cultural expression is the literature of the Caribbean, which is rich and extensive in substance and scope. Douglas Midgett gives the historical and literary dimensions to complement Abrahams' anthropological, linguistic, and folkloric dimensions of the entire West Indian experience. Midgett examines several themes in West Indian literature including historical and con-temporary identity, and the relationship of the people to the land and to their African backgrounds. He is particularly interested in the con-nection between literature and history and in how they can be inter-preted in terms of national identity.

In one of the few studies available on Afro-Hispanic cultures, Norman Whitten focuses on another area of dynamics and change—that of sex and sex roles. Whitten examines several crucial patterns and sexual relationships in the Pacific Lowlands of Colombia and Ecuador, the two countries in Spanish South America with the largest Afro-American communities. He outlines the daily life of the slave in these countries and contemporary views of continuity and change in light of the Afro-Hispanic world view.

A perplexing problem in attempting to restructure black folk culture is the lack of reliable data from blacks. In his methodological essay, Michael Craton presents the results of his oral history investigations in an attempt to retrieve pre-abolition black pasts. In so doing, he suggests the limited reliability of oral testimony in providing information on a specific historical experience.

This volume should be viewed as a point of departure rather than as a definitive statement on the black experience in the Americas. Hopefully, it will expose students and teachers, and perhaps laymen, to new data, concepts, and methods for studying black history. Hopefully, too, readers in Latin American, Caribbean, United States, and Afro-American history will use this work to make comparisons of the black experience in one area with that elsewhere in the Americas.

I thank the contributors not only for their essays but also for their ideas and help in structuring this volume. My appreciation is also extended to several friends in fields with related interests who have been generous with their time and suggestions. They include Sidney Mintz, Franklin Knight, Donald Warren, Bonnie C. Wade, and Carl Degler, all of whom made valuable suggestions on methodology and offered insightful ideas and criticisms. And to Clem, I am indebted for love and faith.

Ann M. Pescatello

NOTES

1. The works of E. Franklin Frazier and H. Orlando Patterson reflect some of the earliest and latest support for that point of view.

2. Beginning with Herskovits and reflected later in the works of W. R. Bascom, Pierre Verger, Janheinz Jahn, E. K. Braithwaite, George Simpson, and others.

3. See, for example, the work of Richard and Sally Price, Ralph Ellison, Dell Hymes, Douglas MacRae Taylor, Roger Abrahams, and the late Roger Bastide for Latin America and the Caribbean. For the United States newly accessible are the latest works of the Cliometricians in the quantitative study of economists Robert W. Fogel and Stanley Engerman's *Time on the Cross,* Engerman and Eugene Genovese's *Race and Slavery in the Western Hemisphere: Quantitative Studies,* and Genovese's *Roll, Jordan, Roll.* (See the Bibliography at the end of this volume.)

4. Sidney W. Mintz, "The Caribbean Region," in *Daedalus* (Spring 1974): 56-57.

OLD ROOTS IN
NEW LANDS

1

Ann M. Pescatello

THE AFRO-AMERICAN IN
HISTORICAL PERSPECTIVE

This essay defines some major historical parameters relevant to the Afro-American experience. The information and ideas to be discussed are ordered into four categories. The first deals with the African heritage of slavery, including the provenience patterns of slavery through time after the start of Euro-African operations; the social, economic, and political relations of Africans among themselves and with Europeans; and slavery as it functioned in African societies.

The second category concerns the Atlantic slave trade. Points considered include the number of slaves involved, the way the trade functioned, and the supremacy of plantations, especially those devoted to raising sugar, as the persistent basis for slavery.

Under the third section is an overview of the south Atlantic system, i.e., the enterprise which involved African labor, European merchandising, and American production. The system of slavery is seen as a variegated one. Views regarding the lack of resistance to slavery throughout most of the Americas are presented, and the role of free blacks and mulattoes in the Americas is discussed.

The final section is devoted to the Afro-American milieus. Under "Old Patterns Remembered" several concepts that functioned in Africa and persisted in America are highlighted. Under "New Patterns Reinforced" is an examination of what happened to the newly freed slave, the attitudes engendered, and the overall pattern of life fostered by these attitudes and economic and social deprivation.

4 Ann M. Pescatello

THE AFRICAN HERITAGE OF SLAVERY: SOCIAL, ECONOMIC, AND POLITICAL CONDITIONS IN THE HOMELAND

In Africa, slavery and slave trading solely among African groups can be documented from the eleventh century. This form of labor was needed primarily to meet the demands of an expanding trade within and outside of Africa.[1] From that time we can also document the development of sophisticated polities along with or in response to the rationalization of economic and social organization.

Arabs, other Middle Eastern groups, and Asian peoples had become involved in African slaving operations at least as early as the eleventh century A.D., but the earliest record of European involvement is 1444. The Portuguese, who had made systematic probes, developed an African commerce and made occasional slave raids along the coast for purposes of permanent occupation. After 1444, Africans from the coasts were carried as slaves over sea routes; this date marks the inauguration of modern traffic in Africans. Since it is the Euro-African relationships in slavery that concern us here, our story will proceed from the mid-fifteenth century.

Provenience patterns in chronological sequence are extremely complicated to follow.[2] It is difficult to determine exactly when shifts in the preference for one group rather than another occur. Determining subtle changes in the composition of slave recruits presents several problems. One complication is that terminology shifted through time. Typologies of groups have varied according to the century of the ethnographer. Individuals might be identified under several rubrics such as place of origin or place from which the slave was shipped. Some terms designating shipments were catchalls; an ethnic or linguistic term used to identify a large group might be applied to others not in that group but shipped with that group. The preferences for Africans, however, were usually quite rational. For example, in American mining areas, efforts were made to secure workers from sections of Africa noted for mining technology. Similarly, in Brazilian tobacco-growing areas, attempts were made to obtain workers who were knowledgeable in the techniques of tobacco-raising. Thus, sudden shifts in demand, arbitrary changes in terminology, procedural alterations in management of the trade, and other elements contribute to the seemingly disjunctive shifts in preference for one group over another. This problem is emphasized here because it is basic to any attempt to trace African heritages in the New World. Table 1 indicates shifts and supplies of slaves through time.

Beginning in the mid-fifteenth century, the dominant slave-exporting region was the *Guine de Cabo Verde,* an area that encompasses present-day Senegal to Sierra Leone. Almost all of this traffic went to Europe (see Table 1). Sixteenth-century African societies from which Europeans derived labor supplies were from the same Senegambia-Guinea-Bissau-Sierra Leone areas and south of the Congo's mouth.

The Atlantic slave trade, which had been underway for some time, did not really acquire momentum until the second quarter of the seventeenth century when plantation systems took root in America. The seventeenth and eighteenth centuries witnessed the rise of prosperous slavetrading city-states in the Niger Delta and along the Dahomey Coast, while the Guinea-Gold Coast-Senegambia commerce underwent tremendous expansion. In the seventeenth century, also, peoples from present-day Angola and Zaire were chief sources for the trade.

The eighteenth century was the apex of the Atlantic slave trade. The trade drew its sources primarily from eight regions: Senegambia (Gambia and Senegal), scarcely changed from its sixteenth-century status; Sierra Leone (but including the coastlines of Guinea-Conakry, Guinea-Bissau, and small parts of Senegal and Liberia); Ivory Coast and Liberia (or eighteenth-century "Windward Coast"); Ghana ("Gold Coast"); Bight of Benin (everything from the Volta to the Benin river, the eighteenth-century core of which was known as the "slave coast" or Togo and Dahomey); Bight of Biafra (centered on the Niger Delta from Benin River on the west to present-day Gabon in the south); Central Africa (or Angola); and southeastern Africa (from the Cape of Good Hope to Cape Delgado, including Madagascar Island (also known as Moçambique).

In the nineteenth century, African sources for slaves followed previous patterns, with some changes. The Angolan sources diminished somewhat, but more slaves were available from southeastern Africa. The main supply areas were Sierra Leone, the Bights of Benin and Biafra, Congo North, Angola, and Moçambique.

What was the nature of these African societies with whom Europeans forged such lucrative deals in human merchandise? What relationship did they have to each other and to the various Europeans?

TABLE 1

Slave Imports/Distribution in Time and Space

Place	Number	Percentage	1451-1600	1601-1700	1701-1810	1811-1870	TOTAL
Overall	9,566,000	100					
Old World:	175,000	1.8	149,900	25,100	—	—	175,000
Europe	50,000	0.5					
Madeira, Canaries, Cape Verde	25,000	0.3					
Sao Thomé	100,000	1.0					
North America:	651,000	6.8	—	—	348,000	51,000	399,000
U.S., British North	399,000	4.2					
America, Louisiana	28,000	0.3					
Mexico	200,000	2.1					
Central America	24,000	0.3					
				British America/Caribbean			
Caribbean	4,040,000	42.2	—	263,700	1,401,300	—	1,665,000
Greater Antilles:	2,421,000	25.3			*French America/Caribbean*		
Haiti	864,000	4.0					
Dominican Republic	30,000	0.3	—	155,800	1,348,400	96,000	1,600,200
Cuba	702,000	7.3					
Puerto Rico	748,000	7.8					
Jamaica	77,000	0.8	—				

	Number	%
Lesser Antilles:	1,619,000	16.9
U.S. Virgin Is.	28,000	0.3
British Virgin Is.	7,000	0.1
Leeward Islands	346,000	3.6
Guadeloupe	291,000	3.0
Martinique	366,000	3.8
St. Vincent, St. Lucia, Tobago, Dominica	70,000	0.7
Grenada	67,000	0.7
Trinidad	22,000	0.2
Barbados	387,000	4.0
Dutch Antilles	20,000	0.2
Bahamas	10,000	0.1
Bermuda	5,000	0.1
South America:	4,700,000	49.1
The Guianas	531,000	5.6
Brazil	3,647,000	38.1
Spanish America (continental)	522,000	5.5

					Total
Dutch America/Caribbean	—	40,000	460,000		500,000
Danish America/Caribbean	—	4,000	24,000		28,000
Spanish America	75,000	292,500	578,600	606,000	1,552,100
Brazil	50,000	560,000	1,891,400	1,145,400	3,646,800

SOURCE: From Philip Curtin, *The Atlantic Slave Trade. A Census* (Madison: University of Wisconsin Press, 1969), Tables 24 and 77, pp. 88-89 and 268, Adapted.

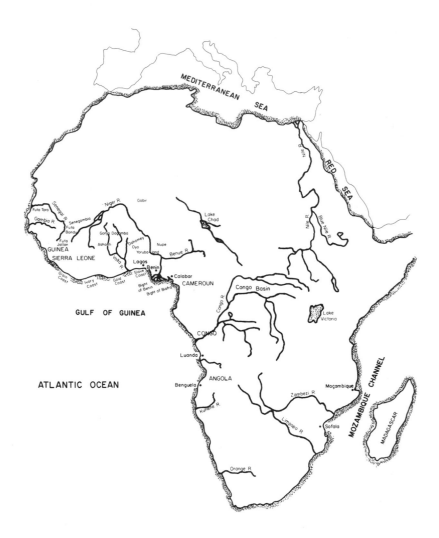

African Culture and Ethno-Linguistic Areas Pertinent to African Movement, Through Time, to the Americas.

It should be emphasized here that, until the nineteenth century, the Portuguese were the only Europeans able to enter and remain in the interior of Africa. Several conditions militated against the involvement of other Europeans—factors such as disease, African political control, African customary law, and social constraints.

The Portuguese were the first Europeans to become actively involved in the commercial venture of slaving. The Kongo Kingdom, with whom the Portuguese developed their first African relationship, was then a loose confederation of tribal organizations under the authority (although not necessarily the suzerainty) of a paramount chief, the Manicongo. The kingdom was divided into six provinces whose hereditary chieftains pledged their allegiance to him. In these areas the village was the basic political unit, ruled by an hereditary headman and including both free people and slaves. Among the slaves were criminals or prisoners-of-war. The government derived income from taxes and labor service; slaves were one of the forms of tribute.[3]

In almost all of the African societies into which the Europeans were invited, and which they later invaded, some form of slavery as a system of labor was already common. This held true until the eighteenth century when several African state units were formed in direct response to the slave trade.

The next area of Portuguese interest was Angola. The first three centuries of Angolan history (c. 1550-1850) were a patchwork of small wars, slave expeditions, and slave commerce. Although some Portuguese troublemakers entered Ndongo (Angola), basically it was local revolts among the Ngola's chiefs which, after 1565, kept the area in constant turmoil. The Ngola was the paramount chief of Ndongo (present-day Angola), as the Manicongo was the paramount chief of Kongo (present-day Zaire.) By the end of the sixteenth century, the entire structure of Ndongo's territorial authority was disintegrating as a result of internal warfare, excessive taxation of tribesmen by their chiefs, inadequate protection of the populace by the chiefs, and enslavement through kidnapping and corruption. African traders encouraged wars and rebellions, while the Portuguese provoked dissension.

In the seventeenth century many changes had occurred. Now, in many areas of western and central Africa, kings and chiefs, whose predecessors had relied on irregulars or temporary conscripts from their own vassals or allies, developed professional armies to guard lucrative trade routes. One of the side effects of this professional military establishment was that the slave ranks were swelled by Africans who were captured in more frequent and more destructive wars. By this time, trading structures had changed. Costly middlemen on internal trade routes had now been eliminated by the arrival and enforcement of groups of African merchants settled and trading on the coasts. Thus, the movement of more slaves more quickly gave momentum to the odious trade. Even the Marxist Davidson admits that the trade grew and Euro-Americans succeeded in obtaining millions of African workers, for "in the master-servant organization which operated in many states and societies. . . . West African chiefs and kings regularly turned war captives and certain classes of law breakers into slaves."[4]

By the late seventeenth-early eighteenth century, expanding trade had encouraged new coastal markets and power centers controlled by Africans as middlemen between European seamerchants and African inland merchants. From the small beginnings of the Euro-African trade until the 1650s, slaves came from two sources: "either they were persons who had lost their civic rights, in the state that sold them, by sentence of the courts, or they were citizens of another state who had lost their rights through capture in war."[5] From the 1650s on, however, the sources—as had the patterns of provenience—changed.

The mid-seventeenth century is an important time frame for marking changes in African societies. Within Africa the authority of several old empires had disintegrated, European-African commercial opportunities had expanded, and the European trading nations had chartered national trading companies—all of which revolutionized slave-trading operations and slavery itself. Thus, it is from the latter part of the seventeenth century that changes in many African societies can best be documented.

Eighteenth-century African societies from which Ibero-America was acquiring its manpower were in the Bight of Benin, (the "slave coast" of present-day Togo and Dahomey). Here the Abomey Kingdom was in ascendance and was soon to assert its control over the major port town of Whydah. The period of the most active trading under Abomey rule coincided with the first prolonged struggle for power between the Hueda and the Fon, in the late 1720s and early 1730s, thus providing an easy captive commodity for trade. It also earmarks a shift in slavetrading operations and growing reliance on European firearms for slaving.

The Dahomey Kingdom, which was established on the Guinea Coast in 1727, was a relatively new monarchy. Its leaders had emerged from an aggressive local clan that had asserted control over numerous ethnic groups in an area where a power vacuum had existed. They swiftly elaborated a trade organization, a stable currency, and an efficient administration. Polanyi argues that when Whydah emerged as the chief entrepôt of slaves, the

> unexpected localization of the slave trade and the economic pressure of slavers' fleets off the coast undermined the inland status of Dahomey. Never before had the slave trade forced itself on an inland state of West Africa as a concern dominating its total existence. Internally and externally the supply situation was unprecedented in . . . numbers involved and the social wreckage caused. Not a few scores of slaves at the most were brought up annually from stray *slattees* (chained groups of slaves for sale in a market place), but many thousands of slaves were channeled in spurts of hundreds of organized *coffilas* (slave *coffles* or chain gangs). This would not have been possible without fortified lodges erected against local pillagers, even though such settlements would still be at the mercy of the concerted action of African ruler. Other requirements of the trade were procedures and manipulations of transporting, keeping, barracooning, subsisting, and branding adult human beings in the mass.[6]

Hence, for Dahomey defense and slavetrading were inseparable, since she was surrounded by militarily prepared states.

Whydah achieved prominence because of ecological factors: a climate created by decreased precipitation and dry-hot local trade winds allowed cereals to flourish. Thus, Whydah became both a large-scale food exporter to neighboring areas and a warehouse for surplus foods. The demands of the slave trade necessitated the institutionalization of that surplus and, concomitantly, an organized bureaucracy, both of which permitted the development of that trading port institution.[7] For the first quarter of the eighteenth century, Whydah remained a superbly organized unit whose very success made her subject to conquest by the Fon of Abomey (i.e., Dahomeans). The Fon had entered West Africa's slave trade as both suppliers and brokers, and they began selling directly to ships anchored off the coast. They gradually usurped control as a result of the rivalries of and insufficient naval support for European powers, and by the 1740s, Whydah had become a Fon colony.[8]

Ashanti, like Dahomey, was a "state" society which at first was economically dependent on European guns to maintain armies for continuous warfare and slave raiding. Earlier, both "states" had enjoyed a village culture with self-sufficient territorial units linked by ethnic, linguistic, and descent-group ties.[9] The acquisition of firearms near the end of the seventeenth century had made it possible for Akan-speaking peoples to combine "matriclan segments . . . under the leadership of Osei Tutu resulting in the formation of the Ashanti Confederacy."[10]

The Ashanti distinguished three groups of servants: foreign-born slaves, pawns, and pawns-become-slaves. The tribe's conception of the slave's economic function as well as his degree of sociopolitical freedom, however, differed from that held by the Ibero-Americans. As Norman Klein has pointed out, the primary determinant of condition for the "foreign-born" slaves (*odonko*) was not economic production but social status. Several factors militated against the development of the *odonko* into a social class. First, they lacked lineage membership, and thus they could be depersonalized and treated as a commodity. Secondly, since the Ashanti's economic enterprises were on a small scale, large groups of slaves who would live and work together were never needed. Furthermore, ritual execution of slaves at funerals where entire villages had to provide sacrificial victims liquidated potential labor forces. Ashanti society did provide for *odonko* assimilation by marriage with a free citizen.

The pawn (*awowa*) was really a debtor who was "leased" to his creditor. The pawn-become-slave (*akoa pa*), however, was a genuine slave, for lineage members were not allowed to redeem a pawned kinsman. The *akoa pa* was sold outright to the creditor, and his condition was similar to that "of the Roman or American Negro slave," since his lessee-creditor became "a master for life and in perpetuity."[11]

The Ashanti Confederation, begun as a movement of national resistance to other African states, developed into a vast organization for slave raiding and trading. This process was simplified by access to an inexhaustible supply of slaves made available through their northern conquests as well as through their conquest of peoples between themselves and the sea. Fage claims that these conquests were launched largely to eliminate chiefs and merchants of other tribes and to keep profits of the gold and slave trade for themselves.[12]

At the same time, the Angolans were continuing their monotonous march along the slave routes. *Pombeiros* (Portuguese-African slave traders) ranged through the interior, bartered for and acquired slaves, occasionally fired a local war to buy prisoners, and then marched their spoils to Luanda port for sale. Accounts of Portuguese Angola describe corps of slaves utilized as domestic servants or in private armies of slave dealers; as laborers on manioc plantations or farms; as workers in clearing lands around towns and fortresses; and as part of a craftsman class. Generally, these forms of slavery may have been more common to African tribal groups than to American plantations. The sources for this slave population were similar to those which supplied overseas traders: peoples displaced as a result of extensive disintegration of ethnic units through warfare, revolts, and violence; natural calamities; and outright barter arrangements.

Africans who were to be shipped to America were held in Luanda's warehouses, barracoons, or open corrals. Many were marched from the deep interior and so arrived emaciated and exhausted; they were then tended and fattened so that they could withstand the rigors of the Atlantic crossing. If voyages were delayed, captives were used in municipal and agricultural tasks.

Despite the burgeoning trade, Europeans rarely were able to penetrate inland in most of West Africa. There were several reasons. Local rulers held tight control over their lands; diseases were fatal to foreigners; African coastal middlemen jealously guarded their positions by preventing direct contact between Europeans and slave-supplying areas; and customary laws, whereby land belonged corporately to the people, prevented African chiefs from allowing European traders to acquire territory.

The arrival of European traders anchored in the Niger Delta saw the development of numerous trading states, mostly from Ijo fishing villages: Bonny, Owome (New Calabar), Okrika, and Brass (Nembe); the Efik state of Old Calabar; and the Itsekirri Kingdom of Warri. Benin, the most important slave market west of the Niger, had a well-organized machinery for merchandising human cargo. It was part of the Niger Delta system and its hinterland, home areas for Africans exported from present-day Nigeria (roughly the area of the Bights of Biafra and Benin).

The socioeconomic structure of numerous Delta tribes had changed significantly by the late eighteenth century. Prior to European contact, each Ijo village had supported 200 to 1,000 inhabitants, and each village was divided into wards or "houses" ruled by a headman chosen through seniority. The economy of the village was based on a dried fish and salt trade with peoples from the hinterland, mainly Ibibio and Ibo. Ibibio's sociopolitical organization resembled that of the Ijo, with each village containing about 500 people. The Ibo had federated village groups of up to 5,000 inhabitants each, headed by a "president." Some lived in even larger communities with more centralized political structures. Once the sparsely populated Ijo became involved in international slavetrading, their two populous neighboring groups became supplies for slave markets.

Of the many internal changes in social and economic organization which Ijo states underwent in the eighteenth century, the most significant was the growth of "house" rule, although the forms of political authority among the states differed.[13] Slaves in each of the Ijo states also lived under relatively different standards. For example, in the strong monarchy of New Calabar, a slave who was successfully integrated could rise to the highest position, for in this society competition was allowed and ability was the major criterion for leadership. In Old Calabar, where authority was divided and where the real power of community lay with a secret organization (the Egba Society) whose members were chosen by wealth and age, slaves were relegated to plantations. The oppression of slaves and refusal to permit them to participate in society fomented revolts in Old Calabar. In New Calabar, the slaves were not as repressed; moreover, they lived in their masters' compounds and so had little chance to organize for revolt. The house system was not without cruelty, however:

> . . . ear cutting in its various stages, from clipping to total dismemberment; crucifixion round a large cask; extraction of teeth; suspension by the thumb; Chilli peppers pounded and stuffed up the nostrils, and forced into the eyes and ears; fastening the victim to a post driven into the beach at low water and leaving him there to be drowned with the rising tide, or to be eaten by the sharks or crocodiles piecemeal; heavily ironed and chained to a post in their master's compound . . . and reduced to living skeletons; impaling on stakes; forcing a long steel ramrod through the body until it appeared through the top of the skull.[14]

Densely populated Iboland (formerly Biafra) was an important source of slaves during the eighteenth century and, to a lesser extent, the nineteenth. A significant element in the Ibo scheme for enslavement was the universally respected and feared Arochuku Oracle of the Aro. The Aro were a subsection of the Ibo in whose territory resided the Oracle, or Ibo supreme deity, and as such commanded great respect among the Ibo and Delta states.[15] In a politically decentralized land, the Aro maintained a highly complex and centralized commercial system fortified by its religio-political leadership. As representatives of the Oracle, they settled in small colonies among each of the tribes, first as mediators and soon thereafter as traders. This scattering was possible because they were the only people who could safely travel. Aro quarters were established in most Ibo towns, and their oracle became the medium through which slaves were obtained for exportation from Delta ports.[16]

Other West African sources for the nineteenth-century trade centering in the Bights opened up as a result of the disintegration of the Oyo Empire, the Yoruba civil wars, and the chronic turmoil that arose from *jihads* occurring in northern Nigeria. Oyo had emerged as a twin kingdom with Benin sometime in the fifteenth century. During the seventeenth century, it expanded into an empire after it developed light cavalry which allowed her extended sway over most of Yorubaland. Oyo was divided into a number of provinces, including those of Yoruba proper, the Egba, the Ijebu, and the Ekiti. The Yoruba traditionally discouraged both individual and groups from acquiring unchecked power. Hence, Oyo devised a complex political structure of title grades and palace societies through which authority was exercised.

In Oyo the political authority of the Alafin, . . . as we have already seen, was considerably restricted by the Oyo Mesi who exercised right of life and death over him. Should their leader, the Basorun, declare: "The Gods reject you, the people reject you, the earth rejects you"—then the Alafin was forced to commit suicide. The device was frequently resorted to in the eighteenth century when the role of the Alafin became excessively tyrannous. Both the Alafin and Oyo Mesi were checked by the Ogboni, a secret society composed of both religious and political leaders, devoted to the worship of the earth. The head of the society had right of access to the Alafin, and the society itself judged any case involving the spilling of blood which was considered an offence against the earth. Furthermore, the society had to sanction certain decisions of the Oyo Mesi, including the rejection of the Alafin.[17]

This pattern did not generally hold true for other Yoruba kingdoms where each town was a separate entity ruled by an Oba from one of the ruling lineages.

In the smaller towns, all the non-ruling lineages supplied chiefs, who together with heads of various cults and societies formed a council which exercised considerable control over the acts of the Oba. Since most lineages as well as associations, whether political or religious, were represented on the council the people of the town had a voice in their government.[18]

By the first quarter of the nineteenth century, Oyo authority had collapsed as a result of several long-standing causes. Among them were the inadequacy of traditional political institutions in an empire as large and prosperous as Oyo; the increasing despotism of the Alafin which caused his elimination and total usurpation of power by the Oyo Mesi's Basorun; and declining military strength. Army defeats in the North had severed Oyo from her traditional sources of slaves, thus causing economic deterioration and forcing her to look southward for slaves to other Yoruba-speaking states, an action that fostered hostility and eventually rebellion. This situation was further aggravated by fears that the Fulani (Muslim) religious revolutions in Hausa-land would move southward. All of these factors combined to cause irreconcilable factional differences. A rebellion detonated a series of wars which, in turn, encouraged open hostilities between Yoruba kingdoms and subgroups. These hostilities persisted throughout most of the nineteenth century.

The Yoruba and other unfortunate West African groups caught in the vise of civil wars became sources for the Atlantic trade. Lagos, which had barely existed before the 1830s, assumed importance in export commerce. Also appearing on the slaving coasts were Afro-Brazilians who settled permanently in Bight of Benin ports and whose trade included spoils of the Yoruba civil wars as well as Hausa refugees from the Fulani campaigns.[19]

The southeastern area of Africa supplied substantial cargoes to Ibero-America in the nineteenth century, largely through the efforts of the Yao, East Central Africa's greatest traders of the eighteenth and nineteenth centuries. In nineteenth-century Yao society, status and power were determined by the number of followers a man controlled. Authority rested with the eldest living brother who was also a chief. Thus, a complex kinship web was created which was simultaneously an atomistic process because it encouraged dissension through male competition for succession.[20] An ambitious individual could attract followers through success as a trader, and in the nineteenth century, Yao territorial chiefs engaged in a substantial commerce in slaves:

> The single family may rapidly become a large state . . . daughters are the great hope of a rising village. . . . In course of time he [the headman] adorns his position by acquiring wealth. He may shoot some buck and get possession of their skins. With these he goes to the Mangoni country and buys slaves. . . . The female slaves thus bought are his junior wives, and he keeps them busy in hoeing the farm, and all such female duties. The male slaves he employs in farming, building, making baskets, sewing garments, and such masculine pursuits. He keeps all these people strictly at their duties, and at the same time welcomes an opportunity of selling them at a profit. The gain thus realised he lays out in purchasing more people. If his daughters were unmarried, he would give them slave-husbands.[21]

The slave trade became integral to Yao society. Slaves were considered "a man's goods and chattels, to do with mainly as he pleased," keeping some and putting the rest into slave caravans going to the coast.[22] Female slaves were particularly useful in augmenting their captor's family. Consequently, the Yao tended to keep captive women and feed their male captives to the slave trade. Acquiring women either through raiding or trading was a common feature of nineteenth-century Yao life, since a Yao man's greatness was always measured by the number of his wives and slaves.[23]

In summary, it may be stated that slaving was familiar to most African "states" and that it can be documented at least as early as the eleventh century. From that time until the latter half of the seventeenth

century, African slavetrading and slavery were adjuncts to state formation, economic needs, religious ceremonies, and other functions of
cultures in change. After the impact of the Europeans began to be
felt (although not until the mid-nineteenth century did medicines make
it possible for most Europeans to penetrate inland beyond the coastlines), the pattern of slavery and slavetrading seemed to change considerably. New African states developed with an economic dependence
on firearms. The mobility created by this new trend led to the dominance of some states, and thus enabled the form and content of African
slavery to be reordered.

THE ATLANTIC SLAVE TRADE

With the exception of the even more massive migration of Europeans to America in the nineteenth and twentieth centuries, the Atlantic
slave trade seems to have represented the greatest intercontinental
migration in history. Iberia's colonies in America absorbed some 4.2
million of the 9.5 million souls transported in the trade; 1.55 million
went to Spanish America and the rest to Brazil. In carriage and con-
sumption of slaves (see Table 1), the Caribbean colonies of Great
Britain, France, and to a lesser extent the Dutch and Danes, had an
equal share of the trade but within a more constricted time frame.
Total slave imports to French America (1.6 million) were matched by
British Caribbean imports (1.66 million). Three major British areas
imported the bulk of slaves: Barbados, 387,000; the Leeward Islands,
346,000; and Jamaica, 747,500. All of the rest of the British Caribbean
took the remainder (184,500) for the entire duration of the trade.[24]
    The Atlantic slave trade was not only of demographic importance,
but it also was at the core of an economic system in which Africa supplied the labor, Europe the entrepreneural expertise, northern North
America food and transport, and South America precious metals and
raw materials. The institutions and ideas of slavery had developed
and coincided with the fifteenth- and sixteenth-century revolution in
maritime science and technology. The Europeans combined naviga-
tional skills with firepower, giving them a naval hegemony almost
anywhere in the world. This revolution was accompanied by a revolution in transport costs; ships could carry more cargo, more swiftly,
over longer distances, and for less money.[25]

According to Philip Curtin, the "South Atlantic system" was established by the beginning of the seventeenth century. Plantations based on sugar cultivation were much larger than their Mediterranean prototypes. Their characteristics were passed from one geographical setting to another, and their seedlings were transplanted to the Caribbean and later to southern North America, first by the Dutch and later by the English, French, and other European entrepreneurs. Tobacco, cotton, cacao, coffee, rice, indigo, and other agricultural products used slave labor, but it was sugar which created the greatest demand for Africans in the Caribbean. The Dutch initially were responsible for creating this sugar-qua-slave situation, first in Brazil, later in the Caribbean. Having been driven from Brazil in the 1640s, Dutch planters and merchants moved their operations and techniques for planting, harvesting, processing, and marketing sugar to the Caribbean.

These operations required a massive labor supply. Since Europeans and the Amerindians they encountered were exceedingly vulnerable to disease, whereas the Africans came from a disease environment to which they had built up immunities, the desirability of acquiring Africans was enhanced.[26] From the middle of the seventeenth century until the end of the eighteenth century, nearly 4 million Africans were shipped to the British, French, and Dutch Antilles (Table 1), primarily to work the sugar plantations.

THE SOUTH ATLANTIC SYSTEM AT WORK IN AMERICA: AFRO-AMERICAN LIFE AND LABOR IN LATIN AMERICA AND THE CARIBBEAN

While slavery, as a system of labor, was not the only social and economic framework within which the African-born or African-descendant American lived and worked, it was the most common labor system for the Afro-American. Slavery, as the major system of labor functioning in societies integral to the South Atlantic system, was neither a static nor a monolithic institution, but rather consisted of internally variegated coercive labor systems, to which the victims often learned to adjust.

External factors also affected the evolution of slavery throughout the Americas: fixed environmental features, such as the geographic ones of climate and topography, and more variable factors such as ecology, demography, or disease environments, as well as social, political,

TABLE 2

Colored Populations in the Americas
for the Last Full Census (1950)

Region	Colored Population	Colored as Percentage of Total Population
THE CARRIBBEAN		
Commonwealth (former British)	2,280,000	86
French (excluding Haiti)	540,000	93
Dutch	140,000	88
Virgin Islands	24,000	92
Haiti	3,080,000	99
Cuba	1,470,000	27
Dominican Republic	1,630,000	77
Puerto Rico	550,000	25
MIDDLE AND CENTRAL AMERICA		
Mexico	120,000	05
Guatemala	8,000	[less than .01]
Belize	34,000	56
Honduras	50,000	33
El Salvador	[less than 1,000]	—
Nicaragua	100,000	09
Costa Rica	30,000	04
Panama (including the Canal Zone)	190,000	22
SPANISH AMERICA: CONTINENTAL		
Colombia	2,917,000	26
Venezuela	1,620,000	32
Ecuador	330,000	10
Peru	110,000	01
Bolivia	12,000	—
Paraguay	10,000	01
Uruguay	60,000	03
Argentina	15,000	—
Chile	3,000	—

Region	Colored Population	Colored as Percentage of Total Population
BRAZIL	17,529,000	33
OTHER SOUTH AMERICA		
(British Guiana) Guyana	184,000	47
(Dutch Guiana) Surinam	102,000	47
French Guiana	22,000	76
NORTH AMERICA		
Canada	22,000	—
United States	14,894,000	10

SOURCE: From Angel Rosenblatt, *La población indígena y el mestizaje en América,* I (Buenos Aires: Nova, 1954), Table I and pp. 145-146; and Herbert S. Klein, "Patterns of Settlement of the Afro-American Population in the New World," in *Key Issues in the Afro-American Experience* (New York: Harcourt Brace Jovanovich, 1971), 115. Adapted.

and economic conditions. In addition, slavery functioned differently in the Americas, depending on whether it operated in a slave society (seventeenth-century Barbados, eighteenth-century Haiti, nineteenth-century Cuba) or in a nonslave society (sixteenth-century Mexico, eighteenth-century Curaçao, or nineteenth-century Trinidad).[27]

The African in America—black and mulatto, slave and free—experienced a wide range of relationships and activities which had little to do with juridical and theoretical constructs. "Slave" and "slavery" were concepts theorized and practiced in almost all societies and, as we have seen, were integral to many African groups. For all of these groups, slavery in the broadest sense signified a relationship in which one human being held another in part or in toto as property. In theory, the perceptions of most cultures regarding slavery were relatively close both legally and practically. It was not until international commercialization and technological-managerial innovations induced changes in labor systems that practices deviating greatly from theorized ideals can be documented. Perhaps the major distinguishing feature between slavery as practiced in Europe, Asia, Africa, Amerindian societies, and early Euro-American societies, and slavery after the Atlantic slave trade-South Atlantic system was that slavery ceased to be an internal or a limited, externally influenced economic process. Instead, it became a system whereby alien powers created and imposed from without economic institutions that relied on an alien and immobile labor supply.

The types of economic activities in which Afro-Americans were engaged depended on the various time periods, places, extenuating sociocultural considerations, and market demands involved. On a scale of more free to less free, those Afro-Americans performing interstitial and marginal economic tasks were likely to be more mobile than those bound to the production of a single crop for external gains. The typology of slavery—in perceived order of more free to less free— included domestic work; artisan and skilled labor; mining—placer and deep pit; cattle ranching; small-scale farming, such as tobacco, indigo, rice, and cotton; and plantation work, such as cacao, sugar, and coffee.[28]

In terms of its longevity, profits produced, slaves consumed, and areas of production and distribution, sugar was the major crop for which systems of slave labor flourished. The sugar economy was particularly dominant in northern Brazil, Cuba, parts of Mexico, and throughout most of the Caribbean. A major feature of this key one-crop economy is that sugar is labor-intensive. Furthermore, during the season all labor must be concentrated on sugar lands and all the rest of the land is left fallow. In addition, since sugar mills were small and cane difficult to transport, planters had to concentrate labor in a small area. Hence, the labor supply had to remain under firm control, i.e., servile, for once the labor supply shifted from slave to nonslave it was difficult to control it and therefore difficult to control use of the land.

Despite its repressive nature, and the extent and duration of the institution, throughout the Americas there was relatively little resistance to slavery.[29] The most frequently documented examples of slave resistance in Latin America occurred in Brazil, although there were some uprisings throughout colonial Mexico and nineteenth-century Cuba.[30]

Throughout most of the Caribbean, slave resistance was negligible. As an explanation for its absence in the Leeward Islands, one of Britain's three major slave centers, Elsa Goveia suggests that slave laws were rigidly enforced and specifically tailored to make almost any kind of organized resistance impossible.[37] The only major area of resistance in the Caribbean seems to have been Jamaica. Patterson attributes this situation in Jamaica to a number of factors, namely, the island's heavy ratio of black slaves to whites; the heavy population of slaves who had been born freemen and were enslaved as adults; the fact that the Akan peoples from whom Jamaica acquired many of its slaves came from a highly developed militaristic regime; the general inefficiency and smugness of Jamaican whites; the maltreatment of slaves; the favorable geography allowing hiding places; and the motivation of social, political, and other forces, such as abolitionism, near the end of the eighteenth century.[32]

The lack of resistance to slavery elsewhere raises some important points. One is that the runaways had varied motivations and were not necessarily rebellious. For example, in some instances the flight of urban slaves was concerned as much with their in-group problems as with their discontent with their owners. Another important point is one raised by Bowser concerning colonial Spanish America: "However widespread and serious the runaway problem was, its importance has obviously been exaggerated, otherwise the institution of slavery would have collapsed under the strain."[33]

Scholars have not only raised serious questions to the ideas that the fugitives had a single motivation (i.e., maltreatment) and that the runaway problem was pervasive, but are also now questioning the dimensions of slave insurrections, revolts, and rebellions. They are asking: "Just how dangerous were the slave populations?"; "How serious was the danger of rebellion?"; "How severe was the problem of black/mulatto resistance?". The answers to these questions require careful scrutiny of documentary sources, as well as quantitative analysis of the numbers involved, the instances of disturbances, the extent of alliance between the free black and slave population, and the like.

The post-abolition life and labor of the blacks in the Americas can be better understood by considering the fact that slavery was not the only condition for blacks and mulattoes. There were a considerable number of free black men and women in every society in America. A small number of Africans had come to the New World as free persons; many others had been given or had earned their freedom; and a large number were descendants of both these groups. A recent study has shown that the free population was sizable in northern Brazil, Curaçao, Martinique, and Puerto Rico, and more moderately so in southern Brazil and Cuba.[34]

It is easier to identify freedmen than slaves because many freedmen were literate, articulate, and expressive of elite ideals. Before any conclusions can be reached, however, several variables have to be considered. These variables include the growth rates of the free colored communities, their size relative to the general community and to slave populations, and the avenues to freedom.

Some patterns can be seen throughout the Americas. Cohen and Greene have suggested that until the mid-eighteenth century the free colored were more capable of increasing through natural means, than both the black slave and free white communities. This pattern seems to have been the case more often in tropical than in temperate climates. In addition to natural increase, the free coloreds added to their numbers through their self-purchase of freedom and the legal provision of free birth for children of mixed marriages.

Several changes in the status of freedmen occurred through time. Initially, more females than males were manumitted, and gradually the ratios of females to males manumitted decreased. Another change, in later decades was away from the early patterns of self-purchase. This trend was more common during periods of economic development and the growth of interstitial and other service opportunities for which there was insufficient white labor. Under this system more males than females acquired their freedom. Another avenue to male freedom was meritorious service to the master or heroic performance in the military.

The growing restrictions on manumission in slave societies seem to have been a response to the imminent demise of the Atlantic slave trade and therefore of the major source of sustenance of slave labor. For Cuba, this growing demise of the slave trade occurred during the early nineteenth century just as her sugar economy was beginning to boom. In areas where agricultural developments had induced the growth of occupations which could be filled by freedmen, the whites, particularly those belonging to the nonelite stratum, began to fear increasing economic and social competition. In addition, the dread of slave revolts had been growing and, after the Haitian Revolution, developed into a quiet hysteria. No more shocking prospect could be envisoned than a massive slave uprising triggered by a dissatisfied free colored population.

The growing restrictions on manumission after the mid-eighteenth century created conflicts between free blacks and slaves, and even more so between free blacks and mulattoes. For the sake of their own self-preservation as a group, the free coloreds realized that it was in their best interests to ally with whites rather than with their black brethren. Increasingly, the free colored aspired to elite positions occupied by whites and emulated ways of acquiring that status. More and more, the established free colored communities began to be aware of the distinction between free mulattoes and free blacks. In particular, the newly freed tended to be black and to be encompassed in the psychological and economic environment of lingering servitude. An indication of the complexity of social and economic relationships among freedperson's can be seen in the following hierarchical ordering:

Freedmen Hierarchy
(in the New World)

Newly freed

1 hired-out slaves (two types)
2 slaves in the process of self-
   purchase of freedom
3 slaves almost free
4 slaves freed but still in debt to
   their masters or others
5 slaves newly freed
6 newly freed with someone or
   rest of the family still enslaved
7 long-free but unsuccessful and
   dependent/marginal

Established freed

1 small farmers
2 artisans
3 restauranteurs and tavern-
   keepers/purveyors of entertainment
4 traders
5 transporters and communications controllers
6 merchants
7 those involved in much wholesale and most retail trade
8 slaveowners

A case for the antipathy between free mulatto and free black, or newly freed and established freed, could be developed in the growing concept of class consciousness. But to do so involves several problems, not the least of which concerns the concept of class in the eighteenth century. On the one hand, advancement from premodern to modern development in these slave societies encouraged the growth of numerous groups of established free colored in society, each of which occupied an accepted economic-social stratum. On the other hand, some established free coloreds were not satisfied with that intermediary position and tended to emulate the elite, which was predominantly white. This pattern seems to be characteristic in most contemporary

Latin American and Caribbean societies: the middle class perceives itself less as a "middle" class and more as in transit to the "upper" class.
    As slavery came to an end during the first half of the nineteenth cen-
tury in most colonies, the newly freed were in a precarious and inse-
cure position. Their position was not helped by the role the established
free communities played as members of the militia and as supporters
of the white plantocracies.
    The ranks of the free colored communities grew as a result both of
manumission and natural reproduction. Although they played interstitial roles in society, opportunities for advancement were limited,
because in almost all of these colonial societies social and economic
mobility and opportunity in general were circumscribed. In such an
environment, economic competition and social conflict rationalized
by race were inevitable.

THE AFRO-AMERICAN MILIEUS

Old Patterns Remembered

    The Africans brought with them to the Americas a rather complex
history of social, political, and economic organization as well as a remembered past of slavery within their own local ethnic units. Their
utilization of their traditions in the Americas depended on a complex
of external and internal variables. The internal variables were very
much intertwined with the cultural patterns of various ethnolinguistic
groups. One of these important variables was the concept of market.
The market always was vital to West Africans, especially to the women who provided the food and other products for cities and towns.
This pattern of market activity—of control of the production and distribution of market products—was common throughout parts of Latin
America, especially Brazil, and the Caribbean, particularly Haiti.
    Another pattern had to do with concepts of property. For example,
in Dahomey, the West African area with the greatest ethnic influence
in Haiti, there were three kinds of property. In essence, everything,
even one's person, belonged to the king, although at the risk of retribution of his ancestors the king was proscribed from claiming things
and people. Two other types of property were collective and individual.
The *sib* or extended family collectively owned property which was administered by the oldest male member. Private property could be held
by either male or female. The Dahomean view of private property was

that it included houses built, trees and produce planted, and the like and that it belonged to the person who worked it, regardless of who owned the land. The Dahomeans also set up complex rules for inheritance of private property.[35]

In general, private rights to usefully occupied or cultivated lands was commonly recognized throughout West Africa. Unoccupied land was usually of the first type, belonging to the king or tribe. It was *not* to be kept idle at the "owner's" whim; therefore, it *could* and *should* be occupied. Squatting on these types of lands—which throughout most of the Caribbean meant crown or metropolitan lands—became a common practice in the West Indies but was considered quite illegal by European standards. This conflict between African and European notions of property was intense. In British areas, it was heightened by the fact that while white owners were willing to sell their lands to blacks, they wanted to sell large plots, whereas the blacks wanted only a few acres. The European view was that land should be held for profitmaking purposes, while the Africans maintained that it should be utilized.[36]

Another cultural heritage from African societies was in the area of sexual mores and marital relationships. Sexual relationships between African males and females were more akin to pre-Council of Trent (1526), medieval European Christian "common-law" situations. Throughout most areas of the Caribbean (there is good evidence for Haiti and Jamaica), Africans were reluctant to enter into the institution of Christian marriage. As Curtin has pointed out, Jamaican women considered Christian marriage a sign of subordination and slavery to the male. While they were ready to accept the heavy responsibilities of their role in "African-style marriages," they were unwilling to accept Christian marriage. This attitude became "too well established to be easily changed. . . . In the long run, this turned out to be one of the most deep-seated of Jamaican Negro attitudes."[37]

Two other cultural heritages were those of language and of religion. Language evolved as a patois of the grammatical forms common to West African societies and the vocabulary of the European ruling classes in Latin America and the Caribbean. Festivals, holidays, and religious celebrations were all based in African ceremonies and rites. Religious ceremonies, beliefs, and other elements associated with Afro-Caribbean life have been the most residual African elements in the Caribbean. It was in the religious sphere that a leader could emerge who could transcend ethnic boundaries and garner support from the diverse groups. In that role, religious leaders provided an alternative to the white ruling class representatives and a channel for preserving African values. The European efforts to eradicate Africanisms were strongest in the area of religion, for it made good political sense to undercut the base of support for the growth of African leaders in their servile environment. Not until after abolition did many Africans move to the established European churches, since the need for ethnic leadership had, presumably, been removed.

The Africans had fundamentally different religious beliefs from the Europeans, and these beliefs largely determined how they perceived the world. In essence, religious conversion could be seen as the ultimate device of social control. Furthermore, the African perception of man and his relationship to the world and his fellow-man is distinctly different from the Western. Authority systems and conceptions of good and evil for Europeans and Africans seemed diametrically opposed. In a world in which the spiritual is integral to the temporal, a constant struggle against malevolence was a major mechanism for moral control in the African environment. For the black man this translated into a spiritual struggle against the white world to be undertaken at any opportunity. The same perception functioned in Africa among different ethnic groups.

From the mid-seventeenth until nearly the mid-nineteenth century, most of the Africans brought to the Caribbean and Latin America comprised many ethnic groups from the West and Central African Negro and Bantu language families. While each group had a cultural ethos which made one group more acceptable than other groups to white owners, they were generally representative of a similar milieu. These different ethnic groups amalgamated, assimilated, and adapted to each other to form a fairly identifiable Afro-Caribbean, Afro-Latin American culture which transcended their ethnic-tribal-national differences. It is possible, with qualifications, to view this process as similar to that of the integration of European ethnic-tribal-national groups into their new American homelands. European and African groups were seeking survival in an alien world. While the elements of force and servility were missing in the European circumstance, in both situations an environment of coercion existed. The end result has been the assimilation of Europeans into a dominant Euro-American culture and the amalgamation of African groups into an Afro-American culture.

New Patterns Reinforced

Several events occurred throughout the Americas in the late eighteenth and nineteenth centuries which changed the course of economic development in societies that depended on coercive labor systems. The Haitian Revolution of 1789 was followed within a few decades by the outlawing of the slave trade and, within the first half of the nineteenth century, by the abolition of slavery in most Latin American and Caribbean countries. In 1888, when Brazil became the last country in the Americas to outlaw slavery, the "peculiar institution" ceased to exist in law.

After abolition in the respective American nations, certain new patterns affecting the life and labor of Afro-Americans began to emerge. As can be seen in Tables 1 and 2, shifts in black and white populations had already occurred throughout the Americas. These shifts were not only among cultures but, later, from rural to urban areas within a culture.

Another pattern that emerged, and that created difficult circumstances, was that no reparations were paid ex-slaves after abolition.[38] Newly freed workers tended to remain in their old areas of settlement. If, as in Brazil, they immediately fled the countryside for the cities, they soon returned to the old plantation regions, for they lacked the money and skills to become urban laborers.[39] Once they returned to the countryside, because they owned no land and had no way to acquire new skills, they were forced into neoservile conditions of debt peonage and sharecropping.[40] This pattern was reinforced, particularly in Brazil, by the immigration of white Europeans to the cities and to farming areas. Later, especially after World War I, the black and mulatto populations began large-scale migrations to urban areas. Many of these populations in the Caribbean began inter- and intrahemisphere movements, going to the United States and to other areas of the Caribbean.

The experiences of the blacks and mulattoes under slavery, especially those in plantation areas, affected their post-abolition existence in several characteristic ways. First, under plantation slavery they were accustomed to group rather than individual work and to a type of labor that was constantly supervised under authoritarian rules. This experience militated against the development of attitudes conducive to an individual free worker in an urban industrial economy. Concepts of time, voluntarism, mobility, and the ethos of dignity in work, all of which were tenets of European industrial society, were alien to the worker strapped to an authoritarian system. Thus, the involvement of the ex-slave in modernizing nations was hindered.[41]

A second effect of the slave experience emerged in rural areas. It was one thing for the ex-slave to work his own plot of land for subsistence, but it was quite another to work someone else's land as a matter of survival. Prior to final abolition, free blacks and mulattoes had disdained plantation labor because it was synonymous in their minds with slavery. This association of place and work persisted after abolition. Habits were hard to break; ex-masters found it difficult to avoid "ordering" their now free workers, and ex-slaves found it difficult to avoid acting subservient. In addition, the freedman preferred to grow subsistence produce rather than to cultivate crops for market. Contrary to expectations, the freedmen did not form European-type classes of yeomen, tenants and small farmers, and artisans, nor did they live in accordance with the European concepts of peaceful and socially useful lives.

A third effect was encouraged by the master classes. Inasmuch as the Euro-Americans were often unable or unwilling to provide social services for their own ethnic groups, it is not surprising that they were remiss in providing education, medicine, and other public welfare for the ex-slaves. Prior to abolition, most estates had not been centers of elegance and enlightenment for either white or black. Dietary, medical, educational, and other amenities of civilization had been sorely lacking throughout many plantation areas. This was the case in much of Brazil, for example. The situation persisted after abolition, but when services were extended to the privileged classes, they were withheld from the ex-slaves. Lack of social action by the elites was the natural consequence of their derogatory attitudes toward their former workers. The established churches alone stepped in to help the ex-slaves.

The question of race consciousness and conflict in contemporary race relations has emerged from these circumstances and patterns. It has been suggested that racial problems have been the least severe in Latin America, less severe in the Caribbean, and most severe in the United States. This suggestion requires some analysis here.

Curtin has suggested that "in Jamaica the race question [beneath the surface of every Jamaican problem] was often hidden behind other issues while in the American South other issues tended to hide behind racial conflict."[42] The attitude of the elites toward the blacks was ambivalent, but it may be generalized that they showed less discrimination against black females than against males. As possible reasons for their greater prejudice towards males, Curtin argues that as the minority race the whites were isolated and were in constant fear of an alien black majority.[43] Most important, Curtin contends that once Jamaica moved into new socioeconomic arrangements in the mid-nineteenth century and once a more permanent social life was introduced to the estates, prejudice became rampant.[44] In a phenomenon new to the plantation scene, the white wives imposed and encouraged the new attitudes and became the arbiters of new color standards.

In general, the British Caribbean colonies more closely resembled each other and stood in sharp contrast to British North America with regard to manumission and the rights of mulattoes and freedmen. Unlike the continental United States, the British Caribbean colonies recognized and made provisions for the mulattoes' relationships and activities. Jordan has suggested that the key to understanding this difference lies in the relative number of whites and blacks in given areas. He posits that because the British Caribbean whites were engulfed by blacks, they had to live in a more phlegmatic environment. He says that this environment was reinforced by the extremely high ratio of men to women which "contributed to the acceptability of miscegenation."[45] Another factor was the proximity of the British Caribbean to American societies of Iberia, especially those of Spain, which had a highly developed hierarchical social structure.

In his comparison of the Brazilian and United States racial pattern, Degler suggests that, unlike Brazil, the United States has had a long history of both customary and legal segregation of the races.[46] He also maintains that "the absence of the caste line or the acceptance of miscegenation is only the most obvious difference between race relations in Brazil and the United States."[47] Differences in slave systems, he states, are not fundamental to explanations of contemporary race relations; rather, in America they have been a result of historical circumstances.[48] If this is truly the case, then what are the roots of race relations and basic differences and similarities between cultures in the Americas? Degler suggests that, at least for Brazil, the principal difference is the mulatto escape hatch. The existence of the mulatto and society's development of a place for the mulatto is "a symbol, actually a condensation of a range of relationships between black and whites and attitudes toward one another."[49] Degler's argument implies that whatever biological, economic, or other circumstances generated the mulatto groups in the Americas, the need to recognize and continue that social stratum was crucial in Brazil as a racial leavening. Further, Degler theorizes that recognition and acceptance of the mulatto as a member of a special intermediary racial stratum has permitted the black race to become assimilated and accepted and to rise in Brazilian society. The lack of legal recognition of the mulatto stratum in the United States, he concludes, is a major difference between Brazil's and the United States' racial relations.

The Spanish-American situation has also been somewhat different from that of the United States. Although the Spanish, like the Portuguese, dissuaded racial mixing, the Spanish had a propensity for the Roman practice of hierarchically ordering society on the basis of place of birth and parentage. This ordering inevitably acquired racial overtones which resulted in fixed positions on the social scale for each degree of color and racial mix. As Davis has noted, in the long run the Spanish (and Portuguese) "were distinctive in their final acceptance of the inevitability of intermixture."[50] In his view Latin America "took concubinage as a matter of course;" masters acknowledged their mistresses and gave them special privileges. The belief was that "each step toward whiteness was a progression in status . . . [making] possible a slow assimilation which, in time, brought a relative degree of tolerance of racial diversity."[51]

In the French and Dutch colonies, free mulattoes ultimately formed a large class. Even so, they were not able to progress toward the status of whites because "unlike the Spanish and Portuguese, the Dutch and French attached the stigma of slave descent to any man with the slightest trace of Negro ancestry."[52]

Other scholars have made more specific points about these cultures. Hoetink has distinguished between two Dutch colonies, Curaçao and Surinam. Curaçao permitted a much more tolerant relationship between master and slave than Surinam. This relative benevolence was possible because Curaçao was a mercantile colony and not plantation-based. Moreover, the landowners did not have much capital and those who had slaves owned only a few. In contrast, Surinam had vast plantations with numerous slaves, a situation which created a great deal of fear in the planters. Yet, Surinam developed a strong mulatto middle class in the absence of a white one, something which did not happen in Curaçao. Hoetink suggests that this development had its origin in the 1773 Amsterdam stock market "crash" when almost all non-Jewish white planter families left the area, leaving the only non-Jewish white community almost entirely male. Since the Jewish residents inter-married with each other, the white males turned to common-law mar-riages with African women. The offspring of these marriages were given most benefits available to white children and became an elite of mulatto intelligentsia, bureaucrats, and the like. In Curaçao, the freedman population had already been considerable. This element readily fell into a hierarchical pattern of economic and social relation-ships in which business was dominated by Jews and government by Protestants.[53]

It is hoped that this outline of the Afro-American's heritage and experience will provide a framework for comparison and contrast among cultures and across time. The essays that follow deal with par-ticular patterns and problems in the Afro-American experience, the roots of which are in the historical past discussed here.

NOTES

1. For an elaboration of early African history, see Ann M. Pescatello, ed., *The African in Latin America* (New York: Alfred A. Knopf, Inc., 1975), pp. 3 ff.

2. For a discussion of the provenience patterns of the trade, see Philip Curtin, *The Atlantic Slave Trade. A Census* (Madison: University of Wisconsin Press, 1969).

3. For information on Portuguese Africa, see James Duffy, *Portuguese Africa* (Cambridge, Mass.: Harvard University Press, 1961).

4. Basil Davidson, *A History of West Africa* (New York: Anchor, 1966), p. 215.

5. Basil Davidson, "Slaves or Captives? Some Notes on Fantasy and Fact," in *Key Issues in the Afro-American Experience,* vol. 1, Nathan I. Huggins, Martin Kilson, and Daniel M. Fox, eds. (New York: Harcourt Brace Jovanovich, 1971), pp. 54-73.

6. Karl Polanyi, *Dahomey and the Slave Trade* (Seattle: University of Washington Press, 1968), p. 22.

7. Ibid., p. 117.

8. Colin Newbury, *The Western Slave Coast and Its Rulers* (Oxford: Oxford University Press, 1961), pp. 17-29 passim.

9. A. Norman Klein, "West African Unfree Labor Before and After the Rise of the Atlantic Slave Trade," in *Slavery in the New World,* Laura Foner and Eugene Genovese, eds. (Englewood Cliffs, N.J.: Prentice-Hall, 1970), pp. 87-93.

10. Ibid., p. 88.

11. Ibid., pp. 90-91.

12. J. D. Fage, *Introduction to the History of West Africa* (Cambridge, Mass.: Cambridge University Press, 1962), p. 97.

13. See G. I. Jones, *The Trading States of the Oil Rivers* (London, 1963). The "house," or "canoe house," to distinguish it from the ward or house of the fishing village, was

based on possession of a canoe equipped for war. The "canoe house" consisted of a wealthy trader, his children, and all his slaves. The house also had a fleet of canoes to bring slaves from interior markets to the coast. The large amount of capital necessary for such a venture tended to concentrate economic and therefore, political, power in the hands of a few. To reinforce such power, the head of a house encouraged its members to þranch into houses of their own. The house system appealed to Europeans because they were assured of trade with men of established reputations.

14. M. H. Kingsley, *West African Studies* (London, 1899), p. 535.

15. S. J. Ottenberg, "Ibo Oracles and Inter-group Relations," *Southwestern Journal of Anthropology* 14 (Autumn 1958): 295-314.

16. K. Onwuka Dike, *Trade and Politics in the Niger Delta, 1830-1835* (Oxford University Press, 1956).

17. Michael Crowder, *A Short History of Nigeria* (New York: Praeger, 1966), pp. 86-87, 110.

18. Ibid., p. 59.

19. Also see Pierre Verger, *Les Afro-Américains* (Dakar: IFAN, 1952), pp. 11-104; and J. F. de Almeida Prado, "Les Relations de Bahia (Brésil) avec le Dahomey," *Revue d'histoire des colonies* 41 (1954):167-226, although it lacks sources. For a full discussion of changing socioeconomic patterns on the "slave coast," see Newbury, *Western Slave Coast.*

20. Edward A. Alpers, "Trade, State and society Among the Yao in the Nineteenth Century," *Journal of African History* 10 (1969):409.

21. D. MacDonald, *Africana: or, The Heart of Heathen Africa* (London, 1882), vol. 1, p. 76.

22. Alpers, "Yao," p. 411.

23. MacDonald, *Africana,* vol. 1, p. 154.

24. Curtin, *Atlantic Slave Trade,* p. 268.

25. See Carlo M. Cipolla, *Guns, Sails, and Empires: Technological Innovation and the Early Phases of European Expansion, 1400-1700* (New York: Pantheon, 1966). See also J. H. Parry, *The Age of Reconnaissance* (London: Weidenfeld and Nicolson, 1963).

26. Philip D. Curtin, "Epidemiology and the Slave Trade," *Political Science Quarterly* 83 (1968):190-216.

27. The term *slave society* implies that the entire social, economic, political, and cultural structure has slavery as its basis. The term *nonslave society* implies the existence of slavery as one form of labor in a society but the overall social and economic relationships in that society are not dictated by the presence of slavery.

28. For a comprehensive look at the life and labor activities of the blacks and mulattoes in Latin America, see Pescatello, *African in Latin America,* pp. 59-194 passim.

29. See Pescatello, *African in Latin America,* pp. 195-220 passim.

30. For an excellent study on Mexico, see David M. Davidson, "Negro Slave Control and Resistance in Colonial Mexico, 1519-1650," *Hispanic American Historical Review* 46 (August 1966):235-253. For Cuba, see Franklin Knight's excellent *Slave Society in Cuba During the Nineteenth Century* (Madison: University of Wisconsin Press, 1970).

31. Elsa Goveia, *Slave Society in the British Leeward Islands at the End of the 18th Century* (New Haven: Yale University Press 1965), p. 245.

32. H. Orlando Patterson, *The Sociology of Slavery* (London: MacGibbon and Kee Ltd., 1967), pp. 273-283.

33. Fredrick P. Bowser, "The African in Colonial Spanish America," *Latin American Research Review* 7:1(1972):77-94, 84.

34. David W. Cohen and Jack P. Greene, *Neither Slave Nor Free. The Freedmen of African Descent in the Slave Societies of the New World* (Baltimore: Johns Hopkins University Press, 1972), Tables 1-3, and chapters passim.

35. Melville J. Herskovits, *Dahomey, An Ancient West African Kingdom* (New York: J. J. Augustin, 1938), passim.

36. Philip Curtin, *Two Jamaicas. The Role of Ideas in a Tropical Colony 1830-1865* (New York: Atheneum, 1970), pp. 113-114.

37. Curtin, *Two Jamaicas,* p. 25.

38. Herbert S. Klein, "Patterns of Settlement of Afro-American Population in the New World," in *Key Issues,* Huggins, Kilson, and Fox, eds., vol. 1, pp. 99-115, 114.

39. Ann M. Pescatello, "Brazilian Checkmate," unpublished paper delivered at the Southern Historical Association, 1970.

40. Ibid.

41. Ibid.

42. Curtin, *Two Jamaicas,* pp. 172-173.

43. Ibid., p. 174.

44. Ibid., pp. 174-175.

45. Winthrop D. Jordan, "American Chiaroscuro: The Status and Definition of Mulattoes in the British Colonies," *William and Mary Quarterly* 19:2(April 1962):183-200.

46. Carl Degler, *Neither Black Nor White* (New York: Macmillan, 1971), p. 5.

47. Ibid., p. 6.

48. Ibid., p. 92.

49. Ibid., p. 225.

50. David Brian Davis, *The Problem of Slavery in Western Culture* (Ithaca: Cornell University Press, 1966), p. 275.

51. Ibid.

52. Ibid., p. 278.

53. Harry Hoetink, "Diferencias en Relaciones Raciales entre Curazao y Surinam," *Revista de Ciencias Sociales* 5:4(December 1961):499-514.

Mary C. Karasch

2

THE AFRICAN HERITAGE OF RIO DE JANEIRO

In the first half of the nineteenth century, African slaves dominated the streets of the city of Rio de Janeiro. On a typical day in the heat of the afternoon, when their masters avoided the sun, African slaves sat in the doorways or worked in the streets. Observing the slaves, foreign visitors like the Englishman Luccock felt that they had landed in Africa instead of the capital of Brazil. There were so many blacks that travelers estimated they made up as much as two-thirds of the population. But until the 1849 census of Rio, there was no means of calculating the exact proportion of blacks or African-born slaves in the population of the city. According to the reasonably accurate 1849 census, Rio had a significant percentage of slaves in its population; moreover, two-thirds of the slaves were African-born (Table 1).[1]

Given the numerical predominance of black Africans in the population, it is startling that historians know little about their identity. Scholars interested in African origins or cultural survivals have turned to the Northeast: historians from Nina Rodrigues to Verger have established the origins of Bahia's slaves and their significant contribution to Brazilian culture.[2] The result is a serious omission. As this study will illustrate, Rio was a major center of African culture in the nineteenth century. In fact, until the dispersal of many of Rio's slaves to the coffee areas in the 1850s, the city had one of the most important concentrations of African slaves in Brazil. Moreover, it had a different blend of African ethnic groups than did Bahia, a blend that must have influenced the evolution of Cariocan culture in a way distinct from the Bahian. In addition, the city served as the major market-

TABLE 1

Slaves in the City of Rio de Janeiro in 1849

| | NATIONALITY | | | | | | SEX | | |
	Brazilian		African		Brazilian	African	Male	Female	TOTAL
	Male	Female	Male	Female					
Sacramento	2,437	2,709	5,566	3,503	5,146	9,069	8,003	6,212	14,215
São José	1,707	1,755	4,261	2,634	3,462	6,895	5,968	4,389	10,357
Candelaria	1,149	1,089	4,772	1,530	2,238	6,302	5,921	2,619	8,540
Santa Rita	1,716	1,495	6,577	2,516	3,211	9,093	8,293	4,011	12,304
Santa Anna	2,280	2,653	4,632	3,275	4,933	7,907	6,912	5,928	12,840
Engenho Velho	1,749	1,736	4,252	2,022	3,485	6,274	6,001	3,758	9,759
Gloria	1,239	1,185	2,788	1,567	2,424	4,355	4,027	2,752	6,779
Lagoa	826	789	1,514	932	1,615	2,446	2,340	1,721	4,061
TOTAL	13,103	13,411	34,362	17,979	26,514	52,341	47,465	31,390	78,855

place through which slaves from Central and East Africa were distributed to the interior provinces of Rio de Janeiro, Minas Gerais, and São Paulo, where the coffee plantations employed slave labor. Thus, Rio was closely connected with the innumerable slaves who were imported into Brazil prior to 1850 and with the great coffee boom of the nineteenth century.

The focus of this study, therefore, is on the newly imported Africans, specifically, their experience and adaptation to Brazilian slavery in the city of Rio de Janeiro. It is hoped that the description of the Africans' resistance to slavery and to the loss of their culture will illuminate the difficulties of adaptation that newly imported slaves experienced not only in Rio but wherever they were brought into the New World.

The identity and origin of the Rio slaves are most difficult to establish inasmuch as they came from many parts of Brazil and Africa. They were not a uniform homogeneous group in nationality, color, age, or sex. As a result, it is not possible to classify or identify them completely, but the following section should clarify the complex nature of Rio's slave population. On the whole, the terms employed are drawn from fugitive advertisements in the newspapers. Since the owners wanted to identify clearly their escaped slaves, the masters' descriptions are a valuable source for the variety of slaves in the population.[3]

One of the most common ways of identifying a slave was according to nationality. This was particularly true of African slaves, who were distinguished by a brand mark or tattoo peculiar to a given people. On the other hand, the term *crioulo (crioula)*[4] was generally sufficient to indicate that the person was a black born in Brazil, which in turn signified that the fugitive spoke Portuguese and in general followed the customs of Brazil. As further identification of a Brazilian-born black, an advertisement listed his place of birth as well as his accent. A fugitive born in Pernaguá, São Paulo(?), was described as "natural de Pernaguá," and he spoke with a Paulista accent.[5] Similarly, slaves who were born in other provinces in Brazil were usually designated as "natural de Bahia, Pernambuco, Minas Gerais." More infrequent was "Crioulo de Loanda, São Thomé, Angola," or "Moçambique," which indicated that the slave had been acculturated in one of the Portuguese African territories. Although African-born, he was expected to speak Portuguese and to be familiar with Portuguese customs.[6]

Quite distinct from the *crioulos* but also born in Brazil were the Indians and Indian-African mixtures. Although Indians were more commonly enslaved in the interior provinces, some did appear as slaves in the city. In 1819, the traveler Leithold observed some Botocudo Indians, who were used as slaves in Rio, and even as late as 1856, Indians were still "made merchandise of."[7] Unfortunately, more information on the Indian slaves is not available. In fact, it is possible that one observer may have confused mixtures of blacks and Indians *(Cafuzo, Cafuza)* with Indians. Although the slave *Cafuzos* were largely peculiar to the interior provinces, the traveler Pohl noted that some also lived in Rio. According to the artist Debret, the term *Ariboco* was used for black-Indian mixtures.[8] On the whole, slave Indians and *Cafuzos* were not common in Rio, since these terms rarely occurred in the sources consulted.

As a reflection of their importance in the city, African slaves were most common in advertisements for fugitives. Instead of following the American practice of giving slaves the master's surname, the usual formula was to use a Christian name plus the slave's place of origin, or his occupation, or another descriptive word. The designations "Joaquim Cassange," "Catharina Rebola [Libolo]," and "João alfaiate [tailor], Nação Congo" served to identify different slaves. If the slave had a brand mark, that too was printed; for example, Joaquim Mujau (Yao) had PR branded on his chest. Other advertisements described tattoos, such as those of Antonio Moçambique, who was clearly marked with a star on each cheek.[9]

Thus, if a slave's nationality, such as Mujau or Yao, was clearly identifiable, it was generally included in the advertisement. But if the master knew only that the slave was of African origin, he advertised him with the designation "de Nação," preceded by his Christian name. This practice probably arose from the common formula of Christian name plus "de Nação" and place of origin, such as "Maria, de nação Caçange."[10] In many cases the Christian name was not known, and the slave was identified only by the general term "negro [negra] de nação," indicating his African birth.

Other ways to call attention to African nationality were the terms *buçal* or *negro novo (negra nova)*. These designations indicated that the slave was African-born and was not yet acculturated. *Negro novo* further revealed that the slave had just been imported. On the other hand, *buçal* could be applied to a slave no matter how long he lived in Brazil if he did not learn the Portuguese language and customs of the masters. When Miguel, *nação* Monjolo, disappeared, his master suspected that he had been kidnapped because he appeared to be a *buçal* slave. After ten years in his master's house, he still could not (or would not) speak Portuguese.[11]

In contrast, if the slave learned Portuguese and comported himself as a Brazilian-born slave, he received the special term *ladino (ladina)*. Frequently, a Christian name plus *ladino* was sufficient to identify a slave, but sometimes the phrase also included the slave's African nationality, such as "Ladino de nação Camundá."[12] Moreover, the above terms were qualified to indicate the slave's degree of assimilation. The African who had acquired some Portuguese and some knowledge of the ways of the masters was designated *meio buçal, meio ladino,* or *meio novo,* indicating that he was at least partly assimilated. Sometimes his degree of fluency in Portuguese was also included, ranging from "speaks little of the language" to perfect fluency.

Final categories dealing with African nationality were those involving freed persons. A freedman who had been born in African was known as an *Africano forro (Africana forra)* or *Africano liberto (Africana liberta)*. Although freed persons, of course, did not appear in advertisements for fugitives, they commonly advertised their services in the newspapers. Since they were freed persons, they were clearly distinct from the group of *Africanos livres* (free Africans). The *Africanos livres* were slaves captured by the British in the slave trade and entrusted to the Brazilian government, which distributed them to private individuals who were to care for them and train them for freedom. At times, these so-called free men also fled from their caretakers, and so they too were listed in the fugitive slave advertisements. Such advertisements ran much like the others: "Fled on the fourteenth of the month, the 'Africano livre' Oracio, age 8 to 9."[13]

Besides nationality, one of the most common means of identification was color, terms for which ranged from almost white to dark black. In addition to general and racial categories, color descriptions included skin tones, such as bronze *(fula)*. To designate a black man, particularly an African, two terms were used interchangeably: *prêto (preta)* and *negro (negra)*. Frequently, the Christian name of a slave was not given, but rather the formula *prêto* or *negro* plus African nationality: "huma preta de Nação Cassange."[14]

The mixtures of white and black had a number of designations, only some of which were used in advertisements for fugitives and in notarial records. The most common term for black-white ancestry was *pardo (parda),* at times qualified as *pardo escuro* (dark) or *pardo claro* (almost white). Less common was *mulato (mulata),* with the same qualifiers. On the other hand, the diminutive ending appeared more frequently with *mulato*—that is, *mulatinho*—to indicate a child of black-white ancestry.[15]

Another mixture that entered the records was *cabra,* which denoted black-mulatto ancestry. Although Debret claimed that *bodé* was the male term and *cabra* the female, advertisements applied *cabra* to both sexes. João and Joaquim and a mother and her child were all called *cabra.* Most likely *bodé* was applied to male slaves because it is the term for male goats, while *cabra* is used for female goats. In the want ads *cabra* was the preferred term for both sexes.[16]

The third important way of identifying a slave was by age categories. In general, adult slaves were so designated in unqualified terms: "um negro," "um prêto," "um pardo," "um mulato." Unless a specific age was included, these individuals were assumed to be prime slaves in their twenties or thirties. Older slaves in their forties generally had their ages stated, such as Maria, who was thirty-eight to forty years old.[17] Although the racial terms do not of themselves imply age, an age meaning seems to have attached itself to them as they were used in the newspapers, since special names were given to nonprime slaves.

On the whole, young black men and women, generally under twenty years of age and of African birth, were called *moleque* and *moleca.* Although today *moleque* signifies a young black boy, the term was then used for all males between the ages of eight and even up to twenty-four. It was not a precise age term, and the evidence suggests that black men in their twenties received this appellation if they were short and youthful in appearance. For these men it must have had a derogatory connotation, as it does today. Moreover, the very young or short *moleques* frequently had the diminutive ending attached—*molequinho*—while older men received the opposite—*molecão,* or sometimes *molecote,* a name for a large-sized boy. Given the high percentage of young black slaves in the population, the term *moleque* appeared most frequently in the want ads.

On the other hand, *moleca* (feminine) was used infrequently. Perhaps young slave girls did not run away so often, or possibly they matured more quickly and merited the term *preta* or *negra.* In the advertisements for slave nurses, young girls who were still teenagers were generally designated *preta,* qualified by "ainda rapariga" (still a young girl). Moreover, these advertisements suggest that teenage girls were the preferred nurses.[18] But young girls also appeared in the advertisements for fugitives and were generally identified as "negrinhas," "mulatinhas," or "cabrinhas." If they were very young, their age was given to distinguish them from older girls. Occasionally, very young boys also received a similar appellation, such as *mulatinho* or *negrinho*; but *moleque* in its various forms was the preferred term for boys.

Slave children under five or six had a special term, *cria,* which was a term used for the young of an animal, such as a calf. On the slave ships, unweaned children were simply called *cria,* while those who were weaned but under five or six were designated *cria de pé,* or "standing child."[19] When these children appeared in the want ads for fugitives, they generally were reported to have been accompanied by their mothers. When Maria *mulata* fled, she escaped with her year-old daughter, who was "very white."[20] The term *cria* was used most frequently, however, in the notices for slave nurses, where the masters noted whether the advertised woman had a surviving baby or not. The common formula was "For sale a black nurse with child" or, as the case might be, "without child."[21] In the notarial records, the term *cria da casa* was frequently given as an explanation for freeing a slave. It indicated that the person had been reared in the household.

Part of the reason that children appear so frequently in the want ads is that a large proportion of children was imported into Rio in this period. Although Klein claims that children formed "a very small number of passengers of the slave cargoes," his conclusion is clearly based on the nature of his documents, which do not distinguish between adults and children, since only very young children were so designated in the 1795 to 1811 customhouse records.[22] On the other hand, a German traveler, Freireyss, reported in about 1815 that most of the imported slaves were children, generally from eight to ten years of age. Other respected travelers support his impression. Spix and von Martius described children from six years of age on sale in the slave market of the Valongo. In 1822, Maria Graham depicted one slave warehouse where the boys and girls were not over fifteen, and Debret portrayed the actual purchase of a child in the Valongo. In about 1827, C. Brand found over 300 children between the ages of six and thirteen in one warehouse, while the store next door held 50 boys. Even in 1848 there was still a market preference for young persons. Elwes, for example, wrote that boys of twelve to fourteen generally sold the best, since they were easily trained.[23] Another probable consideration was that children could serve for a longer period of time than a man of thirty or forty.

It is not surprising, therefore, to find in the records of slaves being imported into Rio a close correlation with the travelers' reports. In a sample from the 1830s and 1840s of slave ships captured by the British, "boys and girls" outnumbered individuals classified as women or men. In one ship alone, the *Duqueza de Bragança,* 80 percent of the cargo was made up of boys and girls; but of a total of eleven ships, the average cargo was about 60 percent boys and girls (Table 2).[24]

TABLE 2

Age and Sex of Imported Slaves, Rio de Janeiro

	Adults	*%*	*Boys and Girls*	*%*	*Total*	*%*
Male	1,188	32.4	1,491	40.7	2,679	73.1
Female	324	8.8	662	18.1	986	26.9
TOTAL	1,512	41.2	2,153	58.8	3,665	100.0

In Africa, Dr. G. Tams also recorded the proportion of children in the trade on the coast of Angola. In the two ships, he noted, children were in the majority. One of the vessels, of about twenty tons, held 105 "little children," the eldest being under seven. They had to be small, since the hold was divided into decks only twenty inches in height. In the *Corisco,* a larger brigantine of eighty tons, children were crammed into the hold. When it was captured in the trade, most of the children were like skeletons, and smallpox and the itch had broken out among them.[25]

In addition to the market preference for children and teenagers, there was a sex bias, which in some cases was reinforced by factors of supply in Africa. Certain slave-trading peoples—for example, the Cokwe and the Yao—kept the women and sold the men and boys. After 1830 in particular, the Cokwe demand for female slaves corresponded with a Brazilian demand for males. Thus, slave caravans traveling to the interior markets of Bihé or Kasanje (Cassange) sold the

females to the Cokwe in exchange for wax and ivory but kept the males
to carry the wax and ivory to the coast. On arrival in a port, they sold
the "legitimate" goods to "legitimate" traders and the slaves to Brazilian slavers. The Yao likewise kept the females to incorporate into
their society and traded or sold the males to the coast for export to
Brazil.[26]

Since African males tended to be sold to overseas traders, while the
women were often kept in Africa, Rio faced the problem of a sexually
unbalanced slave population. Yet, there was no drive in Brazil to import slave women. Brazilian planters and slaveowners preferred to
import boys and men, who could be used in a variety of occupations—
in the fields, at hard manual labor, in the mines, or in domestic service.
As a result, it is not surprising that almost 75 percent of the slaves in
the sample are male.[27] Whether the supply or demand factors were
more critical in influencing this preference for males is difficult to determine, but the cargoes were certainly more sexually unbalanced than
in the eighteenth century.

Table 2, based on a sample of 3,665 slaves from eleven ships, further
clarifies the age and sex breakdown for slave cargoes for at least the
period of the late 1830s and early 1840s.[28]

These import patterns explain, in part, why the city of Rio did not
have a balanced slave population in respect to either age or sex. According to the 1849 census (Table 1), only 60 percent of the slaves were
male. On the other hand, Brazilian-born slaves had a relatively equal
sex ratio and, one presumes, a fairly normal age distribution among
both sexes. However, African men outnumbered African women
almost two to one, and the slave group tended to have a higher proportion of young people, especially of young boys and men.

The above categories based on nationality, color, sex, and age help
to clarify the diverse nature of Rio's slave population as well as to
suggest some conclusions. Although slaves coming from various parts
of Africa contributed to the diversity of the population, the domestic
coastal and interior slave trade also brought Brazilian slaves into Rio.
Particularly after 1840, slaves from Bahia, Pernambuco, Ceará,
Maranhão, and other provinces in the Northeast were mentioned more
frequently in the newspapers. In short, the Brazilian-born slave population encompassed individuals from many different provinces and
regions. Since there were racial mixtures in other parts of Brazil, as well
as in Rio, the slave population was also diverse in color. Indians,

TABLE 3

**Total Population of the Eight Parishes of Rio de Janeiro
1849
Civil Status**

Parishes	Freemen	Freedmen	Slaves	Total	House-holds
Sacramento	25,435	2,206	14,215	41,856	5,054
São José	15,412	1,638	10,357	27,407	2,671
Candelaria	9,949	194	8,540	18,683	1,825
Santa Rita	18,095	1,413	12,304	31,812	2,964
Santa Anna	23,190	2,687	12,840	38,717	4,352
Engenho Velho	9,758	1,367	9,759	20,884	2,386
Gloria	8,168	723	6,779	15,670	1,461
Lagoa	6,312	504	4,061	10,877	981
TOTAL	116,319	10,732	78,855	205,906	21,694

cafuzos, mulatos, and *cabras* in varying degrees of mixture all contributed to the slave group. Certain assumptions to the contrary notwithstanding, the want ads alone illustrate that masters did not necessarily free their slave children, even those who could pass as whites. The image of black slaves did not apply to racially mixed Rio, even considering its large African population, since African women so frequently entered the records with mulatto children. In other words, "slave" did not necessarily equal "black."

Yet, as the census and other records suggest, a significant percentage of the slave group—as high as two-thirds in 1849—was African-born. Although it is difficult to establish the complete picture of the ethnic origins of this African population, part of the identification process, at least in broad geographical terms, has been done by Herbert S. Klein and Philip D. Curtin. After examining Rio's customhouse records on slave imports from Africa, Klein established that for the period 1795-1811 the majority of slaves came from Portuguese West Africa, that is, Cabinda, Angola, and Benguela.[29] Using British records on known slave ships entering the port of Rio, Curtin computed the percentage of slaves entering Rio from various points in Africa between 1817 and

1843. His figures illustrate the continuing importance of Angola and Mozambique as suppliers in the trade. They also reveal that Congo North (Klein's Cabinda) and Mozambique were far more important than in the period 1795-1811. His percentages are compared with Klein's in Table 4.[30]

TABLE 4

**Percentages of Slaves Coming from Portuguese
Africa, 1795-1811, 1817-1843**

	Curtin (1817-1843)	*Klein (1795-1811)*
West Africa	0.8	1.1
Senegambia and Sierra Leone	0.1	
Bight of Benin	0.2	
Bight of Biafra	0.3	
S. Thomé and Principe	0.2	
West Central Africa	71.1	95.8
Congo North	25.4	
Angola	45.7	
Mozambique and Madagascar	24.5	2.7
Unknown	3.7	0.4
	100.1	100.0

While these figures clearly establish that the majority of Rio's African-born slaves came from what is now Portuguese Africa, they no more than define the immense geographical area in which the diverse origins of Rio's African slaves must be pinpointed. In nineteenth-century Sierra Leone, S. W. Koelle carried out a linguistic study of the languages spoken by slaves captured and freed by the British. Koelle's results have provided modern historians with valuable information on the peoples of West Africa who were caught in the slave trade. Unfortunately, only a few of the groups from Portuguese Africa appear in his sample.[31] Where, then, can a comparable list be found to fill in the gaps in his information?

When the British were involved in suppressing the slave trade to Brazil in the first half of the nineteenth century, the Brazilian government helped them to capture various ships that were taken into Rio. The problem was what to do with the slaves, since it was impractical to return sick and weary slaves to Africa. The compromise was to put them under the control of the Brazilian government, which was to see that they received proper care and were given their freedom. Being responsible for these slaves, the government kept reasonably careful records on them, beginning with information on their African origins. In part, this procedure was necessary for identifying and keeping control over the *Africanos livres* given as political gifts to important individuals who, theoretically, were to train them to receive freedom. Unfortunately, only 26 percent were freed by 1869. Yet, because the government kept ultimate control over the remainder and used their nationalities and brand marks for identification, information on specific African ethnic groups has survived.[32]

The records of the captured ships on which these slaves were imported rarely identified them by African nationality, but the records are of critical importance because they establish where the ship traded on the coast of Africa. Without such information, one can only guess at the ethnic origin of a particular slave. The case of the *Brigue Especulador* illustrates the procedure. Her ship's papers, held at Itamaratí's archive, reveal that she took on cargo near the port of Benguela.[33] Beginning at Benguela, then, it is possible to establish through her list of slaves that the majority of the cargo came from the Ovimbundu plateau and the states tributary to Bailundu. Not all information is as complete as that for the *Brigue Especulador,* but knowing the port of origin is a definite aid in establishing what peoples came to Rio.

Thus, the *Africanos livres* records form the core of the sample of 5,384 individuals, but some additional data on ethnic origins came from want ads, a police list of fugitives (1826), license requests from street sellers, and notarial records.[34] Because the port of origin is unknown, these data are less useful except as they fill in some additional ethnic groups. Although the problems in the sample make it difficult to calculate the exact proportions of various groups in the Rio slave population, at least it further pinpoints the identity of some of the slaves and where they came from. However, the percentages for each major group are relatively close to Curtin's (Table 5).

No matter where they came from in Africa, the slaves shared a common experience in the Middle Passage to Rio. Whether crammed in a small coasting vessel or in one of the steamships that carried over a thousand slaves, they crossed the Atlantic in increasingly record times

TABLE 5

African Origins

Region	Total	Percentage
I. West-Central Africa		
Angolan place names	1,276	23.7
Angolan ethnic groups*		
Quicongo	141	2.6
Quimbundo	398	7.4
Lunda-Quioco	37	0.69
Ovimbundu	287	5.3
Ganguela	97	1.8
Nhaneka-Humbe, Ambo, Herero, and Xindanga	23	0.43
Congo place names	1,078	20.02
Congo-Brazzaville	326	6.1
Gabon	146	2.7
Congo-Kinshasa (Zaire)	6	0.1
Tentative Angola-Congo	96	1.8
Two possible identifications in West Central Africa	23	0.43
Total West Central Africa	3,934	73.997
II. West Africa	260	4.83
III. East Africa	1,059	19.7
IV. Unidentified	131	2.4
TOTAL:	5,384	

*Angolan classifications are based on José Redinha, *Distribuição Etnica da Província de Angola* (Angola, 1969).

to be unloaded in the warehouses of the slave market or on lonely beaches unknown to the abolitionists. Entering the Bay of Guanabara, the slaves had their first experience of slave life in the Valongo market. If allowed to be on deck when pulling into port and to the first stop at the customhouse, many of the slaves must have reacted like those on the slave ship that the traveler Ellis observed sailing into the harbor of Rio:

Our passing, however, appeared to affect them but little. The greater part of these unhappy beings stood nearly motionless, though we did not perceive that they were chained; some directed towards us a look of seeming indifference; others, with their arms folded, appeared pensive in sadness; while several, leaning on the ship's side, were gazing on the green islands of the bay, the rocky mountains, and all the wild luxuriance of the smiling landscape.[35]

Once such slaves were landed, they were counted at the custom-house and then led through the streets to the Valongo district, where newly imported slaves were quartered. At that time, the Valongo was bounded on one side by the beach, where small lighters unloaded their cargoes, and on the other by hills and virgin forest. In the early period, when tropical vegetation still surrounded the Rua do Valongo (c. 1820s), Dos Santos pictured the "very excellent houses" that lined the street. Schlichthorst described these same houses as "palaces," but they also served as warehouses for newly imported slaves. While the family of the slave dealer lived on the upper floors, the ground floor of the "palace" housed the slaves. A typical establishment, as described by Schlichthorst, had a large vestibule that opened on to a patio with low benches, where the slaves lived. Since the family lived above, these houses were kept "very clean," and fresh sea breezes eliminated bad odors.[36]

On the other hand, few European travelers paint such a romantic picture of the Valongo. The general impressions their emotional descriptions give are those of unbearable filth, barbarity, and stench. The residents of the Valongo and the newspapers of the time also inveighed against the barbarous conditions in the warehouses for the *negros novos*.[37] In part, what affected these differences of opinion was the period when slaves were imported. Most abuses occurred in periods of heavy importation when the market was not equipped to handle large numbers of slaves. The government's campaigns to confine new slaves to enclosed warehouses may have added to the problem, creating situations of crowding and discomfort whenever a slave ship brought in a new cargo.

When the traveler C. Brand visited the Valongo, a cargo of slaves had just been landed; his description, therefore, illustrates conditions in a period of heavy importation. At the time he saw the Valongo in

1827, almost twice as many slaves were being imported into Rio than in 1825 when Schlichthorst described it. Brand's observations provide a sharp contrast:

> The first flesh-shop we entered contained about three hundred children, male and female; the eldest might have been twelve or thirteen years old, and the youngest not more than six or seven. The poor little things were all squatted down in an immense wareroom, girls on one side, and boys on the other, for the better inspection of the purchasers; all their dress consisted of a blue-and-white checked apron tied round the waist; . . . The smell and heat of the room was very oppressive and offensive. . . . It was then winter [June]; how they fare at night in the summer, when they are shut up, I do not know, for in this one room they live and sleep, on the floor, like cattle in all respects.[38]

Whoever wanted to buy a slave went to one of these slave shops to deal with the slave merchants. In the largest warehouses, a buyer found slaves arranged like an audience in a theater pit, with the oldest (thirty to forty years old) in the highest and back rows, since they were the least valuable. The middle seats were occupied by prime slaves from fifteen to twenty years of age, while the front and lowest were filled by children of four or five. According to MacDouall, the children were the most numerous. In the smaller shops, the slaves were casually arranged on mats or benches along the walls. The slaves were either already divided by age and sex, or the overseer ordered them to organize themselves on the approach of a buyer. In other houses slaves were frequently divided into rooms by sex, the women and girls in one room, the men and boys in another.[39]

When a buyer entered the warehouse, the slaves were exhibited, handled, examined, and haggled over—much as any other commodity. Once agreement was reached and credit terms arranged, the buyer could walk home with his new slave. According to the traveler Rugendas, new slaves awaiting sale at the Valongo were frequently impatient to know their fate. Thus, when they were finally sold, they considered the sale a "true liberation" and accompanied their new master with much goodwill.[40] They were undoubtedly relieved to escape the crowding, the filth, and the confinement of the warehouses.

For these newly imported Africans, the slave market was the beginning of their introduction to Brazil and to their lives as slaves. Perhaps the greatest consequence of their experience in the slave market was the influence it had on their desire to accept or to reject their new situation. In other words, the Valongo not only determined the slave's ultimate destiny but also his conception of it. As such, it was one of the most critical points in his life, affecting where he would live, whom he would serve, and even whether he would live or die an early death.

After entering his new master's home or property, the almost immediate reaction of a new slave was some form of resistance, such as stubbornness, refusal to work, or running away. As in most slave societies, slave resistance was not limited to one form: there were as many types of resistance as there were individuals who did not passively accept their condition as slaves. The city of Rio saw the usual forms of passive resistance to slavery, such as work stoppage, sabotage, theft, and crime. Except in the case of crime, little information survives on passive resistance to slavery other than indirect evidence from the elite's stereotypes of slaves as lazy, inefficient, childlike, and unwilling to work. Violent resistance, such as slaves killing their masters, entered the police records, but in this period in Rio, violent resistance was largely on an individual basis. Unlike Salvador, Bahia, in 1835, Rio did not have an organized slave revolt. Most slave violence in Rio took the form of individual crimes, sometimes against the masters but far more often against other slaves, freedmen, soldiers, or poor men in the city.

The term *resistance* suggests but does not completely define the extent to which Rio's slaves tried to escape their bondage. Given the number of fugitive slaves and *quilombos* (settlements of escaped slaves, see below, p. 52) in and about the city, one might suppose that the prominent characteristic of slave life in Rio was withdrawal rather than violent resistance. Slaves simply ran away and hid in the nearby mountains or lost themselves among the poor of the city. Others formed their own villages and tried to live free and independent lives. Some left Brazil and returned to Africa, while others committed suicide, believing that thus they would return to their homeland.

Whatever form of withdrawal they chose, however, it is evident that the slaves were not interested in "making it" on the terms of Cariocan society. Basically, they wanted freedom and would take risks that imposed severe penalties if they failed. If one allows the slave to express (indirectly through the documents) whether he did or did not want to be a slave, one is not surprised at the number of those who evaded, or tried to evade, their condition. They were not content with their so-called humane Brazilian masters, nor did they passively accept their enslavement. In fact, African slaves in particular were quite maladjusted to life in Rio and the conditions of servitude.

In using the records of slave fugitives there are two problems: limited statistical material and an abundance of want ads dealing with fugitives from all of the major contemporary newspapers. *O Diario do Rio de Janeiro,* a daily whose pages deal almost exclusively with advertisements, particularly regarding slaves, indicates the magnitude of the fugitive problem. In addition, there are two police documents from 1826 that give some statistical idea of the number of fugitives captured in that year. These documents comprise the record of expenses incurred in sending escaped slaves from various parts of the court to the Calabouço (a prison), as well as the police list of fugitives and other criminals.[41]

The expense record immediately supports the impression of a significant fugitive problem. Considering that it deals only with those slaves who were caught and sent to the Calabouço in 1826, the total of 925 men, women, and children must reflect a much larger number of escapees, some of whom must have succeeded in avoiding the police and the slave hunters. Yet, it also seems that the percentage of successful escapes must have been low, since the *Africanos livres* records reveal that no more than 2 percent of 11,008 persons fled and escaped capture.[42] It seems that while there were many fugitives, many were caught, whipped in the Calabouço, and returned to their masters. Although attempted escape was common, successful escape was not.

As Table 6 illustrates, the vast majority of fugitives in 1826 were African-born—almost 85 percent—whereas Brazilians contributed only 6 percent to the total. These figures certainly substantiate Schlichthorst and A.P.D.G.,[43] who commented on the problem of newly imported slaves escaping. Probably the reason so many Africans failed was that they were unfamiliar with the terrain and were easily recaptured by slave patrols composed of ex-slaves and Indians.

Related to the fugitive problem were the *quilombos.* In fact, many of those imprisoned in 1826 were captured while living in small settlements of escaped slaves. In the police records the inhabitants of *quilom-*

TABLE 6

**Nationality of Fugitive Slaves Compiled
from the Police List of 1826**

West Central Africa		*East Africa*	
Ambaca	1	Macua (Makua)	6
Angola	51	Moçambique	186
Cabundá (Umbundo)	12	Quelimane	9
Camu(n)dá (Umbundo)	1	Senna, Mecena (Sena)	3
Benguela	107		
Boma	2	TOTAL	204
Cabinda	66		
Cassange	55		
Congo	125	*West Africa*	
Ganguella (Ganguela)	4	Bissão (Guinea-Bissau)	1
Mahume, Mohumbe		Cabo Verde (Cape Verde	
(Humbe)	5	Islands	1
Coumbe (Humbe)	1	Calabar	7
Rebolo, Rebolla (Libolo)	40	Mina	26
Loanda (Luanda)	2	São Thomé	1
Camindongo (Camundongo)	3		
Mohange(?)	5	TOTAL	36
Quissamã (Kisama)	3		
Maçange (Sanga)	1		
Sanga	1	*Brazilian-born*	
Songo	1	Crioulo	44
Monjollo (Tyo, Teke)	13	Pardo, mulato	8
		Cabra	4
TOTAL	499		
		TOTAL	56

African-born, not identified	
Quicame(?)	1
Prêto buçal or negro novo	29
De Nação	7
TOTAL	37

Total African-born:	776	84%
Total Brazilian-born:	56	6%
Unknown nationality:	93	10%
TOTAL	925	

SOURCE: AN, Cod. 359, Livro 1°, Polícia, Suprimentos de Despêsas com Escravos Fugidos, fols. 1-74.

bos, called *quilombolas* or *calhambolas,* were so designated because the penalties for them were more severe than for other fugitives. The fate of a *chefe* or head of a *quilombo* was to be whipped to death.[44] This severity was imposed because of the masters' fear of another Palmares,[45] but most of the *quilombos* around Rio were relatively small in size, with only five, ten, or twenty individuals who merely wanted to live in freedom. The greatest threat they posed to the city was theft or armed robbery. At times, they even existed with the help of free men, who traded with them for food or forest products. The authorities, however, regarded the numerous *quilombos* in Tijuca, the Morro do Destêrro (Santa Teresa), Corcovado, and Lagoa as evils that had to be eradicated. Throughout the period, the *quilombos* were raided many times but were never eliminated. Although the police once caught 200 slaves in one raid, most of the time they captured only small groups. Thus, while the *quilombos* were generally small in size, they were numerous. Most important, the *quilombos* testify to the slave's desire to control his own life and to live outside of slavery— even "in the greatest misery," as Walsh described a group caught in the hills behind Rio.[46]

While the majority of Africans who wanted to escape slavery fled into the hills, a minority sought to withdraw completely from Rio and from Brazil. Although most Africans could only dream about their homeland, a few managed to return permanently. Typical of the dreamers was a freedman whom Bremoy met on a road in the Corcovado area. When he approached the man, who was sitting with his eyes fixed on the ocean in the distance, Bremoy recognized him as a carpenter who had worked for him. Bremoy asked why he was so far from the city; the man answered in Portuguese, "I am praying the waters to take my 'saudades' to my dear land." His master had freed him three months before, and he had come to live in a place where he could look at the ocean and feel close to his country. He showed Bremoy four carved figures which he said represented his uncle who was a king, his father, his wife, and his baby whom he had never seen. At that time, he was saving money to buy his passage to Angola. When Bremoy returned six months later, the cabin was abandoned, and he never learned if the carpenter had gone back to Africa.[47]

The carpenter was not the only skilled craftsman who hoped to see Africa again. Following peak years of white immigration in 1849 and 1850, Consul Hesketh reported to London that white competition had affected the "free coloured workmen or artificers of this place, who are discontented at the reduction of wages in consequence of the influx of white competitors, and are desirous to return to Africa." He noted that an "intelligent free African" had applied to the British consulate for the protection of the British flag to transport himself and "a large number of his countrymen" to Ambriz (Angola), declaring that there were more than 500 other free Africans who refused to go to any place but Africa.[48]

A more dangerous method was to seize a boat and attempt to escape to Africa. In 1850, the English ship *Rifleman* detained a launch filled with nine blacks, including a woman and a *moleque* of sixteen years. They said they belonged to people living in Campos in the province of Rio, and they intended to sail to Africa. According to the British, they would not have survived the voyage because they had water for only six or eight days.[49] Possibly their action was typical of many unplanned, desperate attempts to escape to Africa by sea.

On the other hand, one well-planned and successful voyage to Africa has entered the historical record for Rio. When the Quakers Candler and Burgess visited Rio in 1852, they received a delegation of free blacks, who had learned of the nature of their antislavery mission. In "strict privacy" at the office of an English shipbroker, who had their confidence and who acted as an interpreter, eight or ten Minas from the coast of Benin told their story. Many years before, they had been captured and sold into slavery in Rio. By "very hard labour" they had earned enough to buy themselves; now they wanted to charter a ship for Africa. They had their passage money, and they desired information about any danger from slave traders on the African coast. Sixty of their companions had already reached Badagry the previous year. The broker verified this fact, showing Candler and Burgess the charter under which they had sailed. The following is part of the copy printed by the Quakers:

On the 27th of November, 1851, It is agreed between George Duck, Master of the British brig called the Robert, Al [*sic*], and Raphael Jose de Oliveira, free African, that the said ship shall receive in this port, sixty-three free African men (women and children included in this number) and their luggage, and shall proceed to Bahia, and remain there if required fourteen days, and then proceed to a safe port in the Bight of Benin on the coast

of Africa, . . . and deliver the same on being paid freight, here
in this port, the sum of Eight Hundred Pounds sterling, to be
paid before the sailing of the next British packet.[50]

Possibly these Minas were Hausas, since Candler and Burgess received
a paper written in Arabic from one of their "chiefs," who was described as a "Mahommedan." Unfortunately, Candler does not say
whether the second group also made it safely back to Africa.

The incident was not an isolated or exceptional occurrence. As late
as 1869, Gobineau reported that Muslim Mina slaves still formed savings societies to accumulate funds, buy their freedom, and return to
Africa. He also noted that it was less common by 1869, since many
preferred to continue working in Salvador, Bahia, or Rio de Janeiro.[51]

Most African slaves, of course, did not realize their dream of returning to Africa, and those who escaped frequently failed to avoid
recapture. For most Africans, no matter by what means or with what
intensity they resisted slavery, the result was the same: they had to
adapt to being a slave in a foreign city. Moreover, their masters forced
them to adopt a new language and a new culture. They were forbidden
to speak their African language and were forced to acquire the proper
subservient deportment.

The result of this forced assimilation was the loss of a rich heritage; yet, despite discrimination and laws, certain elements of African
culture did not die out at the masters' command. While a whole culture
could not be transferred to Rio and remain unchanged, some aspects
continued to be important in the lives of the people. In time, they
were generalized in Cariocan culture, accepted by the masters or by
slaves from other cultural traditions, and passed down to the next
generation of slaves and to their modern descendants. The question is,
if the masters forced assimilation, how could Cariocan slaves continue
their African religious practices, or music, or dances? Were there institutions that safeguarded these traditions and that served as mechan-
isms of transmission from one generation to the next? Moreover, what
were these important institutions within slave society?

First, African slaves tended to maintain some features of the political
institutions they had known in Africa and to organize themselves in
political groups similar to those in Africa. Under one organizational
pattern, if a king, a chief, or his sons were transported to Rio, the
political group was centered around the traditional leaders. Travelers

recorded descriptions of these individuals holding court in the streets of Rio and deciding the "gravest questions." They observed African princes sitting on stones in the streets, surrounded by their subjects who came to consult them. At one street corner, Walsh saw a curbstone which he was told was the throne of a young Angolan prince, who held court there every evening and on Sundays and holidays. Besides making decisions on matters for which he was consulted, he also passed judgment, and if punishment was deserved, one of his officers administered it with a stick.[52]

Other African leaders likewise received the homage of their subjects whether holding court or passing in the street. The special form was to kiss the hand, often accompanied by a bending of the knee. A man's poverty evidently did not determine his status. Dabadie knew an old former *negro de ganho* (black for hire, or streetseller) who had been a king in Africa. Although he wore rags, his subjects never failed to salute him and ask for his blessing. Schlichthorst saw the subjects of an African prince give him presents, which he regarded as the voluntary tribute of loyal subjects. This tribute frequently took the form of contributions to the purchase of his freedom.[53] Consequently, a man's prior status in Africa—if high enough—could influence his manumission in Rio.

When a former king or son of a king died, his funeral was celebrated with great ceremony. Processions, drums, firecrackers, and dancing accompanied the ritual at a slave church, such as Lampadosa, followed by burial in the churchyard or a cemetery. Just as at any king's funeral, three dignitaries, who represented each of the African "nations" in Rio, attended the rites and paid him honor. Debret has provided a graphic representation of the funeral of a king's son that he saw in about 1830.[54]

The presence of national delegates at a funeral points to the political divisions that existed among the African slaves of Rio. Walsh estimated that there were eight or nine "castes" in Rio, each having a separate language and loyalty. Since they maintained national loyalties, they also continued the old feuds that perhaps had led many of them to be enslaved. As Ruschenberger summed up their situation: "Common misery has not caused the negroes to forget the feuds of their tribes, for they have brought mutual and perhaps hereditary hatred with them, and it is supposed that the safety of the whites, whose numbers are very small, depends upon this circumstance."[55]

In much the same words, Schlichthorst observed that their first
loyalties went to their nation, and if they fought, it was over an old
African issue. Moreover, they continued to remember their "native
land" even after many years in slavery. According to Schlichthorst,
their favorite words were "minha terra e minha naçào" (my land and
my nation), and pride in their national origin made them exclaim "Eu
sou Congo!" (I am a Congo) with the same spirit as an Englishman.
When Scherzer asked three *Africanos livres,* who were "hearty of
aspect and neatly clothed, who had been so carefully tended by the
State," if they preferred their present situation to their own home,
they all replied that "they longed to return to Quillimani [Mozambique],
where it is hardly requisite to work above six months."[56]

While many Africans tried to reconstruct traditional political forms
in Rio, others had to adapt their African forms to conditions in Rio.
Those whose leaders had not come with them had to choose new leaders
or establish new loyalties, perhaps to another African ruler. Walsh
found that men from the Congo elected a king from amongst themselves and submitted to his decrees. In a later period, the authorities
permitted the election of "national governors," if approved by the
police. These men thereafter had the responsibility of maintaining
peace and good conduct among the members of their national groups.[57]

Exactly what the election of a king in Rio entailed is not quite clear,
especially in the early period. Did the elected king have decision-making
powers over his subjects? Could he demand tribute from them to buy
his freedom? Could he sit in judgment over them? The travelers suggest that African princes did have these powers and the respect of their
subjects. But did newly elected "national governors" or kings and
queens have the same powers? Or were the coronations of kings and
queens merely rituals, conferring no more powers than those possessed
by a Carnival king of the 1970s? One might speculate that the coronations were meaningful only to the slaves themselves, who tried to re-
create in Rio some semblance of African royalty and kingship. On the
other hand, the ceremonies were peculiarly Brazilian and had been in
existence since colonial times.[58]

One coronation that has entered the historical record took place on
October 8, 1811, in the church of Nossa Senhora da Lampadosa, one
of the famous slave churches of Rio. Caetano Lopes dos Santos and
Maria Joaquina, both of the "Cabundá nation" (Umbundu), were
crowned king and queen. They had been "elected by their nation"

and approved by the chief of police. In testimony thereof, the chaplain of the brotherhood and the "crowned kings" of the other African nations signed the coronation document.[59]

As far as the historical record reveals, the major duties of the kings and queens crowned in the church of Lampadosa were to preside over religious festivities and to represent their "nation" at various events and in the massive religious processions held in the city in that period. On religious feast days, at important funerals, or on any occasion, the "royal" couple represented their African subjects and led the festivities. In their own African celebrations, the king and queen presided over the theatrical dances known in Rio as *congadas* or *cucumbis.*

According to Théo Brandão, there were two major types of dances that generally went under the name of *congadas.* The first, *a congada* or *auto dos Congos,* was a warrior dance between two nations, including the visit of ambassadors and the death and resurrection of an ambassador or king's son. The second, *o congado* or *reinado dos Congos,* celebrated the election and coronation of a king and queen and included a procession with dancing representatives of religious brotherhoods and African "nations." Generally, the coronation dance ended with other dances, among them warrior dances, and storytelling ballets that related remembrances of Africa.[60]

The striking feature of any account of a *reinado dos Congos* is the mixture of Afro-Brazilian elements. African divinities and Catholic saints, and Catholic priests and African *feiticeiros* (religious specialists, priests) played important roles. The king and queen were crowned in the church by the Catholic priest, while the drums beat, and the *feiticeiro* with his snake and charms accompanied the royal couple in the procession. Thus, on the Christian feast day of the Three Wise Men, the slaves used to celebrate the coronation of their king and queen and perform the dances of Africa.[61]

The question is, of course, how the Catholic church could accept so easily this coronation ritual, as well as the participation of the *feiticeiro.* Eventually, in about 1820, the government passed laws forbidding large gatherings of slaves, and the laws soon did away with the political-religious ritual of *o reinado dos Congos.* But until this ban was imposed, it was one of the major institutions that kept alive memories of Africa in a Brazilian setting.

In addition to African political institutions, there existed among the slaves in Rio an organization whose origins are obscure but which played a significant role in slave society. Combining both African and Brazilian elements and incorporating slaves, freedmen, and even whites, it served many functions, but its major purpose was protection. As the Brazilian army and police protected the masters, so this group organized in response to the slaves' need for some form of physical security, especially since they were forbidden to carry arms. It was generally known for the particular style of fighting practiced by its members, called *capoeira, capoeiragem,* or simply *jogo.*[62]

The origins of *capoeiragem* in Rio are not wholly clear. One theory is that it arose among the slaves who carried goods in large baskets on their heads, known as *capoeiras.* While working in the streets, on the beaches, and in the markets they learned to protect their goods and themselves by delivering forceful blows of the feet and head. This form of fighting paralleled a dance form, and by the nineteenth century the *negros de ganho* and all types of porters used the *capoeira* both as a dance form and as a deadly method of combat against their enemies. It was so effective and dangerous that the government tried to restrict its practice by publicly whipping its practitioners.[63]

But *capoeiragem* was not simply a dance-fight. By the time of Dom Pedro I, the *capoeiras* had evolved into organized brotherhoods, or at least gangs, that protected the slaves in their territory through their ability to defend themselves by this technique.[64] At that time, each *confraria,* or brotherhood, of *capoeiras* was known as a *malta.* Each *bairro* of the city had its *malta* with its own leader and its own name— that is, Cadeira da Senhora in the parish of Santa Anna, Três Cachos or Flor da Uva in Santa Rita, Franciscanos of the *bairro* of São Francisco, Flor da Gente of Gloria, Espada of Lapa, Monturo or Lusitanos of Santa Luzia, São Jorge or Lança of the Campo da Aclamação, Santo Inácio of Castelo, and Ossos of Bom Jesus do Calvário. In turn, the *maltas* divided into two rival groups that frequently engaged in fights, respectively known as the Nagoas and the Goyamus.

The professionals or leaders of the *maltas* appear to have been freedmen and fugitive slaves, though mulattoes and whites sometimes took over the leadership, particularly in the second half of the nineteenth century. Factors other than color seem to have determined the chiefs of the *maltas,* especially qualities of leadership and skill in combat.

The *maltas* appear to have had many of the characteristics of secret societies. In fact, Itier was probably referring to them when he discussed the secret societies of Rio that were headed by freedmen and whose purpose was to protect the slaves.[65] He claimed that the masters feared a revolt because of the slaves' ability to organize these societies. Since the *maltas* had secret rituals with oaths and prayers (an African influence?) and characteristic signs and greetings, their activities further suggest the organization of an African-style secret society.

On the other hand, the *capoeiras* openly participated in parades. Notable white politicians used them as protection from attack. The *capoeiras* also helped politicians to obtain votes or to disrupt elections. Others served as hired killers for political or other reasons. Even the police, who were ordered to break up their meetings and arrest them, protected them and used their services. The most famous service of the *capoeiras* to the city of Rio occurred in 1828, when they aided the government in suppressing the revolt of the Irish and German mercenaries. When the foreign soldiers rampaged through the city, the *capoeiras* attacked, forcing them back to their quarters, where the army encircled and subdued them. The *capoeiras* were also credited with defending the royal palace at Quinta da Boa Vista. In a later period, *capoeiras*—at least those from Bahia—were recruited to fight in the Paraguayan War, where many distinguished themselves.[66]

Given their ability to fight armed European mercenaries and troops in Paraguay, one must ask why the *capoeiras* did not become a focus for revolt in the city of Rio. The answer probably lies in the nature of their organization and their basic orientation toward defense. Their division into relatively autonomous *maltas* that fought each other as rival street gangs militated against their ability to organize as a whole. In addition, their goals and ideology never seem to have risen above mere defense of the small group to the wider objective of a full-scale slave revolt. But this is all conjecture, since there is no information to confirm or deny the possibility. The *capoeiras* may have plotted many revolts that never reached fruition and so left no record. Or they may have considered revolt impossible in the face of the well-armed military forces and police stationed in Rio.

Whatever the reasons, the *capoeira* filled an institutional need— protection—that the elite did not provide through its police or military forces. In much the same way, the other political institutions formed by the slaves ensured their role in decisions that affected their own groups, whether through traditional chiefs or elected leaders. In short, the slaves of Rio created political institutions to govern themselves (independent of elite institutions) that had their own particular characteristics, often of an African origin.

If slaves kept alive African political institutions, they also continued to practice their traditional religions. Although African slaves did actively participate in the church and sons of freedmen did become priests, many Africans found it difficult to cast off their ancestral religions. Superficial changes were easily made, but ingrained patterns of thinking and belief were difficult to put aside. What tended to occur was either a total rejection of Luso-Brazilian Catholicism or a synthesis of two or more religious systems.

In the 1820s, Leenhof testified to the strength of African religious practices in the city of Rio when he wrote that those practices indicated a deep religious spirit that could only with difficulty be shaped to Christianity.[67] Unfortunately, only scattered references to nineteenth-century African religious practices survive in the travel accounts, a situation that makes it difficult to establish much about African religions in Rio. Since slaves were arrested for practicing *candomblé,* police persecution tended to drive the religions underground. When they emerged again in the twentieth century, they had undergone so many changes that their form in the nineteenth century cannot easily be reconstructed.

African religious specialists, frequently termed *feiticeiros,* as in the *congadas,* do appear in the records. In fact, a stereotype of one appears as a fictional character, Pai Raiol, O Feiticeiro. Machado depicted him as an evil man having absolute power over the slaves because of his supernatural art, which he had learned in Africa. He hated all whites and plotted the destruction of his owners.[68] But this is a master's viewpoint of the African religious specialists, who in fact mainly practiced divination, made medicines and charms, or conducted *candomblé* sessions.

One of the earliest references to African religious leaders appears in Tuckey, who wrote that newly imported Africans had the "most sanguinary contests" because they were convinced that their "priests" could make them invulnerable.[69] How they did this he does not say, but the probable procedure was to make a powerful charm to protect them from enemies. Another form of specialist in Rio was the diviner. No matter what form of divination he used, he was frequently consulted by the slaves in all matters relating to their future security. One

Mina slave, who consulted the diviner prior to playing the lottery, was probably typical of those slaves who went to the diviner to learn the future or to understand the past.[70] Because of the number of health problems—real or imagined—among the slaves, black barber-surgeons, "doctors," or herbalists were also common. The learned French doctor, Imbert, inveighed against the faith Brazilians put in *feiticeiros,* magic, spirits, and quack doctors. Debret graphically portrayed one of these "doctors" at work on a patient in the streets of Rio. Besides medical treatment, the "doctor" also sold his patients talismans and amulets. Walsh also described a black "doctor," who treated his patients on the steps of a church. When MacDouall visited the shop of a black barber-surgeon, he reported that every such place had an *obi* charm (a large ram's horn with a painted red tip filled with magic ingredients to prevent evil and black magic), made by "old negro women."[71]

In addition to "priests," diviners, and herbalists, certain religious specialists seem to have combined various powers in one person. The "African conjurer" whom Ewbank mentions as having been arrested for "candombe" *(candomblé)* probably spoke with the spirits about the future and also made charms or medicines. Ewbank examined the objects captured by the police when the "conjurer" was arrested. They included the following items: two small wood statues with jointed arms covered with blood and feathers, iron prongs and stone knives used as "sacrificial implements," goat horns, ivory tusks, animal skeleton heads, boxes of colored dust, rattles, bundles of herbs, and a scarlet cap and gown. According to Ewbank, the "conjurer" was a Mina slave, who would be flogged because it was said that the conjurers took the savings of slaves and encouraged them to rob or poison their masters.[72] Evidently, the masters feared the power of these individuals, since they enforced serious penalties against them.

In part, too, the fear of African religious specialists was probably linked with a general Brazilian fear of witchcraft and evil spirits. Since the *feiticeiros* consulted spirits and made charms, one would suspect that the Catholic masters believed that their slaves were consulting the devil and practicing black magic. For example, two mulattoes were arrested for "necromancy," which suggests anything from communication with the spirits of the dead to witchcraft and black magic.[73] Since many of the slaves came from parts of Africa where a belief in witchcraft was particularly common and was sometimes the reason for their enslavement, one suspects that this practice was also true of Rio.

It could be surmised that slaves resorted to various practices connected with harmful spirits or charms to eliminate their masters or at least to make them more benevolent. When an overseer was killed at night by some slaves in Tijuca, they left his body in the middle of a road. When others passed the corpse the next morning, they made "bizarre gestures" and threw branches of greenery and some money on the body. Possibly the green branches were from the garlic tree, which slaves commonly used to placate an angry master. According to Maria Graham, they believed that the bark of this tree would make their masters kind to them again.[74] Perhaps in this case they were placating the spirit of the dead overseer so that he would not return as an evil spirit to harm them.

Regrettably, there is no evidence of the form of the religious ceremonies or of the ritual involved. It could be that they were similar to a contemporary *candomblé* with dancing, prayers and hymns in an African language and offerings of food, liquor, and tobacco; but this is guesswork. It is only possible to describe in general terms some of the beliefs and rituals that slave women passed on to slave children. A belief in spirits, whether of ancestors or nature spirits, was quite common. In fact, descendants of Angolan slaves in Rio still referred to spirits in the twentieth century by the African names of Quilimo *(nkilimo)* and Cassuto.[75] Numerous studies have pointed out the syncretisim of Yoruba gods with Catholic saints, but one would suspect that at least in nineteenth-century Rio the dominant African religious influence was that of the ancestral or nature spirits. In turn, this emphasis on spirits may explain the popularity of the spiritualist Umbanda religion in the twentieth century.

With their belief in spirits, it is not surprising that the slaves used diviners to interpret a man's connection with the spirit world—that is, to contact spirits of the dead or in nature to establish the influences for good or harm in a man's life. Consequently, charms or amulets or medicines were devised to influence the spirits for good or evil. If a man's sickness was attributed to an evil spirit or to another man, the diviner would act as a healer and take steps to eliminate the harmful influence and thus cure the sick man. If a spirit were involved, a ritual would be performed to drive out the harmful spirit; but if an unknown person were involved, the diviner might search out the witch who had caused the illness. Because of the use of charms by the barber-surgeons and other black "doctors," the slaves most likely continued to believe in unnatural causes for sickness. If a man died, they may have believed that witchcraft was the cause of death. Or others might have felt that the spirits of the dead brought about death. In short, their beliefs in the causes of illness and death probably influenced them to seek other healers in preference to the Brazilian doctors. When the French doctor Imbert failed to cure a black women, the black woman went to a *feiticeiro*. Later, her master wrote to Imbert that the illness had left her.[76]

Considering the diversity of peoples who entered Rio, each bringing their own belief systems, one can merely point to a generalized belief in spirits and reemphasize that the Africans brought with them viable religious systems that did not disappear with baptism. African beliefs and religious identities continued to exist alongside the Catholic Church. Although slaves might join in processions and enter churches, they also consulted the spirits. Because of their limited religious instruction in Catholic beliefs, they usually imposed their own beliefs on the external rituals of the church. They confused the Christian God with their remote creator god, the Christian saints with powerful spirits, the souls in purgatory with ancestors, and so forth. As the nineteenth century continued, so did the process of syncretism, the slaves adopting the external rituals of Catholicism but also incorporating their own beliefs. The result was the development of independent religious institutions among slaves, freedmen, and lower class freemen that served their special religious needs. Although technically members of the Catholic Church through baptism, they turned to the African cults for their religious life.

In addition to the traditional African religions, Islam, the religion of the Minas, also continued to survive in Rio. According to Gobineau in 1869, most of the Minas, if not all, were Muslims; they only appeared to be Christians. Because their religion was not tolerated, they kept it hidden. They submitted to baptism and took Christian names, but they continued to guard their religion and to transmit their beliefs brought from Africa "with a great zeal." They were able to do this because they studied Arabic and read the Koran, which was commonly sold in French bookstores in Rio. Although the Koran was expensive, the poor slaves made "great sacrifices" in order to buy a copy. In fact, Gobineau estimated that the number of Korans sold annually in Rio amounted to one hundred and that Rio's Muslim community was second in size only to that of Bahia.[77]

Since religion, whether Islam or a traditional African religion, was highly valued, it is to be expected that it would continue to play a major role in the lives of the slaves. Closely associated with religious practice and also highly valued were music and dance, both important to African life in Rio. In fact, African music and dances were an essential part of the atmosphere of the city. Instead of adopting their masters' music and dances on a wide scale, African slaves continued to sing and dance and play their own instruments. One of the best descriptions of how slaves spent a Sunday in the Campo de Santana in 1808 comes from Robertson, a British merchant, who felt that there was nothing else like it outside of Africa:

> Onward pressed the groups of the various African nations, to the Campo de Sant'Ana, the destined theatre of revelry and din. Here was the native of Mosambique, and Quilumana, of Cabinda, Luanda, Benguela, and Angola. . . .
>
> The dense population of the Campo de Sant'Ana was subdivided into capacious circles, formed each of from three to four hundred blacks, male and female.
>
> Within these circles, the performers danced to the music which was also stationed there; and I know not whether the energy of the musicians, or that of the dancers was most to be admired. You might see the cheeks of an athlete of Angola ready to crack under the exertion of producing a hideous sound from a calabash, while another performer dealt blows so thick and heavy on his kettledrum, . . . Eight or ten figurantes were moving to and fro in the midst of the circle, in a way to exhibit the human frame divine under every conceivable variety of contortion and gesticulation. Presently two or three standing in the crowd appeared to think there was not animation enough; and with a shriek or a song, they rushed in and joined the dance. The musicians played a louder and more discordant music; the dancers, . . . seemed wrapped in all the furor of demons; . . . every looker-on participated in the sibylline spirit which animated the dancers and musicians; the welkin rang with the wild enthusiasm of the negro clans.[78]

As this quotation shows, the drum was widely used in Rio in many sizes and shapes. In one of his paintings, Rugendas depicted a *capoeira* dance, which was accompanied by a slave in a sitting position playing the drum between his legs with his hands. In another, which portrayed a procession of slaves, the black drummer carried a European-style drum upon which he was beating with two sticks. Evidently some of these drums were large and loud, for a justice of the peace in 1833 requested that the city slaves be forbidden to play them because they attracted slaves from the neighboring plantations.[79]

More common than the drums was the instrument known in Rio as the marimba. It was a small, easily portable instrument that slaves carried while they worked. Because it was less noisy than the large drums, it was better tolerated by the masters, and so it was common to hear at least one slave in a household amusing himself with this instrument. Ruschenberger described the porters, who sat at the doors of private homes, spending hours "nodding over their own music, produced with about the same effort required to twirl the thumbs." He also distinguished between two types of marimbas which were then common in Rio:

> [The first] is generally made of some light species of wood, and may be compared to the toe part of a shoe. On the flat side, or sole part, are secured nearly in their centres, eight pieces of steel wire about six inches long; their ends curve upwards, and being of different lengths, form an octave. The longer ends of these keys play free, and when touched, vibrate a sleepy kind of note, which can hardly be called disagreeable.

The second kind of marimba he described, which was painted by Chamberlain, had the keys placed on a thin board secured to a coconut shell; this type he regarded as more musical. In Angola, Monteiro similarly described both of these instruments, except that he noted that glass beads ornamented the first variety, while the second was made from a gourd. He might have been writing of Rio when he observed that "the blacks are excessively fond of these instruments everywhere in Angola, playing them as they walk along or rest, and by day or night a 'marimba' is at all hours heard twanging somewhere."[80]

Another instrument that was played in that period was the *berimbau*. In nineteenth-century Rio, it was common to see African porters carrying loads on their heads while they played the instrument with their hands, as may be seen in Chamberlain's paintings. But at that time, the instrument apparently was not called a *berimbau*. Debret described it as an Angolan violin, a natural identification since Chamberlain also portrayed a slave playing the *berimbau* and holding it like a violin.

In the sources it was generally referred to as an *urucungu* or *aricungo.* According to the historian Coaracy, this instrument was the *oricongo,* which was also described by Monteiro in Angola. In fact, Monteiro's description fits both the modern *berimbau* and the instrument being played by a blind beggar in a Debret illustration:

> A musical instrument sometimes seen is made by stretching a thin string to a bent bow, about three feet long, passed through half a gourd, the open end of which rests against the performer's bare stomach. The string is struck with a thin slip of cane or palm-leaf stem held in the right hand, and a finger of the left, which holds the instrument, is laid occasionally on the string, and in this way, with occasional gentle blows of the open gourd against the stomach, very pleasing sounds, and modulations are obtained.[81]

Slaves played other instruments, such as wooden or metal flutes and almost any object that would serve as a percussion instrument. However, the most popular (or at least those that travelers most commonly depicted) were the African drums, the marimba, and the *oricongo.* Accompanied by these instruments, or *a cappella,* African slaves sang the songs of their homeland. As Schlichthorst wrote, the memory of their "native land" formed the basis for many songs that embarrassed Europeans who heard their longing for their own country ("essa saudade da patria"). Among the songs of the blacks that Schlicthorst collected in Rio was this one:

Vou carregando por meus pecados	For my sins I am carrying The luggage of a white man
Mala de branco p'ra viajar,	so he can travel,
Quem dera ao Tonho, pobre do negro,	Who will give to Tony, poor black,
P'ra sua terra poder voltar![82]	The chance to return to his own land!

What the slaves commonly sang about their masters and slavery in their African languages has not survived, but they surely expressed their opinions while laboring under heavy burdens. As one old slave song in Portuguese expressed it:

A vida de prêto escravo	The life of a black slave
É um pendão de pená:	Is a burden of pain;
Trabaiando todo dia:	Working all day:
Sem noite pra descansá.[83]	Without the night to rest.

While songs and instruments were enjoyed in themselves, they were most popular when combined with dances. As Robertson described them, African dances were great social occasions which combined all three art forms, but the slaves also danced on any occasion individually or in small groups. One popular dance of that period was the *lundu,* which was adopted by the Portuguese and taken to Portugal, where even the best society of Lisbon danced it. In Rio, the *batuque* (samba) seems to have been the most popular. The dancers Robertson described above were evidently doing one form of the *batuque,* which is similar to the *batuco* described by Monteiro in Angola. He divided the *batuco* into two forms: the first was danced by the people of Ambriz and Congo, and the second by Bunda-speakers around Luanda. The former appears closest to the dance described by Robertson. Monteiro's description is as follows:

A ring is formed of the performers and spectators; "marimbas" are twanged and drums beaten vigorously, and all assembled clap their hands in time with the thumping of the drums, and shout a kind of chorus. The dancers, both men and women, jump with a yell into the ring, two or three at a time, and commence dancing. This consists almost exclusively of swaying the body about with only a slight movement of the feet, head, and arms, but at the same time the muscles of the shoulders, back, and hams, are violently twitched and convulsed.[84]

Thus, both Robertson and Monteiro recorded a circular dance form with marimbas and drums and multiple dancers of both sexes moving in and out of the circle.

The second form of the *batuco* that was found around Luanda—and that possibly gave rise to the *lundu*—was also done in circular form with marimbas and drums. But only two dancers—a man and a woman—entered the circle and "shuffle their feet with great rapidity, passing one another backwards and forwards, then retreat facing one another, and suddenly advancing, bring their stomachs together with a whack." When they finished, another couple took their place. Possibly this motion is the one Rugendas tried to depict when he portrayed a man and a woman dancing toward each other in the dance he called the *lundu*. This would also explain APDG's belief that the dance as performed by blacks was indecent.[85]

Whatever the names of the dances, they were clearly of African origin and were performed in the streets of Rio on the slightest pretext. Dr. Imbert complained about the "voluptuous" dances he met with whenever he walked through the streets of the city. Frequently, slaves earned money by performing their national dances and songs for other slaves or even for travelers such as Maria Graham. In any marketplace or area where slaves congregated, there were dances. When Walsh lived in Rio, there was still a small, green yard near São José where slaves could dance unharassed on Sunday evenings. By Dabadie's time, they had to seek out the beaches, but even then they risked problems with the police; arrests for dancing the *batuque* appear throughout the police records.[86]

In the early period, however, African dances were tolerated, if not approved, and the travelers Robertson, Ouseley, and Luccock recorded their celebrations. This open toleration of African forms of entertainment was not to last. The African dances, music, and songs were pushed underground, while the masters turned to Europe for inspiration and denied the heritage in their midst by means of police repression or by ignoring what they did not want Europeans to see. The European travelers fortunately recorded what were to them strange and unusual customs. Moreover, they caught these individuals in a difficult period of transition, when tattooed men with filed teeth adopted European styles of dress and spoke the Portuguese language but at the same time pursued African modes of entertainment and worshipped the old gods. Foreigners not only revealed the problems of acculturation and assimilation which the slaves encountered, but they also illustrated that the masters could not live untouched by the vital cultures around them. Acculturation was a two-way process in Rio, but the masters for too long denied the African contribution. While they preferred to seek their identity in white Europe, their black mistresses and nurses ensured that their children owed as much to Africa as to Europe. Miscegenation frequently accomplished what force failed to do; that is, to incorporate the child into Cariocan society. But the child's African mother also ensured that her offspring would remember its African heritage. In many ways, and despite laws and repression, elements of the African heritage survived in Rio, eventually drawing even white men to participate in the religious rituals, to dance the *batuque-samba,* and to play African instruments.

NOTES

1. The most complete printed version of the census appears in a travel account, Hermann Burmeister, *Viagem ao Brasil através das províncias do Rio de Janeiro e Minas Gerais,* trans. Manoel Salvaterra and Hubert Schoenfeldt (São Paulo, 1952), p. 325. However, there is an error for the parish of Santa Anna, which makes Burmeister's printed totals by sex incorrect. At other points in the census, there are mistakes in addition or printing errors. This printed version must therefore be correlated with other sources to check for errors. The final printed version that appears in Table 3 is the result of careful comparison with the following printed sources that give abbreviated versions of the census: Joaquim Norberto de Souza Silva, *Investigações sobre os recenseamentos da populaçaõ geral do Imperio e de cada provincia de per si tentados desde os tempos coloniaes até hoje feitas em virtude do aviso de 15 de Março de 1870* (Rio de Janeiro, 1870); *Almanak* (Laemmert) *Administrativo Mercentil e Industrial do Rio de Janeiro para o anno bissexto de 1851,* pp. 236-240; and Arquivo Nacional, *Relatorio do Ministerio do Imperio,* 1851, pp. 22-23 (Hereafter cited as AN). To date, the original of the census has not been located.

2. Some influential writers on Bahia's African origins are: Manuel Raymundo Querino, *Costumes Africanos no Brasil* (Rio de Janeiro, 1938); Raimundo Nina Rodrigues, *Os Africanos no Brasil* (São Paulo, 1932); and Pierre Verger, *Flux et reflux de la traite des nègres entre le golfe de Bénin et Bahia de todos os santos du dix-septième au dix-neuvième siècle* (Paris, 1968).

3. *O Diario do Rio de Janeiro* has the longest and best selection of fugitive advertisements. *O Correio Mercantil* and *O Jornal do Comércio,* as well as other newspapers, also carried these advertisements, but *O Diario* is by far the best source. In fact, one has the impression that entire issues were devoted almost solely to the buying, selling, renting, or hunting down of slaves. Thus, most of this discussion is based on the advertisements of the *Diario do Rio,* and only specific cases will be cited.

4. After each term the feminine form will be given in parentheses. For male slaves, the masculine form was used; for female slaves, the feminine.

5. *Diario do Rio,* I, No. 20 (June 20, 1821), 136.

6. Slaves who already spoke Portuguese came to Rio from Angola or Mozambique. F. Torres Texugo, *A letter on the slave trade still carried on along the eastern coast of Africa, called the province of Mosambique . . .* (London, 1839), p. 15, described the *ladino* slaves of Mozambique, who spoke fluent Portuguese. In Angola, however, there were people who spoke Portuguese without having learned it from white men. When Monteiro met a literate African secretary, who had learned to read and write Portuguese from other Africans, Monteiro thought he was from "Ambaca, or some other province of the interior of Angola, where a great many of the natives at the present day can read and write Portuguese, transmitted from father to son since the olden time." Joachim J. Monteiro, *Angola and the River Congo* (London, 1875), I, 223.

7. Theodor von Leithold and L. von Rango, *O Rio de Janeiro visto por dois prussianos em 1819,* trans. Joaquim de Sousa Leão Filho (São Paulo, 1966), p. 38; Thomas Ewbank, *Life in Brazil* . . . (New York, 1856), p. 323.

8. Johann B. von Spix and Carl F. P. von Martius, *Viagem pelo Brasil 1817-1820; Excertos e Ilustrações* (São Paulo, 1968), pp. 24-25, describe and illustrate a *cafuza* woman of the interior. Jean B. Debret, *Voyage pittoresque et historique au Brésil: Séjour d'un Artiste francais au Brésil* (Rio de Janeiro, 1965), II, 1; and João E. Pohl, *Viagem no interior do Brasil,* trans. Teodoro Cabral (Rio de Janeiro, 1951), p. 82, noted that *cafusos* were rare in the city and that they regarded the black slaves with displeasure.

9. *Diario do Rio,* I, No. 1 (August 1, 1821), 7; I, No. 23 (June 25, 1821), 160; II, No. 1 (October 1, 1821), 5-6; *Correio Mercantil,* I (September 2, 1830), 52; and *Diario,* III, No. 5 (December 6, 1821), 20.

10. *Correio Mercantil,* I, No. 6 (August 25, 1830), 24.

11. *Diario do Rio,* II, No. 22 (October 25, 1821), 176.

12. Ibid., I, No. 22 (June 23, 1821), 153.

13. Ibid., XIX, No. 13 (January 17, 1840), 4.

14. Ibid., I, No. 2 (June 2, 1821), 7.

15. The want ads illustrate that nearly-white slaves were not uncommon in Rio. *Diario do Rio,* II, No. 12 (October 13, 1821), 95, has an ad for two slaves designated as *mulato claro.* One of them was so white that he could pass as a white man in terms of skin color and type of hair. Since hair was a racial indicator, the hair style frequently identified racial mixtures in the advertisements for mulattoes. The straighter the hair, the whiter the slave.

16. Debret, *Voyage pittoresque,* II, 1; *Diario do Rio,* III, No. 22 (December 29, 1821), 89; III, No. 10 (December 13, 1821), 40; and I, No. 8 (August 9, 1821), 60.

17. *Diario do Rio,* II, No. 4 (October 4, 1821), 31.

18. Ibid., I, No. 1 (July 2, 1821), 5.

19. AN, Cod. 242, Termos de contagem de escravos vindos da Costa d'Africa, 1795-1811.

20. *Diario do Rio,* II, No. 4 (October 4, 1821), 31.

21. Ibid., I, No. 20 (July 24, 1821), 157; I, No. 23 (July 28, 1821), 180.

22. Herbert S. Klein, "The Trade in African Slaves to Rio de Janeiro, 1795-1811: Estimates of Mortality and Patterns of Voyages," *Journal of African History,* X, No. 4 (1969), 542. His data come from AN, Cod. 242, Termos de contagem de escravos vindos da Costa d'Africa, 1795-1811, which I also consulted for age data.

23. For children in the trade and in the warehouses, see the following travelers: G. W. Freireyss, *Viagem ao interior do Brazil nos annos de 1814-1815,* trans. Alberto Löfgren (São Paulo, 1906), p. 65; J. B. von Spix and C.F.P. von Martius, *Viagem pelo Brasil,* trans. Lucia Furquim Lahmeyer (Rio de Janeiro, 1938), I, 113; Maria Graham, *Journal of a Voyage to Brazil* . . . (London, 1824), p. 227; Debret, *Voyage pittoresque,* II, pl. 23; Charles Brand, *Journal of a Voyage to Peru* . . . (London, 1828), p. 13; and Robert Elwes, *A Sketcher's Tour Round the World* (London, 1854), p. 28.

24. The records from these eleven ships are located at Itamaratí, III, Coleções Especiais, 33, Comissões Mistas (Tráfico de Negros), Latas 2, 4, 10, 12, 13-14, 16, 19, 25, 28.

25. Dr. G. Tams, *Visit to the Portuguese Possessions in Southwestern Africa,* trans. H. Evans Lloyd (London [1845]), I, 300.

26. Joseph C. Miller, "Cokwe Trade and Conquest in the Nineteenth Century," in *Pre-Colonial African Trade,* eds., Richard Gray and David Birmingham (London, 1970), p. 182; and Edward A. Alpers, "Trade, State, and Society Among the Yāo in the Nineteenth Century," *Journal of African History,* X, No. 3 (1969), 411-412.

27. In 1814-1815, the traveler Freireyss (*Viagem,* p. 65) calculated that three-fourths of the imported slaves were male. This percentage also holds true for the late 1830s and early 1840s. See Table 2.

28. See n. 24 above for the sources on the eleven ships, whose papers are held at Itamaratí.

29. Klein, "Trade in African Slaves," p. 540.

30. Philip D. Curtin, *The Atlantic Slave Trade: A Census* (Madison, 1969), p. 240.

31. Sigismund W. Koelle, *Polyglotta Africana . . .,* ed. P.E.H. Hair and D. Dalby (London, 1854; rpt. Sierra Leone, 1963), cited in Curtin, *The Atlantic Slave Trade,* pp. 251-264.

32. AN, *Relatório do Ministério dos Negocios da Justiça,* 1869, p. 134.

33. Itamaratí, III, Coleções Especiais, 33, Comissões Mistas (Tráfico de Negros), Lata 14, Maço 3, Embarcação Especulador, 1836-1839.

34. AN, Cod. 359, Polícia, Suprimentos de Despêsas com Escravos Fugidos, 1826; *O Diario do Rio, passim.* Evidence of some African nationalities also came from "For Sale" advertisements. Divisão do Patrimonio Histórico e Artistico do Estado da Guanabara, 6-1-43 to 6-1-48, Escravos ao Ganho, 1833-1885 (hereafter cited as PHAEG). AN, Seção, Legislativa e Judiciaria, Livros do 1° Oficio de Notas, Nᵒˢ200 a 550 de 23 de setembro de 1808 a 26 de setembro de 1916; and Livros de Escrituras, Registros de Protestos de Titulos, apontamentos e outros que se encontram no Cartorio do 1° Oficio de Notas da Justiça do Distrito Federal, 1651-1852. For the records where the ship lists are held, see the following: AN, Cod. 400, Polícia, Obitos de Africanos, 1834-1840; Ijᵉ-524, Africanos Livres com Cartas de Emancipação, 1845-1864; Ijᵉ-467, Cartas de Libertação, 1831-1844; Ijᵉ-471, Ofícios, Relações e Processos sôbre Africanos Livres, 1834-1864, Cod. 184, Protocolo das conferências da Comissão Mixta sôbre o Tráfico de Escravos, 4 vols., 1819-1840, Ijᵉ-469, Escravatura, Correspondencia de diversos authoridades, 1824-1864; and Cod. 398, Polícia, Africanos remettidos á correção, 1834-1835.

35. William Ellis, *Polynesian Researches . . .* (New York, 1833), III, 256.

36. The following authors give physical descriptions of the Valongo: Luiz Gonçalves dos Santos, *Memórias para servir à história do reino do Brasil* (Rio de Janeiro, 1943), I, 42; C. Schlichthorst, *O Rio de Janeiro como é, 1824-1826,* trans. Emmy Dodt and Gustavo Barroso (Rio de Janeiro, 1943), p. 130; Graham, *Journal of a Voyage to Brazil,* p. 227; Freireyss, *Viagem,* p. 64; Spix and von Martius, *Viagem pelo Brasil,* I, 113; see also Ender's watercolor of a street in the Valongo with its columned houses walled up into slave warehouses, in Gilberto Ferrez, *O Velho Rio de Janeiro através das Gravuras de Thomas Ender* (São Paulo, n.d.), p. 125.

37. BN, II-34, 26, 3, "Parecer de João Inacio da Cunha . . . dirigido a Jozé Bonifácio de Andrada e Silva, sobre . . . o Cemitério dos Prêtos Novos" (Rio de Janeiro, 1822); and "Rio de Janeiro," *Aurora Flumenense,* II, No. 145 (January 23, 1829), 598.

38. Brand, *Journal of a Voyage to Peru,* p. 13.

39. The following travelers describe the arrangement of slaves in the slave shops: John MacDouall, *Narrative of a Voyage to Patagonia and Terra del Fuégo* . . . (London, 1833), p. 25; Brand, *Journal of a Voyage to Peru,* p. 13; Edmond Temple, *Travels in Various Parts of Peru, Including a Year's Residence in Potosi* (London, 1830), II, 503; and Thaddeus Bellingshausen, *The Voyage of Captain Bellingshausen to the Antarctic Seas 1819-1821,* trans. Frank Debenham (London: Hakluyt Society, 1945), I, 71-72.

40. João Maurício Rugendas, *Viagem Pitoresca através do Brasil,* trans. Sérgio Milliet (São Paulo, 1941), p. 138.

41. AN, Cod. 359, Livro 1°, Polícia, Suprimentos de Despêsas com Escravos Fugidos, fols. 1-74; and AN, Cod. 360, Polícia, Escravos Fugidos, 1826-1827.

42. Mello Barreto Filho and Hermeto Lima, *História da Polícia do Rio de Janeiro: Aspectos da Cidade e da Vida Carioca 1831-1870* (Rio de Janeiro, 1942), p. 75. Only 4 percent of the *Africanos livres* from the *Duqueza de Bragança* successfully escaped between 1834 and 1864; 5 percent from the *Rio da Prata,* 1835-1864; and 3 percent from the *Patacho Cezar,* 1838-1864. See AN, Ij⁶-471. In 1869, of a total of 11,008 *Africanos livres,* only 191 had successfully escaped, or 1.7 percent. See AN, *Relatório do Ministério dos Negocios da Justiça,* 1869, p. 134. There is no way of knowing how many *Africanos livres* tried to escape but failed.

43. Schlichthorst, *O Rio de Janeiro como é,* p. 136; and APDG (full name unknown), *Sketches of Portuguese Life, Manners, Costume, and Character* (London, 1826), p. 301.

44. Debret, *Voyage pittoresque,* II, 139.

45. Palmares was Brazil's classic *quilombo* that lasted throughout almost the entire seventeenth century in the backlands of Pernambuco and Alagoas. See R. K. Kent, "Palmares: An African State in Brazil," *Journal of African History,* VI, No. 2 (1965), 161-175.

46. On the *quilombos,* see: AN, Cod. 359, Livro 1°, Polícia, Suprimentos de Despêsas, fols. 1-74; Gustavo Barroso, "Os Quilombos da Tijuca," *Revista O Cruzeiro,* XXX, No. 21 (March 8, 1958), 43, 48; Schlichthorst, *O Rio de Janeiro como é,* p. 137; Fernando Bastos Ribeiro, *Crônicas da polícia e da vida do Rio de Janeiro* (Rio de Janeiro, 1958), p. 71; Elysio de Araujo, *Estudo Historico sobre a Policia da Capital Federal de 1808 a 1831* (Rio de Janeiro, 1898), p. 112; and R. Walsh, *Notices of Brazil in 1828 and 1829* (London, 1830), II, 343.

47. H. Furcy de Bremoy, *Le Voyageur Poète, ou Souvenirs d'un Français dans un coin des deux mondes* (Paris, 1833), II, 110-111.

48. Great Britain, Foreign Office, *British and Foreign State Papers,* 1851-1852, Vol. XLI, "Correspondence of Great Britain, Relative to the Slave Trade, 1851," 378.

49. F. Dabadie, *A travers l'Amérique du Sud* (Paris, 1859), p. 50.

50. John Candler and Wilson Burgess, *Narrative of a Recent Visit to Brazil . . . to Present an Address on the Slave Trade and Slavery* (London, 1853), pp. 38-39.

51. Georges Raeders, *Le Comte de Gobineau au Brésil* (Paris, 1934), p. 75.

52. Schlichthorst, *O Rio de Janeiro como é,* p. 140; Eugenio Rodriguez, "Descrizione del viaggio a Rio de Janeiro della flotta di Napoli," trans. and ed. Gastão Penalva, in *A Viagem da Imperatriz* (Rio de Janeiro, 1936), p. 53; Debret, *Voyage pittoresque,* II, 153; and Walsh, *Notices of Brazil,* II, 339-340.

53. Dabadie, *A travers l'Amérique du Sud,* p. 56; Schlichthorst, *O Rio de Janeiro como é,* p. 140; and Debret, *Voyage pittoresque,* II, 153.

54. See pl. 16, Debret, *Voyage pittoresque,* II, 153-154; and Alexandre J. de Melo Morais Filho, *Festas e Tradições Populares do Brasil,* rev. and ed. Luís da Câmara Cascudo (Rio de Janeiro, 1967), pp. 427-431.

55. William S. W. Ruschenberger, *Three Years in the Pacific.* . . . (Philadelphia, 1834), p. 30; see also Walsh, *Notices of Brazil,* II, 330.

56. Schlichthorst, *O Rio de Janeiro como é,* p. 140; and Karl von Scherzer, *Narrative of the Circumnavigation of the Globe* . . . *in the Years 1857, 1858, and 1859* . . ., trans. from the German (London, 1861), I, 140-141.

57. Walsh, *Notices of Brazil,* II, 340; and Luiz de Aguiar Costa Pinto, *O Negro no Rio de Janeiro* (São Paulo, 1952), p. 240.

58. A richly dressed black king and queen appear in watercolors of the late eighteenth century, one of which depicts the coronation ceremony. Carlos Julião, *Riscos iluminados de figurinhos de brancos e negros dos uzos do Rio de Janeiro e Serro do Frio* (Rio de Janeiro, 1960), pl. 36-39.

59. The document is printed in Melo Morais Filho, *Festas e Tradições,* p. 399.

60. Théo Brandão, "Influências Africanas no Folclore Brasileiro," *Revista Brasileira de Folclore,* VIII, No. 21 (May-August 1968), 141.

61. One description of a *Reinado dos Congos* appears in Melo Morais Filho, *Festas e Tradições,* pp. 395-400.

62. Except where otherwise noted, the following discussion of *capoeiragem* comes from Ribeiro, *Crônicas da Polícia,* pp. 23-33. Supplementing Ribeiro is Adolfo Morales de los Rios Filho, *O Rio de Janeiro Imperial* (Rio [1946]), pp. 51-54. Other information may be found in the following: Araujo, *Estudo Histórico sobre a Polícia,* pp. 55, 59, 62; PHAEG, 40-3-78, Capoeiras, 1836-1861; APDG, *Sketches of Portuguese Life,* pp. 304-306; João Fernando de Almeida Prado, *Tomas Ender, pintor austríaco na Côrte de D. João VI no Rio de Janeiro* (São Paulo, 1955), pp. 299-302; for arrests for *capoeiragem,* see AN, Cod. 401 (327-328), Polícia, Devassas, 1809-1817; and for *capoeira* in Bahia and the role of the *capoeiras* in the Paraguayan War, consult Querino, *Costumes Africanos,* pp. 270-278.

63. By *portaria* of October 31, 1821, those who practiced *capoeira* were to receive corporal punishment—that is, a public whipping. Querino, *Costumes Africanos,* p. 278. In 1822, Dom Pedro I wrote a letter reprimanding the police for their failure to control and prevent *capoeiragens.* He also ordered that any slave who was caught engaging in *capoeira* be taken immediately to the closest place and there be given 100 lashes. To encourage enforcement, any soldier who caught a *capoeira* would be given four days leave. Letter of Dom Pedro I to Carlos Frederico Bernardo de Caula, February 6, 1822, reprinted in Almeida Prado, *Tomas Ender,* pp. 300-301.

64. Querino, *Costumes Africanos,* pp. 271-272, notes that Bahia also had similar divisions by *bairros,* each *bairro* having its own national flag and *capoeira* defenders.

65. Jules Itier, *Journal d'un Voyage en Chine en 1843, 1844, 1845, 1846* (Paris, 1848), I, 49-50, 62.

66. Roberto Macedo, *Notas Históricas* (Rio de Janeiro, 1944), pp. 136-137; and Querino, *Costumes Africanos,* pp. 275-278.

67. Carlos de Leenhof, *Contribuições para a história da guerra entre o Brasil e Buenos Aires nos anos de 1825 a 1828,* trans. L. Brockmann (São Paulo, 1946), p. 96.

68. João Baptista A. Imbert, *Uma Palavra sobre o Charlatanismo e os Charlatões* (Rio de Janeiro, 1837), p. 15, observed that the Brazilians put their faith in *feiticeiros.*

Raymond S. Sayres, *The Negro in Brazilian Literature* (New York, 1956), p. 176, discusses the fictional character of the *feiticeiro* in Brazilian literature.

69. J. K. Tuckey, *Tuckey's Voyage. An Account of a Voyage to Establish a Colony at Port Philip in Bass's Strait,* in Sir Richard Phillips, ed., *A Collection of Modern and Contemporary Voyages and Travels* (London, 1805-1810), I, No. 6, 15.

70. Charles Expilly, *Le Brésil tel qu'il est* (Paris, 1864), pp. 88-89.

71. For black doctors, see: Imbert, *Charlatanismo,* pp. 13, 23; Debret, *Voyage pittoresque,* II, 142-146; Walsh, *Notices of Brazil,* I, 415; MacDouall, *Narrative of a Voyage,* p. 316.

72. Ewbank, *Life in Brazil,* pp. 406-407.

73. Ibid., p. 327.

74. Maria Graham, "Correspondência entre Maria Graham e a Imperatriz Dona Leopoldina e Cartas Anexas," trans. Américo Jacobina Lacombe, *Anais da Biblioteca Nacional,* LX (1940), 160.

75. Étienne I. Brazil, "O Fetichismo dos Negros do Brasil," *Revista do Instituto Histórico e Geográphico Brasileiro,* 124, tomo 74, parte 2 (1911), 237.

76. João Baptista A. Imbert, *Manual do Fazendeiro ou Tratado Domestico sobre as Enfermidades dos Negros* (Rio de Janeiro, 1839), II, 124-125.

77. Raeders, *Le Comte de Gobineau,* pp. 74-76.

78. John Parish Robertson and William Parish Robertson, *Letters on Paraguay . . .* (London, 1838), pp. 164-169.

79. Rugendas, *Viagem,* pl. 4/18-19; Schlichthorst, *O Rio de Janeiro como e,* p. 118; PHAEG, 6-1-25, Escravidão, fol. 12.

80. Travelers who described the marimba include the following: Ruschenberger, *Three Years,* I, 28-29; Sir Henry Chamberlain, *Vistas e Costumes da cidade e arredores do Rio de Janeiro em 1819-1820,* trans. Rubens Borba de Moraes (Rio de Janeiro, 1943), p. 108; Monteiro, *Angola,* II, 138-139; Schlichthorst, *O Rio de Janeiro como é,* p. 141; Leenhof, *Contribuições,* p. 96; Debret, *Voyage pittoresque,* II, 129, p. 41.

81. For the *berimbau,* consult: Chamberlain, *Vistas,* pp. 112-113; Vivaldo Coaracy, *Memórias da Cidade do Rio de Janeiro* (Rio de Janeiro, 1965), III, 348; Debret, *Voyage pittoresque,* II, 129, pl. 41; Ferrez, *O Velho Rio,* p. 164; Max Radiguet, *Souvenirs de l'Amérique espagnole . . .* (Paris, 1856), p. 261; Imbert, *Manual do Fazendeiro,* II, 363; and Monteiro, *Angola,* II, 139. Finally, Brandão clearly identifies the *aricungo* as the *berimbau.* Adelino Brandão, "Contribuições Afro-Negras ao Léxico Popular Brasileiro," *Revista Brasileira de Folclore,* VIII, No. 21 (May-August 1968), 121.

82. Schlichthorst, *O Rio de Janeiro como é,* pp. 176, 178. Richard Mazzara assisted me in translating the songs.

83. Morales de los Rios Filho, *O Rio de Janeiro Imperial,* p. 62.

84. Monteiro, *Angola,* II, 136-138.

85. Ibid.; Rugendas, *Viagem,* pl. 4/16-18; and APDG, *Sketches of Portuguese Life,* pp. 288-290.

86. Dabadie, *A travers l'Amérique du Sud,* p. 55; Imbert, *Manual do Fazendeiro,* II, 363; Graham, *Journal,* p. 166; C. S. Stewart, *A Visit to the South Seas . . .* (London, 1832), p. 83; Walsh, *Notices of Brazil,* II, 337. Arrests for dancing the *batuque* appear in AN, Cod. 360, Polícia, Escravos Fugidos, 1826-1827.

Ann M. Pescatello

3

PRÊTO POWER, BRAZILIAN STYLE: MODES OF RE-ACTIONS TO SLAVERY IN THE NINETEENTH CENTURY*

Throughout the nineteenth century, the Brazilian government had so weakened the foundations of the institution of slavery that when the final decree of abolition came (1888) it caused little disturbance in most areas of the country. Abolition without compensation meant economic disaster for some planters and social dislocation for many freedmen, but it also signaled victory for Afro-Brazilian abolitionists.[1]

Most scholarship heretofore has concentrated on the *causes* for the abolition of slavery and the campaigns against the slave trade and slavery itself, usually from the viewpoint of Brazilian and foreign governments.[2] Few scholars have focused on the specific roles of the Afro-Brazilians themselves. In order to redirect the focus from governments and toward the individuals and groups involved, this essay examines the contributions of Afro-Brazilians to nineteenth-century re-actions against slavery and toward the ultimate goal of abolition.

This approach requires an examination of the various nineteenth-century modes of re-action to slavery in Brazil within the context of each of the different protest movements that arose. It also requires a discussion of the types of re-action within the perspective of an historical continuum as well as an examination of the nature of changes in these

---

*Research for this essay was conducted in the summer of 1969 and during a special research trip to Brazil, December 1969-February 1970. OHI, when used, refers to Oral History Interviews conducted during that time span.

A few short excerpts from this essay were published earlier in *The African in Latin America,* edited by Ann M. Pescatello. Copyright © 1975 by Alfred A. Knopf, Inc.

re-actions that occurred throughout time and space. In terms of the human elements involved, the emphasis here is solely on the Afro-Brazilian participants in these protest movements. In terms of time and place, the modes of re-action are grouped into primarily two types and two time periods: the armed uprisings of the Northeast in the early nineteenth century and the pacific intellectual organizations of the South later in the century.

A proper understanding of the material that follows requires some elaboration of concepts and terms, problems of methodology and sources, and the situation in Brazil in the final decade before abolition. The term *abolition* as used here is synonymous with the phrases "abolition of the slave trade" or "abolition of Negro slavery"; *emancipation* is the action of setting an individual free from the *patria potestas* or from slavery; and *manumission* is essentially the same action of releasing liberating individuals from bondage or servitude. Abolition implies a wholesale end to a particular trade, system, or institution, while emancipation and manumission suggest the freeing of an individual or group from an existing trade, system, or institution. The antislavery movements in Brazil, particularly during the nineteenth century, ranged from those which fought for individual manumission, to campaigns for the emancipation of certain groups, to demands for total abolition of the trade and system. Those efforts were not so much revolts against a system, but rather diverse re-actions to the economic and social institution of slavery.[3]

Central to this discussion of re-actions is a group in Brazilian society who by blood, generation, or fixed social position was a cultural symbiosis of the African and Brazilian. There is little agreement on what these American descendants of Africans should be called; the term Afro-Brazilian is adopted here since it is used more in an ethnic sense vis à vis assimilation than in a racial sense. The term *black* is eschewed, for it is not sufficiently precise: few of this group were really black in color. Furthermore, since the "re-actionaries" included not only first-generation Africans but descendants of Africans and mulattoes as well, the word Afro-Brazilian is more appropriate to the groups discussed.[4]

Another problem is that these individuals and groups re-acted against the Brazilian system of slavery for many disparate and often unrelated reasons. Some of the re-actions involved a simple issue, but others touched on a complex of social, political, religious, and economic factors. Their occurrence at particular times and places is connected with factors such as the ratio of slaves to masters and of "blacks" to "whites"; the relationship of new recruits to old slaves and of Africans wrenched from their own "free" society to descendants of Africans born into a slave system and socialized within it; the "family" or societal environment of the newly recruited African slaves; the situation of slaves in Brazil, either urban or rural; and even larger national concerns of an economic or political nature peripheral to the slaves' interests.

For an examination of modes of re-action within the context of an historical continuum—in this case the nineteenth century—the usefulness of the comparative method is not explicit. However, the apparent changes in re-action throughout the period do suggest implicit comparisons and contrasts both within Brazil and with other slaveholding nations. The comparative method is still rife with pitfalls and imperfections and usually has been applied to larger models. Nonetheless, if we accept the assumption that underlying all of these modes of re-action was the desire for release from a particular system, it is possible to imply comparisons for times and places. This assumption, in turn, depends on sources that are as varied as the movements themselves. Most scholars have relied on secondary accounts for their presentation of the protest movements. In fact, however, there exists an extensive body of primary documentation, both oral and written, some of which has been used in this study.

Finally, a brief statement on the general Brazilian background for final abolition is in order. Throughout the nineteenth century, and particularly after midcentury, numerous entrepreneurial, technological, and other changes had altered the plantation production systems that had formed the basis of Brazil's economy and society. Coffee had replaced sugar as Brazil's primary export, thus inducing a shift in political power from the northern sugar magnates to the southern coffee planters. This shift had important implications for social change in both old and new plantation regions and also in the urban areas. Moreover, new European ideas on modernization and industrial currents had enveloped Brazil and brought her to the threshold of modernization. All of these economic and sociological changes would have special impact on Brazil's desire to convert her labor force from slave to free.[5] With this enormous impetus for change and its concomitant results in the growth of a free labor system, the precise role of the Afro-Brazilians in bringing about final abolition is not readily ap-

parent. It is hoped that the following discussion on the nature of the
modes of re-action and their historical continuity will elucidate this
role.*

The literature on abolition in Brazil reveals that many individual
and group Afro-Brazilian challenges to slavery emerged after the
seventeenth-century mulato Padre Antonio Viera first raised his voice
against bondage.[6] In the early period, the slaves sought freedom from
bondage by fleeing from the plantations into the *sertão* (backlands),
establishing *mocambos* or *quilombos* (settlements of fugitive slaves),
and participating in slave revolts or armed insurrections. Some even
resorted to abortion and suicide as avenues of escape. As early as the
sixteenth century, numerous vagabond bands *(vadios)*, composed
mainly of mulattoes and mestiços, had challenged the authorities and
encouraged slaves to escape from their "repression." The military
offered a legal avenue of re-action for in the army a slave could become a free Brazilian.[7]

The earliest and most successful form of re-action was the flight of
slaves and their organization into *quilombos*. The most famous of
these—Palmares—lasted from 1603 to 1697 as a center of sustenance
and security for its inhabitants.[8] The *mocambo* at Palmares was preceded by at least 50 years of slave flights and attempted rebellions
by Africans newly arrived from the Angolan-Congo area who organized themselves into *ki-lombos* and *mocambos*.[9] Although this form
of re-action continued throughout the following centuries, it ceased
to be a significant threat to Brazilian plantation development after the
destruction of Palmares and the execution of its "prince" Zambi in
1695.[10]

Organized uprisings and flight from the plantations continued to be
the most common type of re-action. Fugitive slaves were a problem
for several decades from the end of the sixteenth century. They invariably sought shelter in mountainous areas not too far from the towns

---

*In addition to black/mulatto freemen in Brazil there were three categories of slaves:
(1) domestic "servants" in the large cities; (2) a large urban class of *negros de ganho,*
i.e., those employed in a modified form of slavery whereby they lived apart from their
masters, arranged their own employment, and remitted a fixed sum per week to their
masters (in rural areas, they were known as *campairos* who lived on their own, worked
owners' *estancias,* and sometimes owned their own cattle); and (3) plantation slaves.

and farms, and from those havens they conducted raids and destroyed several small farming units in Bahia and Pernambuco.[11] Similar actions occurred throughout the seventeenth century in the provinces of Bahia, Paraíba, and Rio de Janeiro, and also throughout the eighteenth century in numerous provinces. In 1719, Negroes revolted in Minas Gerais with the avowed intent of annihilating the whites. A similar insurrection of fugitive blacks from São Thomé in São José de Maranhão in 1772 resulted in such widespread attacks on the populated areas that government troops, in an extremely costly campaign, were sent to subdue the rebels. Not all uprisings by the Afro-Brazilians were focused merely on freeing the slaves. For example, a political separatism was the goal of the Conspiração dos Alfaiates (tailor's conspiracy) in 1798 led by the Afro-Brazilians Lucas Dantas, João de Deus, and Luis Gonzaga das Vírgens, who sought equality for all Brazilians.[12]

Slave upheavals increased in the nineteenth century, especially in the North in the early decades. These movements took several forms: some were separatist in character, seeking political independence from the central government; a few may have been concerned with asserting the authority of Islam over Christianized or pagan blacks; and others were preoccupied with the process of abolition, although their first concern was usually the emancipation of slaves within a particular region. Surprisingly, little research of a monographic nature has been done on these movements, despite the availability of substantial primary documentation, particularly for the Bahian revolts and their leaders.[13]

Of the various nineteenth-century armed insurrections, attempts at seizure of power, and similar movements, nine occurred in Bahia between 1807 and 1835. Ramos, citing Rodrigues, indicated that many of these revolts were primarily religious in nature, but this conclusion no longer seems valid. These uprisings involved a complex mix of Muslim Hausas and their *alufás* (political-religious leaders), Yoruba and Kwa-speaking groups, some elements of the Ogboni society, and a back-to-Africa group. Thus, it is impossible to agree with Ramos that the revolts were simply a continuation of the long religious struggles of Moslem Negroes in the Sudan who had been transplanted with slaves to Brazil and who conducted their campaigns not solely against whites or masters, but also against blacks who refused to join their movements.[14] Granted, many rallied to the cause of a *jihad*, and religious and cultural values did play an extremely important part in the development or destruction of slave societies per se. But it must be recognized that the movements were too complex to have been motivated solely for a religious purpose and that these rebellions were not singular in intent.[15] Even the movements led by the militant Muslim Hausas were most likely not plotted solely for the conversion of their brothers to Islam, thereafter to allow them Allah's resigned contentment in their state of bondage. It is more likely that the Hausas *(Ussa),* many of whom were literate in Arabic, allied in their revolts with Christian and animist Yoruba, Gegé (Ewe), and others to buy freedom for individuals or to work for the liberation of all slaves.

The roots of the nine major Bahian rebellions lay in a long tradition of Afro-Brazilian dissatisfaction with their condition, and their immediate prelude was a conspiracy of 1806. Little is known of this incipient revolt because, as a result of a raid on a "conspirator's house," the rebellion was defused and the government ordered the arrest of all slaves found in the streets after the 9 P.M. curfew if they did not have a letter from their masters or were not accompanied by their owners.[16] The first of the re-actions commonly refered to as the "nine Bahian revolts" occurred on May 28, 1807. The uprising was elaborately planned, with each section of the city placed under the charge of an emissary or agent of the conspirators whose functions were to direct black slaves from the plantations into rebel quarters in the city of Salvador and to perform the diversionary tactic of harassing the whites. Correspondence between African conspirators in Bahia and Santa Amaro in the Recôncavo (a sugar area in the state of Bahia) was intercepted on May 27 and the governor of Bahia informed. The leaders were subsequently captured, tried, and executed. At the same time, two troublesome *quilombos* on the outskirts of Salvador city, Cabula and Nossa Senhora dos Mares, which the governor had ordered destroyed in March, were finally eliminated.[17] The confiscated evidence as well as the betrayal of the plotters by other blacks indicate a polarization of the racial groups in the conspiracy. Thus, the theory that the singular avowed purpose of all blacks was to destroy all whites in their path for the sake of Allah is further discredited.[18]

In the following year, on September 26, 1808, in the town of Jaguaripe, and again on January 4, 1809, groups of Hausas and members of Yoruban and Dahomean slave groups from the plantations and the cities revolted. They wreaked great destruction in Salvador, especially within a twelve-mile distance from the city, until they were forced to retreat to the countryside and were finally defeated by government troops.[19] This failure was not a deterrent. Secret Hausa, Yoruban, and Dahomean societies such as the Ohogobo and Ogboni—powerful associations utilized as defense groups by the migrant Africans in the Americas—began plotting other revolts. Their activities and the preceding uprisings were preludes to the large-scale revolt that occurred on February 26, 1814, when Hausas moved on the city of Salvador, burned homes, and killed every white who resisted. In the suburb of Itapoan, meanwhile, plantation slaves fired the houses and *senzalas,* or slave quarters, of their masters.[20] On February 12, 1816, a relatively widespread revolt erupted in the areas of Crauassu, Guaiba, Itatinga, and Legoa; the revolt was ended through betrayals by Africans and military expeditions sent by the governor, Conde dos Arcos.

There were no other major re-actions until 1826 when a cluster of uprisings occurred. First, a group of Yorubas fled Salvador and established a *quilombo* in Urubú, not too far interior from the city. The leader of this movement was a black woman named Zeferina who directed the Yoruba in numerous assaults on plantations and towns in that area of Bahia. According to the confessions of captured Yorubas, numerous insurrections had been planned against the government and their slave masters for the purpose of emancipation and the eventual abolition of the institution of slavery.[21] Elsewhere, the Yoruba and other groups attempted to carry out those plans in various sections of the Recôncavo, including Cachoeira, where Africans had chosen a king of the Afro-Brazilians replete with monarchical paraphernalia.[22] In areas closer to Salvador city, such as Pirajá, a *quilombo* of fugitive slaves successfully resisted the attacks of small government military forces.

The Yorubas continued to oppose the Brazilian regime's slavocracy, again rebelling in 1827, 1828, and 1830. In 1827, a group of Yoruba slaves fled their plantations, sacked and burned houses in the suburbs of Salvador, and fled into the bush country outside the city limits. The resistance lasted only a few days but was a prelude to three separate revolts which occurred in the Recôncavo the following year and continued into 1829. Insurrections were occurring so easily and frequently that slaveholders finally appealed to the Bahian governor for more substantial and effective police protection. On April 1, 1830, in Salvador, a small band of Yorubas armed themselves and 100 other blacks, attacked the police station at Soledad in a Salvador suburb, and swept through the city before losing a significant percentage of their contingent.[23]

The final and most severe of the Bahian revolts took place on January 24-25, 1835. The extensive plans for this revolt included the participation of slaves from the entire Recôncavo area, many of whom had in the nights before the uprising fled the plantations for Salvador.[24] (The style of the revolt was much like that adopted by the Mau Mau of East Africa in the 1950s.) In the revolt of 1835 in Bahia, the plans called for the rising of the Africans under Chief Arrumá (or Alumá)*; a takeover of the lands; and the massacre of whites, Creole Negroes, and African blacks who refused to join the so-called *jihad*. Mulattoes were to be spared but would be forced into servitude. The Hausa Muslims moved against the mulattoes and Creole blacks precisely because Islam had not been successful with them. Conspiracies were planned in Moslem temples and their movements were established under *alufás* or *marabús,*** who exercised absolute authority over the blacks.

The 1835 revolt was quickly quelled after two free Africans warned the authorities; police squads and military units, alerted in both city and countryside, encountered numerous rebellious groups and forced them into retreat and then surrender.[25] Thereafter, intensive searches were conducted throughout the city, all with the certainty that the "religious rebels" would reopen the fighting. It has been suggested that many of the leaders were Muslim "crusaders" who wore *patuás* (charms) to protect them from death, that Bahia was the seat of the *Iman* in Brazil, and that a banner and the robes worn at Muslim ceremonies were designated as war costumes. It has also been suggested, however, that the plan was instigated solely against whites and for the purpose of eliminating slavery, that the conspirators planned to establish a queen after exterminating all of the Europeans and that they enlisted the support of all the blacks and mulattoes without concern for their religious affiliations.[26]

In an analysis of these Afro-Brazilian re-actions and their implications for the final abolition of slavery, several points should be considered. In all of these reactions, it has been difficult to determine

---

*This word could also be a corruption of *ulema* (council of political-religious leaders) in code.

**Marabús resemble North African *marabouts* (political-religious leaders).

whether they were merely a series of separate uprisings, a core of related urban revolts, or part of the broader historical cycle; whether they were concerned with achieving emancipation for their own groups or abolition of slavery for all Afro-Brazilians; and whether they were religious or secular in nature.[27] The Afro-Brazilian leaders should be studied to discern their ideas and influence in these causes. These leaders include António and Balthazar, Luiza Mahin (Luis da Gama's mother), Belchior, Gaspar da Silva Cunha, Domingo Marinho de Sa, Luis *(Sanim)*, Manoel Calafate, Aprigio, Cornelio, Pedro Luna, Pacifico *(Licutan)*, Elesbão do Carno *(Dandara)*, and Francisco de Lisboa. Ramos states that all of the above and other leaders were Muslim Hausa who preserved the ceremonies and teachings of Islam in their native language. This is not true; in fact only Luis *(Sanim)* and Pedro Luna were Hausa.

Other points should be considered. The names of these slaves indicate neither recent arrival from Africa nor Islamic membership. Census and other statistical data also appear to show that the Africans imported into Brazil during the latter half of the eighteenth and first half of the nineteenth centuries were overwhelmingly of Bantu or non-Islamic "Negro" origin.[28] More importantly, of those Africans who landed at Bahia there was a heavy percentage of non-Islamic groups. This fact does not, of itself, negate the possibility that small Muslim groups were instigators of secular revolts against Brazilians. Nonetheless, the recent arrival of these Africans would preclude their ability to attract adherents as quickly, as devotedly, and as numerous as Ramos and others claim. Since the conspirators gathered at the homes of Luiza Mahin and others, it is suggested here that she and her friends had maintained residence in Brazil for sufficient time to have acquired such an establishment and to have attained such a following.

Another important point is that the pervasive impact of Islam is questionable. The majority of West African immigrant groups such as the Akan, Fon, Yoruba, and Ibo were not adherents of Islam, and it is their ancestors who apparently populated the Northeast. The Yoruba—Gegé (or Ewe), Nagôs—and Kwa tongues are among many African tongues preserved today; they in particular are the lingua franca for most Afro-Brazilian religious rites, which, incidentally, bear little resemblance to Islamic ceremonies. Neither the Hausa nor much Islamic influence has endured in Brazil, probably because their major vehicle, African religions, had already syncretized their animism with a ritual Catholicism that enabled Africans to maintain their individual and ethnic identity. And, too, it is difficult both culturally and politically to reconcile the concepts of "establishing a queen" and of matriarchal leadership—as exemplified by the position of Zeferina, Luiza Mahin, and others—with the role of the woman and her basically inferior position in Islamic tradition. Finally, other blacks considered male leaders such as Pacifico or Dandara, while noted as *alufás,* to be primarily secular agitators in whom discontented slaves found an adviser and an avenue to escape.[29]

The seeming cooperation among sundry black groups; the singularity of purpose in killing whites and *pardos,* and destroying *senzalas* and masters' homes; the organization of cadres and the recruitment of captains solely to lead slaves away from their plantations or release them from urban bondage—all of these factors negate the belief of Ramos and other earlier scholars that the revolts were merely Muslim holy wars. There is ample written documentation, oral tradition, and a full folklore repertoire from which scholars can reconstruct the causes and effects of the Bahian and other northern revolts. And these sources clearly point to the fact that the revolts were secular re-actions against slavery or, perhaps, for other power purposes.[30]

Another point which scholars have thus far ignored is the ethnic and numerical composition of the blacks involved in these uprisings. In the events of 1807, the "many" Negroes who were captured and punished were Hausa and Mandinka, while those taken prisoner at the *quilombos* consisted of 78 blacks, some of whom were free Negroes.[31] In the 1809 uprisings, "after offering fierce resistance" the Hausa, Yoruban, and Dahomean were defeated, "losing some 80 prisoners and a much larger number of casualties."[32] In the 1814 revolt, some 500 to 600 Hausa, "heavily armed Negroes participated," while references to smaller insurrections in the intervening years cite groups of less than 50 or 100. The 1826 uprising of the Yoruba and some Dahomeans (likely Fon) included "large" groups in various points of the Recôncavo, including Cachoeira, and other towns near Salvador, such as Pirajá. Exact numbers are unknown, but earlier efforts of several *capitáes do matto* failed because they underestimated the size of the African contingents.[33] Documents on the 1827 encounter note that the police wounded or killed eight of the fugitives, while reports on the revolt of 1830 referred to a small band of Yorubas and about

100 other blacks.[34] And, as the police records demonstrate, at least three-fourths of the 1835 conspirators were non-Islamic West Africans belonging to at least seventeen different groups, although predominantly Nagôs (Yoruba). The numbers mentioned in the actual revolt period itself include "sixty noisy blacks," "some forty dead and innumerable wounded," and all but "six Africans" left by the end of the battle in the early hours of January 25.[35] In view of Bahia's position as a center of the African slave trade as well as possessor of one of the largest slave populations in Brazil (see Tables 1 and 2), these figures would indicate not widespread slave conspiracies but rather small-scale agitation by radical groups such as is true of the United States today. The notion that the blacks were so disgruntled as to revolt *en masse* without disciplined, widespread leadership is not a feasible one, especially if seen in the light of the natural conservatism of human beings.

Other variables that historians should consider are the occupational concerns and geographical locations of the blacks and mulattoes who engaged in surrectionist activities. It would appear that the majority of participants were either free blacks and mulattoes or semi-independent *negros de ganho*.[36] These *negros,* primarily Yorubas, Gegés, and Hausas, were artisans and performed almost every type of job from porter, stevedore, printer, and mason to sculptor, sign painter, vendor, and shopkeeper. By virtue of their positions, they were not so intimately involved with whites that they could work to gain each other's freedom. This group of blacks and mulattoes, with a large measure of freedom and lacking close personal contact with the Bahian whites, were involved in the uprisings. Other Africans, primarily domestic and plantation slaves, were more intimately bound into the entire structure of slave society, repeatedly refused to join the revolts, and often warned their masters that a revolt was about to occur.[37] It would appear that more impersonal relations between master and slave, more urban-based *negros novos,* and more involvement with each other's problems were likely to foster revolts. It is also possible that those involved were not recently arrived "Muslim" Africans but blacks and mulattoes who were more familiar with the situation, more knowledgeable as to how to acquire armaments, and better able to make contacts and plan for mass emancipation by flight. Those Afro-Brazilians involved in re-actions to slavery were primarily those who had lived

Ann M. Pescatello

TABLE 1

The Afro-Brazilian Population, 1600-1888
(Rough Estimate)

Year	African (pure) Slaves	Freedmen	Mixed	Total
1600				13,000-15,000
1650	33,000			50,000 (slaves) plus
1700				100,000 (slaves) plus
1798	1,361,000	406,000	221,000	1,988,000
*1817-				
1818	1,930,000	585,000		2,515,000
1819	1,107,389*			
1823	1,147,515			
1850	2,500,000			
1864	1,715,000			
1873	1,542,230			
1882	1,272,355			
1885	1,000,000			
1887	637,602			
1888	500,000			

SOURCES: Mauricio de Goulart, A escravidão africana no Brasil (Sao Pãulo, 1950), 106; Rollie Poppino, Brazil, The Land and People (New York, 1968), 169-170; A. Ramos, Introdução a Antropologia Brasileira (1943), I:322 (of the 1817-1818 total, prêtos constituted less than 15 percent of the 585,000 free; whereas mulattoes accounted for only 202,000 of the 1,930,000 slaves); Stein, Vassouras, 294 (note the discrepancy of 820,000 slaves from 1817 to 1819; obviously there are inaccuracies)*; Stein, Vassouras, 294-295; Curtin, Atlantic Slave Trade, 207-245 passim. It is not possible here to go into a detailed analysis of Curtin's "census" reports which, obviously, do much to draw Afro-Brazilian figures more accurately.

SOURCES: Stein, Vassouras, 295. Also see Curtin, Atlantic Slave Trade, 240.

in the cities where life was less arduous than on the plantations and where leisure and exposure to more permissive lifestyles encouraged associations and plotting for freedom.[38]

TABLE 2

The Afro-Slave Populations, 1819-1887 (Rough Estimate)
in Bahia, Pernambuco, Rio, and São Paulo Provinces

Year	Bahia[1]	Pernambuco	Rio de Janeiro	São Paulo
1819	147,263	97,633	146,060	77,667
1823	237,458	150,000	150,549	21,000
1872	167,824	89,028	292,637	156,612
1873	165,403	106,236	301,352	174,622
1882	132,200	84,700	268,881	130,500
1885	158,000	66,000	218,000	128,000
1887	76,838	41,122	162,421	107,829

1. The provenience of slaves entering Bahia from 1801 to 1830 has been estimated in one source as 70,000 to 75,500 "Sudanese" (or Negro), and 104,000 to 111,500 "Bantus" (Congo-Angola). See L. Vianna Filho, *O Negro na Bahia* (1946), 98-99 and tables therein. See my note 28 at the end of this essay.

One other rebellion in Bahia, the "middle-class" political separatist revolt of 1835-1837, involved several Afro-Brazilians. Among them was a mulatto, Francisco Sabino Alvares da Rocha Vieira, the Chefe da Republica Bahia de 1837, who gave his name to the movement— *A Sabinada*. Vieira was a physician, professor of medicine, and owner of the *Novo Diario da Bahia*; he and his colleagues sought political independence, one of the goals of which incorporated the abolition of slavery.[39] He was joined by other Afro-Brazilians such as Francisco Xavier Bigode, Nicolau Tolentino, Luiz Gonzaga Pau Brasil, and a major, Santa Eufrásia.

According to oral tradition as well as official documents, minor plots and insurrections occurred throughout other areas of Brazil during the early decades of the nineteenth century. The blacks involved were imprisoned, whipped, condemned to forced labor, or deported to Portuguese penal settlements in Moçambique, Angola, and Benguela.[40] While the Bahian revolts are the most well-known, Afro-Brazilian re-actions elsewhere in Brazil were also significant, although many were conducted in conjunction with other causes. In Pernambuco, abolition was an ingredient in both the 1817 and 1824 insurrections, the former promoting the progressive emancipation of all slaves and the latter the abolition of the slave trade. Neither, however, was specifically concerned with the abolition of slavery per se. The 1823 uprising in Recife, although a popular movement with numerous grievances, was composed primarily of *pardos* and *prêtos* under mulatto Captain Pedro da Fonseca da Silva Pedroso. In the *Cabanada* revolts of 1832 in Alagoas and Pernambuco and of 1835 in Pará, numerous blacks were involved, and one article in the program of those insurrections demanded liberation of all the slaves.[41] In another famous revolt, the *balaiada* (1837-1840), which developed in Maranhão, the first leaders were the mulatto Raymundo Gomes, the African Cosme who commanded 3,000 slaves, and the Afro-Brazilian Manoel Franciso dos Anjos Fereira, the major ideologue of the uprising[42] whose nickname, *balião,* gave the movement its name and who, himself, was the organizing genius. Nonetheless, the movement was essentially an amalgam of forces in re-action to the provincial and national governments.

A later but little known so-called revolt prior to the final decade of the abolitionist campaigns occurred in 1874 and was known throughout the North as the *quebra-kilos*. Initially caused by the introduction into Brazil of the metric system, it later came to include a significant number of blacks and coloreds captained by the initiator of the revolt, the mulatto João Vieira, better known as João Carga d'Agua. Another black, Manoel do Carmo, also joined the revolt. They and the other Afro-Brazilians expanded their protests, marched on the public square, seized a number of hostages, and demanded that the local council president grant them their liberty and release to them the registry books in which newly born slaves were registered.[43] Their demands were met.

Throughout the nineteenth century, blacks and mulattoes engaged in numerous violent movements, many of which were separatist or not specifically abolitionist in character. Their leadership, however, was often Afro-Brazilian, and their demands often included a measure for emancipation or abolition.

This incessant violence became less frequent as the century progressed. As Brazil's economy and society changed, the re-actions against slavery as represented by Afro-Brazilian armed movements were diverted into more organized, less violent modes of re-action which coincided with growing external pressures and increasing internal reexamination of the institution of slavery. If nothing else, these Afro-Brazilian uprisings were physical precursors to the more philosophically oriented movements culminating in the events of 1879-1888.

In the second half of the century, Afro-Brazilian leaders were more and more becoming involved in pacific protests and incipient abolition campaigns such as the one which the black Manoel Roque, a shoemaker with little education, established in Bahia. He succeeded in securing the freedom of a number of slaves.[44] Another Afro-Brazilian, the mulatto Professor Francisco Alvares do Santos, from 1862 and for more than a quarter century thereafter, worked toward abolition and later organized the Sociedade Libertadora Dois de Julho.[45] From the late 1860s abolitionist societies were organized throughout the most heavily populated slave areas, particularly in Bahia and even more so in Rio de Janeiro which became the center of the abolitionist campaigns. The shift from violent to pacific modes of re-action, first recognized in the activities of men such as Roque and Alvares do Santo, reached its pinnacle with firebrands such as da Gama and Patrocínio.

The final abolition drive, launched in 1879 with the program of Joaquim Nabuco, owed its intensity to the preceding decades of re-action, the diverse areas of abolitionist activities, and the extensive aid of a few generations of Afro-Brazilian abolitionists.[46] From 1879 to 1888, free mulattoes and blacks joined Brazil's leading white citizens to effect the total abolition of slavery. Ironically, the decades of agitation had slowly whittled down the absolute numbers of slaves, so that when total abolition was decreed, it affected only about 500,000 Afro-Brazilian slaves instead of the 2.5 million that existed in 1850. These were mainly in Rio de Janeiro, Minas Gerais, and São Paulo provinces, areas with two-thirds of Brazil's slave population.

The first of the major Afro-Brazilian contributors to the final campaign was Luiz Gonzaga Pinto da Gama (1830-1882), son of the famed Luiza Mahin and precursor of the final phase of abolitionist activities which began in his native São Paulo.[47] Luiz de Gama's concern for his fellow blacks likely stemmed from his own experience. Da Gama's wealthy nobleman father had lost his fortune gambling, and on November 10, 1840, sold his son into slavery on the ship *Saraiva*. Before the *Saraiva* sailed, however, Luiz was removed by authorities from the vessel and boarded in a student residence in São Paulo, the city where he later achieved success as a journalist, politician, abolitionist poet, and lawyer. As a Paulista lawyer, he assumed the defense of cases involving slaves and was responsible for acquiring the freedom of hundreds of Afro-Brazilians through legal means.[48] In 1847, 1856, 1861, and 1862, da Gama was involved in movements to release blacks from bondage in the province of Minas Gerais, and by the mid-1860s, he had begun his polemics against slavery. His vitriolic lampoons of such manifestations of inferiority as the mulattoes' *caiado* (the use of whitening powders in an attempt to lighten one's skin) complex were carried in the pages of the *Diabo-coxo* and *Cabrião*.[49]

Da Gama attained national prominence as an abolitionist after he raised objections to the manifesto on manumission written by the first Republican Congress in Rio de Janeiro on July 2, 1873. One of the terms of the manifesto stipulated that each province would grapple with and solve the problem of slavery independently and gradually through conciliatory measures designed to appease slaveowners. Da Gama, representing the municipality of São José de Campos, protested against the idea on the grounds that it condoned oppression and crime. His substitute motion affirmed the rights of slaves to revolt and demanded full, immediate, and unconditional abolition of slavery.[50] Da Gama's motion was defeated. Nevertheless, for nearly a decade thereafter, he remained one of the few outspoken advocates for the absolute illegality of slavery and the principle of unconditional abolition. In the mid-1870s, he joined the staff of *Radical Paulistano,* a newspaper that published the abolitionist arguments of the intellectuals, including Rui Barbosa, and that became a forum for da Gama's own commentaries on abolition. Under the pseudonyms Getulino, Afro, or Barrabraz, he contributed satirical poems on Brazil's social and political life which spared neither white nor black in their condemnation of inequities.[51] Later, da Gama and Rui Barbosa collaborated to demand the emancipation of all children born to slaves.[52]

Da Gama did not live to see any of opinions on abolition vindicated, although by the time of his death in 1882 a general movement against slavery had acquired strength in São Paulo. Da Gama's apostolic dedication was passed on to the audacious and virulent law school graduate, Antônio Bento de Souza e Castro. Bento's journal, *A Redempção,* became the center of a network of informants and volunteers who abducted slaves from the *fazendas* to asylum in São Paulo city or its port of Santos. Bento ultimately lost faith in the legal process as an avenue to abolition and began to help slaves escape. Many prominent citizens aided Bento in his efforts, and in many cases their homes in the cities or the interior served as hiding places for fugitive slaves. Students, politicians, clerks, typographers, merchants, cabbies, and a lay brotherhood of Negro workers joined the movement. By 1886,[53] the movement had achieved such success that in the final two years prior to abolition slaves fled the plantations en masse.[54]

The large numbers of ex-slaves required areas in which they could live and function. In a place known as Jabaquára, in a hilly section of Santos, a quarter was established by an ex-slave, Quintino de Lacerda who, as *intendente,* had achieved reknown in the movement. Together with Santos Garrafão he controlled the Quilombo de Jabaquára with its houses and shelters for slaves. De Lacerda was joined by other young educated Afro-Brazilian men such as Arthur Carlos, who worked among the São Paulo slaves, and a man with the assumed name of Antonico, who slipped into the *senzalas* at night to organize escapes.[55]

Before Luiz da Gama's death and while the movement against slavery accelerated, a publication entitled *Gazeta de Tarde* (July 10, 1880) appeared, founded by the Afro-Brazilian José Ferreira de Menezes and by Joaquim Serra. The publication was dedicated to a detailed recording of the abolitionist movement, not only in Rio de Janeiro but also in the provinces, and it was devoted almost entirely to the cause. Thus, it printed such works as Nabuco's *Memória* which was presented to the Congress in Milan, Magalhães Lima's articles reprinted from Lisbon's *O Seculo* which urged Portuguese immigrants in Brazil not to own slaves, constant accounts of the cruelties suffered within the institution, and the proceedings of the meetings of the Abolitionist Confederation. Ferreira de Menezes gave both his time and money as a lawyer in Rio de Janeiro and as a political writer; he had been a contributor to another journal dedicated to abolition, the *Gazeta de Noticias,* founded by another Afro-Brazilian, Ferreira de Araujo.

Among the intellectuals and artists who had long been dedicated to the abolitionist cause was the mulatto poet and student of São Paulo's law school, Antônio de Castro Alves, who recited his fiery abolitionist verses at special festivals. Another mulatto, Carlos Gomes, was one of Brazil's foremost composers; his opera *O Escravo* contributed to the abolitionist cause. Gomes became an activist in the campaigns and his name was a great publicity aid. In keeping with the dramatic techniques of the movement in an opening scene of a pageant given in Gomes' honor he formally manumitted a slave and gave him money collected by Patrocínio and Rebouças.[56]

The Afro-Brazilians André Pinto Rebouças and José Carlos do Patrocínio were two of the most famous abolitionists. Rebouças (1835-1898), a reputed Bahian engineer, mathematician, and poet, had been involved in the abolitionist movement since 1868.[57] In his diary of July 1867, Rebouças wrote of a projected law which would establish a tax of 5$000 for agricultural slaves and 10$000 for urban slaves, thereby producing some 12,000 *contos* as a base for emancipation. His diary entry of June 15, 1869, reads: "I hope in God that I shall not die without having given to my country the most exuberant proof of my dedication to the Holy Cause of Emancipation." On April 11, 1870, Rebouças noted his participation in a session to found a society to fund the emancipation of slaves, and on April 15 he amplified this idea with a law proposed for the same purpose. Entries in his diary from April 1879 on, concerning conversations with Viconde de Lage, Viconde de Itaborai, and the Conde d'Eu, reveal his dedication to abolition, but it was not until May 21, 1880 that he began an intensive period of abolitionist propaganda.[58] By this time Rebouças had come to the attention of Dom Pedro after serving as an engineer in the Paraguayan war and constructing some of the first railroad lines in Brazil. He and his brother Antonio gained access to the imperial palace and achieved fame for engineering projects such as the Rio water works, rail lines, and execution of technical articles. Rebouças was to use this accessibility as a vehicle for their cause.

As a writer Rebouças contributed more than 120 articles, many of which appeared anonymously, to both the abolition press and to general journals such as the *Gazeta da Tarde, Folha Nova, Jornal do Comercio,* and *Novo Mundo.*[59] Through his commitment to manumission, Rebouças became associated with Patrocínio, Nabuco, Gomes, and Barbosa. In his diary he later noted the date July 9, 1880, as marking the beginning of nearly a decade of his concentrated dedication to the cause of abolition. His first article, entitled "Carlos Gomes e Emancipação," dealt with the relationship between Gomes' work and efforts to obtain manumission. It appeared in the July 9, 1880 issue of *Jornal do Comercio,* and two weeks later he wrote his first article for the *Gazeta da Tarde* on the same subject. On July 25, 1880, as friends and

allies, Rebouças and Gomes organized the first full conferences devoted to the cause of emancipation. The conference was conducted in
Rio at the São Luiz Theater.[60]

On September 28, 1880, Rebouças and Nabuco founded the Sociedade Brasileira Contra a Escravidão; Nabuco was elected president
and Rebouças treasurer. The society augmented Brazil's numerous
emancipation associations formed for the purpose of protecting and
ransoming slaves. The Sociedade Brasileiro Contra a Escravidão
preferred peaceful and legal means in its major task of propaganda
and aided Africans who had been shipped clandestinely into Brazil.
Rebouças was totally committed to the cause; he financed many of the
functions and supported the various organs of abolition such as the
journals and societies. He prepared the first numbers of the new society's monthly, *O Abolicionista,* which strengthened the abolitionist
press which at that time consisted of the *Gazeta da Tarde,* the *Gazeta
de Noticias,* and other lesser known sheets.[61] In 1881, the Associação
Central de Imigração sponsored a journal publishing "Notas," "Arti-
gos," and "Noticias" as another aid against slavery.

Rebouças and Nabuco traveled to Europe for a brief time, specifically
to study antislavery techniques. In 1882, Rebouças formed the Club
Nabuco in an unsuccessful effort to elect Nabuco as a deputy to the
National Congress from the capital's First District.[62] During the next
few years, Rebouças worked steadily, both alone and in concert with
José do Patrocínio and several others. On May 12, 1883, they established the Abolitionist Confederation with Rebouças as treasurer and
Patrocínio as speaker. Their purpose for the confederation was not
only to create a central propaganda force for abolition but also to
unite the various emancipation societies in direct action against slavery.[63]
Henceforth, slaves were kidnapped and, after 1884, shipped to Ceará,
landed by *jangadeiros* (craftsmen), given false manumission papers;
their freedom was arranged on presentation of these papers to a sym-
pathetic magistrate.[64]

The confederation was the movement's first organization with
salaried personnel, although there remained extensive fraternal secrecy
and the like. The first step in the centralized program was the organization of speeches, theatricals, concerts, and liberty parties at which
emancipation certificates were presented. Confederation agents clandestinely urged Afro-Brazilians to leave plantations, falsified docu-

ments that declared the free state of slaves, hid fugitive blacks and mulattoes, or aided their escape to Ceará.

The prime mover of this more forceful activist movement was José Patrocínio (1854-1905) whose operational motto was "slavery is theft." Offspring of a black slave and a Portuguese priest, Patrocínio was born and raised in Campos, Rio de Janeiro, and as a young man moved to Rio city to earn a pharmaceutical degree.[65] His early life was quite different from Rebouças in that Patrocínio received very little formal education as a young boy, supported himself in Rio with money earned from tutoring or as a subapprentice at the Santa Casa de Misericordia Hospital, and supplemented this income with a small monthly stipend from his vicar father or aid from friends.

Patrocínio began writing verse and joined the staff or the *Gazeta de Noticias* in 1877 where, under the pseudonym Proudhomme, he composed political verse on subjects such as the Chamber of Deputies debates. Prolific also under the pen names Justinio Moneiro and Notus Ferrão, he produced a number of plays, newspaper editorials, and articles. His novel condemning *fazenda* slavery, *Mota Coqueiro, ou a Pena de Morte,* appeared in 1877. Reflecting on the maltreatment of free Negroes in Rio and incensed with his slaveowning father, Patrocínio commenced abolitionist agitation and was soon fired from the paper.[66] Shortly thereafter, when his friend Ferreira de Menezes died, Patrocínio was given 15:000$000 by his father-in-law, Capitão Emiliano Rosa de Senna, owner of substantial real estate in Praia Formosa. Patrocínio then bought and became editor of the *Gazeta da Tarde* and later the *Cidade do Rio.* Thus, in his journals, in lectures, and in meetings Patrocínio launched mobile and written crusades against slavery. He traveled to Ceará and campaigned for abolition in Acarapé, which on January 1, 1833, became the first Brazilian municipality to achieve full emancipation. After abolition in Ceará, Patrocínio wrote to Victor Hugo that one Brazilian law now declared that no more slaves were to be born in Brazil and "Thanks to the efforts of the abolitionists in Ceará, another law will be made—no more slaves will die in my country."[67]

Patrocínio had initiated a series of meetings in Ceará and had given impetus to the Liberation Society in Ceará. An added feature of the movement in Ceará was the organization of the Jangadeiros of Fortaleza —many of whom were free blacks—under Francisco do Nascimento.

Thus began intensive resistance and sabotage of the transporting of slaves to ships destined for the South.[68] Since *Jangadas* were the only vessels that could ply the heavy breakers outside the northern harbors, the jangadeiros' refusal to transport slaves ended, for all practical purposes, the coastal slave trade. In 1886, Patrocínio successfully ran as a Confederation candidate for alderman in Rio's municipal chamber, and on September 1, 1887, he inaugurated the *Cidade do Rio,* a militant abolitionist paper.[69]

With the spiraling abolitionist activities from 1883 on, it was merely a matter of time before abolition was a *fait accompli.* This is not to ignore the realities of the larger society: numerous Afro-Brazilians were opposed to abolition, and among the abolitionists there were intensive conflicts over methods and goals. In fact, prior to the establishment of the Confederation there were only three mulattoes in the abolitionist party. Moreover, in many recorded instances free men of color, themselves slaveholders, were indifferent or opposed to abolition.[70] For example, in 1884 a black, one of thirty candidates for the Bahian Chamber, published a document requesting his election in the name of slavery.[71] Among the abolitionists some different techniques did arise, as can be seen in the diverse methodologies of Rebouças and Patrocínio. Rebouças was the quiescent idealist of the movement as well as one of its most important financial backers; Patrocínio, the emotional orator, dominated meetings and advertised his status as a "poor black man." While Patrocínio was the popular agitator and revolutionary spokesman, Rebouças embodied the "spirit" of emancipation. Destpite their differences these two men worked harmoniously.[72]

At the successful end of the abolition movement, and despite the fact that slavery had thrived under the monarchy, both Patrocínio and Rebouças reacted, in their own ways, against the establishment of a republic. Rebouças accompanied Pedro II to Portugal, considering himself a debtor of the Empire; Patrocínio, feared the possible revival of slavocracy, in the relative rapidity of the legalizing of abolition, and on September 23, 1889, called a conference directed against Republican slavocrats and initiated the *Guarda Negra da Rendentôra.*[73]

From this essay it is clear that Afro-Brazilian re-actions to slavery in Brazil varied in style, form, numerical and ethnic composition, and especially purposes. The goals were just as diverse, ranging from the emancipation of individuals or groups working within a slave system, to abolition of the Brazilian coastal slave trade, to abolition of the Atlantic trade, to abolition of slavery. The Afro-Brazilians not only participated in all of these activities but often provided the leadership for them as well.

But was there historical continuity in these Afro-Brazilian movements, a continuity sufficient to enable Afro-Brazilians to be effective in bringing about final abolition? In a larger sense, it would appear that there was little continuity in the movements, for the needs of the Afro-Brazilians and the "content" of the movements in the Northeast in the early part of the nineteenth century were quite removed from those of their southern counterparts at the end of the century. More important as an indication of the lack of historical continuity, in the organizational sense of the word, is that the evidence demonstrates that few, if any, of the early movements had a clearly defined program of social and political protest vis-à-vis the system of slavery. Not until the later intellectual-dominated movements in the South were protests defined into programs for abolition. In addition, the very diversity of the early movements, their sporadic and often singular, small-scale goals, prevented the development of a strong and enduring abolition program. Indeed, it may be posited that well-defined protest programs did not exist until the 1850 abolition of the Atlantic slave trade. Once the supply source for slaves was permanently destroyed, programs with continuity and cumulative effect could be developed because the number of goals had been reduced and the human variables neatly contained.

A cumulative effect was not felt until the final decade prior to abolition. It was possible at this time because of the momentum the various programs generated, the much wider scale and often interrelated nature of the protests, the enormous increase in communications for publicizing the movement, and the acquiescence of influential planters to the abolition of what they considered to be an ineffective system of labor. Abolition did not occur simply because of the demands and pressures of a racial or ethnic force. Economic and social changes in Brazilian society as a whole had made it responsive to the efforts of Afro-Brazilians, to the requirements of a modernizing nation, and to its demand for a system of free labor.

In another sense there *was* historical continuity and cumulative effect. The final abolition decree of 1888 (without compensation to slaveowners) was possible, in part, because Afro-Brazilians had often and relatively consistently protested their situation. The various modes and phases of Afro-Brazilian re-action ultimately contributed to the end of slavery in Brazil.

NOTES

1. Richard Graham, "The Causes for the Abolition of Negro Slavery in Brazil: An Interpretive Essay," *Hispanic American Historical Review* (HAHR), XLVI, 2 (1966), 123-137, noted that many ex-slaves went to the cities and were unable to find jobs. A general depression hit the countryside and encouraged excessive government lending which, in turn, benefited urban groups such as bank managers, company promoters, and stock manipulators (p. 137).

2. See, for example, Graham, "The Causes"; P. A. Martin, "Slavery and Abolition in Brazil," HAHR, XIII (May 1933), 151-196; Evaristo de Moraes, *A Campanha Abolicionista, 1879-88* (Rio de Janeiro, 1924); Osorio Duque-Estrada, *A Abolição (esboço historico, 1831-88)* (Rio de Janeiro, 1918); Sud Menucci, *O Precursor do Abolicionismo no Brasil: Luiz Gama* (São Paulo, 1938); Robert Toplin, "Upheaval, Violence, and the Abolition of Slavery in Brazil: The Case of São Paulo," HAHR, XLIX, 4 (1969), 639-655; Leslie Bethell. *The Abolition of the Brazilian Slave Trade* (Cambridge, 1970); Robert Toplin. *The Abolition of Brazilian Slavery* (New York, 1972); Robert Conrad. *The Destruction of Brazilian Slavery* (Berkeley and Los Angeles, 1972); Peter Eisenberg, *The Sugar Industry of Pernambuco* (Berkeley and Los Angeles, 1973).

3. "Revolt" implies an aggressive, violent action. Most of these movements, it appears, were formed out of a sense of passive resistance which took the reactionary forms of flight, abortion, suicide, or merely resistance to attempts to destroy *quilombos,* etc. It should be made clear, however, that the term *re-action* is used in the literal sense of reactivating (a) previous pattern(s) of resistance to or actions against something. It should *not* be given its modern negative connotation of conservative politico-military action against something of which we are in favor. Use of the term *re-action* is crucial, I believe, to the concept of the historical continuum context.

4. The designation *Negro* is also rife with confusion. Theoretically, it should refer to those members of linguistic groups, or their descendants, from the vast geographical sector of Africa who are the "true" or Sudanese Negro peoples as opposed to the other great linguistic group, the Bantu. See Joseph Greenberg, *The Languages of Africa* (Bloomington, 1963) and S. W. Koelle, *Polyglotta Africana* (London, 1854). In Brazil, the term *Negro* has been used for *prêtos* (blacks), *pardos* (dark, brown), and *gente d'côr* (people of color); sometimes for *crioulos* (more correctly denoting Portuguese born in Brazil, but also extended to mixed-bloods); and sometimes for *Africanos*.

5. See Richard Graham, *Britain and the Onset of Modernization in Brazil, 1850-1914* (Cambridge, 1968); Joaquim Nabuco, *O Abolicionismo* (Rio de Janeiro, 1938); *O Abolicionista: orgão da Sociedade Contra a Escravidão,* 1-14 (November 1, 1880-December 1, 1881); and *O immigração,* 1887-1888.

6. Antonio Vieira, in Maranhão, the first Sunday of Lent, in Afranio Peixoto (ed.), *Vieira Brasileiro* (Paris, 1921), I, 220-221.

7. Documented participation of blacks/mulattoes in the Brazilian militias begins with the collaboration of the Afro-Brazilian Henrique Dias' black regiments against the Dutch in the seventeenth century. See José Antonio Gonçalves de Mello, *Henrique Dias: Governador dos pretos, crioulos, e mulattos* (Recife, 1954).

8. Also called *ladeira* or, more popularly, *mocambo* from the Ambundu *mu-kambo* (hideout) which was the original designation for *quilombo* (from the Jaga *Ki-lombo,* or war camp). *Palmares,* which became the *nom de guerre* for the fugitive slave settlements in Alagoas-Pernambuco, originally meant no more than an area covered by palm trees. See Renato Mendonça, *A Influencia Africana no Portugues do Brasil* (Rio de Janeiro, 1937), 267; and Giovanni Antonio Cavazzi da Montecuccolo, *Istorica descrittione de 'tre regni Congo, Matamba e Angola* (1687), 207. Kent notes that there were about ten major *quilombos* in colonial Brazil, of which seven were destroyed within two years of being formed. One in Minas Gerais lasted from 1712 to 1719; the "Carlota" in Mato Grosso lasted from 1770 to 1795; and Palmares. R. K. Kent, "Palmares: An African State in Brazil," *Journal of African History* (JAH), VI, 2 (1965), 161-175. Schwartz, however, refers to several others that seemed to have endured in various forms, such as those of Jaguaripe (1588-1627?) and Buraco de Tatú (1743-1763), both in Baía. Stuart Schwartz, "The *Mocambo:* Slave Resistance in Colonial Bahia," *Journal of Social History* (JSH), III, 4 (Summer 1970), 313-333; see especially 324-325, 327-333.

9. The earliest record of armed re-action is in a letter from Padre Nóbrega to Governor-General Tomé de Sousa (July 5, 1559), in Serafim Leite (ed.), *Cartas dos Primeiros Jesuiticos do Brasil* (1954), III, 101.

10. For more thorough discussions of Palmares, see Edison Carneiro, *O Quilombo dos Palmares 1630-95* (São Paulo, 1958); Ernesto Ennes, *As Guerras dos Palmares* (1938); and Ennes, "The Palmares 'Republic' of Pernambuco: Its Final Destruction," *The Americas,* V (1949); "Relação das Guerras feitas aos Palmares de Pernambuco no tempo do Governador d. Pedro de Almeida," *Revista do Instituto Historico e Geographico Brasileiro* (RIHGB), XXII (1859), 303-329; and Kent, "Palmares." A few years ago, some Afro-Brazilian towns were discovered in the areas of Alagoas and Pernambuco states. In 1969, a backlands village of 1,200 "pure" blacks, descendants of a *quilombo,* were discovered after having isolated themselves for a few centuries. A personal communication from Donald Warren, Jr.

11. See René Ribeiro, "Relations of the Negro with Christianity in Portuguese America," *The Americas,* XIV, 4 (1958), 458; and Vicente do Salvador, *Historia do Brasil, 1650-1627* (São Paulo, 1961), 315. Other published primary sources available to the student in the role of Afro-Brazilians and their resistance are the six-volume *Documentos historicos do Arquivo Municipal: Atas da Camara (Bahia)* (Salvador, 1949); and the *Documentos Historicos da Biblioteca Nacional de Rio de Janeiro* (Rio de Janeiro, 1950). Documentary evidence is also available in the *Cartorio dos jesuiticas* in the Arquivo Nacional da Torre do Tombo (ANTT); codices of the *Relação da Bahia* in the Biblioteca Geral da Universidade de Coimbra (BGUC); and the codices and maços for Bahia and Rio de Janeiro in the Archuivo Historico Ultramarino (AHU), all in Portugal.

12. For further information on these formations and activities, see Pedro Thomas Pedreira, "Os quilombos baianos," *Revista Brasileira de Geografia* (RBG), XXIV

(1962), 79-93; Schwartz, "The *Mocambo*," especially 319-327; and A. Ruy. *A Primeira Revolução Social Brasileira* (n.p., 1942), 144-150. Of the thirty-four conspirators tried in court, twenty-three were *pardos* (ten freeborn, four freed, and nine slaves) and one African.

13. Rodrigues and Ramos, initiators of the field of Brazilian black studies, indicated that materials for these movements were difficult to find. This is not so. The best sources available in English are the sketchy travelers' accounts. Those in Portuguese appear in the citations following discussions of specific movements. In the past few years, two students from Columbia University have undertaken studies specifically of the nineteenth-century urban revolts in Brazil. A student at the University of California at Berkeley has also been working in Bahian archival materials pertinent to the 1800-1835 period, and a few students in African history at the University of California at Los Angeles are working on the African backgrounds, in Africa, to the Bahian revolts. There are also copious oral and written sources available. In Bahia alone, the Archuivo Publico in Salvador has several thousand police documents on the revolts of 1806-1835; they are included in four volumes and each contains from 1,000 to 1,200 sheets in long hand. Other records include the voluminous correspondence between the governors of Bahia and the *senhores de engenho* in petitions and other correspondence. The laws of the province, year by year, are another indicator of the "revolts" of the blacks and the measures taken to repress them and punish the offenders. Trial records are also available at the Archivo Publico, Bahia, as are facsimiles of the documents found in the possession of "black revolutionaries." An excellent additional source is the folklore and oral traditions of the Bahianas, especially the words to the *capoeira* texts.

14. There are many references to these movements, especially those of 1807-1808, 1809, 1814, and 1816, in accounts other than those found in the Bahian archives. These supplementary accounts, primary and secondary, include the Arabic script manuscripts of the movements and the works of Pierre Verger. See also Etienne Ignace Brasil, "La Secte Musulmane des Malês et leur Revolte en 1835," *Anthropos,* IV (1909), 99-105, 405-415. For activities of returned "brasileiros" to Africa, see David A. Ross, "The Career of Domingo Martinez in the Bight of Benin, 1833-1864," JAH, VI, 1 (1965), 79-90.

The Fulani *jihads* of northern Nigeria (beginning in 1725) were, in effect, great prose-lytizing wars that reached their peak in the nineteenth century, especially 1804-1840. Many prisoners were sold into the foreign slave trade so records of sales, plus our knowl-edge of African forms of slavery, should not surprise the reader vis-à-vis the similar activities noted in a few of the nineteenth-century Brazilian campaigns. Dissenters of the religious motivation schools concerning the Brazilian *jihads* include A. Jurema, *Insur-reções Negras no Brasil* (n.p., 1940), which contains a more socioeconomic view of class struggles. This position is also espoused by C. Moura, *Rebelião nas Senzalas* (n.p., 1958). For further information on the *jihads,* see especially M. G. Smith, "The Jihad of Shehu Dan Fodio: Some Problems," in I. M. Lewis (ed.), *Islam in Tropical Africa* (London, 1966), 408-424; H. Smith, "A Neglected Theme of West African History: The Islamic Revolts of the Nineteenth century," in Jan Vansina, Raymond Mauny, et al. *The Historian in Tropical Africa* (London, 1964); and M. R. Waldman, "The Fulani Jihad—A Reassessment," JAH, VI, 3 (1965), 333-335; and John Ralph Willis, *"Jihād Fī Sabīl Allāh*—Its Doctrinal Basis in Islam and Some Aspects of Its Evolution in Nine-teenth-Century West Africa," JAH, VIII, 3 (1967), 395-415.

There are numerous new works devoted to this subject, and an extensive literature has developed, with suggestions as to the secular motivations of leaders and participants in the *jihads*. Given the theories of J. S. Trimingham and I. M. Hogben that the wars were more socio-racial than religious since they involved *rimbe* or assimilated free groups who were not "pure Fulani," it is possible that the Brazilian movements were heavily influenced by these secular elements of the African *jihads* and that they have been misinterpreted as "religious" in orientation. Incidentally, *jihad* literally means a disciplined exertion in the way of Allah and has been simply translated as "holy war" by scholars.

15. See Astolfo Serra, *A Balaida* (Rio de Janeiro, 1946); Vianna, *A Sabinada;* and Vicente Licínio Cardoso, *Margem da historia do Brasil* (São Paulo, 1933).

16. Ignacio Accioli de Cerqueira e Silva, *Memorias historicas e politicas da provincia da Bahia,* 4 vols. (Bahia, 1919-1930), I, 346.

17. Orders from the governor of Bahia as cited in Eduardo A. de Caldas Britto, "Levantes de prêtos na Bahia," *RIGH Bahia,* XXIX (1903), 69-90, 72. The plan of revolt, I am told by a leader of an Afro-Brazilian cult group in Salvador, was partially written in Arabic.

18. This is confirmed in the archives cited above, in the notes, police, and trial records contained therein, and in the Arabic-character documents preserved there. Oral tradition, as relayed to me in interviews (January 1970): folklore materials in the archives of the Afro-Bahian and folklore centers in Salvador; and "texts" of Afro-Bahian cult ceremonies indicate the abolition and emancipation content of these movements.

19. As cited in Alvares do Amaral, *Resumo chronologico da Bahia* (Salvador, n.d.), 6.

20. Of the 500 or so Hausas, who *were* the revolt, the leaders were publicly hung in the Praça Piedade. Others were deported to Portuguese Africa, a fate many felt was worse than death since they were removed from their homeland. Orders of the Conde dos Arcos in the Archuivo Publico, Bahia (Caldas Britto), 78-81.

21. *Justiça,* Dockets A1-C1 series in the Archuivo Publico, Bahia, police and trial documents. Some are cited in Brasil, "La Secte Musulmane," 406-414.

22. It has been noted in oral tradition that when the "African king" was captured he wore a crown and an old-fashioned green velveteen mantle that had a golden cock embroidered on it, and he carried a red flag. OHI, January 1970, Salvador.

23. About 50 dead, many others taken prisoner.

24. From the report of January 29, 1835, of the Salvadorean police chief Gonçalves Martins to the governor of Bahia, as republished from the *Diario da Bahia* in the *Jornal do Commercio,* Rio de Janeiro (February 10, 1835). A letter from Bahia (January 31, 1835) to the *Jornal do Commercio,* Rio de Janeiro, also published (February 10, 1835), noted that all life was at a standstill and that it was a serious, long-planned revolt put down by the armed forces. See also R. Nina Rodrigues, *Os Africanos no Brasil* (São Paulo, 1932), 19-32; and R. K. Kent, "African Revolt in Bahia: January 24-25, 1835," in JSH, III, 4 (Summer 1970), 334-356.

25. The *Officios* 19:384 and 19:385b, as cited in Brasil, "La Secte Musulmane," 409-415.

26. A letter from Gonçalves Martins revealed a substantial documentary account of activities in a rather bastardized Arabic script. The letter also indicated that the insurrection had had a long gestation period, with absolute secrecy, and had involved several tribal groups. Analyses of the documents can be found in Vincent Monteil, "Analyses des 25 documents arabes des Mâles de Bahia (1835)," *Bulletin,* Institut Funda-

mental d'Afrique Noire (IFAN), XXIX, 1, 2 (1967). Also, R. Reichert and A. B. Abdel-ghani, "Os documentos árabes no Arquivo Publico do Estado da Bahia, la série: Textos coranicos," *Afro-Asia* (University of Bahia), II (1966); and R. Reichert, "L'Insurrection d'esclaves de 1835 à la lumière des documents arabes des Archives publiques de l'Etat de Bahia, Brésil," *Bulletin,* IFAN, II, 1, 2 (1967).

27. Of immediate reference to the "nine Bahian revolts," six were urban in origin and orientation—1809, 1814, 1816, 1826, 1830, 1835; three more were more "suburban" and rural in tone—1808, 1827, 1828-1829; and other near or immediately abortive "revolts," such as 1807, fit both categories. No single monograph on the 1807-1835 period is available to sort out these theories more systematically.

28. Philip Curtin, *The Atlantic Slave Trade. A Census* (Madison, 1969), Table 62, 207; Table 69, 240. During 1701-1810, Angola supplied 68 percent of the slaves imported into Brazil, and from 1817 to 1843, Angola and Congo together accounted for nearly 68 percent. At the same time, figures indicate that of some 605,500 Africans from Costa da Mina (or areas more likely to have Islamic influence), as many as 515,000 could have entered Bahia between 1701 and 1810. Whether they remained is a point of conjecture since from the 1690s to the 1750s the demand for slaves in the gold mines of Minas Gerais might merely have flushed the Africans through Bahia. In the years 1817-1843, Bahia seems to have taken less than 14,000 of its 55,000 total from areas of possible Islamic influence. Curtin, *Atlantic Slave Trade,* 207-243 passim, and sources cited therein. Pierre Verger, *Bahia and the West African Trade* (Ibadan, 1964), 205, indicates that there was an extremely large-scale Yoruba importation into Brazil from the latter third of the eighteenth century.

29. Oral traditions today as cited to me in OHI, January 1970. The trial proceedings as noted in Rodrigues, *Os Africanos,* contain written materials for the investigation of these movements. Also Verger, *Bahia,* and his *Notes sur le culte des orisa et vodun* (Dakar, 1957), point to the traditional leadership of women in Afro-Brazilian cult activities, definitely a part of the non-Islamic Yoruba culture.

30. In a brief trip to Brazil (December 1969-February 1970), I interviewed several Afro-Brazilian cult leaders of both Nagô (Yoruba) and Gegé (Ewe) religious groups. Their traditions indicate that the nineteenth-century revolts were far from solely concerned with Islamic precepts. The cult leaders felt that the insurrections were movements for the abolition of slavery and attainment of political control.

It would have been desirable to identify and to reprint portions of the testimony of the several cult leaders whom I interviewed in the states of Bahia and Pernambuco, and the two whom I interviewed in Rio de Janeiro city. However, the testimony was given with the explicit request that it not be directly quoted, nor the names of the interviewees made public, for they were afraid that *any* discussion of revolts and political intrigue, albeit more than a century old, would be misconstrued by a military government that is trying to subjugate the Afro-Brazilian elements of Brazilian culture. In such contexts, the scholar faces the hazards of modern politics at cross-purposes with the "pursuit of truth."

31. Caldas Britto, "Levantos de prêtos," 72; narrative song, untitled, in the Recôncavo about Cabula and Nossa Senhora dos Mares, played and sung for me in January 1970 by two troubadors of Bahia. Basic concepts in the song line are freedom, fugitive camps, pity for the *capitão mor* and his soldiers, and dreams of return to Africa!

32. As cited in Artur Ramos, *The Negro in Brazil* (Washington, D.C., 1939), 46. This rising has also been attributed to the secret Yoruba society, Ogboni.

33. Ultimately, a whole detachment of soldiers was required since the numbers of Africans were substantial. As cited in Nina Rodrigues, *Os Africanos,* 76.

34. *Justiça,* A1-C1: Archuivo Publico, Bahia.

35. Ibid. The police records in the APB show that 236 Afro-Brazilians were brought to trial: 165 Nagos, 21 Haussas, 6 Geges, 16 Tapas, 3 Gurmas, 5 Bornos, 3 Cabindas, 4 Congolais, 1 Camarao, 1 Barba, 3 Minas, 2 Calabars, 1 Jabu, 1 Mondubi, 2 Benim, 1 parda, and 1 *cabra.*

36. In fact, all of the leaders except Luiz *(Sanim)* were freed persons. Belchoir and Gaspar owned hostels, and their liaison who provided them refuge, Domingo Marinho de Sa, owned the building in which the initial contact was made between insurrectionists and police.

37. "A person of integrity" sought out the governor and informed him that "a Negro of mine told me that the slaves of the Ussa nation are planning to revolt." As quoted in *A Illustração,* Bahia (June 1836) on the revolt set for 7 P.M. on May 28, 1807. This was the case with almost every uprising and even travelers commented that "some Negroes . . . did not wish to join" or that "colored troops were used in suppressing them" [the revolts]. See Prince Maximillian Wied Neuwied, *Viagem ao Brasil* (São Paulo, 1940), 450-451; and Henry L. Koster, *Travels in Brazil, 1809-1815* (Philadelphia, 1817), 2 vols., I, 214. Also see Brasil, "La Secte Musulmane," 409ff., on informers of the 1835 revolt.

38. Similar situations existed in West Africa. For example, in the Niger Delta states where plantation and "house" system types of labor existed, those slaves and freeborn living in the towns were more prone to revolts than those on the plantations.

39. Vianna, *A Sabinada;* and João Gualberto Ferreira Ladislão dos Santos Titára, *Paraguassú* (Bahia, 1835).

40. See "Correspondencia da Corte de Portugal com os Vice-Reis do Brasil," *Publicações do Archuivo Nacional,* III (1901), for orders from the court to the viceroy at Rio de Janeiro on deporting "these ruffians."

41. Several revolts against the Brazilian imperial government, varied in content, occurred in Para, Sergipe, Pernambuco, and Rio Grande do Sul. For the roles of Afro-Brazilians in the nineteenth-century affairs, see Walter Spaulding, *A Revolução Farroupilha* (São Paulo, 1939); Astolfo Serra, *A Balaida;* Vianna, *A Sabinada*; and Aderbal Jurema, *Insurreições Negras no Brasil* (Recife, 1935).

42. As cited in Ramos, *Negro in Brazil,* 39.

43. Ibid., 40.

44. Its formal organization was known as the Sociedade Abolicionista Bahiana, formerly the Sociedade Libertadora Bahiana, founded in 1883. Its name changed four years later.

45. He was a mathematician who supposedly had access to two-thirds of the students of mathematics in Salvador and formed a "patriotic battalion" consisting of himself and the students.

46. For some excellent cartoons and caricatures of the abolitionists, see Angelo Agostini's ridicule of proslavery elements in *Revista Illustrada.*

47. One of da Gama's literary precursors was Antonio Gonçalves Dias (1823-1864) whose "A Escrava," "A Meditação," and was his translation of Victor Hugo's *Bug-Jargal*

sounded the first few notes of emancipation sentiment. The first, which appeared in 1846 in *Arquivo,* discusses the melancholy slave and cruel master. The second (see his *Obras,* III, 3-128) is an allegory which suggests that what is created by man is unworthy because it is created by slaves and slaves are incapable of great achievement. The last is about an African prince in slavery. See his *Obras Posthumous,* ed. by Antonio Henrique Leal (São Luiz de Maranhão, 1868).

48. Graham, *Britain and the Onset of Modernization,* 182n.1.

49. Both of these were journals of satire and humor, the *Diabo-Coxo* lasting from October 17, 1864, to November 24, 1865, and the *Cabrião* from October 30, 1866, to October 1, 1867.

50. Sud Mennucci, *O Precursor do Abolicionismo no Brasil, Luiz Gama* (São Paulo, 1938), 159-160; and Morães, *A Campanha Abolicionista,* 251.

51. His *Bodaradda,* one of his more famous poems, is a ridicule of mulattoes. For a fuller exposition of his writings, both prose and poetry, see *Trovas Burlescas e Escritos em Prosa* (São Paulo, 1944). He had also been preceded by Afro-Brazilians such as Silva Alvarenga, Teixeira e Souza, and Tobias Barreto, each of whom was never as seriously involved. However, Barreto's poem, "A Escravidão," (either 1866 or 1868) was one of the few major poems concerning slavery.

52. *Recepção do Sr. Senador Ruy Barbosa no Faculdade de Direito no Dia 18 de Dezembro de 1909.* See the *Revista da Faculdade de Direito de São Paulo,* XVII, 160, for Barbosa's speech and comment.

53. See Graham, "The Causes for the Abolition of Negro Slavery," and *Britain and the Onset,* 172. According to Richard Morse, *From Community to Metropolis,* São Paulo city in 1855 had only 4,075 slaves; in 1872, 3,424 slaves; and in 1887 only 439 slaves (p. 159).

54. Ibid., 132-133. Within a year of March 1887, and as a result of the Paulista planters' own Emancipation Society, voluntary manumission had freed 39,538 of the province's slaves. The newspapers of the period are rife with such information. See, for example, the *Gazeta da Tarde,* 1882-1888; *A Redempção,* all of 1887 and 1888; *Cidade do Rio,* October-December 1887; the *Rio News,* October-December 1887; *Diario de Santos,* October-December 1887; and *Correio Paulistano,* October-December 1887.

55. Santos, *Os Republicanos,* 177-182; Dornas, *A Escravidão no Brasil,* 185; and Moraes, *A Campanha Abolicionista,* 269. Also see *Annaes da Câmara* (São Paulo, 1888), I, 51ff.; *Diario de Santos* (May 1888); *Cidade do Rio* (January 1888); and *O País* (November 23, 1887).

56. Evaristo de Moraes, "Pedro II e o Movimento Abolicionista," RIHGB, CLII (1920), 334-339.

57. Also famous as a bontanist, astronomer, geologist, hygienist, philanthropist, philosopher, etc. See Duque-Estrada, *A Abolição,* 271ff.

58. For a chronological exposition of his involvement, see his *Diario e Notas Auto-biograficas* (Rio, 1938).

59. However, he noted them in his *Diario* and in additional publications (several articles on economic and social themes).

60. Symbolic manumission seems to have been widespread. For example, on the anniversary of St. John's Day, the Free Masons' Grand Lodge in Rio, composed of the most influential statesmen and proprietors, manumitted a number of slaves by purchasing them.

61. Carolina Nabuco, *The Life of Joaquim Nabuco* (Stanford, 1950), 71-72. Major sources for the opinions and attitudes of Afro-Brazilians on slavery and abolition can be found in *O Abolitionista, Gazeta da Tarde,* and *Gazeta de Noticias;* the political caricatures of Angelo Agostini in the *Revista Ilustrada;* and other papers such as the *Jornal do Comercio* or the American edited *Rio News,* which were helpful to the abolition movement.

62. Nabuco went into exile briefly and in 1885 was elected to the Chamber.

63. Duque-Estrada, *A Abolição,* 93-95. A manifesto was drawn and representatives of fifteen societies signed it. It was read to the public, presented to Parliament, and then edited by Patrocínio and published in the *Diario Oficial.*

64. Duque-Estrada, *A Abolição,* 121.

65. His mother, Justina Maria do Espirito Santo, was a respected vendor of fruits and vegetables who was, apparently, maltreated by José's father, João Carlos Monteiro, a vicar and well-known orator.

66. Moraes, *A Campanha Abolitionista,* 372. Patrocínio lampooned his father as a re-enslaver of poor coloreds.

67. Duque-Estrada, *A Abolição,* 119. The primary impetus was probably a new tax law which made the value of a slave less than the tax of a slave.

68. Nabuco, *The Life of Joaquim Nabuco,* 81. An example of the "nuts and bolts" type of historical research that needs to be done on the entire subject of nineteenth-century abolition movements is the case of Ceará. Slavery was abolished there on March 25, 1884, but very little is known of *how* it was abolished, *who* was involved (how many, their composition, the motivations and the techniques), problems encountered, issues involved, and the like. We need studies that fall under the rubric of price history; social history of the common man; and urban, rural, regional, local, demographic, and immigration history.

69. Some of the contributors were Aluizio Azevedo, author of *O Mulatto* and *O Cortiço;* Coelho Neto, Olavo Bilac, Paulo Ney, and Guimarães.

70. Letter from Rebouças (March 10, 1882) to Joaquim Serra, quoted in his *Diario,* 36.

71. Fonseca, *A Escravidão,* 137, 145-156, 148-149.

72. Rebouças noted that he and Patrocínio swept theaters and posted bills; were editors, reporters, reviewers, and distributors; and were even barkers at fairs. *Diario,* 293.

73. Rui Barbosa, *A Queda do Imperio,* II, 77-93, 141-149, 293-300. Among the studies needed are penetrating biographical analyses of the men, white and Afro-Brazilian, involved in abolition.

4

B. Edward Pierce

THE HISTORICAL CONTEXT OF NENGRE KINSHIP AND RESIDENCE: ETHNOHISTORY OF THE FAMILY ORGANIZATION OF LOWER STATUS CREOLES IN PARAMARIBO[1]

The family system of lower status Creoles, or the Nengre of Paramaribo, Surinam,[2] is similar to that of other Afro-American proletariats. The common characteristics of these systems include: (1) variable mating forms, including legal marriage, nonlegal coresidential unions, and nonlegal extraresidential unions; (2) a high degree of conjugal instability; (3) a high incidence of households headed by single females; (4) the pivotal position of females in kinship, domestic, and residential groups; and (5) the frequent inclusion of distant consanguineals in the household. In addition, the factors that have provided the bases for causal explanations of these characteristics in other Afro-American family systems (i.e., the West African heritage of polygyny, the slave and plantation systems, economic marginality, systems of land tenure, and a high incidence of migratory wage labor) are all pertinent in the Surinamese case.[3] Since all of these factors are apparently relevant to an explanation of Nengre family organization, none of them, taken singly, is an adequate causal explanation of this particular family system, or for that matter, of Afro-American family organization in general.

My initial research on Nengre family organization resulted in a contemporary, synchronic analysis of kinship and residence with the aim of demonstrating that distinctive patterns of kinship provide the Nengre with important referents for manipulating their domestic and residential relationships (Pierce, 1971). As work on this synchronic study progressed, I developed an interest in gaining a diachronic or historical perspective on Nengre family organization. This essay represents my initial attempts to come to grips with some of the problems involved in reconstructing the (ethno) history of Nengre family organization.

As is the case in other areas of Afro-America, there is little direct historical evidence on the family system of the Surinamese slaves or their emancipated descendants, the Nengre. Consequently, a diachronic perspective on Nengre family organization can only be acquired through heavy reliance on inference from indirect evidence. This inferential reconstruction will be successful only if the conceptual framework within which it occurs is rigorously defined. Published studies of Afro-American family organization are of limited aid in this regard since they generally rest on inadequate concepts of "the family" and simplistic ideas about causal factors that account for continuity and change in family organization.

Family organization is defined here as the sociocultural system which results when a society's members participate in the groups and networks formed by the articulation of the kinship, domestic, and residential domains. Kinship is the collective cultural or cognitive map of the biological network. Domesticity refers to the domain of activities that must be performed in order to sustain the lives of the members of a household. Residential relationships are concerned with the problem of who lives with whom.

Buckley (1968:490) describes sociocultural systems as being complex and adaptive, and he defines complex adaptive systems as being negentropic and internally and externally open. Thus, it may be suggested that the important characteristics of a family system are that it maintains its structural integrity through time, it consists of components or domains that are reciprocally related and mutually interdependent, and the system as a whole persists or changes in response to external influences or causal factors. Externally derived change-producing factors can impinge on the domain(s) of kinship, domesticity and/or residence, and changes in any of these domains will produce corresponding changes in the others.

The external influences or causal factors include ecological and demographic variables which have a significant effect on residence and domestic patterns, and externally derived cultural inputs which have a significant effect on the ways that a society's members think about the family. These constitute the environing field of the system of family organization. Considerable insight into the historical development of the Nengre system of family organization can be acquired by determining significant changes that have occurred in its environing field.

The point of departure for our consideration of the historical development of Nengre family organization will be a discussion of significant aspects of the contemporary system. The data on which this summary discussion is based were gathered by means of the traditional anthropological techniques of participant observation, intensive interviews of key informants, and a household census. This discussion of the contemporary system will be followed by a consideration of the historical development of Nengre family organization in the context of its environing field. It must be emphasized that this reconstruction is tentative and preliminary. There are enormous collections of relevant archival materials in Surinam and Holland that I have not had the opportunity to examine.[4]

THE CONTEMPORARY NENGRE FAMILY

Nengre families manifest variable conjugal, domestic, and residence patterns. This variability is closely associated with ranked status. As is the case in other Caribbean societies, the Nengre manifest and evaluate status in terms of what Wilson refers to as the respectability prestige system (1969:71). Respectability encapsulates societywide status-determining criteria which are based on metropolitan (i.e., Dutch) behavioral norms. In a familial context, respectability entails the maintenance of a neolocal, primary household based on a legally sanctioned monogamous marriage in which the husband-father provides support and the wife-mother engages in domestic and child-rearing activities.

Statements by informants indicate that the Nengre consider the respectable form of household as ideal and that most attempt to organize their own domestic and residential relationships accordingly. However, because of such factors as poverty, the necessity of supporting and caring for dependent consanguineals, conjugal dissolution, and early pregnancy, many Nengre households manifest one or more of the following Afro-American patterns: single female headship, nonlegal coresidential conjugal union, matrifocality in kinship, domestic, and residential relationships, and consanguineal extension. Several scholars have interpreted these patterns as a reflection of social disorganization or pathological deviation from Euro-American norms (Frazier, 1939; Glazer and Moynihan, 1963). However, evidence on Nengre social organization indicates that this population has a viable kinship system which is distinctive, and provides a charter for both respectable Euro-American and typical Afro-American households.

The Nengre currently consider three types of conjugal union to be socially significant: legal marriage, living-together unions, and outside unions. Legal marriage is formalized by religious and civil ceremonies and an elaborate wedding reception, and is considered to be maximally respectable. Living together, a nonlegal coresidential conjugal union, is not considered particularly prestigious, but it is regarded as completely legitimate. An outside relationship is a nonlegal union between a male who is a partner in a legal marriage or living-together union and an extraresidential female; such unions are not approved of despite their frequent occurrence.

Living together and outside unions do not entail binding legal rights or obligations, and they can be dissolved at will by either spouse. On the other hand, legal marriage involves rights and obligations that can only be terminated through divorce, which is prohibitively expensive. Because of the expense and permanence of legal marriage, Nengre couples generally establish living-together unions initially. They delay legal marriage until they are financially secure and have assured themselves that their relationship will endure.

Many adult Nengre of both sexes are conjugally unstable. Some of these are without mates, while others are in the process of establishing or dissolving living-together unions, in which case the partners are not coresident but refer to each other with reference terms for spouses.

Surinamese law requires a mother to register the names of her children with the civil government at birth. A father who is not legally married may grant legal recognition to his children by a living-together or casual mate if she grants him permission to do so. A child who receives paternal recognition inherits a patrinymic and is considered to be legitimate. If a man is legally married, paternal recognition of all children born to his wife during the marriage is automatic.[6] A man who is a partner in legal marriage or a living-together union never recognizes his children by outside mates. Paternal recognition is currently becoming more important than it was in the past, but even today the stigma that attaches to children who bear their mothers' surnames is minimal.

The potential for conflict between affinals is high. While the Nengre have reference terms for close affinals, they are not considered to be "family people" or true kinsmen. Relevant genealogical space is bilaterally structured and includes all third ascending and descending generation and closer lineals and all parents' parents' siblings' children's children (second cousins), and closer collaterals. The incest taboo is bilaterally extended to include second cousins and closer consanguineals. A Creolized reference terminology of English, Dutch, and Portuguese provenience embraces all known kinsmen within this domain.

The Nengre consider two types of consanguineal kinship groups to be significant. All living kinsmen within two ascending and descending generations and five degrees of genealogical distance are members of the "closeby family." The closeby family is an exogamous, kindred-type network, the members of which are tied to ego by reciprocal rights and obligations. Few, if any, Nengre know all of their relatives within the theoretical limits of the closeby family, and ties between fourth- and fifth-degree consanguineals are very weak, even when knowledge of the relationship exists. The "root" is a cognatic descent group of four generations which consists of all the descendants of a great grandparent. Roots are identified with the plantations or rural areas in which they originated, and are of religious significance in that they are the groups within which possessing spirits and ancestral ghosts are inherited and worshipped. Roots are frequently spoken of as if they were corporate, but at present, they do not have corporate functions.

The bilateral structure of Nengre kinship occurs because descent is simultaneously traced through agnatic and uterine linkages in the patrilateral and matrilateral segments of genealogical space. However, the relationship between a father and child is considered to be fundamentally different from that between a mother and child. This difference is reflected in the fact that different terms are used for the two types of relationships. The Nengre consider themselves to be related to their fathers through "blood" and to their mothers through the "belly" or the womb.

According to the Nengre folk theory of reproduction, a male deposits blood in the belly or womb of a female at conception. The blood is the essence from which the fetus is formed and the medium through which immutable physical and behavioral characteristics are transmitted. Food taboos are also inherited patrilineally because foods that are incompatible with a father's blood are thought to be incompatible with the blood of their children. After depositing his blood in the belly of the mother, the father's active involvement in prenatal development ceases.

The mother's womb is the receptacle within which the fetus develops. When impregnated, she assumes the task of providing a suitable environment within which the fetus develops. In addition to maintaining her own health through proper diet, cleanliness, and the like, she must avoid eating foods that are prohibited to the father of her child since they will produce skin irritations and ultimately leprosy if ingested in great quantity.

Paternal and maternal obligations to dependent children are analogous to male and female reproductive roles. Ideally, fathers provide support for their dependent children while mothers care for, nurture, and nourish them. Care, nurture, and nourishment provide the basis for more cohesive and intimate relationships than support. As a result, virtually all Nengre feel a closer relationship to their mothers than to their fathers, and ties betwen kinsmen related through belly or uterine linkages are stronger and more cohesive than those joining kinsmen through blood or agnatic linkages. Genealogical knowledge of matrilineal relatives is usually much more extensive than that of other segments of genealogical space. Kinship and domestic activities tend to occur within uterine networks, and if consanguineal household extension occurs, uterine relatives are much more likely to be incorproated than those joined to the household head by agnatic or mixed networks.

In the spring of 1969, a household composition survey was carried out on fifty-eight randomly selected Nengre households that were located in the residential district in which my dissertation field research was based. The results are summarized in Tables 1 and 2.

The composition of sample households varies considerably. Typical Afro-American patterns of household organization occur frequently.[7] Peripheral household members are joined to female core members most frequently, to both members of conjugal cores less frequently, and to male core members least frequently. Household extension involves consanguineals much more frequently than affinals. Consan-

TABLE 1

Core Structure and Basic Household Type Among the Nengre

	Type of Household			
Core Structure	*Nonextended*	*Primary*	*Extended*	*Total*
Single Male	3	0	3	6
Single Female	3	8	8	19
Living Together	3	9	5	17
Legal Marriage	2	5	9	16
				58

Core = single household head or household head and coresident spouse.
Nonextended household = housenold containing only core members.
Primary household = household containing a core and children.
Extended household = household containing a core and relatives other than or
        in addition to children.

TABLE 2

Patterns of Household Extension

Total number of household members	317
Total number of core members	91
Total number of peripherals	226

Affinal peripherals	4
Bilateral children of conjugal core	93
Primary or uterine consanguineals of female core member	110
Nonuterine consanguineals of female core member	9
Primary or uterine consanguineals of male core members	10
Nonuterine consanguineals of male core members	0

guineal extension occurs through uterine networks much more frequently than through nonuterine networks. These data indicate that
there is a close correlation between Nengre kinship and residence.

HISTORICAL PERSPECTIVE

The first successful attempt to settle Surinam was made by Lord
Willoughby of Parnham, who claimed it for England in 1650 and established a sugar colony there. The colony was taken over by a Dutch
fleet in 1666 during the second Anglo-Dutch war. From 1667 until
1975,[8] Surinam was a part of the Kingdom of the Netherlands, with
the exception of two brief periods during the Napoleonic wars, 1795-
1802 and 1804-1814, when England again established control. During
the early stages of Surinamese colonization, a plantocracy of diverse
provenience developed consisting of British, Dutch, French, Germans,
Northwest European Jews, and Sephardic Jews from Brazil. Van Lier
(1949:33-48) indicates that planters of differing national origins tended
to form separate subsocieties.

The Dutch conquest of Surinam was initiated by the Dutch West
India Company after it had lost control over the Pernambuco Region
of Brazil in 1650. From 1667 until 1794, the Dutch West India Company maintained a monopoly on the importation of slaves to the colony,
after which the slave trade was opened to traders from all Western
European countries. In 1808, when she had reconquered Surinam for
a brief period, England outlawed the importation of slaves from Africa
to her colonies in the New World. Holland reaffirmed the British
position when she again gained control of the colony in 1814, but the
clandestine importation of slaves continued for more than a decade
thereafter.

Several authors of early descriptions and travel accounts of Surinam
have discussed sources of provenience of the slave population. Van
Lier (1949:122-124) and Wooding (1972:17-50) have synthesized this
information. The provenience terms indicate that slaves were imported
to Surinam from the West African coast between Senegambia and
Angola. However, on the basis of clusterings of tribal provenience
designations, it appears that a majority of the West Africans who were
shipped to Surinam came from the region of the Ivory, Gold, and Slave
Coasts.[9] This hypothesis is supported both by the fact that, after 1650,

Dutch military and commercial activities were centered in El Mina on the Gold Coast, and by a consideration of the provenience of African-isms in Nengre supernaturalism.

The urban Nengre believe the soul consists of dual aspects: the *kra* and the *djodjo*. *Kra* is an Akan and Ewe term for soul, and *djo* is the Fon term for god. Two larger categories of *winti* or possessing spirits are *Kromanti* and *Papa*. *Kromanti* is an altered form of Coromantyn, the slave port on the Gold Coast, and *Papa* or *Pawpaw* was an impor-tant slave port on the Dahomean coast. The names of many particular *winti* come from the same general area: Vodu (Fon), Loko (Fon), Opete (Akan), and Leba (Fon) are some of these. The urban Nengre have a system of day names which is almost identical to the Ashanti system.[10] Anansi, the Akan spider trickster, is the major character in a genre of folk tales told by the Nengre at wakes. While numerous ex-plicit African elements have been retained in the Nengre magico-religious complex, it is important to note that these are combined into a total configuration that is Surinamese rather than African.

In spite of the retention of explicit Africanisms in Nengre super-naturalism, West African cultural patterns are not manifest in Nengre kinship and residential patterns. No Nengre kinship terms appear to be of African provenience. Genealogical space is bilaterally structured and the incest taboo is bilaterally extended. The frequent occurence of conjugal instability and a variety of mating forms can be more plausi-bly explained in terms of the Surinamese external environing field than as a survival of West African polygyny. It is tempting to inter-pret the differentiation of agnatic and uterine linkages in Nengre de-scent and the relative cohesiveness of relationships in uterine and sororal networks, as opposed to agnatic and fraternal networks, as being derived from the Ashanti descent system. As will be seen presently, however, this descent system can be explained as a consequence of customs and laws connected with the Surinamese system of slavery.

Most scholars who have interpreted the Afro-American family in terms of systems of slavery have minimized or completely discounted the importance of African cultural influence to its development. The fact that research has failed to yield explicit African cultural survivals in Nengre kinship and residence does not indicate that African cultural influence on this family system was negligible. Rather, it indicates that explicit manifestations of kinship and residence at a surface level are responsive to change in the Surinamese external environing field. Comparative analysis of Surinamese and various West African kinship systems at a deeper structural level would probably reveal a close relationship between them.[11]

Until the end of the eighteenth century, Surinamese society consisted primarily of masters and slaves. According to Stedman (1796:280), an estimated slave labor force of 50,000 at the height of the plantation period in Surinam declined at the rate of 5 percent per year so that it was necessary to import 2,500 Africans annually. The abolition of the slave trade in the early nineteenth century forced Surinamese planters to rely on reproduction within the Surinamese slave population to renew the labor force. The significant consequences of these changes were a noticeable improvement in the treatment of slaves during the nineteenth century and the simultaneous increase in the ratio of births to deaths within the slave population. Despite this improvement in the condition of slaves, this population was never able to maintain itself.

A major distinction within the slave population was drawn between "Saltwater Negroes" who were imported from Africa and Creole Negroes who were born in Surinam. During the seventeenth and eighteenth centuries, when a large proportion of the slave population consisted of Saltwater Negroes, tribal loyalties appear to have provided an important basis for the organization of interpersonal relationships among slaves. As the number of Saltwater Negroes decreased, tribal loyalties were supplanted by plantation affiliation as a determinant of social organization (Van Lier, 1949:162). The attachment of Creole Negro slaves to their plantations is reflected in the following statement by Teenstra (1848:42): "Negroes are extraordinarily attached to the place of their birth, the graves of their elders and their close relations. The yard on which they have played as children is holy to them so that they dislike leaving the plantation on which they were born."[12]

It should be noted that contemporary urban Nengre consider themselves to be mystically attached to the places where they were conceived and to the plantations where their cognatic descent groups or roots developed.

A second basic distinction within the slave population was between slaves owned by individuals, a majority of whom lived in Paramaribo, and slaves who were owned by the plantations to which they were attached. The proportional representation of the urban slaves to the total population of Paramaribo, and to the total slave population of

Surinam, varied. In 1791, 8,000 of a total Paramaribo population of 11,500 were slaves, and the total Surinamese slave population was 53,000. In 1830, there were 8,500 slaves in the total urban population of 15,265, and the total slave population of the colony was 48,784 (Van Lier, 1949:31, 151). While the proportional representation of slaves in the population of Paramaribo declined during this period, the percentage of urban slaves in the total slave population increased largely as a result of a decline in the colonial slave population. Freed slaves continued to move toward Paramaribo in increasing numbers following emancipation in 1863.

According to Van Hoevel (1854:138), individually owned urban slaves were much more fortunate than those who were bound to plantations, although their circumstances were also wretched. Some of these slaves worked as domestics in the households of their masters, but a large number were made to go out and seek jobs, or were rented out to others by their masters. Salaried and artisan slaves were required to bring their masters a specified amount of money each day. Some masters permitted these slaves to keep the remainder of their pay, but others took all that their slaves earned and gave them provisions, or more frequently, a set amount to be used for the purchase of provisions for themselves and their children. Van Hoevel (1854:76) estimates that the funds that slaves received for their provisioning generally varied between fifty and seventy cents per week. He states that this amount was completely inadequate, especially for women who had to support and care for themselves and their children. Many slave women were forced to work for their masters on Sunday, the only free day that was allowed them, or to turn to prostitution in order to acquire the funds necessary for minimal survival.

Working conditions for slaves varied on different types of plantations. Conditions on sugar plantations were generally the worst, especially during the relatively short seasons during which cane was harvested and sugar was refined. On coffee and cotton plantations, workloads were lighter. On wood plantations, which were situated further from the coast, conditions for slaves were most favorable because of light workloads and isolation and independence from masters who resided closer to the coast (Van Hoevel, 1854:144).

Most plantations had a few domestic and artisan slaves, but the great majority of plantation slaves worked in the fields for at least nine hours per day, six days a week. Instead of the money which many individually owned slaves received for their provisioning, plantation slaves were given minimal provisions which were supposed to be supplemented by their own spare time efforts at raising food on small plots provided by the plantations. Generally, slaves on plantations with resident owners received better treatment than slaves on plantations run by administrators because the administrators were more interested in the quick maximization of profits than in the maintenance of the capital that the plantation's slave force represented.

The Surinamese slave system was based in part on Roman law, in part on custom, and in part on colonial proclamations and statutes. Adequate provisions for enforcing the proclamations and statutes pertaining to slavery were never made, however. It was only in 1851, when it was certain that Holland would emancipate the slaves in the near future, that anything resembling a comprehensive slave code was developed.

During the seventeenth and eighteenth centuries, most of the measures that were passed appear to have been designed to maximize the difference in status between free and slave, and to keep the slaves under control. Sexual relationships between white females and slave males were forbidden and were punishable by the death of the latter. Slaves who met whites on the street were required to stand aside and make way for them. Whites and slaves were prohibited from keeping company or gambling with one another. Slaves were forbidden to carry weapons. Slaves darker than mulattoes were not allowed to wear shoes, stockings, or jewelry. Each slave was to be branded with the mark of his master. Slaves could not go onto the street at night without a letter of permission from their masters, and they were required to carry lighted lanterns to announce their presence. Throughout the period of slavery, religious dances of all types were forbidden, as was the gathering of large crowds of slaves at funerals (Van Lier, 1949:141-142).

The growth of abolitionist sentiment in the Netherlands and the emancipation of slaves in the British colonies in 1834 and the French colonies in 1848 caused a reevaluation of the Surinamese slave system. At the insistence of the Dutch metropolitan government, the colonial government of Surinam passed a comprehensive slave code in 1851. The code defined rights and obligations between masters and slaves, minimal requirements for the care and provisioning of slaves, maximal workloads for slaves, maximal punishments that could be exercised against slaves, and penalties for the infringement of these rules. The

Surinamese planters accepted this code with a surprising degree of willingness because it was seen as a means of postponing the inevitable emancipation of slaves and because it was not at all stringent.

The slave code of 1851 made inadequate provisions for the welfare of slaves. Van Hoevel maintains that the stipulated workloads for field slaves were almost twice as onerous as maximal workloads for manual laborers in the Netherlands (1854:213), and that the minimal food allowance for adult slaves according to the law contained a tenth of the protein consumed by an ordinary Dutch soldier (1854:183). The maximal punishments that could be given slaves were extremely severe, and the penalties for slaveowners who exceeded these limits were very light. The major inadequacy of the slave code was that the governor, who was given the responsibility for enforcing its provisions, was not given the means for doing so.

Throughout the period of slavery, Surinamese slaves could secure their freedom through manumission. Manumission occurred in one of three possible contexts. It occurred most often when European males purchased the freedom of their common-law slave wives and children. In other cases, manumission was granted by masters as a reward for faithful service by domestic slaves. During most of the period of slavery, it was possible for slaves to purchase their own freedom, but relatively few of them were able to do so (Van Lier, 1949:100).

In spite of various governmental attempts to control manumission through the imposition of manumission taxes, requirements that manumission requests receive governmental approval, and the outlawing of self-purchase between 1832 and 1851, the free Creole population grew steadily. In 1738, there were an estimated 598 free Creoles in Surinam. By 1812, this population had grown to 3,075 and was larger than the European population. By 1830, there were 5,041 free Creoles in Surinam as compared with a European population of 2,500 (Van Lier, 1949:97-98; Teenstra, 1842:5-9). Almost all of the free Creoles resided in Paramaribo.

The free Creole population was differentiated on the basis of phenotype and legal position into four status categories: freeborn colored, manumitted colored, freeborn Negro, and manumitted Negro. As was the case in other colonial slave societies in the New World with significant populations of free Creoles, Caucasoid phenotype and free birth were accorded more prestige than Negroid phenotype and freedom through manumission. The colonial government issued procla-

mations which placed restrictions on free Negroes but not on freeborn
or manumitted coloreds, and free Creoles who had been manumitted
were subject to restrictions that did not apply to those who were freeborn. It is not possible to determine whether phenotype or legal status
was the more important status-determining criterion, but it can be
assumed that phenotype was of more immediate relevance in ascribing
status because of its visibility as compared with the relative difficulty of
determining legal status.

As of 1830, the free Creole population consisted of 3,974 individuals
categorized as colored and 1,094 classified as Negroes (Van Lier,
1949:98). No data are available on the relative sizes of the manumitted
and freeborn segments of the free Creole population. However, it is
probable that the rate of manumission was always much lower than
the birth rate within the free Creole population. As a result, Creoles
born into freedom almost certainly outnumbered those who were
manumitted throughout the period of slavery.

Within the free Creole population, there was a colored elite that
mixed relatively easily with Europeans, and a "middle class" consisting of Jewish, colored and a small number of Negro clerks, bureaucrats, and shopkeepers. Lower status free Creoles, most of whom were
manumitted Negroes, formed a proletariat consisting of manual laborers
and gardeners who sold produce raised on provision grounds close to
the city (Van Lier, 1949:114-116).

New World slave systems have been compared in terms of economic
factors (Williams, 1944) and the distinction between Iberian and Northwest European cultural heritage (Tannenbaum, 1947). Hoetink (1967,
1969) has effectively demonstrated that these approaches should be
combined. In a comparison of the slavery and race systems of Curaçào
and Surinam, he suggests that, although both of these areas were subject to cultural influence from the same colonizing power—i.e., Holland—ecological, demographic, and geographic differences in the two
areas caused significant differences in severity of treatment of slaves,
frequency of manumission, relative size of free and slave populations,
and the like. While the comparison suggests that Surinam's slave system
conformed more closely to the Northwest European model than Curaçào's, it is necessary to recognize that the slave society of Surinam was
similar in certain respects to those based on Iberian cultural influence.

A substantial racially mixed free Creole population developed early
in Surinam and was maintained until emancipation through extensive

sexual relationships between European males and slave females and frequent manumission. High-status free Creoles interacted freely with Europeans and occupied important political positions because of the transitory nature of European society (Hoetink, 1969:183). It is important to remember that the size, importance, and relatively great social mobility of the free Creole population were attributable to ecological and demographic factors rather than to Latin influence via Iberian colonizing powers.

The civil and legal aspects of the Surinamese slave system were clearly of Northwest European provenience. During most of the period of slavery, the colony lacked a comprehensive slave code. Governmental control of the treatment of slaves by masters was minimal, and governmental decrees and proclamations pertaining to slavery were aimed at maintaining repressive control over the slave force. Slaves were legally defined as property rather than as persons. Unlike the Spanish and Portuguese colonies where the Roman Catholic church and the crown were protectors of slaves, Christian denominations had little, if any, influence on the Netherlands' colonial policy. Moreover, Dutch royalty did not become concerned with the welfare of slaves until abolitionist sentiment became very strong in the nineteenth century. While the baptism of slaves was mandatory in the Iberian colonies, the government did not encourage missionary work among the Surinamese slaves by Moravians and Roman Catholics until emancipation was recognized as inevitable.

Little information is available on the mating patterns of Surinamese slaves. Because they were not legally recognized as human beings, slaves could not enter into legally recognized marriages, and consorts could be sold separately if their master desired (Van Hoevel, 1854:52). Blom reports that conjugal unions between plantation slaves were not ceremonially sanctioned, and he implies that both male and female slaves frequently had continuing sexual relationships with several mates at the same time (1787:393). It can be assumed that mating patterns among urban slaves were similar to those of plantation slaves in most respects. However, the proportion of Europeans and free Creoles to slaves was greater in Paramaribo than in rural areas, with the result that slave females mated and formed conjugal unions with free males much more frequently in the city than on the plantations.

Most Europeans who went to Surinam were single, or they left their wives at home. Usually, they bought or rented female slaves or established nonlegal conjugal unions with free Creole women whom they took as housekeepers and sexual consorts. While these unions were not legally recognized, many of them were extremely durable and stable.

Teenstra (1842:48) describes mating among free Creoles as follows: "Most Creoles live unmarried, having in addition to a housekeeper, two or three concubines outside of the house, for the colored women are nowhere less proper in their behavior to men than in Surinam although they are very faithful in the absence of legal marriage.[13] He also states that because some free Creoles considered marriage as too final and permanent, they prevented their daughters from marrying legally until they had lived together with their prospective husbands and were sure that their unions would endure.

While this information is not extensive, it suggests that important features of the system of mating among contemporary urban Nengre were already present during the period of slavery. Among the slaves and free Creoles, conjugal relationships appear to have been unstable. The data presented indicate that members of both of these populations formed conjugal unions that were comparable to the living-together and outside relationships that are entered by the Nengre today. Religiously but not legally sanctioned unions became possible for slaves in the nineteenth century. Legal marriage, while comparatively rare among free Creoles, was theoretically possible and was engaged in by members of the elite segment of this population.

Surinamese slaves were not regarded as having any relatives other than a mother, and the status of the mother determined the status of her children. In speaking of the children of European fathers and slave mothers, Stedman (1796:88) makes the following comment: "In Surinam, all such children go with their mothers: that is, if she is in slavery, her offspring are her master's property should their father be a prince, unless he obtains them by purchase."

In the same vein, Teenstra (1842:23) says that white directors were generally discouraged from creating stable unions with female slaves belonging to the plantations on which they were employed since this caused a loss of authority and could tempt them to purchase their consorts and children from the establishment.

It was customary in Surinam not to sell slave children and their mothers separately, although it sometimes occurred if a plantation was to be liquidated or if the owner was returning to Europe (Teenstra, 1848:102; Van Lier, 1949:157). Proclamations forbidding the separate selling of mothers and children were issued in 1782, 1821, and 1850. The last of these proclamations stated:

> Slaves, during the life of their mother and as long as they belong to the slave class, may never be separated from her through purchase, barter, giving or in any other manner be placed in the ownership of a third party in such a way that they will not be reunited with their mother.—Children can never be separated from their mother, or the mother from her children. (Van Hoevel, 1854:52)[14]

This proclamation did not apply if a mother or her children were manumitted, since, legally, a slave and a free person could not be related. In addition, if a mother were convicted of a crime, her children could be sold away from her as punishment. In spite of these exceptions which could provide legal justification for the separate selling of slave mothers and children, it is probable that the customs and proclamations forbidding it were generally adhered to.

The inviolability of the bond between a slave mother and her children was the only feature of the family organization of slaves that was legally validated by the Surinamese slave system. As a result of this feature, households and kinship groups had a matrifocal or matricentric character that was externally imposed. Given the high degree of conjugal instability that characterized the slave population, it is logical to assume that male consorts would be peripheral or absent in many Surinamese slave families.

The Proclamation of 1850 specified that the slave mother and her children should remain together for as long as she lived. Following her death, it is probable that her children would continue to reside on her plantation in some cases. Intergenerational extension of matrifocal ties would produce descent groups consisting of a core of uterine relatives with children of male members who selected mates from their own plantations. While they are not localized or corporate, urban Nengre roots are structurally equivalent to these descent groups which can be hypothesized to have existed among slaves on plantations.

In retrospect, many important features of urban Nengre family organization appear to have been present, or at least were foreshadowed, during the period of slavery in Surinam. These include: a high degree of conjugal instability and the possibility of legal marriage for free Creoles; emphasis on the closeness of uterine and sororal as opposed to agnatic and fraternal linkages; and the probable existence of matrifocal households and cognatic descent groups with a supernatural attachment to their place of origin.

Three population segments of the Surinamese slave society are relevant to this analysis: lower status free Creoles, individually owned slaves from the urban area, and plantation slaves. Demographic, ecological, and status differences between these segments undoubtedly caused differences in modes of family organization, but the historical data are not sufficiently detailed to enable systematic comparison. Distinctive characteristics of kinship and residence of all three of these population segments were probably combined as emancipated plantation slaves migrated to Paramaribo and mingled with emancipated urban slaves and lower status free Creoles to form an urban proletariat.

During the period of slavery, Dutch colonial policy was directed toward the maximization of profits from plantation agriculture and the maintenance of as great a difference as possible between the slave and free statuses. As plantation agriculture became less profitable and abolitionist sentiment in Europe increased, Holland's colonial policy in Surinam underwent significant change. Following emancipation in 1863, a colonial program of "Assimilation Politics" was adopted. The aim of the new program was to make Surinam an overseas replica of Holland and to impart Dutch culture to the Surinamese Creole population. Behavior patterns such as conjugal instability and nonlegal conjugal unions, speaking Surinamese Creole, and going without shoes and stockings were now discouraged. The Dutch language, Christianity, formal education, and European manners and morals became highly valued and, at least theoretically, were accessible for the first time to a large majority of the Surinamese population.

The program of Assimilation Politics was naïve in its basic assumptions and impossible to execute without the expenditure of tremendous resources. It was abandoned before it had a chance to work because it was realized that Hindustani and Javanese indentured laborers, who were imported to Surinam following emancipation, were unwilling to abandon their own cultures. The result of Assimilation Politics was to establish the Dutch behavior patterns that it sought to inculcate as highly valued respectable forms of behavior for Creoles, and later, for upwardly mobile members of other ethnic groups.

Prior to emancipation, Surinamese planters feared that, when given their freedom, slaves would abandon the plantations to which they had been attached because of laziness and an aversion to their former owners. During the late nineteenth and early twentieth centuries, a majority of the previous plantation slave population did, in fact, migrate to Paramaribo. However, the evidence suggests that the urban migration of Creoles was not a result of the causes advanced by the planters. Rather, it was a result of the continuing decline in Surinamese plantation agriculture that had begun at the turn of the previous century, and of the replacing of the slave labor force by the importation of approximately 72,000 indentured laborers between 1853 and 1939.[15] While it is probably true that many slaves disliked plantation agriculture and were attracted to the city, the economic situation in Surinam following emancipation was such that most ex-plantation slaves were forced to become urbanized regardless of their wishes.

After emancipation, previous city slaves were joined by those who were moving in from the plantations to form a rapidly growing urban proletariat which was the nucleus of the contemporary Nengre population. The number of uneducated and unskilled Creoles seeking work was much greater than the number of nonagricultural jobs available. The urban unemployment problem became more acute when, following the expiration of their contracts of indenture, Chinese, Hindustani, and Javanese indentured laborers began moving to the city and into nonagricultural pursuits.

The slave forebears of the contemporary Nengre population were economically powerless in that they had no control of the profits produced by their labor. While emancipation gave them this control, it did not assure them a secure economic position. For most of the period that has elapsed since emancipation, the Nengre have been economically marginal because of low wages and limited occupational opportunities. Emancipation did produce a very significant change in the legal status of ex-slaves and provided them with a limited number of opportunities for upward mobility. Yet, it did not appreciably alter the external environing field so as to produce sudden dramatic alterations in Nengre kinship and residential patterns.

Since emancipation, Surinam has been faced with a problem of chronic unemployment. From time to time, increased economic activity and foreign aid have provided temporary relief. Between the 1870s and 1930s, gold mining and the harvesting of wild rubber were important nonagricultural industries. During the 1920s, bauxite mining became a major industry, and its importance has increased continually since then. Several long-term construction projects such as the Zanderij Air Field, which was built by the U.S. Army during World War II, and the Afobakka hydroelectric dam, which was built after the war, have provided large numbers of jobs for skilled and unskilled laborers. In addition to these indigenous sources of employment, the petroleum refining industry of Curaçào, and the postwar reconstruction and industrial boom that followed it in Holland, opened up many jobs for the Surinamese.

Most of the occupational opportunities mentioned above are for males and involve spending considerable periods of time in the interior of Surinam or in other countries. The urban Nengre have taken these jobs more frequently than members of other ethnic groups. As is the case in other Afro-American populations, male absenteeism has been an important factor in perpetuating matrifocal patterns of kinship and residence within the Nengre population.

While matrifocality and other traditional Afro-American patterns of mating, domesticity, and residence are manifestations of continuity in the historical development of the Nengre family system, the system has undergone significant change since the period of slavery, and particularly since the 1930s. As will be recalled, the Nengre have adopted selected Dutch social patterns as canons of respectability during the postemancipation period. In a familial context, respectability requires the maintenance of a neolocal primary household based on legal marriage in which the husband-father provides support and the wife-mother engages in domestic and child-rearing activities. With the rapid development of educational and occupational opportunities in Surinam since the 1930s, increasing numbers of Nengre have been able to conform to standards of respectability in family organization. The contemporary Nengre kinship system, described in the first part of this essay, is sufficiently flexible to provide institutional validation for a wide variety of domestic and residential arrangements ranging between traditional Afro-American and respectable Euro-American polar extremes.

CONCLUSIONS

The historical development of the Nengre family system has been conceived of in terms of adaptation to a complex, changing environing field. The foregoing analysis suggests that factors affecting the organization of Nengre families can be subsumed within three general categories: (1) African cultural survivals of a general nature which have subsequently operated to selectively filter adaptive responses at a deep structural level; (2) Euro-American acculturation in general and Dutch cultural influence in particular which have become increasingly significant in the postemancipation period; and (3) historical events, phenomena, and ecological and demographic factors that are unique to Surinam. Cultural influences from China, India, Indonesia, and the parent nations of smaller Surinamese ethnic segments appear to have had negligible effects on Nengre family organization. In this regard it can be noted that African slaves and European masters coexisted in Surinam for two hundred years before the importation of indentured laborers, and that the boundaries between ethnic segments are very impermeable.

Because past conditions and responses to them have limited the possible variety of responses to subsequent changes in the external environing field, a consideration of historical factors is essential to an adequate analysis of Afro-American family organization. However, as this study has demonstrated, simplistic historical explanations are inadequate. All factors cited as causes in the literature on the Afro-American family are relevant in the Nengre case. No single historical source or condition or contemporary ecological or demographic factor can be expected to provide an adequate explanation of the urban Nengre or any other Afro-American system of family organization.

NOTES

1. The information on which this essay is based was gathered during two field trips to Paramaribo, Surinam. The first of these (October 1967-May 1969) was devoted to the gathering of data on contemporary urban Nengre family organization, and provided the basis for my dissertation on the articulation of kinship and residence among the urban Nengre. The second (Summer 1971) was devoted to the gathering of primary data on urban Nengre supernaturalism and library research on the history of Surinam. The first field trip was financed by NIMH Fellowship 1F1-MH-35, 792-01 and Grant Attachment MH 13, 771-01. The second was financed by grants from the National Geographic Society and the Committee on Faculty Research Support of the Florida State University, Tallahassee, Florida. I am grateful to these agencies for making the research possible.

2. In Surinam, the term *Creole* is utilized to designate an ethnic segment that is defined in terms of European and/or African descent, and participation in the national social and cultural system of the coastal area. Approximately 70 percent of the Creole population resides in and around Paramaribo, the capital and only true urban center of the country, and a substantial majority of this population is lower status, economically marginal, and Afro-Caribbean in cultural orientation. Lower status Creoles are referred to as Nengre both by themselves and by others.

3. During the 1930s and early 1940s, explanations of the Afro-American family stressed historical factors such as the survival of West African cultural patterns (Herskovits, 1941) and disorganizing effects of slavery systems (Frazier, 1939). Later, contemporary ecological and demographic patterns provided bases for explaining salient features of Afro-American family organization. These explanations are based on factors such as: systems of land tenure (Cohen, 1954; Clarke, 1953), a division of labor that causes prolonged separation of the sexes or migratory wage labor (Gonzales, 1969; Kunstadter, 1963; Otterbein, 1965), and economic marginality (Clarke, 1957; Smith, R. T. (1965). M. G. Smith (1966) compares the family systems of five Caribbean communities in terms of differences in the structuring of relationships of conjugality and parenthood. Valentine (1968) critically evaluates analytical schemas which emphasize the disorganization of Afro-American families and those which focus on poverty as a cultural determinant of family organization.

4. Since this essay was submitted for publication, two important analyses of Surinamese Creole family organization have appeared. William F. L. Buschkens (1974) has amassed an extensive body of ethnohistoric data on the family organization of Paramaribo Creoles in a much more ambitious analysis than is represented here. My criticisms of Buschkens' work stem from his definition of family organization which is based primarily on residence, secondarily on domesticity, and peripherally, if at all, on kinship. This definition results in what I consider to be a superficial analysis of contemporary Creole family organization, and in an overemphasis on patterns of continuity in Creole family organization as manifest in such patterns as instability of conjugality, consanguineal household extension, and matrifocality. I am unwilling to conclude, as Buschkens seems to, that the family system of Paramaribo Creoles has not changed significantly since the early stages of the period of slavery.

I would agree with Bushkens that there have been numerous important continuities in the historical development of the Creole or Nengre family system. I think, however, that it is also necessary to recognize that historical events and phenomena such as the decline of the plantation system, emancipation, the migration of many lower status Creoles to Paramaribo, Dutch colonial policies such as Assimilation Politics, and the decreasing isolation of Surinam from U.S. and Western European acculturative influences have had significant effects on Creole residential, domestic, and kinship patterns.

Brana-Shute (1974) has studied the organization of familial and extrafamilial relationships of lower status Creole males in Paramaribo. His concept of family organization is similar to that of Buschkens, but Creole family organization is not the primary focus of his analysis. Brana-Shute's research deals with the important problem of the articulation of males within an Afro-American society. With regard to this focus, his analysis is detailed, thorough, and sophisticated.

5. When missionary work was begun among Surinamese slaves by Moravians and Roman Catholics in the latter part of the eighteenth century, missionaries encouraged

converts to become partners in religiously sanctioned marriages. These marriages were not recognized by the colonial government since slaves were not permitted to enter into legal contracts. Older informants stated that religious marriages persisted until as late as the 1950s.

6. The legally married husband of a female is the father of her children by different males. In the field, I encountered a case in which a legal wife deserted her husband for another man who was older and richer. During the ten years that she lived with the latter, she bore him four children. Since divorce had not occurred, the children had the surname of their mother's husband, rather than their own father, and the husband was theoretically the children's legal guardian.

7. For concise summaries of the literature on recurrent patterns of Afro-American household organization, see Kunstadter (1963) and Otterbein (1965).

8. From 1667 until 1954, with the exception of two brief periods of British control, Surinam was a colony in the Kingdom of the Netherlands. From 1954 until 1975, it was an internally autonomous commonwealth partner in the Kingdom of the Netherlands. On November 25, 1975, Surinam became a completely independent country.

9. Wooding deals extensively with the tribal provenience of Surinamese slaves. His data are summarized in the following table (adapted from Wooding, 1972:36).

Tribes from Which People Were Imported to Surinam

Sengambia Sierra Leone Liberia	Ivory Coast Ghana (Gold Coast)	Togo Dahomey (Slave Coast)	Nigeria	Cameroon Congo Angola
Foela	(Tebou)	Abo	Nago	Abo
Foeloeppoe	(La Hoe)	Ayois	Ibo	Congo
Conia	Aqueras	(Ardra)		Loango
Sokko	Alquirasche	Fida		Goango
Riemba	Akim	Foin		Pombo
Temne's	Annamaboe	Jaquin		Demakoekoe
Mendees	Asiantijn	Mallais		(Angola)
Pre-Negers	(Accra)	Papa		Guiamba
Gola	Coromantijn	Dahomansche		
(Sierra Leone)*	Delmina			
(Goree)	Fantijn			
(Cabo Monte)	Gango			
Konare	Tjamba			
	N. Zokko			
	Sokko's			
Sokko's	Wanway			

* Names in parentheses are place names, not tribal names.

10.   **Comparison of Day Names in Surinam and Ashanti**

	Surinam		Ashanti (Source: Smith, RT, 1965:131)	
	Male	*Female*	*Male*	*Female*
Sun.	Kwasi	Kwasiba	Kwasi	Akwasibu
Mon.	Kodjo	Adjuba	Kwaduo	A'duowa
Tues.	Kwamina	Abeni	Kwabena	Abenaa
Wed.	Kwaku	Akuba	Kwaku	Akuwa
Thurs.	Yaw	Yaba	Yaw	Yaa/Yawa
Fri.	Kofi	Afi, Afiba	Kofi	Afuwa
Sat.	Kwami	Amba	Kwame	Amma

11. The concepts of surface and deep structure have been developed by the Transformational Grammar School of Linguistics. In the present context, it is sufficient to define surface structure as being manifest at the level of empirical reality, and deep structure as underlying and accounting for the appearance of the empirical manifestation. This distinction is relevant in social anthropology because it clarifies the differences between structural-functionalists such as Malinowsky and Radcliffe-Brown and structuralists such as Levi-Strauss with regard to the definition of structure. Structural-functionalists have been concerned with surface structure of sociocultural phenomena, while structuralists are primarily concerned with deep structure. For an excellent demonstration of such deep structure similarities, see Wilber (1975).

12. Author's translation.

13. Author's translation.

14. Author's translation.

15. Between 1853 and 1872, 5,400 indentured laborers were brought to Surinam through individual initiative. These included 500 Maderian Portuguese, 2,500 Chinese, and 2,400 British West Indians. In 1872, the Dutch government took control of the importation of indentured laborers to Surinam. Between 1873 and 1916, approximately 34,000 Hindustani indentured laborers were brought in from India, and between 1891 and 1939, approximately 33,000 Javanese indentured laborers were imported from Indonesia (Malefijt, 1963:21-22).

REFERENCES CITED

Bascom, W. R. 1941. "Acculturation Among the Gullah Negroes." *American Anthropologist* 43:43-50.

Blom, A. 1787. *Verhandeling van den Landbouw in de Kolonie Suriname.* Amsterdam: J. W. Smit.

Brana-Shute, Gary. 1974. Streetcorner Winkels and Dispersed Households: Male Adaptation to Marginality in a Lower Status Creole Neighborhood in Paramaribo. Ph.D. Dissertation, Gainesville: University of Florida.

Buckley, W. 1968. "Society as a Complex Adaptive System," in W. Buckley, ed., *Modern Systems Research for the Behavioral Scientist.* Chicago: Aldine, pp. 490-513.

Buschkens, Willem F. L. 1974. *The Family System of the Paramaribo Creoles.* The Hague: Martinus Nijhoff.

Clarke, E. 1957. *My Mother Who Fathered Me: A Study of the Family in Three Selected Communities in Jamaica.* London: George Allen Unwin.

Cohen, Y. A. 1954. "The Social Organization of a Selected Community in Jamaica." *Social and Economics Studies* 2:104-134.

Frazier, E. F. 1939. *The Negro Family in the United States.* Chicago: University of Chicago Press.

Glazer, N., and Moynihan, D.P. 1966. *Beyond the Melting Pot: The Negroes, Puerto Ricans, Jews, Italians and Irish of New York City.* Cambridge: M.I.T. Press and Harvard University Press.

Gonzales, N.L. 1969. *Migration and Modernization: Adaptive Reorganization in the Black Carib Household.* Seattle: University of Washington Press.

Herskovits, M.J. 1941. *Myth of the Negro Past.* New York: Harper.

Hoetink, H. 1967. *Caribbean Race Relations: A Study of Two Variants.* London: Oxford University Press.

Hoetink, H. 1969. "Race Relations in Curaçao and Surinam," in L. Foner and D. Genovese, ed., *Slavery in the New World: A Reader in Comparative History.* Englewood Cliffs, N.J.: Prentice-Hall, pp. 178-188.

Kunstadter, P. 1963. "A Survey of the Consanguine or Matrifocal Family." *American Anthropologist* 65:56-66.

Malefijt, A. de Waal. 1963. *The Javanese of Surinam: Segment of a Plural Society.* Assen: Van Gorcum and Company.

Otterbein, K. F. 1965. "Caribbean Family Organization: A Comparative Analysis." *American Anthropologist* 67:66-79.

Pierce, B. E. 1971. Kinship and Residence Among the Urban Nengre of Surinam: A Re-evaluation of Concepts and Theories of the Afro-American Family. Ph.D. Dissertation, New Orleans: Tulane University.

Smith, M. G. 1966. *West Indian Family Structure.* Seattle: University of Washington Press.

Smith, R. T. 1965. *The Negro Family in British Guiana: Family Structure and Social Status in the Villages.* New York: Humanities Press.

Stedman, J. G. 1796. *Narrative of a Five Year Expedition Against the Revolted Negroes of Surinam.* London: J. J. Johnson and J. Edwards.

Teenstra, M. D. 1842. *De Negerslaven in de Kolonie Suriname en de uitbreiding van het Christendom onder de heidensche bevolking.* Dordrecht: H. Lagerweij.

Valentine, C. A. 1968. *Culture and Poverty: Critique and Counter-proposals.* Chicago: University of Chicago Press.

Van Hoevel, W.R. 1854. *Slaven en vrijen onder de Nederlandsche wet.* Zaltbommel: John Norman and Son.

Van Lier, R.A.J. 1949. *Samenleving in een grensgebeid.* The Hague: Matrinus Nijhoff.

Wilbert, Johannes. 1975. Kinsmen of Flesh and Blood: Is the Goajiro Kinship System Indigenous or African? Paper presented in a symposium on Ethnohistory of Afro-Americans in Latin America, 74th Annual Meeting of the American Anthropological Association in San Francisco, December 5, 1975.

Wooding, C. J. 1972. *Winti: een Afroamerikaanse Godsdienst in Suriname: een cultureel-historische analyse van de religieuze verschijnselen in de Para.* Meppel, Holland: Krips Repro b.v.

Michael D. Olien

5

THE ADAPTATION OF WEST INDIAN BLACKS TO NORTH AMERICAN AND HISPANIC CULTURE IN COSTA RICA

Both North American and Costa Rican social scientists have characterized the Central American Republic of Costa Rica as a basically "white" population in contrast to the other Central American Republics in which the Amerind component remains strong. The 1950 census (Dirección General de Estadística y Censos, 1953:34) supports this contrast. The population consisted of 97.65 percent whites (blancos) and *mestizos* (persons of Indian-white admixture), 1.89 percent blacks *(negros),* 0.33 percent Amerinds *(indígenas),* and 0.12 percent Orientals *(amarillos*—primarily Chinese.)[1] It is unlikely that these percentages have changed markedly in the years since this census. Yet, the Costa Rican population is not distributed equally, either geographically or racially. The republic is divided into seven provinces (see Map 1) for administrative purposes. Of these provinces, Limón encompasses the entire eastern coastline from Nicaragua to Panama, as well as most of the eastern lowland hinterland. While the majority of the inhabitants of Limón are white and mestizo, the percentage of whites and mestizos in relation to the rest of the population in Limón is considerably less than in any other province. In 1950, the whites formed 62.69 percent of the Limón population, while the white and mestizo populations of all other Costa Rican provinces ranged from 99.12 percent to 99.89 percent. At the same time, Limón had by far the largest percentage of blacks (33.24 percent in contrast to the other provinces which ranged from 0.03 to 0.25 percent) as well as the largest actual number of blacks

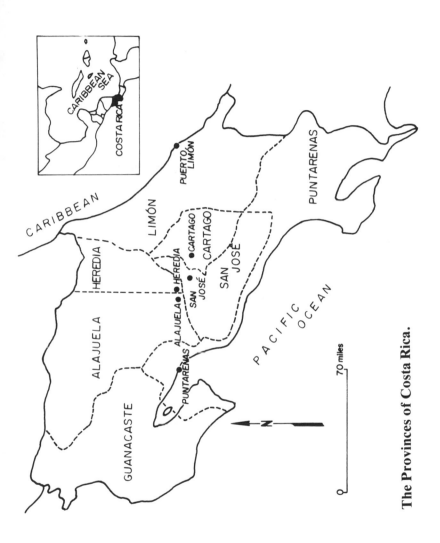

The Provinces of Costa Rica.

(13,749 out of 15,118) in the republic (Dirección General de Estadística y Censos, 1953:34). Costa Rica has an average population density of twenty-three inhabitants per square kilometer. However, because the bulk of this population is clustered in the highlands, Limón Province has a density of only six inhabitants per square kilometer (Ávila, 1964:68, 74).

Costa Rica can be divided topographically into three major areas: the Pacific lowlands of western Costa Rica, the highlands of central Costa Rica, and the Caribbean lowlands of eastern Costa Rica. The Caribbean lowlands are separated from the highlands by a range of volcanoes. Throughout the nation's colonial and early republican history, these lowlands were effectively isolated from the rest of the country due to lack of roads. Until very recently, the only connecting links between Puerto Limón, the capital of Limón Province, and San José, the capital of the country, located in the highlands, have been two daily trains and two daily airplane flights.[2] The only link with either Puerto Limón or the highlands for most rural inhabitants of the Limón hinterland has been by way of the railway. In the many areas not serviced by the railway, travel is carried out on horseback, on foot, by canoe or launch, or via the old "colonial railway" *(burro-carril)*, which consists of mule-drawn carts pulled over narrow-gauge tracks.

Within the lowlands there is considerable racial and cultural diversity. Siquirres marks a racial dividing line along the San José-Puerto Limón railway (see Map 2). West of Siquirres, on the fringe of the highlands, communities with brightly painted wooden, tile-roofed houses are laid out either in a traditional Spanish grid pattern, surrounding a plaza, or surrounding a coffee *beneficio* (processing plant). In this section of Limón Province, the population is predominantly Spanish-speaking and white. East of Siquirres, in the lowlands, the communities are settlements made up of unpainted, corrugated iron-roofed, wooden houses built on stilts, laid out parallel to the rail tracks and are often former United Fruit Company towns. The population is predominantly black. Here Spanish cathedrals give way to small Protestant churches (see Photos 1 and 2).

In the region east of Siquirres, the proportion of blacks decreases the further north one travels from Puerto Limón to Guápiles, an area encompassing Limón's northern rail spur known as the Old Line (Línea Vieja). In the far north, along the Nicaraguan border, are a few scat-

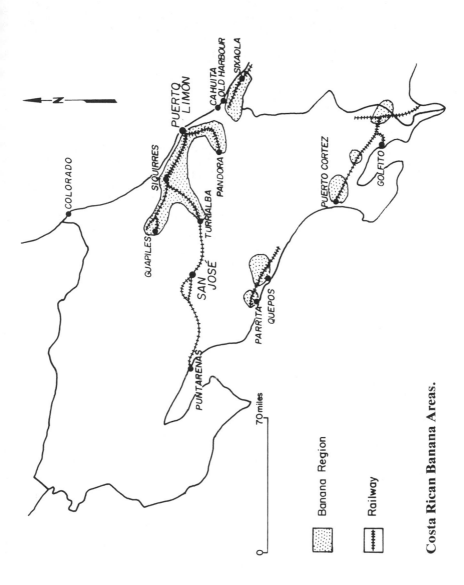

Costa Rican Banana Areas.

Photo 1. Typical Dwelling Unit Along Railway from San José to Puerto Limón.

Photo 2. Contrast of Old and New Style Dwelling Units Along Railway from San José to Puerto Limón.

tered communities that can be reached only by water. The largest community in this area, Colorado, has been populated primarily by migrants from Nicaragua who are a white-Amerind-black admixture. Communities along the southern spur of the railway from Puerto Limón south and west to Pandora have been settled almost exclusively by blacks, as have been the small ports extending south from Puerto Limón to the Panama border. The mountainous interior south of Puerto Limón is populated by remnants of Costa Rica's small indigenous population.

The Chinese constitute a numerically small (approximately 2 percent of the province's population) but economically important segment of the lowlands (see Photo 3). While the Chinese are centered in Puerto Limón where they own many of the restaurants, *pulperías* (grocery stores), *cantinas* (bars), movie theaters, and hotels, there is at least one Chinese family in most small communities of the province. The community's commerce is usually dominated by these local Chinese entrepreneurs. In most towns they own the local *pulpería-cantina,* which also functions as the local movie theater, pool hall, restaurant, hotel, and dance hall. The Chinese also serve as middlemen through whom the imports and exports of the community are channeled.

Photo 3. Contrast of Chinese-owned Bar-Department Store Complex with Black Housing in Puerto Limón.

Limón Province has been settled by four ethnic groups, one of which, the black West Indian population, will serve as the focus of this essay. The reasons why this particular province has such a sizable black population and the relationship of this population to other populations of Costa Rica through time are of special concern here.

THE SETTLEMENT OF THE EASTERN LOWLANDS

The eastern lowlands were neither heavily populated by Spanish settlement during the colonial period, which lasted from the early sixteenth to the early nineteenth century, nor by Costa Rican settlement following independence in 1821. During the colonial period, the Matina Valley was a center for the production of cacao (a pre-Columbian crop) for export. However, most of the small cacao plantations were operated by absentee white landlords who remained in the highlands. A small force of African slaves, probably numbering no more than 200 (Thiel, 1902), and a somewhat larger mulatto population performed most of the work tasks.[3] White settlement in the lowlands was deterred by the availability of land in the highlands, the hostile lowland climate, and the inability of the Spaniards to establish de facto political control over the lowlands.

Throughout the colonial and early republican periods, de facto political control over the eastern lowlands shifted back and forth between the Spanish and the English who were attempting to establish a foothold in Central America through the use of buccaneers and Miskito troops.[4] Fear of the raiders and the high cost of transporting cacao to foreign markets led to the general abandonment of the eastern lowlands by the time of independence. Various attempts by the new government to establish national and foreign agricultural colonies in the lowlands were unsuccessful (Masing, 1964).

Costa Rican interest in the eastern lowlands was not renewed until the 1860s. By this time, coffee had become the important export crop of the young republic. However, one major problem faced the highland coffee exporters. The primary markets for Costa Rican coffee were located in Europe, yet the country's only major port, Puntarenas, was situated on the west coast. Consequently, all exported coffee had to be shipped around the tip of South America at prohibitive costs. The coffee growers pressured the government to construct a port on the east coast and a railway connecting the port with the highlands.

The builder of the Andean railways, Henry Meiggs, was commissioned to build the railway. He was soon discouraged by the difficult terrain and relegated the work of constructing the railway to his nephew, Henry Meiggs Keith, who, in turn, passed the responsibility to his younger brother, Minor C. Keith (Stewart, 1964). It was Minor C. Keith who saw the railway to its completion and developed the eastern port of Puerto Limón. The major work force for the construction of the railroad was recruited from the West Indies, especially from Jamaica which was still suffering the effects of emancipation and the collapse of the plantation system. Migration from Jamaica to Limón began in December 1872 (Meléndez, 1972b:63-64). In order to finance the construction of this railroad, Keith introduced a commercial banana, the Gros Michel, into the eastern lowlands. Bananas began to provide freight for the railway as early as 1880.

Keith merged his holdings in Costa Rica with the Boston Fruit Company in 1899 to form the United Fruit Company. Many of the West Indian blacks who had come to Costa Rica to work on the railroad remained in Limón and were employed by the banana plantations once the railway was completed. Many other blacks migrated from the West Indies to the United Fruit Company plantations at the turn of the century. In 1864, six years prior to the building of the railway, the census (Dirección General de Estadística y Censos, 1964:67) showed only twenty-eight inhabitants in Costa Rica who may have been black: twenty-three "Jamaicans," seven of whom lived in Cartago Province (which at that time included Limón), one "Haitian," and four "Africans."[5] By 1927, when the next census was taken, the number of blacks *(negros)* in Costa Rica had risen to 19,136, of which 18,003 were located in Limón Province. Puerto Limón, with 7,639 inhabitants, had become Costa Rica's second largest community.[6]

ADAPTATION TO NORTH AMERICAN CULTURE (1899-1942)

The position of the West Indian black in Costa Rica from 1899 to 1942 was one of regional importance. He was generally restricted from moving into the highlands and in reality had no part in the wealth, authority, and prestige substructures as they existed in the highlands. On the other hand, the black held an important position in the banana plantation system of the lowlands. For the most part, this plantation system functioned as a self-contained system, independently of Costa Rican institutions.

The majority of West Indian blacks who came to the province of Limón during this period became employees of the United Fruit Company, working on the company's banana plantations, the company's railway, or in the company's port town, Puerto Limón. For as long as they remained employees of the United Fruit Company, the plantation system permeated all aspects of their lives.

The West Indian immigrant filled positions both in the middle and especially at the bottom of the socioeconomic hierarchy. The white managers from the United States held the positions at the top. White peons from the highlands generally were at the very bottom of the hierarchy. Only a few highland whites ever assumed managerial positions with the company.

The demographic data, although not conclusive, suggest that the West Indians did not migrate to Limón as settlers but rather as temporary laborers who came to Costa Rica because the job market was somewhat better than that of Jamaica and other areas of the Caribbean. For example, a study cited by Kepner and Soothill (1935:256) undertaken in the early 1900s found that only 128 banana planters were Costa Rican nationals while 589 were foreigners. The study also reports that a large proportion of these foreign planters were sending remittances to their native countries.

The data from the 1927 census (Dirección General de Estadística y Censos, 1960:63) indicate that Limón Province was the only Costa Rican province with more foreigners than Costa Ricans (see Table 1).

TABLE 1
**Proportion of Costa Ricans to Foreigners in the
Provinces of Costa Rica, 1927**

Province	
Heredia	97.0 Costa Ricans for each foreigner
Cartago	28.5 Costa Ricans for each foreigner
Alajuela	27.7 Costa Ricans for each foreigner
San José	19.7 Costa Ricans for each foreigner
Guanacaste	9.7 Costa Ricans for each foreigner
Puntarenas	5.7 Costa Ricans for each foreigner
Limón	2.2 foreigners for each Costa Rican

Similar proportions also held true for the urban capitals of each province. Whereas the city of Puntarenas, Costa Rica's other major port, had 3.8 Costa Ricans for each foreigner, Puerto Limón had 1.5 foreigners for each Costa Rican. In comparison, all other provinces had a higher ratio of Costa Ricans to foreigners than Puntarenas (Dirección General de Estadística y Censos, 1960:63).

Other demographic data suggest that the laborers who were living in Limón Province did not expect to remain in Costa Rica permanently. For example, most of the people in the province were unmarried males.[7] Only 24.4 percent of the population in Limón Province over the age of fifteen were married (Dirección General de Estadística y Censos, 1960:43).

The average household size for Limón Province was only 2.7 persons, while the average household size for all other provinces of Costa Rica was nearly double that figure. Almost 41 percent of all households in Limón Province consisted of a single person. An additional 21 percent of the households consisted of only two persons.

The above data indicate that the majority of blacks were temporary residents of Costa Rica. Without citizenship, the blacks had little voice in the functioning of the Costa Rican government; however, Costa Rican politics were unimportant to the blacks. The United Fruit Company's foreign managers were able to control Limón Province as they pleased and with little interference from the Costa Rican government. The company constituted the de facto authority in Limón Province.

All of the blacks' needs were fulfilled by the company. The West Indians lived in company houses, received company health services, and purchased supplies at company commissaries. The company railway provided the main and, in most cases, the only means of transportation for the inhabitants of the lowlands. Until very recently, a special company funeral train even carried the dead to the cemetery in Puerto Limón (Nunley, 1950:45).

The West Indian laborer adapted to the plantation's institutions and cultural patterns, both of which differed from those of the Costa Ricans. The company managers of the United Fruit Company acted as buffers, or intermediaries, between the West Indians and the Costa Rican institutions, retarding the West Indians' adaptation to Costa Rican society.

Fearing that the blacks would migrate into the highlands, bringing new diseases[8] and competing with the rapidly expanding white population for jobs, the government, beginning the 1930s, exerted legal and nonlegal pressures to restrict blacks from settling in the highlands. This action further reinforced the blacks' already strong dependence on the United Fruit Company (Duncan, 1972:94; Meléndez, 1972b:79).

Under the protection of the United Fruit Company, the lowland blacks were able to retain their West Indian dialects of English. The ability to speak some form of English enhanced the blacks' chances of finding employment with the company, as the North American managers found it easier to communicate with the blacks than with the Spanish-speaking Costa Ricans. The blacks were given slightly higher rates of pay than the Costa Rican peons for the same jobs.[9]

Even though Catholicism was the official state religion, the West Indians were able to retain their membership in various Protestant churches and religious cults with the support of the United Fruit Company. The larger Protestant churches were instrumental in keeping black children from attending the public schools operated by the Costa Rican government with instruction given in Spanish. Instead, the West Indians sent their children to private schools operated by the Protestant churches. These schools were often built and supported by the United Fruit Company. In 1930, the secretary of education in Costa Rica, Ricardo Fournier, commented on the effects of the private schools (Kepner, 1936:166-167):

> Because of the language difficulty, the children of English speaking Jamaican Negroes frequently go to private schools, in which they often have to pay tuition.
>
> The private schools are really an acute problem for the public education system—it being hard to exercise superivison over them because of the language and because they do not follow government regulations. Some of the schools are in very small villages; thus the only way to force them to conform to governmental requirements would be to increase the number of inspectors. They tend to denationalize their areas. In them the government is unable to teach national ideas and the sentiments of Costa Rica.

In the lowlands during 1927, there were at least thirty-three private schools with a total enrollment of 1,500 students, most of whom were black (Dirección General de Estadística y Censos, 1960:79).

Not all blacks migrated to Limón as temporary laborers on the banana plantations. As with any migrant population, there were many motives for movement. Some West Indians came in search of land and settled or squatted on small farms and survived through peasant farming much as they had done in Jamaica or elsewhere. Other blacks were incorporated into the Costa Rican polity through appointments as local police and judicial authorities. Yet, most of the West Indian migrants were attracted to Costa Rica by the banana plantation system of the Untied Fruit Company. Within the system, the West Indians were able to maintain their West Indian style of life. Little accommodation to the new social setting was necessary. The adaptations that took place were usually adjustments to the peculiarities of the United Fruit Company plantation system rather than to the institutions or lifestyle of the Costa Ricans. Even those West Indians in Limón who were not directly employed by the United Fruit Company were affected by the company and the plantation system. Those blacks who settled or squatted as peasants often were part-time employees or periodically sold bunches of bananas to the company. They were, of course, dependent on the company for their supplies, transportation, medical assistance, and the education of their children.

The West Indians were able to retain almost all of their former traditions. To a certain extent Limón became an outpost of the West Indies, particularly Jamaica. The language spoken was English; Protestant churches predominated. The laborers on both banana farms and peasant farms were similar to the inhabitants of the West Indies. Clothing styles remained the same. Women served as "higglers," or middlemen trading in agricultural produce. Food was basically the same, with many recipes brought over from the Caribbean. Some of the West Indian games, such as cricket, were transported to Limón (Olien, 1967; Bryce-Laporte, 1962). Black nationalism was supported by the Universal Negro Improvement Association (UNIA) in Puerto Limón. This organization was founded by Marcus Garvey who had worked briefly in Limón as a company timekeeper (Cronon, 1955:14).

At the same time, the North American managers represented the prestige culture of the lowlands, and so some of the blacks adopted the North American traits, e.g., baseball became a popular sport and a baseball stadium was constructed in Puerto Limón (see Photo 4). North American, as well as West Indian, holidays were celebrated.

Photo 4. Baseball Stadium in Puerto Limón.

In general, it would seem that the West Indians were able to maintain most of their cultural traditions because the important elements, such as language and work experience, were similar to or the same as those required by the North American managers of the United Fruit Company. Other traits such as particular forms of education, food preferences, religious affiliations, and so forth did not affect banana production; therefore, the West Indian cultural alternatives were allowed to survive, even though they often differed from those practiced by the North Americans.

As early as 1890 in some areas, Panama disease *(Fusarium cubense),* a root disease, began attacking banana plants. There was no means of eliminating this disease. Banana production reached its height in the lowlands in 1913, but thereafter production began to decline as the banana disease spread and as soil depletion occurred. In 1938, another banana disease, sigatoka *(Cercospora musae),* a leaf spot disease, began to spread throughout the lowlands (Olien, 1971). The United Fruit Company started to abandon or sell its land in the eastern lowlands and embarked on a policy of acquiring banana land in the western lowlands of Puntarenas Province, an area unaffected by Panama disease (Olien, 1973:269-270).

The company's original idea had been to move its entire operation, including the work force, from the east coast to the west coast, but the plan ran into government opposition. By the late 1930s, the highlands and the Nicoya Peninsula were feeling the effects of increased population pressures and extensive unemployment. The government refused to allow the company to relocate the West Indians on the grounds that it would "upset the racial pattern of the country and possibly cause civil commotion" (May and Plaza, 1958:208). By restricting the movement of blacks, the government was able to provide new jobs for the whites and the mestizos. Even today the company workers in the Pacific lowlands are primarily white or mestizo. By 1942, the United Fruit Company had completely shifted its banana production to the Pacific lowlands.

THE INTERIM PERIOD: 1942-1949

Following the collapse of the banana plantation system, some West Indians returned to the islands, but many remained in Limón. For some, the second generation, this was the place of their birth. Many settled on the land vacated by the company. Even though the land had been exhausted by the company and banana disease had ravaged the best farming areas, land still remained plentiful in the lowlands. Some of this land was suitable for commercial banana production.

As the company pulled out of Limón, it divided its banana lands into small plots that were then sold or leased to the small planters. The company promoted the belief that the small plots would succeed where the large plantations had failed because an individual would be intimately acquainted with the intricate problems a particular patch of land presented (Shouse, 1938:29).

Through the collapse of the plantation system, the West Indians were transformed from rural proletariats into landholders. At the same time, they began to become citizens of Costa Rica and their patterns of adaptation were considerably altered. They no longer had foreign administrators who formed a buffer between themselves and the nation, nor were they now part of a social system that provided for all of their needs outside of the Costa Rican institutions. Once the United Fruit Company relocated, the blacks came into direct contact with the Costa Rican national institutions and cultural patterns, and from that time on they began to adapt to these patterns.

The Costa Ricans began to make their presence felt throughout the lowlands, especially in the larger towns such as Puerto Limón and Siquirres, as whites from the overpopulated highlands began to settle in Limón. Whites purchased land from the West Indians who in turn migrated to the smaller lowland towns, Panama, Nicaragua, Honduras, or the West Indies in search of work. Cacao and hemp *(abacá)* became the new export crops of the lowlands. Chinese and white merchants established shops, bars, and restaurants which now performed the functions of the company commissary stores. Catholicism began to spread, as did the Spanish language.

Pressure was exerted on West Indian families to send their children to government-sponsored "Spanish" schools. Yet, in spite of the pressure for the nationalization of the lowlands, West Indian traditions continued. "Quadrille" dances were popular and the UNIA was the most active organization in the lowlands. The *Jamaican Daily Gleaner* and the *Panama Tribune,* both English language newspapers, were widely read (Bryce-Laporte, 1962:67-68).

While the West Indian traditions flourished, the process of "Costaricanization" had been set in motion. The Revolution of 1948 brought about accelerated change.

ADAPTATION TO COSTA RICAN CULTURE:
1949 TO THE PRESENT

Following the presidential election of 1948, Costa Rica was thrown into a civil war between the conservatives, representing the old aristocracy and personalist politics, and more liberal elements advocating a democratic political structure, social reforms, and changes in the national economy (Rodríguez, 1965:20-21).

Eventually, the reformers emerged victorious, and a provisional junta was established for eighteen months with José "Pepe" Figueres as head. During its incumbency, the junta put into effect a number of basic reforms that have become institutionalized and have resulted in considerable internal structural change. The junta dissolved the Costa Rican army, leaving only a police force to maintain order; it banned the Communist party which had sided with the conservatives during the Civil War; and it levied a capital tax that fell most heavily on the rich. The junta also nationalized the banking system and paved the way for a civil service organization to end the recruitment policies of the conservatives which had been based on favoritism. The new constitution of 1949 gave women the right to vote, modernized education, and provided for social welfare (Rodríguez, 1965:22).

Many of the blacks had fought with the reformers at the side of Figueres; some had lost their lives. It was the junta that attempted to provide the Limonenses with greater participation in Costa Rican life (Olien, 1972b:237). Restrictions on the movements of blacks into the highlands were abolished, thus marking the beginning of equal legal status for blacks. Figueres also set the wheels in motion for the improvement of education. Prior to 1951, all of Limón Province had only six public schools—all at the primary level. Once Figueres was elected president to serve a full term in office, forty-seven schools were built in one year. By 1960, there were eighty-two elementary schools and a *colegio* (secondary school) in Puerto Limón. Blacks have been hired as teachers at all levels, and black teachers, leaders, and professionals have been given government scholarships for study abroad (Bryce-Laporte, 1962:70-72).

Since the revolution, the West Indians of the lowlands have been increasingly influenced by Costa Rican society and culture. The blacks have begun to absorb more of the values of the highland whites and have obtained a position in Costa Rican society as a whole, and not just within the context of a single region. The West Indians are no longer foreign migrant workers but have become Costa Rican citizens (see Table 2).

TABLE 2

Number and Percentage of Costa Ricans and Foreigners Living in Limón Province, Costa Rica, 1927, 1950, 1963

Status	1927[1]		1950[2]		1963[3]	
	No.	%	No.	%	No.	%
Costa Ricans	10,000*	31*	30,260	73	63,238	92
Foreigners	23,000*	69*	11,000	27	5,146	8
TOTAL	33,000*	100*	41,260	100	68,384	100

*Approximate
1. Dirección General de Estadística y Censos, 1960:63.
2. Dirección General de Estadística y Censos, 1953:105.
3. Dirección General de Estadística y Censos, 1966:442.

Some West Indians living in Costa Rica have never bothered to apply for Costa Rican citizenship. In 1950, shortly after the revolution, there were over 7,000 "British" living in Limón Province, most of whom were West Indians (Dirección General de Estadística y Censos, 1953:108). The 1963 census (Dirección General de Estadística y Censos, 1955:443-449) lists 1,837 Jamaicans for all of Costa Rica. Of these, 1,812 were born in Jamaica, 1,584 of whom have lived in Costa Rica for fourteen years or more. These figures suggest that it is primarily the older blacks who have not obtained citizenship.[10] In general, the greatest changes since the revolution have occurred among the younger blacks. The older blacks have tended to change slowly. Part of the West Indian tradition which has been maintained disappears as each generation dies off. The second generation, and especially the third and fourth generations, have more readily adapted to Costa Rican culture.

In Costa Rica, required attendance in the public Spanish-speaking schools has proven quite successful as an acculturating force. Classes are taught in Spanish, and attendance is compulsory through six years of primary education. Primary and secondary education is free and is supported by money from the government, although parents must provide school uniforms for the children.

While the Costa Rican public schools are the dominant educational force in the lowlands, private English schools continue to operate and negate some of the acculturating force of the Spanish schools. The private schools tend to emphasize and perpetuate ethnic differences. Students attend the English schools during the half-days in which they are not attending the public schools. The students study essentially the same academic material covered in the public school, but instruction is given in English. Until recently, the Spanish high school in Puerto Limón was the only secondary school in the lowlands, but now several other larger towns also have secondary schools. To attend the university, lowland students must move to the highlands.[11]

Spanish has become the dominant language of the lowlands. It is the lingua franca used between strangers. Although many West Indians speak English, most are also able to speak Spanish. Limón Province, however, remains the only area in Costa Rica in which English is spoken by a large number of persons (see Photo 5). As reflected in Table 3, a comparison of Limón Province and San José Province (located in the highlands) shows an interesting contrast (Dirección General de Estadistíca y Censos, 1953:53).

Photo 5. Example of Daily Movie Advertisement Used by Each of the Movie Theaters, Puerto Limón. (Note insertion of *h* in the word *old,* reflecting the Jamaican dialect of English.)

Michael D. Olien

TABLE 3

Languages Spoken in Limón and San José Provinces,
Costa Rica, 1950*

Province	% Speaking Spanish	%Speaking English
San José	99.01	0.43
Limón	63.88	32.12

*Last census to include such information.

Further census data support the hypothesis that the younger, public
school educated generations are influenced most by Costa Rican culture. As shown in Table 4, the percentage of English-speaking peoples
in Limón increases with age (Dirección General de Estadística y Censos,
1953:34-35):

TABLE 4

Age of Resident and Language Spoken as Mother Tongue,
Limón Province, Costa Rica, 1950

Age Category	% Speaking Spanish	% Speaking English	% Speaking Other Languages
Under 7 years	70.76	25.52	3.72
7-9 years	65.68	30.49	3.83
10-14 years	65.40	30.80	3.80
15-19 years	68.85	26.45	4.70
20-24 years	70.90	24.21	4.89
25-34 years	64.52	31.51	3.97
35-44 years	64.56	31.72	3.72
45-54 years	58.43	37.44	4.13
55-64 years	40.93	54.75	4.32
65 years and over	32.37	64.56	3.07

Unfortunately, none of the government census data takes bilingualism into account. The great majority of blacks speak a West Indian
dialect of English as well as Spanish, and many of the lowland whites
speak some English.

It would appear that the linguistic acculturation of the West Indians has been considerable since the United Fruit Company's domination of the region. However, a West Indian who claims to speak Spanish to a census taker is often still quite limited in his ability to use the language. Analysis of school records from all of the primary schools in Puerto Limón, whose West Indian population is generally regarded as the most acculturated of the lowlands, reveals that the black children have considerable difficulty in public school because of the language. Forty-six percent of all black children have had to repeat one or more grades because of language difficulties (see Table 5).

TABLE 5

Number of Grades Repeated in Primary Schools in Puerto Limón, Costa Rica, by Ethnic Group, Due to Language Difficulty, 1965 (_N_ = 1,958)

Number of Grades Repeated	%White* (N = 973)	%Black* (N = 967)	%Chinese* (N = 18)
No grades	70	54	67
One grade	22	30	6
Two grades	6	11	11
Three grades	2	4	11
Four grades	0	1	6
TOTAL	100%	100%	100%

*Percentages have been rounded off to the nearest whole number.

While Spanish is replacing English as the prestige language of the lowlands, the process of linguistic acculturation is far from complete.[12]

The Protestant churches still retain large congregations as they did during the United Fruit period, but the Catholic church has begun to make converts among the blacks. The Protestant churches[13] constitute a force that has acted to counterbalance the various agents of acculturation in Costa Rican society. They continue to hold services in English and maintain the English schools. Yet, Catholicism has grown rapidly in the lowlands, partly as a result of increased settlement in the lowlands by Catholic highlanders, and partly from the growing acceptance of the state religion by some blacks.

One other institution in particular has attempted to maintain West Indian traditions, namely, the UNIA (see Photo 6). The UNIA sponsors cultural programs, dances, an annual May Pole dance and lawn party, and a parade to celebrate Jamaican Independence Day. It is also one of the two organizations in Puerto Limón that has a burial plan for blacks (Olien, 1968:87). The organization is comprised solely of blacks. However, it appears to be supported mainly by the older generations and is seen as something of an anomaly by the younger generations of blacks who have been influenced by Afro-American interests in the United States. Some of Limón's university students have founded a group known as El Comité de Estudiantes de la Cultura Negra (AFROTSCO) which promotes the blacks' African, rather than Jamaican, heritage.[14]

Photo 6. Headquarters of the Universal Negro Improvement Association, Puerto Limón.

CONCLUSIONS

The West Indians' adaptation to the lifestyle and culture of Costa Rica differs from the adaptation to Spanish culture experienced by blacks in many parts of Latin America. Specifically, the blacks in Costa Rica adapted first to North American culture, which was much like West Indian culture and which tended to retard acceptance of Costa Rican Hispanic tradition. The integration of the West Indian into Costa Rican society began only after the United Fruit Company abandoned the eastern lowlands in 1942.

Since the collapse of the lowland banana plantations and the Revolution of 1948, there has been considerable structural change in Costa Rican society. A redistribution of wealth occurred throughout Limón Province in the form of landholdings. Formerly landless plantation laborers, many of them West Indians, assumed ownership of sections of the abandoned plantations.

Positions of power and prestige in the lowlands were vacated by the North American administrators. These positions were, in turn, filled by Spanish-speaking whites who began migrating to the Limón region from the highlands as they became the merchants and administrators of the province.

Since the Revolution of 1948, many aspects of West Indian adaptation to Hispanic culture have been accelerated. As citizens of the country, the younger generations of blacks now send their children to public schools, speak Spanish, and consider themselves Costa Ricans. Their position in Costa Rican society had been transformed from that of "foreign laborer" on foreign-owned banana plantations to that of "Costa Rican" filling positions at the middle and bottom of the wealth, authority, and prestige substructures.

NOTES

1. The 1950 census was the last Costa Rican census to differentiate by color or *raza* (race). Later census questionnaires have not collected information about race.

2. Recently, a highway has been completed between San José and Puerto Limón and has facilitated travel between the two centers.

3. Sometimes Spanish colonists convicted of a crime were sentenced to work on the plantations of Matina for a particular number of years; see, for example, Costa Rica, Archiva Nacional (1793). For more information on the African blacks, see Meléndez (1966, 1972a) and Olien (1972a).

4. For more detailed treatment, see Floyd (1967), Olien (1967, 1970), Parsons (1954), and Helms (1975:213-216).

5. The 1864 census did not distinguish the population by race; yet, it can be assumed that the Haitian and the four Africans were most likely black. Some of the Jamaicans may have been white. The important point, however, is that the number of blacks was very small.

6. Only San José, the capital, with 50,580 persons, was larger (Dirección General de Estadística y Censos, 1960:36).

7. The census shows 9.4 percent more males than females, the highest proportion of males to females of any Costa Rican province (Dirección General de Estadística y Censos, 1960:62).

8. Especially malaria and yellow fever.

9. Putnam (1913:107) recorded that the West Indian blacks received fifteen cents an hour on the docks for night work and ten cents an hour for day work. The Spanish-speaking Costa Ricans received twelve and one-half cents an hour for the same night work and eight and one-half cents an hour for the same day work.

10. Of the 1,837 Jamaicans living in Costa Rica, 1,702 were living in Limón.

11. A branch of the university was opened in Puerto Limón in 1975 but has only very limited offerings.

12. Only recently has any scholarly research been undertaken on black speech in Limón (Wolfe, 1970). As a result, it is still difficult to make comparisons of Limón English with that of Jamaican English.

13. These include the larger Anglican, Baptist, and Methodist churches, as well as Bahai, the Church of God, the Church of God of the Prophecy, the Evangelical Pentacostal church, Jehovah's Witnesses, the Salvation Army, and the Seventh Day Adventists.

14. While more racially mixed couples are now seen in public in San José than ten years ago, without access to adequate census data it is difficult to estimate whether miscegenation has actually increased. Unfortunately, data on the racial composition of households are not collected by the Dirección General de Estadística y Censos.

REFERENCES CITED

Avila, Fernando Bastos. de. 1964. *La inmigración en América Latina.* Washington, D.C.: Unión Panamericana.

Bryce-Laporte, Roy S. 1962. Social Relations and Cultural Persistence (or Change) Among Jamaicans in a Rural Area of Costa Rica. Thesis, Institute of Caribbean Studies, University of Puerto Rico.

Costa Rica, Archivo Nacional. 1793. Colonial document, C.E. No. 5787, August 26. San José, Costa Rica.

Cronon, Edmund D. 1955. *Black Moses: The Story of Marcus Garvey and the Universal Negro Improvement Association.* Madison: University of Wisconsin Press.

Dirección General de Estadística y Censos. 1953. *Censo de población de Costa Rica, 22 de mayo de 1950.* San José, Costa Rica: Ministerio de Economía y Hacienda.

———. 1960. *Censo de población de Costa Rica, 11 de mayo de 1927.* San José, Costa Rica: Ministerio de Economía y Hacienda.

———. 1964. *Censo general de la república de Costa Rica, 27 de noviembre de 1864.* San José, Costa Rica: Ministerior de Economía y Hacienda, 2nd ed.

———. 1966. *Censo de población, 1963.* San José, Costa Rica: Ministerio de Industria y Comercio.

Duncan, Quince. 1972. "El negro antillano: immigración y presencia." IN: *El Negro en Costa Rica,* Carlos Meléndez and Quince Duncan, editors. San José, Costa Rica: Editorial Costa Rica, pp. 89-132.

Floyd, Troy S. 1967. *The Anglo-Spanish Struggle for Mosquitia.* Albuquerque: University of New Mexico Press.

Helms, Mary W. 1975. *Middle America: A Culture History of Heartland and Frontiers.* Englewood Cliffs, N.J.: Prentice-Hall, Inc.

Kepner, Charles David, Jr. 1936. *Social Aspects of the Banana Industry.* New York: Columbia University Press.

Kepner, Charles David, Jr., and Jay Henry Soothill. 1935. *The Banana Empire: A Case Study of Economic Imperialism.* New York: The Vanguard Press.

Masing, Ulv. 1964. Foreign Agricultural Colonies in Costa Rica: An Analysis of Foreign Colonization in a Tropical Environment. Ph.D. dissertation, University of Florida.

May, Stacy, and Galo Plaza. 1958. *The United Fruit Company in Latin America.* Washington, D.C.: National Planning Association.

Meléndez Ch., Carlos. 1966. "Los origenes de los esclavos africanos en Costa Rica." Sevilla: XXXVI Congreso Internacional de Americanistas, vol. 4, pp. 387-391.

———. 1972a. "El negro en Costa Rica durante la colonia." IN: *El Negro en Costa Rica,* Carlos Meléndez and Quince Duncan, editors. San José, Costa Rica: Editorial Costa Rica, pp. 55-85.

———. 1972b. "Aspectos sobre la inmigración jamaicana," IN: *El Negro en Costa Rica,* Carlos Meléndez and Quince Duncan, editors. San José, Costa Rica: Editorial Costa Rica, pp. 55-85.

Nunley, Robert F. 1960. *The Distribution of Population in Costa Rica.* Washington, D.C.: National Academy of Sciences-National Research Council, Publication No. 743.

Olien, Michael D. 1967. The Negro in Costa Rica: The Ethnohistory of an Ethnic Minority in a Complex Society. Ph.D. dissertation, Unviersity of Oregon.

———. 1968. "Levels of Urban Relationships in a Complex Society: A Costa Rican Case," IN: *Urban Anthropology: Research Perspectives and Strategies,* Elizabeth M. Eddy, editor, Athens, Ga.: Southern Anthropological Society Proceedings, No. 2, pp. 83-92.

———. 1970. *The Negro in Costa Rica: The Role of an Ethnic Minority in a Developing Society.* Winston-Salem, N.C.: Wake Forest University, Overseas Research Center, Developing Nations Monograph Series, No. 3.

———. 1971. The Ecological Adaptation of a Plantation to a Changing Environment. Paper presented at the annual meeting of the American Anthropological Association, New York.

———. 1972a Ethnohistorical Research on Colonial Black Populations in Costa Rica. Paper presented at the annual meeting of the American Society for Ethnohistory, Boston.

———. 1972b. "The Negro in Costa Rica: The Ethnohistory of an Ethnic Minority in a Complex Society, Resumen y Conclusiones." In: *El Negro en Costa Rica,* Carlos Meléndez and Quince Duncan, editors. San José, Costa Rica: Editorial Costa Rica, pp. 233-241.

———. 1973. *Latin Americans: Contemporary Peoples and Their Cultural Traditions.* New York: Holt, Rinehart and Winston.

Parsons, James J. 1954. "English-speaking Settlements of the Western Caribbean." *Yearbook of the Association of Pacific Coast Geographers* 16:3-16.

Putnam, George Palmer. 1913. *The Southland of North America: Rambles and Observations in Central America During the Year 1912.* New York: G. P. Putnam's Sons.

Rodriguez, Mario. 1965. *Central America.* Englewood Cliffs, N.J.: Prentice-Hall, Inc.

Shouse, M. A. 1938. Lowland Hinterland of Limón, Costa Rica. M.S. thesis, University of Chicago.

Stewart, Watt. 1964. *Keith and Costa Rica: The Biography of Minor Cooper Keith, American Entrepreneur.* Albuquerque: University of New Mexico Press.

Thiel, Bernardo Augusto. 1902. "Monografía de la población de Costa Rica en el siglo XIX." IN: *Revista de Costa Rica en el Siglo XIX.* San José, Costa Rica: Tipografía Nacional, pp. 1-52.

Wolfe, Terry A. 1970. An Exploratory Study of the Morphology and Syntax of the English of the Province of Limón. Costa Rica. Thesis, Universidad de Costa Rica.

Mary W. Helms

6

NEGRO OR INDIAN?: THE CHANGING IDENTITY OF A FRONTIER POPULATION[1]

In common with most of Middle America, the various population components of the Miskito Coast of eastern Nicaragua and Honduras, from the time of European contact until the present, have included "Indian," "Negro," and "Euro-American" groups. This essay focuses on the position accorded one ethnic group resident on the coast—the Miskito Indians, as they are known today—within this tripartite division. Most of the analysis will be concerned with the identification of the Miskito by various Euro-American groups as indicated in travel accounts, missionary reports, and government documents dating from the late seventeenth century to the present day. The major point to be explored is the interesting circumstance that the Miskito are considered an "Indian" population in some accounts but a variant of "Negro" in others.

The changing identity of this group essentially reflects the fact that, since the time of contact, the eastern regions of Nicaragua and Honduras have formed a frontier zone or hinterland generally lying beyond effective influence by the Hispanic mainland region of Central America. Instead, this territory has encompassed part of the Anglo-American Caribbean rimland (Augelli, 1962). Consequently, documents dealing with the coast and its inhabitants have been written by both Hispanic and Anglo-American observers. Understandably, these observers have viewed the Miskito from the vantage points of their respective cultures and have not always seen the same thing. At the same time, certain features of the culture pattern of the Miskito have also changed over the last three centuries as the nature of the hinterland has changed. This, too, is reflected in the socio-racial identifications accorded them by the various categories of viewers.

The native inhabitants of the east coast of Nicaragua and Honduras are first mentioned in the narratives of seventeenth-century buccaneers, mainly English and French, who visited points along the isolated shore of the Miskito Coast in the 1670s and 1680s. They traded, cohabited with native women, and hired local natives, who were skilled fishermen, as provisioners for their journeys at sea. In their accounts, the buccaneers refer to the coastal inhabitants who assisted them as Indians and as "Moskitoes" or "Moskito-men"[2] (Esquemeling, 1967:249-255, 341; Dampier, 1968:30-34). These early records also note the presence of Negroes and mulattoes on the coast, particularly at Cape Gracias a Dios. These people are identified as survivors of a slaveship that had been wrecked offshore, although some also were refugees from West Indian plantations or from Spanish mines in Honduras. By the beginning of the eighteenth century, Negro-Indian miscegenation was well established (Esquemeling, 1967; M.W., 1732; de Lussan, 1930).

During approximately the next 150 years, from about 1700 to 1865, information regarding the Miskito Coast and its peoples appeared in two general bodies of material: reports compiled by Hispanic writers of the colonial period and early republican decades, and accounts by English-speaking diplomats, military men, and traders. All of these accounts are concerned more or less with common subjects, including the relationships between native coastal inhabitants and foreign colonial powers. They differ to some extent regarding the areas of contact they emphasize and the socio-racial classification of native peoples.

The inhabitants of the Miskito Coast were of interest to English-speaking writers because of their antipathy toward Spaniards, their eagerness to obtain European material goods, and their willingness to combine these interests by serving as guides and mercenaries for English-inspired raids on Spanish outposts in Central America. The English writers of the period most commonly refer to these coastal inhabitants as Mosquito-men or Mosquito Indians, terms indicating a status of indigenous natives. Within this general classification, subgroups are frequently differentiated in terms of the presence or absence of Negro admixture. Persons with Negro affiliation are termed samboes or zamboes. Those without Negro admixture are frequently referred to as pure or common or unmixed Indians. The following excerpt from the report of Bryan Edwards, written about 1773, shows this classificatory order particularly well. It also clearly denotes the criteria of ancestry, physical appearance, and personality characteristics that underlie the differentiations:

> The Musquito Indians, properly so called, . . . [are] justly remarkable for their fixed hereditary hatred of the Spaniards, and attachment to us, . . . Their present number is from seven to ten thousand fighting men, formed into different tribes, both by nature and policy; by nature, from the general distinction of pure Indians and Samboes; by policy, as living and acting under several chieftains. . . .
>
> The Samboes are supposed to derive their origin from a Guinea ship, which, it is said, was wrecked on the coast about a century ago. Certain it is, that their hair, complexion, features, and make, clearly prove an African ancestry; from whom they have also inherited some of the worst characteristics of the worst African mind; for they are generally false, designing, treacherous, knavish, impudent, and revengeful.
>
> The pure Indians are so called, because they are free from any mixture of negro blood; and their general conduct gives a very favourable idea of Indian nature. They are seldom guilty of positive evil, and often rise to positive good, when positive good does not require much exertion of mind. Their modesty, docility, good faith, disposition to friendship and gratitude, ought to engage equally our regard and protection. (Edwards, 1819:210-211).

A significant addenda to this classification of coastal peoples is found in the account written in 1781 by Stephen Kemble (1885:422) which notes the presence of various native inhabitants other than Miskito in the interior reaches (Hodgson, 1965; Roberts, 1827:115, 146-147; Bell, 1899:2-4). By mid-nineteenth century, these tribes, which were slowly declining in size and significance as the Miskito became more prominent, are identified by English writers under the collective term Sumu. It is also recorded that, in contrast to the Miskito, the Sumu did not approve of miscegenation with foreigners (Bell, 1862).

Still farther to the west, the Sumu bordered on the fringes of Hispanic Central America. In line with the general policy of pacification
and "civilizing" authorized by the Spanish crown, colonial authorities
attempted to resettle and Christianize these natives in mission communities, which also served as a line of demarcation between the Hispanic world of Nicaragua and Honduras and the unconquered (by
Spanish) Caribbean frontier (see map). The missions were singularly
unsuccessful. Their failure is in no small measure attributable to attacks by marauding bands of Miskito who traveled up the rivers from
their coastal haunts to the interior in order to strike at frontier missions and Spanish settlements (Floyd, 1967: Chap. 4; Gamez, 1939:
Chap. 8).

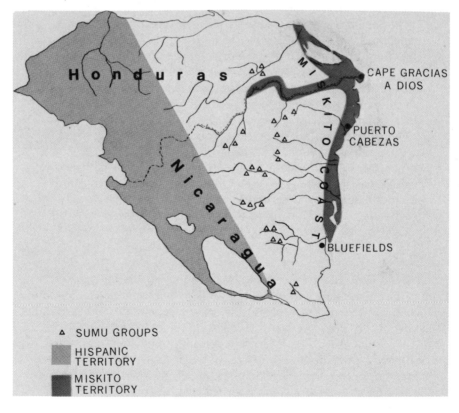

Miskito Coast, 1970.

It is in this context of armed frontier raiders that the Miskito are predominantly viewed by Spanish writers of the time (Costa Rica, 1913:Doc. No. 151, 154, 240). For the same reason, Hispanic accounts also emphasize the Negroid or zambo element in Miskito socio-racial history to a far greater extent than do their English counterparts. This identification reflects the fact that to Hispanic Central Americans the Miskito Coast was a rough, uncivilized region which harbored undesirables, including Englishmen and, especially, escaped Negro slaves. The report of an alcalde mayor of Tegucigalpa written in the early eighteenth century and quoted in translation in Bancroft is indicative of this orientation:

> The sambos have plenty of vessels, provisions, arms, and ammunition, for they are supplied by the English of Jamaica, who egg them onto hostilities against the Spaniards. Their country is also a place of refuge for the mulattoes, negroes, and other evil-doers who flee from justice in the Spanish settlements, and who give them information of the Spanish plans, as well as join them in the execution of their own (Bancroft, 1886:600; cf. Gamez, 1939:85).

There were similar frontiers or enclaves of escaped slaves elsewhere in the Viceroyalty of New Spain, for example, in the mountains of Honduras, along the isolated Pacific Coast of western Mexico, in the hills between Veracruz and Mexico City, and in the vast stretches between Mexico City and the northern mining districts. From these places of refuge bands of marauding Negroes would attack and rob passing travelers and mule trains. (Trans-Isthmian travelers in Panama faced similar problems.) The dangers and terror inspired by such raids confirmed the fear with which colonial Spanish society regarded Negroes, mulattoes, and zamboes in general.

Negroes and persons of either real or imputed Negro admixture, including zamboes, were also placed virtually at the bottom of the legal and social hierarchy characteristic of the Hispanic colonial world (Mörner, 1967:53-68). This degradation reflected the stigma associated with slavery and the fact that many Negroes, mulattoes, and zamboes were of illegitimate birth, or at least were so suspected. The official aversion of the crown to the fruits of Afro-Indian miscegenation (since it showed the obvious failure of the crown's policy of separation for

Indians and challenged fundamental Hispanic concepts of the rightful order of society) led to additional socio-racial prejudice against zamboes. Negroes and persons of Negro admixture also were usually prohibited from carrying firearms. They paid tribute, which was a legal indication of inferiority and subordination, and their movements and dress were restricted by laws requiring evening curfews and forbidding Negro women to wear gold, pearls, or silk (Mörner, 1967). The loyalty of persons of African ancestry also was suspect. Mere rumors of Negro uprisings threw citizens into panic, and we have already noted the aggressiveness of bands of escaped Negro slaves who attacked wayfarers from their redoubts in the hills or forests (Mörner, 1967:75-77). The zamboes had a particularly poor reputation along these lines: "A greater number of robberies and murders are committed by this caste than by all the rest, except the Chino (mixture of Negro and Chinese)" (W. B. Stevenson, quoted in Schurz, 1954:192n.36).

In light of these factors, it is understandable why the terms Mosquito and zambo were frequently used interchangeably by Spanish writers dealing with the Miskito Coast. Their accounts frequently refer to the "Zambo Mosquitos" or "Mosquito Zamboes" as a single classificatory unit (Gamez, 1939:84). To be sure, some sources indicate that zambo, strictly speaking, specifically referred only to those of Negro-Indian admixture, while Mosquito is said to apply broadly to Indians, mulattoes, Negroes, and anyone else in the area (Costa Rica, 1913: Doc. no. 166; cf. Gamez, 1939:83). In actuality, however, the term zambo was used as frequently and extended as broadly in its coverage as the term Mosquito: "On the eastern coast of Nicaragua and Honduras there lived in the seventeenth century a people known among themselves as Misskitoes, and called by the Spaniard Mosquitos, or more frequently sambos, the off-spring probably of cimarrones [escaped slaves] and native women (Bancroft, 1886:595)." Not surprisingly, this single identification of zambo-Mosquito was particularly marked within the context of frontier raids. The historican José Gamez, who generally views the zamboes as separate from the Miskito, notes their commonality in times of attack: "The Zamboes formed a faction distinct from the Mosquito, with whom they were rivals; but when it was a question of invading the territory of the Spanish provinces, they engaged the enemy lines and made their incursions together and in good harmony" (1939:83; trans. M.W.H.).

Significantly, however, the term zambo, when applied by Hispanic observers to inhabitants of the Miskito Coast, lacked certain of the connotations usually attributed to it in Hispanic colonial society. Within the Spanish world the Miskito-zamboes, as fugitive slaves or offspring of such, would have carried the stigma of slavery and, by default of any European religious organization on the coast at this time, of illegitimate birth. However, other areas of restriction and indications of subordination found within the Hispanic system did not apply to the Miskito. They did not pay tribute to the Spanish crown; their movements and dress were not restricted; they owned numerous firearms and were fearful fighters. In short, it is clear that, when applied to the Miskito, the term zambo had significance in the social sense of Hispanic usage (i.e., in terms of slavery stigma, illegitimate birth, general fear of Negroes), but not in any legal sense.

The absence of any legal significance to the term reflects the fact that for the duration of the colonial period the eastern coast of Nicaragua and Honduras was a hinterland that fell outside the effective control of the Spanish crown, even though the crown formally considered it Spanish territory. Consequently, the legal arm of Spanish colonial government did not intrude, and the residents of the coast were free of tribute payments and similar restrictions.

During the first half of the nineteenth century, the Spanish colonies became politically independent of the mother country. Slavery in the newly created Central American republics was prohibited, and terms such as zambo were eschewed in legal usage as all persons now were to be considered equal citizens—at least under the law. In mid-century, the British also relinquished their hold on the Miskito Coast. Miskito raids became things of the past, although the east coast of Nicaragua and Honduras remained significantly outside the Hispanic sphere. Thus, fear of Miskito attack and the role of the coast as a slave refuge no longer existed as concerns for Hispanic Central American society.

By the end of the century, additional changes were occurring in coastal demography and in the overall configuration of social and economic organization. Most important for our purposes were, first, the continued decline of the Sumu tribes, which significantly removed the most "Indian" population of the coast; and, second, the introduction of large numbers of West Indian Negroes to the coast as laborers on commercial banana plantations which American fruit companies began to develop in this frontier region during the early decades of the twentieth century. It would appear that in the eyes of Hispanic Nicaraguan and Honduranan nationals, this new population of West Indian blacks now replaced the "Miskito-zambo" as the most Negroid element on the coast. The arrival of the West Indians occasioned loud outcries by the Spanish-speaking population who deplored the "Africanization" of the Caribbean frontier.

Today these dark-skinned West Indians, or Creoles as they are called locally, form a predominant element in the society of the port towns that also sprang up along the coast in the early years of the twentieth century. In contrast to the Miskito, who as individuals vary greatly in physical appearance today (see below), the Creoles on the whole exhibit more definite Negroid phenotypic features. They also participate in a more town-oriented lifestyle, while the Miskito are still primarily rural.

These changes correlate significantly with changes in attitudes and terminology now applied to the Miskito. During the second half of the nineteenth century and continuing to the present day, the term Miskito (Moskito, Mosquito) Indian generally continued to be used by European and North American missionaries, travelers, and entrepreneurs (Collinson, 1870; Martin, 1894; Mierisch, 1893; Moravian Church, 1849-1887; Moravian Church, 1890-1956). Zambo also is still noted occasionally, again usually by Hispanic writers (Subirana, 1938; Altschul, 1928; Rivas, 1929). However, the criteria used by various outsiders in defining this ethnic group are slowly being amended. For one thing, the Miskito increasingly are being considered within the Latin American context of *indigenas*. This term was introduced to the new republics by legislators and administrators after independence. Generally, it referred to rural peoples who, regardless of racial background, still spoke a native tongue and followed distinctive Indian or native lifestyles rather than adopting Hispanic customs, language, and behavior (Mörner, 1967:6,102). By the late nineteenth century, sociocultural *indígena* criteria became an additional factor in the identification of the Miskito by European, North American, and Hispanic observers, particularly by Nicaraguan and Honduranan government agencies.

For example, the resolution adopted in 1895 by the National Legislative Assembly of Nicaragua, formally admitting the Miskito Coast of Nicaragua into the republic as the Department of Zelaya, still identifies the Miskito by general reference to race (although now as Mosquito

Indians, not as zamboes). The document also appears to view the Miskito as backward peoples bereft of acceptable (i.e., Hispanic) forms of government who are still following their own rather than national customs and are expected to continue doing so. The following excerpts from the document are illustrative:

> Whereas, we have agreed wholly to submit to the laws and authorities of Nicaragua for the purpose of forming part of their political and administrative organization; Whereas, the lack of a respectable and legitimate government is always the cause of calamity to a people, in which condition we have been for so long a time; . . . Whereas, although the constitution of Nicaragua provides for all the necessities and aspirations of a free people, we, nevertheless, desire to retain special privileges in accord with our customs and our racial disposition. In virtue of all the foregoing . . . we hereby declare and decree . . .
>
> Article 3. Natives [*Los indigenas*] shall be exempt from all military service in time of peace and war.
>
> Article 4. No tax shall be levied upon the persons of Mosquitoes . . .
>
> Article 10. The people shall promulgate their local regulations in assemblies over which the Chief shall preside . . . (Nicaragua, 1895:xviii-xix; Hooker, 1945:57-58).

A similar attitude is expressed in the Indianist Yearbook of the Inter-American Indian Institue (IAII), where the Miskito are classified as a "principal" Indian group in Honduras and among the "most important Indian groups" in Nicaragua. Under the heading "Governmental attitude toward the Indians," the yearbook also notes that "Indian legislation" concerning questions of Indian land and welfare was promulgated since the beginning of the twentieth century in both countries and that various "national Indianist organizations" and other agencies are concerned with problems of rural schools, sanitation, and agrarian interests for the Miskito (IAII, 1962:63-64, 84-86).

Similar expressions of interest in education, health, and general community welfare and development are found among Protestant and Catholic missions to the Miskito Coast. The missions (staffed by North Americans), like Nicaraguan government agencies, also appear to view the Miskito of the twentieth century as poor, ignorant, and backward Indians. As the Moravian bishop, Karl Mueller, notes, "even today . . . [the Miskito] prefers the village and the rural mode of life on the savannah or in the bush, to life in the towns, and in this respect he has remained true to the characteristics of his Indian forbears" (Mueller, 1932:33).

Criteria of physical appearance, psychological attitudes and character, and African ancestry are still expressed in the twentieth-century literature. Bishop Mueller discusses these criteria fully:

> There is a marked difference in the outward appearance of the Miskitos [and other regional Indians]. The Miskito or Zambo (the latter name indicates that he is of mixed Indian and Negro blood) is rather tall, well-built, dark, occasionally approaching the black; frequently with hair, which shows his relationship to the Negro race; mentally fairly alert and much more aggressive than his relatives of the other Indian tribes. . . . This mixture of races [Indian and Negro] has increased and has become progressively noticeable through the immigration of considerable numbers of people of African ancestry from the various West Indian Islands. At present there are not many people bearing the signs of unmixed Indian ancestry among the Miskito tribe. It must be said, however, that the usual result of the mixing of races, which is said to be a transmission of most of the vices and few of the virtues of their ancestors, is not confirmed in the case of the Miskitos. On the contrary, they seem to have benefitted very decidedly, both mentally and physically (1932:32-33).

In light of the evidence for increasing sociocultural identification of the Miskito as *indígenas,* it is noteworthy that the Negro racial element is still singled out for emphasis in comments such as Mueller's. However, even as the sociocultural criteria emphasized by outside observers were changing from those associated with zambo to those associated with *indígena,* so, too, is Negro racial identification being tempered. Eduard Conzemius, writing at the same time as Bishop Mueller, noted that the Miskito freely intermixed not only with Negroes, but with peoples of various backgrounds. (Careful reading of the ethnohistorical sources shows that this pattern has occurred since the days of the buccaneers.) The following quote from Conzemius is particularly interesting, since in the first sentence he repeats the truism of Miskito-Negro admixture, while in the next he notes that that admixture, in fact, has been much more widespread:

> [The Miskito] are largely mixed with Negroes, for which reason Spaniards have called them "Zambos," meaning Negro and Indian half-breed, a name which is appropriate.
>   The Miskito readily intermarry with foreigners. They assimilate all races; the children always speak the language of the mother and grow up as Miskito, whether the father be "Creole," "Ladino," [Black] Carib, Negro, Sumu, Rama, Paya, North American, European, Syrian or Chinaman (Conzemius, 1932:12-13).

Conzemius's statement on the general miscegenation common among the Miskito may have been spurred by the probability that at this time (the 1920s and early 1930s), in spite of increasing Negro-Miskito admixture as noted by Mueller, the Miskito as a group no longer were phenotypically the most Negroid population element on the coast, for an influx of West Indians seeking work on banana plantations had begun. Instead, it is quite likely, if present-day observations are at all relevant, that individuals identified as Miskito now showed a wide range of skin color, hair texture, and other physical features which, in sum, rendered them less Negroid in appearance than West Indian Negroes.[3] In the same vein, Conzemius suggests that character and psychological attributes may be ascribed to general contact with foreigners as well as to specifically Negro admixture:

> Contact with foreigners is rapidly modifying the character of the Indians; it has made them less shy and easier to approach, and more hospitable, but on the other hand has made them more pretentious and less reliable and trustworthy. . . . The hybird Miskito differ greatly in character from the pure Indians, owing to their large admixture with Negro blood and their long association with foreign traders and settlers (Conzemius, 1932:105).

Ancestry, physical appearance, and sociocultural charactristics are also important factors in the Miskito's identification of themselves, although the emphasis given these several criteria varies depending on the situation. At the present time, criteria of ancestry and physical appearance are used in a limited context in that they are considered significant factors for determining individual identification only under specific circumstances. Sociocultural (including linguistic) characteristics, however, are used more broadly for general individual, group, and ethnic identification.

Recent ethnographic data obtained from the Miskito village of Asang during my field study of this community in 1964-1965 indicate that ancestry and physical appearance are most likely to be taken into account when questions arise concerning the propriety of proposed marriages (Helms, 1971:82-84, 88-89). I found that traditional marriage rules had been determined largely by kinship terms which separated cross cousins, who were suitable marriage partners, from parallel cousins, who were not. Informants indicated, and missionary reports of the period agreed, that at about the turn of the twentieth century the cross-parallel distinction was dropped and parallel terms were extended to include all cousins. By the time of my field work, this change had resulted in some cases of marriage with technically forbidden cousins.

Currently, in order to make these matches more acceptable any non-Miskito ancestors (parents or grandparents) of the couple involved may be emphasized in order to "lessen" the closeness of the Miskito relationship. It is not hard to find such ancestry in Asang. (Note, too, the significance of these data for Conzemius's statement on miscegenation quoted above.) The original founders of the village (which was established in 1910) included five sisters and two brothers of a Miskito family. Two sisters married Miskito men,[4] but a third married an Englishman originally from Cornwall. After his death, his Miskito widow remarried, this time choosing a Nicaraguan reportedly from Managua. The fourth sister married a Spanish-speaking Honduranan, while the only daughter of the fifth (whose husband had deserted her prior to the move to Asang) married a Spanish-speaking merchant of Jewish extraction. One of the two brothers married the daughter of yet another foreigner who had settled in the community: an American Negro allegedly from Ohio. Although other families gradually settled at Asang, which enjoys a particularly advantageous location, a large number of residents today are related through at least one parent to one or another of these foreigners (Helms, 1971:57-58, 83-84).

In stressing non-Miskito ancestry for purposes of marriage, the Miskito themselves give no special emphasis to Negro as opposed to non-Negro ancestors. However, physical appearance in the sense of light versus dark skin is mentioned occasionally as a factor adding to or detracting from the desirability of a proposed match in that some consider light skin to be preferable to dark. This attitude does not appear to be a major factor guiding choice of spouse and is not likely to be considered sufficiently significant to warrant forming or breaking off specific relationships.

Although ancestry may aid in solving difficult social situations, it is not of importance in determining who is or is not Miskito. Here sociocultural criteria are far more important. To the Miskito themselves, use of the Miskito language as the mother-tongue and proper adherence to Miskito customs—particularly recognition of kinsmen and observance of proper behavior towards relatives—are the crucial points, along with a general pride in Miskito customs and traditions. This pride is also commonly expressed to emphasize ethnic identity and unity when dealing with non-Miskito persons. Frequently, however, the Miskito consciously project an image not of pride but of poverty, need, and helplessness to outsiders, particularly foreigners, in hopes of acquiring some sort of material benefits. In so doing, of course, they reiterate the image of backward, rural Indians which now is imputed to them by government and mission groups.

In conclusion, the Miskito appear to be an example of a racially mixed American Indian-Afro-American "colonial tribe" (Helms, 1969) which over the centuries has gradually become generally identified more as "Indian" than as "Negro" by outside observers. This changing identification can be understood to be largely the result of the changing relationships between the Miskito and various other coastal and Central American peoples over the last 300 years. It is also significant that very few traits of contemporary Miskito culture appear to be distinctly based on an African heritage, the New World slavery experience, or West Indian Negro cultures.

In this respect, the contemporary Miskito stand in contrast to their neighbors, the Black Carib, who live along the Caribbean coast from Stann Creek, British Honduras, to Iriona, Honduras. The Black Carib, a mixed population of escaped African slaves and indigenous natives, also originated in the colonial period. Unlike the Miskito, the Black Carib have become progressively more Afro-American and less Indian in culture pattern and identity over the past centuries (Solien, 1971).

In some areas of social and economic life, however, the Miskito and Black Carib show generally comparable adaptations to the wider socio-economic conditions characteristic of the Caribbean lowland frontier of Central America (Helms, 1971; Gonzalez, 1969). It is beyond the scope of this essay to explore these similarities, but it is important at least to note that they exist (Helms, 1977). Contrasting contemporary identifications as *indígena* and Afro-American, while valid in some contexts, should not be allowed to overshadow the structural and functional similarities between (1) the Miskito and Black Carib and (2) other comparable cultures such as the so-called Bush Negroes of Surinam and French Guiana and the Seminoles of Florida.

NOTES

1. An earlier version of this essay was presented at the 19th annual meeting of the American Society for Ethnohistory, Athens, Ga., October 14, 1971. I would like to thank Michael D. Olien and James W. VanStone for their helpful comments and suggestions.

2. Various spellings are found in the literature of what today is termed *Miskito.* The origins of the word are uncertain. Although there is no evidence that the name existed aboriginally, some authors imply that the term was of pre-contact origin. Other interpretations have suggested that origins may lie in the Spanish phrase *indios mixtos,* referring to the early admixture between natives and Negroes, or in terms for "musket" since the population in question was also distinguished from other natives in the region by virtue of acquiring firearms.

3. In 1964-1965, the 665 villagers of the Miskito community of Asang ranged in skin color from very light ("white") to very dark. Hair texture and nose shape showed comparable wide ranges from "Caucasoid" to "Negroid."

4. Since Miskito genealogies are very short, usually extending back only to include one generation of deceased, it was not possible to obtain details on the ancestry of these strictly "Miskito" persons.

REFERENCES CITED

Altschul, Francisco. 1928. "Informe presentado al señor Presidente de la República Dr. Miguel Paz Baraona, acerca de La Mosquitia Hondureña." *Revista del Archivo y Biblioteca Nacionales de Honduras* 6:280-282, 298-301, 379-382.

Augelli, John P. 1962. "The Rimland-Mainland Concept of Culture Areas in Middle America." *Annals of the Association of American Geographers* 52:119-129.

Bancroft, Hubert H. 1886. *The Works of Hubert Howe Bancroft: History of Central America.* Vol. II, 1530-1800. San Francisco: The History Co.

Bell, Charles N. 1862. "Remarks on the Mosquito Territory, Its Climate, People, Production, Etc." *Journal of the Royal Geographic Society* 32:242-268.

_____. 1899. *Tangweera: Life and Adventures Among Gentle Savages.* London: Edward Arnold.

Collinson, John. 1870. *The Indians of the Mosquito Territory. Memoirs Read Before the Anthropological Society of London, 1867-8-9.* Vol. 3:148-156.

Conzemius, Eduard. 1932. *Ethnographical Survey of the Miskito and Sumu Indians of Honduras and Nicaragua.* Bureau of American Ethnology Bulletin No. 106. Washington, D.C.: U.S. Government Printing Office.

Costa Rica. 1913. *Costa Rica—Panama Arbitration. Documents Annexed to the Argument of Costa Rica.* Washington, D.C.: Gibson Brothers.

Dampier, William. 1968 [1729]. *A New Voyage Round the World.* New York: Dover Publications.

De Lussan, Raveneau. 1930. *Raveneau de Lussan, Buccaneer of the Spanish Main and Early French Filibuster of the Pacific . . .* M. E. Wilbur, trans. and ed. Cleveland: Arthur H. Clark Co.

Edwards, Bryan. 1819. "Some Account of the British Settlements on the Musquito Shore." *In The History, Civil and Commercial of the British West Indies,* 5th ed. Vol. 5. London, Pp. 202-214.

Esquemeling, John. 1967 [1893]. *The Buccaneers of America.* New York: Dover Publications.

Floyd, Troy S. 1967. *The Anglo-Spanish Struggle for Mosquitia.* Albuquerque: University of New Mexico Press.

Gamez, José Dolores. 1939. *Historia de la Costa de Mosquitos.* Managua, Nicaragua.

Gonzalez, Nancie L. Solien. 1969. *Black Carib Household Structure.* Seattle: University of Washington Press.

Helms, Mary W. 1969. "The Cultural Ecology of a Colonial Tribe." *Ethnology* 8:76-84.

_____. 1971. *Asang: Adaptations to Culture Contact in a Miskito Community.* Gainesville: University of Florida Press.

_____. 1977. "Domestic Organization in Eastern Central America: The San Blas Cuna, Miskito, and Black Carib compared." *The Western Canadian Journal of Anthropology* (in press).

Hodgson, Robert. 1965 [1855]. "Some Account of the Mosquito Territory." *In Waikna; or, Adventures on the Mosquito Shore.* S. A. Bard, ed. Gainesville: University of Florida Press. Pp. 354-359.

Hooker, Roberto Montgomery. 1945. *La reincorporación de la Mosquitia desde el punto de vista del derecho internacional y patrio.* Leon, Nicaragua.

Inter-American Indian Institute [IAII]. 1962. "Indians in the Hemisphere Today." *Indianist Yearbook,* Vol. XXII. Mexico.

Kemble, Stephen. 1885. "Report on the Mosquito Territory." *In The Kemble Papers.* Vol. 2:1780-1781. *Collections of the New York Historical Society for the Year 1884.* New York. Pp. 419-431.

Martin, A. 1894. *Handel und Kreditwesen der Moskito-Indianer.* Globus 65:100-101.

Mierisch, Bruno. 1893. "Eine Reise nach den Goldgebieten im Osten von Nicaragua." *Petermanns Mitteilungen* 39:25-39.

Moravian Church. 1849-1887. *Periodical Accounts Relating to the Missions of the Church of the United Brethren, Established Among the Heathen.* Vols. 19-34. London.

_____. 1890-1956. *Periodical Accounts Relating to the Foreign Missions of the Church of the United Brethren, Second Century.* Vols. 1-17. London.

Mörner, Magnus. 1967. *Race Mixture in the History of Latin America*. Boston: Little, Brown & Co.

Mueller, Karl A. 1932. *Among Creoles, Miskitos and Sumos: Eastern Nicaragua and Its Moravian Missions*. Bethlehem, Penn.: Comenius Press.

Nicaragua. 1895. *Documents Relating to the Affairs in Bluefields, Republic of Nicaragua in 1894*. Washington, D.C.: Published by authority of the government of Nicaragua.

Rivas, Catarino, and Carlos Aquilar Pinel. 1929. "Informe, descriptivo, económico y administrativo acerca la Mosquitia hondureña." *Revista del Archivo y Biblioteca Nacionales de Honduras* 7:250-253, 270-277.

Roberts, Orlando. 1827. *Narrative of Voyages and Excursions on the East Coast and in the Interior of Central America*. Edinburgh: Constable and Co.

Schurz, William Lytle. 1954. *This New World*. New York: E. P. Dutton & Co.

Solien, Nancie L. 1971. "West Indian Characteristics of the Black Carib." *In Peoples and Cultures of the Caribbean*. Michael Horowitz, ed. Garden City: The Natural History Press. Pp. 133-142.

Subirana, Manuel. 1938. "Letter of 27 June, 1864 to Juan de Jesús Zepeda, Bishop of Honduras." *In Algunos documentos importantes sobre los limites entre Honduras y Nicaragua*. New York. n.p.

W., M. 1732. "The Mosquito Indian and His Golden River." *In A Collection of Voyages and Travels*. Vol. 6. A. Churchill, ed. London. Pp. 285-298.

Roger Abrahams

7

THE WEST INDIAN TEA MEETING: AN ESSAY IN CIVILIZATION[1]

> A surface polish of civilization the negro can attain, and is attaining; but beyond this it seems doubtful whether he can ever advance . . . the negro will ever remain a race apart. . . . He forms a class by himself antagonistic to many, dissimilar to all.[2]

Stereotypical arguments such as the one above, especially in the use of the ethnocentric term "civilization," is difficult for us to handle today. But the man who made the remark, Charles Rampini, was not an insensitive observer of Afro-American life in Jamaica. To be sure, Rampini was repeating a cliché of the European literature on the Caribbean, but such arguments should not be so easily rejected without examining their basis.

Of course, such a stereotype served as one means of rationalizing slavery. "Civilization" commonly meant an acceptance of European practices and behavior systems; therefore, any variation from Western mores was regarded as uncivilized and was usually deemed animalistic or childlike, and often immoral. Though this kind of stereotypical argument reveals its own shortcomings, it is nonetheless useful insofar as it often points to real cultural differences that have been misapprehended. In fact, it is these very apologists for the plantocracy who, because they were apologists and were attuned to finding evidence for inferiority based on a lack of civilized life patterns, provide us with the evidence that an African conceptual or interactional stream ran very deep and was hardly diverted by enslavement. This consideration is important today as we are still being told that such African "retentions" are either a figment of the imagination or else peripheral to those elements that define the existence and boundaries of "a culture."

It is to this kind of openly prejudiced reports, then, that we may
have to turn to discern whether Afro-American societies and cultures
did in any measure survive in the New World. But to use such data
requires that we distinguish between the observation of cultural differences and their uses for stereotypical purposes. The liberal scholars
of the mid-twentieth century, in their rush to emphasize the commonality of all groups in the great American experience, eliminated the use
of this type of data because it smacked of racist ideology. These scholars
(with the obvious exception of Melville Herskovits and his students)
focused away from African continuities in the New World setting,
assuming that the professed intent of the slavers to deculturate the
slaves was effective to a high degree. Thus, it is strongly implied that,
if there are New World Negro cultures, they arise for the most part
from the shared experiences of enslavement and social exclusion.
Sidney Mintz, who has studied a number of Afro-American communities, expresses this position fully and eloquently:

> enslaved Africans were quite systematically prevented . . . with
> few exceptions . . . from bringing with them the personnel who
> maintained their homeland institutions: the complex social struc-
> tures of the ancestral societies, with their kings and courts, guilds
> and cult-groups, markets and armies were not, and could not be
> transferred. Cultures are linked as continuing patterns of and
> for behavior to such social groupings; since the groupings them-
> selves could not be maintained or readily reconstituted, the ca-
> pacities of random representatives of these societies to perpetuate
> or to recreate the cultural contents of the past were seriously
> impaired. Again, the slaves were not usually able to regroup
> themselves in the New World settings in terms of their origins;
> the cultural heterogeneity of any slave group normally meant that
> what was shared culturally was likely to be minimal . . . [How-
> ever] the slaves could and did create viable patterns of life, for
> which their pasts were pools of available symbolic and material
> resources.[3]

This prevailing view emphasizes that cultural retentions were of necessity very selective and that they were restricted to symbolic behaviors

such as music, dance, and other aspects of folklore. But to relegate such expressive behaviors to the periphery of culture is to ignore the centrality of interpersonal performance in the prosecution of life in the black community. Furthermore, it is to retain an institution-centered definition of culture at the expense of the microbehaviors and the larger interactional systems that provide the formal and informal rules by which groups live on a day-to-day, minute-to-minute basis.

It is just these expressive retentions and adaptations that are crucial to an understanding of the institutions blacks adopted in their various New World situations. One cannot explain certain parallel developments in such areas as religious practice, community governance, economics, even the concepts of the family, simply in terms of the shared plantation and slavery experience. These similarities almost certainly arose because there were shared perspectives and a common conceptual and affective system of which the slave could not be stripped, shared practices and beliefs and behavioral patterns that not only survived but were further developed in the New World setting. The importance of performance throughout Afro-American in the stylization of individual and group relationships cannot be overemphasized. These patterns of performance, models of social organization in the Old World, provided the basic groundwork on which African-like community interactions could be generated (in spite of the loss of their institutional renderings).

To understand this process, it is necessary to look closely at what happened in these New World situations to the folkways of the Africans, and to use whatever evidence is available, including the observations by ethnocentric Westerners. This process does not pose as many problems as it may seem on first glance, for once one acknowledges that the observations are made from a highly biased perspective, separating the ethnocentric from reportage is not difficult. Of course, it must also be remembered that the practices which came to the notice of these Euro-American observers were selected by them not just because they were different but because they confirmed the white stereotype of blacks as well. These may then be an overfocus on the kinds of events that confirmed this convenient European ethnocentric perspective.

This stereotypical dimension can in a sense be regarded as a positive aspect of the history of Africans in the New World, for once it is acknowledged, it is also possible to calculate its effects on the intercultural socialization procedures that arose. That is, if we are to understand the nature of the Negro practices that were and are observed, we must consider at all times the possibility that some characteristics of these occasions may have arisen in response to this European value system in its stereotypical (i.e., negative) dimension.

Interesting in this regard is the widespread West Indian ceremony of the tea meeting, for its history indicates that it was consciously imposed on black West Indian life by white missionary societies who were attempting to counteract certain African practices. In spite of this origin, the tea meeting seems to have been Africanized—or more precisely, *creolized*—almost immediately. It was accepted and incorporated in great part by the British West Indian peasantry, but it was almost immediately adapted by many of them to conform to their attitude toward what a community get-together should be. We can therefore witness a gravitation of a European ceremony toward a pattern of performance that for the most part is African in origin.

The central argument of this essay is that with ceremonies, as with the majority of performance events introduced into Afro-American life from Europe, the focus and uses of the ceremony were changed along with some aspects of the pattern of performance, and that these changes were in accord with the ethical and aesthetic demands of a conceptual system shared by Africans and Afro-Americans. This process can be understood to a degree by reference to the Creole language hypothesis. This hypothesis seeks to demonstrate that English, French, and other New World Negro Creole languages all developed from a West African Creole tongue used by traders, which is perhaps an amalgam of Portuguese and West African features.[4] The adherents of this line of argument point to the large number of underlying similarities among the various New World Creole systems, accounting for the major differences in vocabulary by relexification, the simple substitution of a different word into the phonological and morphological structure of the West African-based language. This word (and phrase) substitution does not necessarily mean that the vocabulary substituted is used with the same system of reference. Indeed, there is good evidence that the process of relexification cannot be understood without taking into account the *calque* (or "loan translation"), words that are translated into their nearest Western equivalent, but that continue to be used in the same system of reference as in Africa. Hence, this process of vocabulary substitution has ramifications for the entire semantic realm, and, as I have tried to demonstrate elsewhere, especially for the area of joking and oratory.[5]

Regardless of whether the Creole language hypothesis proves valid, something like relexification seems to have operated on this larger communication level. For example, in oratorical events throughout English-speaking Afro-America, the oratorical variety of standard English was used but in contexts demanding a different performer-audience relationship than is found in British usage, and for purposes that are in many ways diametrically opposite to the British practices. A number of these differences will be commented upon as the history and practice of tea meetings are described, but a few of these distinctions will be outlined here.

A speaker (or any other performer) is judged in Afro-American communities neither by the power of his ideas not by his ability to keep the audience stimulated and awake, but rather by his ability to heat up audience involvement and counteract this heat with the coolness of his oratory and the logic and knowledge of his argument. Rather than stilling the body to stimulate the mind (especially the conscience), performers attempt to get the whole person and the whole community involved in the performance.

This means that there is a sensed feeling of *complementarity* between the body and the mind, the hot and the cool, the involvement-centered noise of the audience and the ability of the speaker to control this noise through his performance abilities. The principle of complementarity means that opposites are rendered not only in contest or conflict terms, but also as inexorably interrelated, and as not susceptible to being resolved. Performances, then, rehearse these oppositions rather than attempt to harmonize them.

Enjoyment and edification arise simultaneously through the total involvement of performers and audience through *interlock*. Again, the principle of complementarity best explains the relationship of performer and audience. The sense of wholeness of the ceremonial encounter is induced in this aesthetic, not through the carrying out of a set progression of acts (as in the usual Euro-American church service), but through establishing a context in which repetition and redundancy become the rule. This gives an open-ended quality to the Afro-American performance and leads to a (perhaps *the*) major way in which the event is judged as effective—by how long the performers are able to sustain the involvement of the performance. *No sense of closure* is needed or called for.

As a result, this sense of wholeness is accomplished through community involvement rather than through any climax and catharsis.

The units of performance themselves have a conventional sense of completeness (one can generally sense when they are going to begin and end), but the sense of overall continuity in the performance-event overrides the closure effected by those mini-climaxes. Continuity is established between individual performances because between them the audience will perform through some kind of improvised exchange.

Givern this ethico-aesthetical complex of performance expectations, untold relexification can and did occur in the West Indies. Not only was an oratorical register of standard English introduced into many ceremonial proceedings (substituted, I would argue, for similar prestige varieties used for oratory in West Africa), but also numerous traditional performance roles and items, deriving from European antecedents. This blending of superficially European forms and Afro-American interactional patterns will be illustrated in regard to the tea meeting as it developed and exists on various British West Indian islands.

I

The tea meeting began as a testimonial gathering, introduced by Methodist missionaries into the region to teach a European and Christian mode of worship as part of the proselytizing process. The tea service was to serve as a means of counteracting the pagan, uninformed practices of the blacks. Ironically, it soon became one of the most important focal community events in which the very excesses of the African style which it set out to counteract were soon incorporated into its performance, at least in some parts of the British Caribbean. From the few documents we have, it is not possible to demonstrate all of the stages of this development. However, one may hypothesize a probable evolution from these social historical records and from the different ways in which the tea meeting is presently practiced in this culture area.

To makc such an hypothesis, one must understand why the tea meeting was introduced in the first place. From our earliest documents on the slave populations and their social customs, it is evident that Europeans were fascinated by the tremendous energies which the slaves devoted to recreation. For instance, in his wonderfully open-eyed description of Negro life on Barbados very early in the slave period, Richard Ligon not only discussed the black aptitude for making music and dancing, but he also described their Sunday afternoon entertainments.

On Sundaies in the afternoon, their musick plaies, and to dancing they go, the men by themselves, and the women by themselves, no mixt dancing. The motions are rather what they aim at, than what they do; and by that means, transgresse the lesse upon the Sunday; their hands having more of motion than their feet, and their heads more than their hands. They may dance a whole day, and neer heat themselves; yet, now and then, one of the activest amongst them will leap bolt upright, and fall in his place again, but without cutting a caper. When they have danc'd an houre or two, the men fall to wrastle, (the musick playing all the while) and their manner of wrastling is, to stand like two Cocks with heads as low as their hipps; and thrusting their heads one against another, hoping to catch one another by the leg, which sometimes they do: But if both parties be weary, and that they cannot get that advantage, then they raise their heads, by pressing' hard one against another, and so having nothing to take hold of but their bare flesh, they close, and grasp one another about the middle, and have one another in the hug, and then a fair fall is given on the back. And thus two or three couples of them are engaged at once, for an houre together, the women looking on: for when the men begin to wrastle, the women leave off their dancing, and come to be spectators of the sport.[6]

Ligon's fascination was shared by almost every British observer of slave life throughout the plantation period, but subsequent descriptions did not share his delight and openmindedness. Rather, they saw the dances and singing as evidence of all the worst attributes of the African mind. Thus, these descriptions were often flavored heavily with stereotypical responses to the retention of these savage practices. As early as 1707, Sir Hans Sloane observed: "the Negroes are much given to Venery, and although hard wrought, will at nights, or on Feast days Dance and Sing; their Songs are all bawdy, and leading that way. . . . Their Dances consist in great activity and strength of Body, and keeping time, if it can be."[7]

It is evident from the large number of reports, most of which are considerably more detailed than those quoted here, that this ambivalent sense of fascination and condemnation was the major focus of the white's stereotypical image of the African (along with the magical practice of *obeah*). This kind of activity was viewed both as indicative of the continuing depravity of the slaves and a threat to the morality

of white Creoles. William Beckford so saw it: "I have often been surprised to observe how infinitely more the negro appears to be affected
by music and dancing, than the white children . . ., and for this fact I
know not how in any manner to account. The same customs are daily
before the eyes of both; nay, the Creole (white) infants are suffered to
associate too much with those of the negroes: they converse and play
together, and are too apt, as they grow up, to copy their manners and
to imitate their vices."[8]

On the other hand, a number of observers saw the acculturative
stream flowing the other way. They noted with mixed feelings that
native-born slaves were attempting to imitate (without understanding)
the entertainments of the plantocracy. Thus, they were able to use these
entertainments as an index to the degree of "civilization" of the resident blacks. Mrs. Carmichael, one of the great Creole journal keepers,
noted a division between the entertainments given by the African slaves
and those of the native born; those of the native born were imitations
of the more genteel European practices.[9] A number of other observers,
among them the Jamaican planter, H. T. De La Beche commented on
this distinction. He describes the kinds of dances given by those who
most closely imitated the British manners:

> Negroes in giving dances or plays sometimes go to great expense.
> I was present at a dance given by my black doctor, as the head
> negro who attends the hospital is called, which must have cost
> him more than two doubloons (thirty-two dollars). There was
> madeira wine, with liquors of various kinds, and an abundance
> of meat, poultry, fruits, &c. The only money expended on this
> occasion by the guests was a small trifle each to the fiddlers.
> Most frequently the host expects remuneration for his trouble
> and viands, and is paid a certain sum each by his guests.
>
> The following is a literal copy of a negro ball ticket, which
> came into my possession, the ladies and gentlemen mentioned in
> it are the slaves upon an estate adjoining my own, and the per-
> son giving the dance a free man:—
>   "Vere, Hayses, 1824
>
>   "Wm. Gottshalk beg leave to inform the Ladies and Gentle-
> men at Dunkleys, that he intends giving a May Pole dance on
> the 3rd Saturday in May, wherein every attention shall be paid,
> and good accommodation, &c. &c.
>   Ticket————5 Shilling Each.

When a negro wishes to give a dance, he applies for leave to
the overseer, who as a matter of course grants it; the day fixed
upon is almost always Saturday, in order that they may keep it
up during that night and the next day; the dance, or play, as it is
sometimes called, commences about eight o'clock in the evening,
and although contrary to law, continues to daybreak with scarcely
any intermission, those of the old school preferring the goombay
and African dances, and those of the new, fiddles, reels, &c.
The dance is discontinued at daybreak in the morning, and the
guests are then feasted; there is generally also a dinner and sup-
per. The dance recommences the second evening, but does not
continue through the night.[10]

That such dances were widely practiced throughout the British Caribbean is confirmed by the large number of reports to that effect and by
the fact that such dances are still held occasionally in many rural communities. Today they are attended primarily by the older people, and
they are thought of as a relic of past ways. But most important, it was
worldly customs of this kind which the missionaries encountered
when they came to the area in the nineteenth century.

II

The missionaries sought to counteract these "venial" practices with
their strongest weapons. As usual, they reached into their British
armory of devices and came up with the meeting featuring tea and
testimonials, in which the proceeds went to the church.

The tea meeting was probably introduced into West Indian life in
the nineteenth century by Methodist missionaries. Indeed, the tea
meeting seems to have been a nineteenth-century development. The
Oxford English Dictionary, for instance, notes its use as denoting "a
public social meeting (usually in connexion with a religious organization) at which tea is taken," and the only reference to the term in the
dictionary is late in the century.

The earliest, but in many ways the fullest, report we have of this
ceremony appears in Mrs. Lanigan's *Antigua and the Antiguans* of
1844:

The place of all others where the greatest display of colored
beaux and belles are to be found is at the tea-parties given at the
Methodist chapel for charitable purposes.

It being a beautiful moonlight evening upon the last occasion of the kind, we determined to avail ourselves of it, and attend the party whose gastronomic performance was to commence at seven o'clock. Upon gaining the outer wall of the chapel, we found the gate guarded by a few of the "new police," and the porter appointed to receive the tickets of admission, for which the sum of 2s.6d sterling was demanded.

Passing across the court-yard, we stopped for a few moments at an open window, to view the interior. The entertainment was held in the school-room, a large apartment, forming the ground floor of the chapel; the walls of which were hung round with various pictorial embellishments, seen to advantage by the aid of numerous lamps. We entered at that auspicious moment when nearly the whole of the company were assembled, and before the actual business of the evening commenced. The effect was really very picturesque, and the scene would have been worthy of the painter's pencil. The whole of the interior, with the exception of a space all round the apartment, reserved for a promenade, was laid out with tables, placed breadthwise, surrounded by well-dressed groups, and covered with all those delicate "cakes and confections,". . . .

After the prayer, a few hymns were played and sung; during which period, I took the opportunity of walking with my companion around the space already mentioned, in order to obtain a full view of the assembled guests; and then followed some speeches by the missionaries and one or two of the leading members, which afforded much interest to the assembled group.

One old gentleman—a very excellent man, by the way, but rather too much given to prosing while on the pulpit—spoke in favour of the tea-meetings and of the chapel debt, (to pay off which these entertainments were given as one means of raising money). Another preacher gave us a long rambling account of a bowie-knife; paid his compliments to the ladies, which were received with a grin of applause; said how much better it was to have these agreeable parties, and thus raise money, instead of the old way of trudging from house to house, begging to inmates to put down their names for certain sums, and attributing the happy change to the fertile genius of the "tender sex"; and concluded by remarking, that in the course of a week or two there would be a bazaar held at the court-house, for the purpose of raising more cash to liquidate the chapel debt, at which he understood there was to be a *solid lunchtable* spread besides one for confectionary; and although he liked *tea* very well, he liked *lunch* a great deal better.

After Mr. ——— had concluded, a mild, quiet-looking man rose who spoke of social intercourse, referred to Job's sons and daughters; talked of heaven and heavenly enjoyments; and then after a few more speeches, more compliments to the ladies, a few more hymns, and a concluding prayer, came the cloaking, shawling and bonneting, we returned home.[11]

Subsequent reports indicate that the practice became popular but was immediately secularized in several ways. Like the "grand balls," the tea meetings, in some areas, came to be a resource for the entrepreneur who made the arrangements and who charged for them. In time, proceedings were also lengthened into the all-night and sometimes licentious ceremonials characteristic of the earlier Afro-American celebrations. Greville John Chester, for one, notes in his *Transatlantic Sketches:* "Sometimes a cottager in want of money will give a tea, charging a shilling entrance, and the entertainment lasts till sunrise next morning. These teas lead to a great deal of immorality, and the evil is rather increased than lessened by the vociferous singing of the most sacred hymns throughout the whole night."[12]

In a similar vein, the Reverend H.V.P. Brockhurst says of his Guyanese parishioners:

There is another institution, of a pseudo-religious character, which is largely patronized by the natives especially in country districts, and that is the "tea meeting." Instrumental music is allowed in these tea meeting gatherings; the people sing heartily and lustily enough to the sound of the music. Only sacred (or, as some are pleased to call it, "secret") music is allowed, and every thing goes on well for a time, but by-and bye the musicians ("musicianers") play a sacred march, and the friends take up the musical strain by keeping time with their feet or by marching round with a limitation of the number of hops in each bar of the music.[13]

This type of dancing, however, was not common to tea meeting practices elsewhere.

The one element of the tea meeting that seems to have persevered in spite of the numerous changes was the alternation of speeches and songs. That the songs and speeches were secularized in some places is also clear, though the introduction of secular performance pieces necessitated a distinction between *tea meeting* and *service of song,* the latter then conforming more or less to the tea parties as described by Mrs. Lanigan.

The tea meeting likely developed as the major form of entertainment for the community in the last generation of the nineteenth century and flourished until World War II. By the 1960s, it was universally judged moribund, though it is still given on a number of islands. While numerous different kinds of performances developed on each island, it became known primarily for the fine, eloquent speeches which the occasion elicited. These speeches, which certainly originated in congregation distinction and testimonial tradition, became the keynote to the ceremony. The tea meeting is also mentioned in early twentieth-century reports from the farthest reaches of the British West Indies, most notably in two sentimental discussions of the practice on Barbados (where, though the practice is still alive in the countryside, it is reported to be dead by Bridgetown reporters) and in another two from observers on Jamaica. The first of these discussions is as follows:

> . . . the local tea-meeting, which seems to have disappeared from the scene shortly after the conclusion of the first world war, requires, I think, a special note. It was a sort of prolonged concert whose main features were songs, both solo and choral, an abundance of refreshments, and a type of oratory that delighted in the display of resounding polysyllabic words (some of them specially coined for the occasion), and elaborate alliterative allusions to the great names of history and literature. Preparations for the tea-meeting were begun several months before the event, and admission was by ticket: one shilling. The tea-meeting, usually held in a school hall or in the lodge of a friendly society, adorned with evergreen branches and flowers, began at nine o'clock with an oration by the vice-chairman, although for an hour previously the choir-master and his carefully rehearsed choir would have been welcoming the in-coming audience with a

selection fro their repertoire. The vice-chairman would then address the gathering reminding them that he was no great orator "such as Plato or Dido, Demosthenes or Socrates," but only the forerunner of the "man of gladness" who was now to entertain them. Amid great cheering the chairman would then take his seat, and the vice would introduce him, exhorting him as being "fundamental and groundamental enough to take and hold his place like Mark Anthony or Cicero, or Blake or Drake, or Words-worth or Tennyson." etc., etc. "Take it and hold it," he would conclude "until the cock says *Claro Clarum* pronouncing or announcing the break of day." The chairman would then address the audience at some length, after which the vice would intro-duce to the chairman those who would provide the various items of the programme: There would be solos, choruses, monologues, dialogues, and "trialogues." The chairman would comment on each item until the stroke of midnight, when there would be an intermission of two hours for refreshment: large quantities of bread, biscuits, sponge cakes and puddings, with large pots of boiling hot tea and chocolate. Afterwards the songs and speeches would be resumed and continue until daybreak.[14]

In a somewhat more discursive mood, Louis Lynch, former mayor of Bridgetown and Barbadian social historian, notes the demise of this ceremeony in *The Barbados Book*. In addition to giving portions of a number of speeches, Lynch states:

Tea Meetings in Barbados were held usually at night, Sunday night preferably, and were greatly looked forward to by the working-class of both sexes. For the modest outlay of sixpence a cheering cup of rich brew could be obtained, besides several buns, during the course of the evening. There was a kindly old-world custom too of pressing upon the parting guest a few rusks, flaky and delicate in crust, which were prudently wrapped in the wayfarer's pocket-handkerchief to provide comfort and sus-tenance during the long trek home. . . .

Entertainment at these functions usually took the form of vocal items from the ladies and flights of oratory from the men. . . . The theme of the men's speeches might be historical, e.g., "The Battle of Balaclava" declaimed with mime, gesture and much lurid detail, or scriptural, e.g., "David's Lament for Ab-

salom." There was, however, always something educational or
edifying about it in intent and in this lay the social significance
of the Tea Meeting which was not only an opportunity for get-
ting together, eating and drinking, but had as its worthy objective the training in public speaking of those who orated, the
enlightenment of those who attended.

Speeches had to be prepared, quotations memorized, pas-
sages from Holy Writ learnt by heart. . . . It was traditional that
the speeches of the men be highly seasoned with a Latin that
would hardly have won Ciceronian approval. These oratorical
masterpieces were usually the result of weeks of "scorning de-
lights and living laborious days" painfully inflicting upon an
unwilling and often treacherous memory a mass of *memorabilia.*[15]

Martha Warren Beckwith briefly reports tea meetings from Jamaica
from the same period. She too notes the importance of speeches, but
she indicates that the ceremony developed in a different direction in
Jamaica:

. . . forms of folk wit develop under the pressure of social competition as part of the entertainment at group gatherings. The
great occasions for merrymaking are at weddings, at funerals,
and during the special festivals of the Christmas and New Year
season and (a holiday today going out of fashion) of Emancipation Day on August 2. Dancing parties may be given at any time
in private homes, and these are always accompanied by a certain
formality. All-day picnics are held in mid-summer and all-night
"tea meetings" either then or more often at the New Year. A
single entertainer gives this party, to which admission is charged.
At one end of the leaf-covered booth erected for occasion, a
platform is constructed on which sits the "chairman" who is
chosen to preside. Benches for the onlookers range about three
sides. The girls attend in new frocks, wearing ribbons and other
ornaments all of a prearranged color. After a succession of formal toasts and set dances, the "queen" selected for the occasion
is unveiled by the highest bidder for that privilege, and there is
an elaborate cake to be sold in slices or sometimes small cakes in
fancy patterns (called "show bread" or "crown bread"). After
this the night wears through with riddles, games, stories or other

forms of amusement. In Mandeville there is no queen, but the men vie with one another in presenting the girls with "thrupence worth of crown bread," to which the lady is supposed to make some such witty acknowledgement as "I will not eat it. I will not drink it, but I will send it to England to buy a pair of shoes to wear to church, and instead of the shoes crying 'Ne' pass! ne' pass! they will cry "Love! love!' ''[16]

Finally, David DeCamp briefly describes tea meetings on Jamaica in the 1950s and 1960s in his discussion of the practice of mock bidding:

The most colorful of the social events involving mock bidding is the "tea meeting." The tea meeting . . . is simply a fund-raising event, which may be sponsored by any organization. . . . Inside the meeting the crowd can buy food and drink, including tea, of course, but beer and rum are more popular. A program is provided, which can be brought to a halt at any moment by a bid to "mek him stop" and can be got under way again only by the inevitable final bid to "mek him go on." It is this mock bidding which is the real source of revenue, and a successful tea meeting may net more than a hundred pounds. People of all classes attend. . . .

The program is a matter of local tradition and varies from district to district, though very little from decade to decade. . . . The orations and other set pieces in the program . . . are . . . reminiscent of traditional school graduate exercises, and a few features of the program echo considerable antiquity. There is always a veiled queen, for example, and in some communities she is seated in a fishing boat on the stage or is surrounded by farm produce. . . .

The program is presented by local talent, and mainly consists of songs, recitations, and orations, all delivered in exaggerated high style, an elocution-class parody of the prestige standard English stressed by local schools. Exaggerated intonation and rhythm, pretentious vocabulary (often malapropisms) and Latin or pseudo-Latin quotations are all prized. . . . Recitations include nursery rhymes and other pieces from elementary school readers, past and present. Pieces of African or Jamaican origin do not appear. For example, I have never heard an Anancy story as part of a tea meeting program. "The House that Jack Built" is a favorite, as is an old alphabet rhyme constructed on the same incremental pattern, presumably originally taken from some old school textbook. . . .:

A for the apple that was hanging upon the tree.
B for the boy that pluck the apple, that was hanging upon the tree.
C is for the constable that saw the boy that pluck the apple, that was hanging upon the tree.
D is for the dog that chased the constable, that saw the boy, that pluck the apple, that was hanging upon the tree.
E is for the eagle that flout the dog, that chase the constable, that saw the boy, that pluck the apple, that was hanging upon the tree. *Etc.*

The crowd participated during these performances in three ways. First, of course, they bid to stop or resume the program. Second they applaud and encourage their favorite performers.

Applause may take the form of whistling or hand-clapping but most characteristically consists of the shouted syllable "gee!" This is shouted in unison at the end of each couplet or quatrain of a song or poem and at each rhetorical pause in orations and other prose recitations. I have no idea of the origin of the word, not even whether it represents the injection *gee* (from *Jesus*) or, as is claimed by some participants, the alphabetic letter *G*. It is very effective, however, in accentuating the progressively accelerating rhythm of the speaker, comparable to the cries of "Amen! Yes, Lord!" etc. which punctuate the sermon of the revivalist preacher. Booing and hissing sometimes occur but only as good-natured ribbing among friends, not as serious heckling. Only once did I see a performer really disgruntled at being forced to step down because of negative bidding.

Third, the crowd "play the sticks." That is, many of them bring with them . . . a piece of thick bamboo . . . a small stick to beat against the bamboo or to scrape along its side. A few may bring along a large and a small piece of steel pipe for the same purpose. . . . The players match the chanted rhythm of the orator, and the effect is hypnotic. A few skilled stick players can effectively support their favorite speaker by creating such an irresistible rhythm that people jump to their feet and start dancing to the recitation.[17]

III

Quite clearly, the focal element of the tea meeting is the oratory. Just as clearly, the reason this ceremony caught on throughout the West Indies was that it provided the occasion for a public demonstration of speechmaking abilities. But from the speeches given by these observers, as well as those noted in a number of other communities, the style of oratory seems to have been derived primarily from the Afro-American's imitation of British patterns, an imitation that has been viewed as often ludicrous, even by such a schooled investigator as David DeCamp.

The style used in the speeches was the "formal style" of standard English, which was apparently learned from British sources. This style is characterized, as Martin Joos points out, by detachment of the speaker from the audience and by cohesion of text so that the psychically removed audience may easily follow it. Virtually each key word defines the speaker's removal from the audience; the speaker effects this removal by using predominantly elaborate sentence constructions, precise pronunciations, and a self-consciously ornamental diction. The intent of the speaker is to state implicitly that he is there not to interact so much as to inform his audience.[18] This sense of removal also makes the audience focus on the content and form of the text, forcing "the text to fight its own battles. Form becomes its dominant character.,"[19] but other stylistic and content features must be consistent with the form.

In most regards, both the content and form of the speeches given in tea meetings are doubtless derived from this British tradition. This fact does not necessarily constitute evidence of total acculturation to the British model, however, for numerous other facets of the eloquence tradition differ greatly from British practices. An obvious example is a failure of imitation, notably in certain hypercorrections of pronunciation and diction, and in severe misunderstandings of the meaning of some of the most elaborate words and phrases (especially those in Latin and other foreign tongues). On closer examination, it is seen that these "mistakes" do not occur because of failures of understanding by the speakers or their audience, but rather because of a different expectation and attitude toward the ongoing speech event. To be sure, certain of the attributes of formal style are employed, but for purposes and effects that differ in crucial respects from British practices.

The basis of this misunderstanding lies in the stereotypical assumption that Africans brought with them no culture (or that they became deculturated early on) and that this lack included no traditions of eloquence.[20] To the contrary, we have ample evidence that similar eloquence traditions throughout Africa, that effective oratory is regarded as central to the prosecution of life there, and that these patterns of performance were transplanted and acclimatized to the new plantation environment. This is not to say that the speechmaking traditions of Africa and Great Britain did not differ. Where the differences were greatest the African style of performance prevailed, and thus it was that "bad imitation" was attributed to the Afro-American orators.

Perhaps the most important difference between the two traditions lies in the functional expectations of these speeches. As Joos points out, the formal style emphasizes the imparting of information or wisdom and is text-oriented. Therefore, the use of formal style creates a distance between performer and audience which the performer then capitalizes upon in his teaching; his expectation is that the audience will listen in silence, judging the aptness and validity of his argument. This distancing technique is not the norm in Afro-American performances. Rather, any Afro-American performance is expected to elicit verbal and kinesthetic audience participation. An orator must therefore not only inform, but he must also contend successfully with those elements in the environment that would eliminate the coordination of the group—forces such as rudeness, noise, and others vying for the spotlight. A performance is judged in terms of how well it brings about this coordination. The West Indian orator is judged not only by the information *(truth, facts)* he imparts and the copiousness of his delivery, but also by his ability to convert the noise of the audience into a guided, effective, appropriate response to his words.

Thus, part of the expectation pattern of these eloquence performances is that functionally there will be a good deal of noise so that the effective speaker can demonstrate his abilities to bring about decorum and to guide the response in a competititve manner. This aspect provides "the basis of the symbolism of most village rituals. Meetings begin with a call for Conduct, and descend into 'noise' and Creole via argument.''[21] The opposition between the speaker and the audience, in such cases, is seen as a creative and expected one. As Reisman suggests, this opposition may also be viewed as a clash of codes, between manners and rudeness, and between formal standard English and Creole, the Creole being identified in the West Indian mind with noise and contentiousness ("vextation").

The features characteristic of the tea meeting—the eloquent speechmaking, the competition, the all-night duration of the performance, and the alternation between speeches and songs—are not unique to this ceremony. Indeed, this is the modal pattern for the whole series of festive ceremonies surrounding rites of passage and other person-centered rituals. Wedding feasts, first-night wakes, sendoffs, thanksgivings (to celebrate the end of an illness or the return from a trip or some other ending to a transitional event), all share these characteristics of performance. Moreover, in the most formal of these ritual occasion, as does Reisman's study of Antiguan speech.[23] I have siminated to keep the proceedings going. Just as in the tea meeting, this man of words may be called the "chairman" (or "master of ceremonies"). Keeping the proceedings going means maintaining some sense of decorum in the midst of noise, making sure that everyone who wants to speak or sing is given the opportunity, and perhaps most important, if no competitive element has been introduced into the proceeding, ensuring that this is done.

These competitive elements are a matter of ritual and have nothing to do with hostility between individuals. Rather, they are crucial to both the interactional and the aesthetic systems of the group. David DeCamp's article on mock bidding[22] gives an example of one of the play-competition devices used by Jamaicans on virtually every public occasion, as does Reisman's study of Antiguan speech.[23] I have similarly heard a number of other mock-arguments contrived, such as the Vincentian wedding feast in which the bride and groom were chastised and defended for "sticking" the cake with a knife and fork. The Herskovitses registered their experience of culture shock in viewing a first-night wake in Toco, Trinidad, in which the two chairmen had a fight over which hymns were to be sung and in what order—a proceeding which the Herskovitses were informed was "a matter of usage."[24] This competitive pattern can go far beyond simply engineering a mock-argument. In their description of the wake, for instance, the Herskovitses detail the competition that arose during the hymn singing, between the group in the yard and the one in the house. This opposition, often expressed simply by noise in the yard, occurs in many such familial ceremonies throughout this culture area.

While the tea meeting is similar to many other ceremonies throughout the area, all of these others are associated with transitions in personal lives, including marriage feasts and first-night wakes. As discussed earlier, all of these individual-based familial ceremonies are organized around the talents of a man of words who is entrusted not only with entertaining the group but also with keeping the proceedings going and at the desired pitch of participation by those involved. As with the chairmen in the tea meeting, the man of words makes sure that everyone performs who cares to; he does so by registering everyone's name in some way, introducing everyone, and giving some kind of closing remarks.

A large number of the community are called upon to give speeches in an approximation of formal standard English, thus demonstrating the general language ability of the community. These festivities are all associated with the home and the homely virtues; they are occasions in which family and friends sit down together and share food and "talking sweet." The content of the speeches reflects this orientation, and they are most commonly on homiletic themes, emphasizing the conscious value system of the community. Marriage and family solidarity, order, cooperation, deference, responsibility, cleanliness, and so on are rehearsed as they are ritually practiced. These are explicitly rites of incorporation (or reincorproation), and what the celebrant is incorporated into is the extended family system. As far as the formal code and the eloquence are concerned, this means that the formal code and the eloquence are identified with these familial virtues, this conscious ideal system. Not insignificantly, the ceremony is held in the home. In contrast, the tea meeting does not take place in the home, hence, as a nonfamilial eloquence ceremony it is almost unique. The opportunity for eloquence provided by the mission churches also took eloquence out of the house and yard. In a very real sense it produced a traditional amalgamation with the seasonal festivities (like Christmas and Carnival) which are held on the streets and which are notable for their licentious, often antisocial qualities and for their performances primarily in the Creole tongue.

At the risk of overschematizing, the yard-road dichotomy must be briefly described if the present constitution of the tea meeting is to be understood. Though the operation of the matrifocal household system has been somewhat misconstrued, it *is* the modal unit throughout the Negro New World. While many communities, including some peasant communities in the British West Indies, do have a high degree of conjugal stability and, consequently, a responsible resident male in the household, the woman of the household is still the center of family life and the protector of the homely virtues. The woman's role is fixed by agreements made prior to the conjugal union, when the separate domains of the husband and wife are detailed and, in most cases, clearly divided. Most commonly the man must provide the residence for the woman, and it must be substantial if they are to marry. Once provided, this is the woman's domain, and the man is given little sense of place there. In not being permitted their due role in the home, men are not emasculated; rather, they are recognized as different from and opposed to females—though their opposition is expressed in terms of complementarity and interlock.[25]

The man's place is in the fields or rumshop or cardtable at the crossroads. He is judged by how well he keeps company with others, and she by how well she keeps to herself and maintains her house and her household. According to Peter Wilson, women are usually viewed in terms of respectability, while men by their reputation—and their reputation is formed by how many friends they have (of both sexes) and by how much style or "flash" they exhibit in public.[26] Thus, a male may be judged by the conscious and sentimental family-based ideal and by an unconscious ego-centered male ideal. Since both systems emphasize cooperation and sharing, they seldom come into conflict.

Paradoxically, a man may be both approved and condemned by these same criteria. For example, in the distribution of his resources, a conflict often arises between his familial and his friendship obligations. The gravitation toward street-life, even in peasant communities, is expected of men (especially young men), and yet it provides the basis for conflict and rejection within the family unit. This situation leads, among other things, to an often-stated attitude that mother-child love is much stronger than husband-wife love, for children never betray as men do. Thus, even when the men are excellent providers, they feel that time is best spent away from home.

This consideration is pertinent to our present discussion because formal standard English, since it is used in the home-based ceremonies, is associated with the family virtues, the conscious ideals of the community. Street friends are invited into the home on these occasions specifically to hear everyone (especially the men) catechetically perform in accordance with the system of the household, and in the most elevated and content-oriented code in the repertoire, or in songs that adopt the sentimental model of family life (also associated with female attitudes and generally sung by the women). A byproduct is that truth and knowledge and decorum are associated with eloquence, and in contrast (but from the household point of view), ignorance and lies and rudeness are associated with the crossroad and, in crucial ways, with the Creole language (variously called "bad," "broken," and "broad"). In the tea meeting, the two varieties and behavior systems come together, often in interlocking contest. Many of the conflicts in values and ideals are thereby rehearsed in a dramatically creative and entertaining, if not resolving, manner. One of its attractions, then, is in bringing community conflicts to the surface and in playing them out in a dramatically satisfying way by revealing them as complementarities.

The common denominator of the tea meeting is the playful confrontation between "talking bad" Creole and the ornamental varieties of "talking sweet" and between the systems of behavior they symbolically represent. The chairmen are the most direct representatives of the conscious ideal system and are a carryover from the family and house-based rites of passage feasts. Also retained from such occasions is the necessity (a consciously expressed one) to keep the ceremony going all night, and to do so by eliciting the participative energies of the group, generally through a combination of eloquence and playful competition. The practices of hanging flowers and fruits around the hall and of serving midnight refreshments seem to have been a common feature of both public and private occasions in the pre-tea meeting era. The only vestiges of the European church background of the tea meeting are the alternation of speech and song and the use of Biblical subjects for the speeches.

IV

Much of our knowledge of the early tea meetings comes from observing performances on the smaller islands in the British Windwards and Leewards. Meetings are still held, or were until very recently, on Barbados, Jamaica, Union, Tobago, Grenada, Antigua, Nevis, St. Kitts, and St. Vincent. Actual performances have been recorded by DeCamp on Jamaica, by Reisman on Antigua, and by Peter Mallalieu and myself on Nevis and by myself on St. Vincent.[27] The Nevis and St. Vincent traditions will be described here.

According to reports by older Nevisians on Nevis, the tea meeting developed at least as early as the turn of the century into a secularized tradition. A strong division was therefore made between *tea meeting* and *service of song*. The tea meeting was commonly held during mango season (June-September) during the times of the full moon. By report, before World War II, the good tea meeting performers could find a tea meeting on some part of the small island during full moon during that entire period. In this country where *jumbies* (the walking dead) are feared, the moon was important to make night-time travel possible.

The service of song, on the other hand, can be held during any season, but it must come on a Sunday or Wednesday night, and also during a full moon. This service is very similar to the tea meeting as it was first held on the island (once again, by report of the older people). It is commonly held in a church rather than in the meeting hall which is customary for the tea meeting. The service of song is run by a chairman and a vice-chairman who, as at tea meetings, may drink rum in front of everyone. The church is decorated, but not as ornately as for the tea meeting, which typically has the "harbor" of fruits hanging from the ceiling. Furthermore, the serving of *tea* (any hot beverage but usually chocolate, *cocoa tea*) is not obligatory, and the meeting seldom goes on until daybreak. Tickets are sold to benefit the church. The chairmen are not paid for their services either with money or with the special cakes baked for them as part of the payment in the tea meeting.

The chairmen use the same techniques of introducing speakers or songs as they do in tea meetings, but they attempt to keep the speeches solely to Biblical and homiletic subjects. It is assumed that all solo performances given will be similarly circumscribed. After each solo performance a hymn is sung by the church choir; the subject of the solo and the hymn provides the thematic material which the chairmen use for their speeches, at least in their introductory remarks. The major "performances" of the evening are those between the chairman and vice-chairman, and between them and the speakers from the floor, to see who knows scripture best. Furthermore, the "cool" of the men of words is constantly tested by the noise emanating from the audience. A noise is guaranteed to exist because there will almost always be a group (often women) who heckle the speakers from the rear, shouting boasts and deprecatory remarks from the rear of the church, directing them primarily at the chairman. As opposed to the tea meeting, there are no prizes given; therefore, the sense of competition is not nearly as strongly expressed in the service of song.

The Nevis tea meeting provides almost a total résumé of the history of entertainments on the island. The folklore of Nevis, one of the British "Mother Colonies" settled in 1628, derives almost totally from British countryside traditions. At Christmas, for instance, there are touring groups of wassailers, morris dancers, mummers who present folk plays like the St. George play. The tea meeting, on the other hand, has many of the features of the British Spring and Midsummer festivals, for it features not only a king and queen and their court, but also players like the fighting wooers and the bereft mother and baby who perform during the festivities.[28]

All of these performances are regarded as exhibiting the highest abilities of the community. They may be comic and occasionally even obscene, but they must use the Nevisian's approximation of British performance codes, techniques, and patterns. Consequently, the songs gravitate toward the sentimental; indeed, this is what most of them are called, "sentimental songs." The speeches, whether performed by one of the chairmen or a person from the floor, must be in proper ornate and eloquent style. Although these performances and the code in which they are couched are derived from British sources, it would be a mistake to see them as European. Rather, there exists an undeclared war between the performers and the audience, between these forces of decorum and those of rudeness and noise. Furthermore, the outcome is forever in doubt. The outsider may feel that rudeness is usually the winner, for the hall is usually full of uncontrolled sound. Thus, in Nevis the tea meeting is held not for the performances but for the chance to have a confrontation between the crowd and the performers.

In this battle, the king and queen, those who perform in the very middle of the ceremony, provide the median and the norm of sanity for the occasion. They speak as a king and a queen ought, in the most elevated diction and in proper discursive style. Their speeches, however, are satirical, focusing on the ills of the island, the government's lack of responsiveness to the peoples needs, and the whole idea of royalty itself. Significantly, they are the one group of performers who have little trouble commanding the attention of the crowd.

The rest of the evening is a constant battle between the denizens of decorum, represented most fully by the chairmen, and those of chaos, represented by the hecklers. Each attempts to get the attention of the crowd; the bedlam that results has lately led the chairmen who remain on the island to hesitate to play that role.[29]

A number of subsidiary contests are built into this opposition. For instance, the king and queen can be regarded as contesting with each other. They must come from different villages, and at the beginning of the performance they are each picked up at their home by a "Big Drum," a band consisting of fife, snare, and bass drums. These adherents then march with them to the meeting house, and they are jokingly evaluated in terms of how many people each has as an entourage. Later, their speeches and those of their court are judged competitively, though once again the contest is jocular. This is also the tone of what one might call the "battle of the cakes." When tea and cakes are served, the king and queen are called to cut a cake ceremonially, and the process is described in swordplay terms by the chairman, who at the end of the cutting declares a winner.

There are many other contest features. In addition to the battles between the courting couple, numerous other aspects of the battle of the sexes emerge during the performances. Women sing a number of songs about the perfidy of the opposite sex, and men answer in kind. There is a sense of competition between the chairmen, of course, and there are other men of words who arise from the floor, each attempting to show that he, and not any of the chairmen, is "the cock with the brightest comb." Each attempts to show this superiority by making speeches even more grandiloquent and knowledgeable than the next one, or by making a mocking speech in which the irony is often couched in some variety other than the oratorical standard.

The pattern of performance then is one in which dramatic oppositions arise in a number of forms, all of which are in contention simultaneously and all of which everyone heartily enjoys. But these oppositions are not uncontrolled, for as is true of Afro-American performances generally, opposites are viewed not agonistically (i.e., susceptible to being presented in conflict and resolution terms) but rather as balanced complementarities.

This complementarity principle is boldly stated in the major framing action of the ceremony—the coming together in marriage of the king and the queen. The two (with their courts) who come from different towns are brought together at the meeting hall. There they are greeted with a marriage-song:

> Behold the bridegroom cometh
> And may we enter in?
> All sorrows now have vanished
> With veil as white as snow.

Throughout the evening this coupling of the sexes is mentioned constantly; the coupling is expected to be not so much a harmonious as a vigorous and contentious one. In the tea service at the midpoint of the occasion, cakes are cut ceremoniously, as in the West Indian wedding, and with the same type of ritual argument encountered in a nuptial feast. But this is only the primary metaphor for presenting entertaining contentions, in such terms of complementarity.

After the entrance of the king and queen, they and their court and attendants sit on the stage. All subsequent performances take place before them, ostensibly for their pleasure. On one side of the stage, the chairmen sit at a table. The stage, then, is defined as the place of performance and decorum, and the rest of the room is available for movement, noise, and nonsense.

After the court is assembled, the vice-chairman, who is responsible for compiling the list of performers, makes a speech in which he welcomes everyone and calls for volunteers to give their names and the title of their performances. The chairman or the vice-chairman then introduces each act with elaborate words, which are sometimes answered by the other chairman before the performance begins. This speech often serves both to commend the departing performer and to introduce the next.

> Peace then, ladies and gentlemen, my gracious king and queen, and for the advice of the foregone speaker, I now adding to some of his sentiments. I would say *durante bamitsha quo momentum mori;* through your life of pleasure, remember that. After that comes *ecce homo,* here comes the man. Now gentlemen, I beg you attention as we bring before you one Mr._____

for a speech. Mr._____, toil on, and in your toiling rest on the next side at home. [Much applause always follows this little "run" which is used to introduce every performer.] Now, one Mr._____. He's coming, so large and strong, Christian friends, ladies and gentlemen, make way for him along.

At some time early in the evening, when the first onslaught of noise begins to threaten the order of the meeting, one of the chairmen will give the "A is for attention" speech. The form and content of this speech are more standard than those of any of the other speeches from these men.

Decorum! Ladies and gentlemen, we must remember the alphabet and what it teaches. The alphabet of the English language has only twenty-six letters, and there may be times when you have to take plenty of those letters; but tonight we take just six. These six are A, B, C, D, J and P. Ladies and gentlemen, there's attention, that's A. A is for Adam, the first one that God made; that's why A upside down stands for attention. B is for Bethlehem, where Christ was born. So the upside down B stands for Behavior. Ladies and gentlemen, there's more; there's C. C is for Cain, who killed his brother Abel. C upside down, C stands for Conduct. D is for poor old fatherless Daniel who was cast in the lion's den. Turn that upside down, D stands for Decorum. etc., etc. Okay. J. J is for Jesus and Jehovah. Turn it upside down, J stands for Justice. It is a precious for all that brings us all to P. P is for Pharoah, the enemy of the Israelites. Turn the letter P upside down, P stands for Peace. Now ladies and gentlemen, Christian friend and men and brethren you know that Christ himself was lost. And when leaving this earth he said "My peace I give to you. Peace I left with you." Peace eternal, forever, amen.

A number of other performances now ensue from the audience. There are two types of speeches, the comic recitation and the serious and competitive orations. The latter invoke the same kind of speech patterns as those of the chairmen, but in addition they often end with a boast.

Unto the Queen in her Royal Highness; unto the King, in his Royal Majesty; and to all the rest of the Royal Family, allow me to be here. So therefore I must now say *beneficio accura al monastico eventora,* which is to say that stand rest assured in mighty names. Here too I must say, *allamento in dovi,* which is to say I arise from my seat without any doubt. So Mr. Chairman, sir, I must now say I will turn to my topic. My topic will be about King Solomon. King Solomon, you know, he loved many strange women. Woman of the Hahabite, the Hibarite, the Wipparite, the Riparite, the Sybarite, the Zibarite. If there is any cock or hen with a brighter comb than me, tell them I said to come over.

More commonly, such speeches gloss their Biblical texts at great length.

The comic speeches utilize the same conventions and thus the same patterns of expectation. They make their humorous point by suddenly introducing a humorous rhyme in Creole, concerning a subject which is outlandish, especially in this setting.

Mister Chairman, sir, ladies and gentlemen. To the King in his excellent majesty, and the Queen, her royal highness. And all the rest of the family. May God bless them all. Mr. Chairman, sir, ladies and gents, my speech will be about the moonlight night. Mr. Chairman, sir, one night I went walking in the moonlight night. On my way going, I hear a great grunting uunnh!! Mr. Chairman, sir, ladies and gentlemen, I go a little farther, I still hear the same grunting uunnh!! I get frightened now. I go on a little farther, I still hear the same grunting, louder and louder, uunnh!! Mr. Chairman, sir, ladies and gentlemen, when I looked, when I peeked, I see sandfly got a great hoe, digging a chigger out of mosquito toe.

At some point in the middle of the proceedings, at around midnight, someone begins singing:

Blow de fire, le'e' bu'n (let it burn)
Blow de fire, le'e' bu'n
Blow de fire, le'e' bu'n
We all want tea.

Miss _____ put de kettle on
Miss _____ put de kettle on
Miss _____ put de kettle on
We all want tea.

Suppose I sing a funny song
Suppose I sing a funny song
Suppose I sing a funny song
We all want tea.

Huge vats of "cocoa tea" are then brought in and served, while the chairmen auction off the ceremonial cakes. This phase of the performance begins with the king cutting the cake with his "sword" in great mock gravity, proclaiming all the while that he is doing battle for the country. This leads directly to the major speeches, those made by the king, the queen, and their court. These speeches, strongly ironic in tone, make references to the local government's inaction. (Many of the references in the following speech are to the much celebrated visit of Queen Elizabeth and Prince Philip to the island in the winter of 1966.)

King: Tonight, my dear people, I come here into your country to pay you all a visit. I'm passing through your island home tonight, Love to all. I love you all as Jesus Christ loveth the whole world. And tonight, my dear people, I come at your island, to see the condition of your island. I come to you to see the need of the peoples. Tonight, my dear peoples, for the few days I am here, I visit the places, villages and them, see what they are looking like. And my dear people, I buss around to all the villages and them, and I see the conditions are serious. And one night I lay down, and I studied, and I wondered how come all the poor people live here in this country, Nevis. I say my mind. Some of them is only living by the mercy of our blessed Lord and Savior, Jesus Christ. So my dear people, tonight, I must say that when I go back to my island, I promise to you that I will try to develop your island a little better than what it is. I announce that by the year 1968 that your island will be better for the white man's fault. So my dear people, all that I have to hand you on, I ask you all to live with one another in peace. I come to the island, I love your island. You all have love inside here, lovely place, and I love the island, Nevis. So my dears, sleep tonight. I am your king, and you are my dear peoples. So my dear peoples, I will say to you all I love you and I glad to be here with you all tonight.

Queen: Goodnight, ladies and gentlemen. Now, I'm your majesty queen. I do hope you all are looking at me, queenie, for this I know, you all see me in pictures, but you never see me face to face. (much laughter) So small and great please look at your majesty queen keenly tonight. Now I am a tour around the Caribbean. I just take a small flight to Nevis tonight and in a few hours I will be back to Canada. Since I am here for the past few hours, I met a shortage of water around the whole island. So sorry to hear about that. I must do something about that, in the near future. Cotton grows, well I am putting cotton to one dollar and fifty cents per pound this year. (much applause) Shopkeepers, there'll be a little sad news for you. I'll be putting down sugar for three cents per pound. Agricultural men your wages will be improved according to your work. Nurses, around the fifteenth of June, I will give you a higher wages in the hospitals. (Yeah.) All you has to do is pray that the queen arrive back in London safely. As I look around, God knows from the eyes of you all that I'm for you all. Anywhere, I'll do something about that in the near future. Well, I won't take up much of your time because on Nevis life is too hard; you have to go to sleep in the morning. And who all don't see the queen on the stage tonight shall meet me in Charlestown on the 22nd of January. (much tumult) I know you all will want to see the queen, but no money. But I'll make some arrangement to take you poor people in busses to town. So just get dressed and stay by the wayside and I'll tell you all one and what kind of busses I will get for you all. Well I wishing you all a happy 1966, just so that the queen may arrive in England safely, and you all will be better off. Good night, everyone. (much applause.)

After these speeches, the earlier kinds of performances begin again, continuing commonly until cockcrow (otherwise, the audience feels it has been cheated.) The pace slows considerably, and many of the children in the audience fall asleep in their parents' arms. Nevertheless, the speechmaking, noise, and hilarity continue to the very end.

The tea meeting on St. Vincent in the British Windwards is somewhat closer to the earlier church-based ceremonies. It is generally arranged by entrepreneurs, as on Nevis, but for the benefit of a church. The ceremonies are held on three occasions—Christmas, Easter, and August Monday (Emancipation Day)—and the speeches given must be appropriate to these occasions. Thus, on two of the three, the orations must be on Biblical subjects. The major contest which occurs centers on the knowledge of the "facts" of the Bible (or, in August, of history), and each such speech is followed by a hymn or anthem from the choir.

The Nevisian distinction between *tea meeting* and *service of song* is paralleled by the Vincentian dichotomy between *tea meeting* and *soiree party and dance*. Whereas the service of song was the direct descendant of the religious tea service on Nevis, the tea meeting remained religious on St. Vincent since the soiree party served the secular and more licentious function. The soiree party appears to have been a carryover of the entertainments described in the travel literature, the all-night celebrations of a people "much given to venery." These celebrations consisted of short plays, songs, and recitations which tended toward the satirical and the obscene. The soiree party is no longer held, and *concerts* have now taken their place. The concerts are devoted to Shakespearean performances as well as to the older types of playing.

The performers view the Vincentian tea meeting as an open contest between the forces of decorum and rudeness. As on Nevis, there is a strong spatial division between the stage and the rest of the meeting hall, with the stage the locus of order and the meeting hall, of disorder. There is a constant contest between the *orators* on stage and the *pit-*

boys in the audience to see who can confuse whom. The declared intent of the orator is to confuse the audience with his copious abilities, especially in his use of eloquent words and ability to cite facts and truths. Conversely, the pitboys (and other members of the audience) attempt to confuse the orators through *ragging* (little speeches or rhymes in Creole *broad talk* about their superior abilities to entertain) or through rapping (hitting sticks on the benches while chanting something in derision).

The mediators of this conflict are three chairmen, who are individually designated chairman, vice-chairman (or just vice), and secretary. One of the three must introduce and conclude each oration, all the while demonstrating a greater ability to speak well and a firmer grasp of the facts than the orators. In this role they can be challenged by another man of words from the floor, and on occasion they must relinquish their position. This seldom occurs, however, as most of the orators are their pupils, younger men and women to whom they have taught the rules of speechmaking and most of the set-speeches performed.

The chairmen are judged on their abilities to orate better than anyone else, to maintain order, and to keep the ceremony going. (If they cannot maintain interest until cockcrow, they are deemed failures.) Because of this last-named criterion, the secretary is regarded as the most important of the chairmen, for he must get a sufficient number of orators to sign up with him. If there are not sufficient speeches, the chairmen will have to fill in the time with orations of their own.

A noisy reaction from the audience and the pitboys is crucial to the performance. The chairmen are judged on how well they can manipulate this noise. To this end, they attempt to make an arrangement with a leader among the pitboys that, if he can quiet the others, he will be rewarded (with one of the special cakes baked, for the most part, for the winners of the oratorical contest). The chairmen need the noise for a number of reasons. First, they know that the noise generally signifies that the crowd is enjoying itself. As one chairman, Charles Jack of Yambou Village, explained it, "That [the noise] forms part of the entertainment. Everybody there have their time. You have a time for the chairman, you have a time for the orators, you have a time to say poems and rags and so on. You have a time to rap, you have a time for refreshments, you have a time for everything."

Second, the noise, the rapping, and the ragging test the orators. As Jack put it:

The rag will be coming from the others who want to confuse you. . . . You are going on the platform and when someone starts ragging you, now, if you're not one who has very good memory, you're likely to forget what you have to say. You're going on the platform and you begin saying your speech, now you're burst. They could mock you and that is the purpose and that is the main objective of these rhymes, to confuse them.

Unlike the rags in everyday discourse, the rhymes are not directed against the speaker. Rather, they are in boast form:

The foals are in the field,
They're willing to yield.
But watch your step and look for the test,
Leave this giant and come back for the rest.

The idea is to ignite the audience in hilarious response so that the noise will confuse the orator.

As on Nevis, the meeting consists of a series of performances, each of which has its sense of wholeness. The proceedings themselves, however, have an open-ended quality to them. Similarly, the meeting is divided in two by the serving of refreshments, though on St. Vincent the tea and cakes have been replaced by ginger beer and buns since World War II. Finally, as on Nevis, the chairmen are encouraged to drink *strong* rum while they are on stage as a means of increasing their verbal abilities. Ceremonial cakes are used, not to be auctioned, but to serve as prizes for the performers, the head pitboy, and the chairmen.

The speeches of the orators are specifically constructed to appeal to the three most important segments of their audience. The introduction compliments the judges; the body of the speech, with its show of facts and its elocution is a bow to the chairmen; and jokes are interspersed as a means of enlisting the attention of the general audience. The jokes represent a departure from the elevated diction and the hypercorrect standard English pronunciation of the body of the speech; this sudden discontinuity virtually guarantees laughter and, thus, attention.

The primary opposition here, as on Nevis, is between the two codes of behavior—the household and the crossroads ideals—as they are symbolized in two speaking varieties, *sweet* and *broad talk,* and in the two performance behaviors. All of these oppositions are brought into direct conflict for entertainment purposes. As in other Afro-American performances, they are set up as complementarities and are forced into a playful dialogue with each other, thus giving a sense of community interlock. Each person attending has a place in the performance, and all who desire to do so may individually play a part.

V

This history and description of the tea meeting illustrates one common type of cultural development in the New World which arose when Africans encountered European practices that agents of the plantocracy presented as ideal behaviors. Similar developments occurred in other performances, especially plays, (including the widely reported all-night "grand balls"—called *plays* in the West Indies) which the Euro-Americans loved to attend, and wakes which featured European and African riddling, storytelling, and game playing.

In all of these syncretisms, African structural patterns were maintained, even though some of the elements used were European in origin. The insistence on maintaining an open-ended sense of performance, which might have seemed formless and "uncivilized" to the plantocrat- and traveler-observers, constitutes evidence that an essentially African mode of organization persisted in the New World. The sense of continuing oppositions or contrarieties underlining this lack of dramatic closure must have been dismaying to these onlookers, but at the same time the vitality expressed in such a performance structure provoked in them no end of comment and amazement. The dancing and singing simply confirmed their stereotypic notions of the African, but the attention generated to performers by audiences in itself encouraged the maintenance of these ways of interacting. Moreover, in the play patterns involving the interlock and overlap of voices and movements, a viable image of creative community organization was maintained despite the planters' deculturation efforts. The ethnic identity of individual slaves may have been eliminated in the plantation experience, but the commonalities of sub-Saharan African performances and images of community were developed through ceremonies such as the tea meeting. If we are to understand how the Afro-Americans maintained their collective sanity, it seems clear that we must examine the means they used to provide psychological support for each other. Studying public performance should assist us greatly in this effort.

NOTES

1. Material for this essay was collected in 1966-1967 while I was a John Simon Guggenheim Fellow and in the summer of 1968 under the support of NIMH Small Grant #MH S706-01. I am indebted to Peter Mallalieu, William A. Stewart, and my friends and informants on Nevis and St. Vincent, especially Charles Jack.

2. Charles Rampini, *Letters from Jamaica* (Edinburgh, 1873), 80-81.

3. "Foreword," in *Afro-American Anthropology: Contemporary Perspectives,* ed. by John F. Szwed and Norman E. Whitten (New York: Free Press, 1970), 7-8.

4. Keith Whinnom, "The Origin of European-based Creoles and Pidgins," *Orbis* 14 (1965), 511-526; William A. Stewart, "Sociolinguistic Factors in the History of American Negro Dialects," *The Florida F/L Reporter* 5; William A. Stewart, "Continuity and Change in American Negro Dialects," *The Florida F/L Reporter* 6; and Joe E. Dillard, *Black English* (Random House, 1973).

5. "The Training of the Man of Words in Talking Sweet," *Language in Society* I (1972), 15-29; "Traditions of Eloquence in the West Indies," *Journal of Inter-American Studies and World Affairs* 12 (1970), 505-527; "Sense and Nonsense on St. Vincent: Speech Behavior and Decorum in a Caribbean Community" (with Richard Bauman), *American Anthropologist* 73 (1971), 762-772; "Joking: The Training of the Man of Words in Talking Broad," in *Rappin' and Stylin' Out,* ed. by Thomas Kochman, (University of Illinois Press, 1972), 215-40.

6. Richard Ligon, *A True and Exact History of the Island of Barbadoes,* 2d ed. (London, 1673), 50.

7. Sir Hans Sloane, *A Voyage to the Islands, Madera, Barbados, Nieves, St. Christophers, and Jamaica* (London, 1707), vol. 1, xl.

8. William Beckford, *A Descriptive Account of the Island of Jamaica* (London, 1790), vol. 1, 391.

9. Mrs. Carmichael, *Domestic Manners and Social Conditions of the White, Coloured and Negro Population of the West Indies* (London, 1834), vol. 1, 292.

10. H. T. De La Beche, *Notes on the Present Conditions of the Negroes in Jamaica* (London, 1825), 40-41.

11. Mrs. Lanigan, *Antigua and the Antiguans* (1844), vol. 2, 171-175.

12. Greville John Chester, *Transatlantic Sketches* (London, 1869), 80.

13. Rev. H.V.P. Brockhurst, *The Colony of British Guiana and Its Labouring Population* (London, 1883), 387-388.

14. Frank C. Collymore, *Notes for a Glossary of Words and Phrases of Barbadian Dialect,* 3d ed., revised and enlarged (Bridgetown: Advocate Co., 1965), 110-111.

15. Louis Lynch, *The Barbados Book* (London: Andre Deutsch, 1964), 239-243.

16. Martha Warren Beckwith, *Black Roadways* (Chapel Hill: University of North Carolina Press), 204.

17. David DeCamp, "Mock Bidding in Jamaica," in *Tire Shrinker to Dragster,* ed. by Wilson M. Hudson (Austin: The Encino Press, 1968), 150-153.

18. Martin Joos, *The Five Clocks* (New York: Harcourt Brace and World, 1967), 33-34.

19. Ibid., 37.

20. Roger D. Abrahams, "Patterns of Eloquence in the British West Indies," *Journal of Inter-American Studies and World Affairs* (1970).

21. Karl Reisman, "Cultural and Linguistic Ambiguity in a West Indian Village," in *Afro-American Anthropology: Contemporary Perspectives,* ed. by N. E. Whitten and J. F. Szwed (New York: Free Press, 1970), 141.

22. DeCamp, op. cit.

23. Reisman, op. cit.

24. Melville J. and Frances S. Herskovits, *Trinidad Village* (New York: Alfred A. Knopf, 1947), 148. See also George Eaton Simpson, "The Nine Night Ceremony in Jamaica," *Journal of American Folklore* 70 (1957), 330.

25. Alan Lomax, "The Homogeneity of African-Afro-American Musical Style," in *Afro-American Anthropology: Contemporary Perspectives,* ed. by N. E. Whitten and J. F. Szwed (New York: Free Press, 1970), 181.

26. Peter Wilson, "Reputation and Respectability: A Suggestion for a Caribbean Ethnology," in *Man,* 4 (1969), 70-84.

27. It is difficult to discover whether there were similar events on other non-British islands, though many of the events discussed by Errol Hill in his *Trinidad Carnival* (University of Texas Press, 1971) are similar in their focus on eloquence competition. Harold F.C. Simmons' description of the *A-Bwe* (drinking) ceremony on St. Lucia indicates a similar tradition there: "The fete begins with the host welcoming guests, asking for good behavior and a contribution to cover the cost of refreshments. . . . The speeches and songs are in a very Frenchified French Creole, a macaronic language, using many French words and idioms." From "Notes on Folklore St. Lucia" in *Iouanaloa* (Department of Extra Mural Studies, Castries, St. Lucia, 1963), 42. Similar types of gatherings under the name of tea meeting have been reported to me in personal communications, from East Africa and Nova Scotia.

28. Cf. Roger D. Abrahams, "British West Indian Folk Drama and the 'Life Cycle' Problem," *Folklore* 82 (1971), 241-265.

29. Roger D. Abrahams, "Patterns of Performance in the British West Indies," in *Afro-American Anthropology: Contemporary Perspectives,* ed. by N. E. Whitten and J. F. Szwed (New York: Free Press, 1970), 163-180.

Douglas Midgett

8

WEST INDIAN VERSION: LITERATURE, HISTORY, AND IDENTITY[1]

> Poets and satirists are afflicted with the superior stupidity which believes that societies can be renewed, and one of the most nourishing sites for such a renewal, however visionary it may seem, is the American archipelago.
>
> Derek Walcott[2]

Perhaps one of the most perplexing issues concerning West Indian societies is that of identity. This issue has occupied the talents of many writers and political thinkers and has drawn the attention of scholars of the history and society of the area. Some commentators maintain that its resolution would lead variously to healthy psyches, political stability and independence, a sense of social community, and the integration of a potentially major region of the New World. The continued failure to arrive at a distinctive, positive identity is blamed for everything from alcohol abuse to the repeated failure to achieve political and economic integration.

A brief glance at the historical origins of these societies may shed some light on the bases of these problems.[3] The people of the West Indies are products of the most sustained and intense European colonial domination undergone by any present-day population. For some, at least, that process has not yet ended. Moreover, they are products of a process that has resulted in the formation of new societies, that is, the population segments that came to be constituent parts of these societies were none of them indigenous. They arrived from the Old World, and the society that developed very much reflected the relationships between populations resulting from the initial economic structures on which European interests in the area were predicated. West Indian society, viewed as a whole, was always fragmented in terms of political administration and economic ties to the metropole. As the British Colonial Office administered the units separately, so the plantocracies in the individual islands were engaged in economic competition with one another. Internally, too, these were fragmented societies, divided initially between slave and free, white, colored, and black, and evolving (some with subsequent additional population segments) into entities characterized by social, cultural, and structural pluralism. This situation produced an atomized regional structure of increasingly economically peripheral units tied to Great Britain like unconnected points to the hub of a wheel, each internally divided into sections that were often culturally antithetical. Hence, the possibility of integration of the region was severely limited. As Gordon Lewis has noted, in view of this historical development it is ridiculous to criticize West Indians "for their insularism, when in harsh fact the basic responsibility is that of the English themselves who kept the islands unnaturally apart from each other for three centuries or more and then expected them to come together in less than fifteen years."[4]

The kind of integration which many have envisioned and worked toward for decades depends on some basic factors. Some of these factors may well be beyond the realm of West Indian influence. If, for example, continued fragmentation serves the continued "development" of the region as a source of cheap labor for import substitution industries and as a market for consumer products from North America and Europe, then area politicians, however pure their motives, will find it very difficult to buck that tide. On the other hand, much has already been done in one field, although perhaps not specifically directed to the ends suggested here. This endeavor concerns the difficult issue of identity, the creation or manifestation of a vision and unity of purpose that transcends the pettiness of the micronationalism of the current post-Federation West Indies. In this essay some of the directions that this endeavor has taken and might take are elaborated.

In another area, East Africa, Ali Mazrui has discussed the concept of cultural engineering—the process of constructing institutions and ideologies that will enable new nations in that part of the world to embark on nationhood with integrity and sense of purpose.[5] The parallels with the West Indies, while not overwhelming, are suggestive.

Until recently, both areas were under colonial control; both are composed of heterogeneous populations, separated during the colonial period by the nature of the administrative apparatus; and, in both cases, the partial integration of individual members of the non-European population into the colonial political and economic structure was facilitated by an educational process of European design, a programmed alienation process. In his study, Mazrui suggests the utility of the concept for this study of identity in the West Indies:

> Cultural engineering becomes the deliberate manipulation of cultural factors for purposes of deflecting human habit in the direction of new and perhaps constructive endeavors. Sometimes the effort consists in changing cultural patterns enough to make it possible for certain institutions to survive. At other times the purpose of cultural reform is basically attitudinal change. Ultimately, there is the paramount issue of identity, of how people view themselves and how far self-conceptions can be modified in the direction of enlarged empathy.[6]

In applying some of Mazrui's approaches to the West Indian situation, the scope of this essay has been limited to include just two of the areas of his concern, the writing of history and creative literature. These two topics were chosen for a number of reasons, the most important of which is the abundance of literary and historical material available to the researcher. The creative literature of the West Indies is the product of an especially prolific group of writers, particularly during the last quarter century. Historical accounts of the region, abundant and mostly written from a Euro-centric point of view, have begun to attract the attention of many young historians of the area who are bringing decidedly different orientations to the interpretation of these data.

LITERATURE

In his discussion of the relationship between creative literature and nationalism or nationalistic identity, Mazrui suggests three dimensions for consideration: the act of writing itself, the themes employed, and the linkages between, in his case, African literature and other literary traditions, particularly those European.[7] An examination of

West Indian writing along these dimensions reveals a number of aspects that have implications for the formation of identity. The very act of writing in societies that are as profoundly colonial as those in the West Indies is initially an assertion of identity. If that writing moves in directions that diverge from those of the colonizer and are counter to that sector of the society which has controlled access to literacy, then the assertion has particular salience. In a society such as the West Indies which is characterized by cultural ambiguity and social schisms, a number of themes are of obvious importance: the issue of race, the connections with Africa and Europe, and the impact of centuries of slavery, to name just a few. Finally, the relationship to European literature may be viewed from different perspectives: the determination of criteria by which this newly emerging literary output is to be judged, or the development of an indigenous, unique style of expression within the confines of a European literary language. These perspectives, especially indigenous style, are closely tied to questions of particularistic versus universalistic interpretation, a question hardly confined to literature of West Indian expression, but nonetheless one that must be considered after the following discussion.

In the West Indian creative literature appearing during the past twenty-five years, many of the issues noted above have consistently arisen. In these societies where the European custodians of literacy produced almost nothing of artistic merit, much of this recent literary output is the product of blacks and East Indians. Consequently it deals in various ways with the social cleavages and psychological disorientation common in a colonial situation.

Although any consideration of literature from a thematic approach results in some distortion of the works considered, examining the literary output from the perspective a number of themes relating to identity will illuminate these issues significantly. Accordingly, five broad themes that have been given some attention by West Indian writers are discussed, with exemplary material given in each case. These five themes include (1) the relationship of the people to the We Indian physical environment; (2) the use of Africa and Europe as metaphor, the invocation of cultural continuity and racial memory; (3) the reference to historical events in the islands, including the examination of slavery and the struggle, for freedom; (4) present-day issues, including class and color schisms in the societies; and (5) the use of language, particularly the role of Creole or dialect.

The Island Environment

The writer who has gone farthest in an attempt to define the relationship of the West Indian to environment is the St. Lucian poet and playwright Derek Walcott. For Walcott this relationship must be understood if West Indians are to make sense of their position and comprehend their existence. He directly addresses the question of whether the West Indian experience, rooted in a history characterized by human destruction and dehumanized relations, can ever result in anything more than a derivative identity, neither creative nor in harmony with the island landscape.

So it is that Walcott explores features of that landscape, physical and human, and expresses at times a deep love for his homeland. Separation, so much a part of the West Indian experience, evokes the following response:

> I watched the shallow green
> That broke in places where there would be reef,
> The silver glinting on the fuselage, each mile
> Dividing us and all fidelity strained
> Till space would snap it. Then after a while
> I thought of nothing, nothing, I prayed, would change;[8]

As Gerald Moore observes, Walcott is a writer of the small islands; his poetry frequently focuses on those dazzling beaches fronting the rusting, galvanized roofed fishing villages that rim his native St. Lucia.[9] Despite the penetration of his vision (or perhaps because of it), Walcott's portraits of Anse-la-Raye and Dennery reveal an ambiguity that aids in our understanding of the motives of migrants who, in flight from villages in austere London council houses, assert their longing for these small, somnambulant places.[10]

With the exception of *The Sea at Dauphin,* Walcott does not, however, confine himself in his plays to the sea and the villages. Other works explore the aspects of the countryside environment of the peasantry and evoke even more basic elements of the West Indian setting. A striking case is the continual presence of the heavy rain in *Malcochon,* a feature that becomes a device for measuring the pace of the play. Another example is the treatment of the mountainous interior of the island, the domain of the charcoal burner, Makak, in *Dream on Mon-*

key Mountain; this image was fully realized in the televised production of the play by Trinidad and Tobago Television.[11]

Other West Indian writers, mostly novelists, explore the island environments and experiences through vivid portrayals of rural and village life. These works, occasionally referred to as childhood novels, deal in varying detail with coming of age in these settings. In the process, they examine the relationship between the growth of their actors and their comparatively diminished settings. The most important of these works is George Lamming's first novel, *In the Castle of My Skin.*[12] A "childhood novel" only insofar as its protagonist and occasional narrator is a boy growing up in a Barbadian village, this work is a portrait of West Indian society in flux during that period of labor unrest and growing demand for popular political participation before World War II. Despite his preoccupation with these themes, Lamming frequently details the human communion with environment in this setting.

The novels of Michael Anthony, particularly *The Year in San Fernando* and *Green Days by the River,* lack the pointedness and concern with larger issues that characterize Lamming's work.[13] In their depiction of coming of age, or perhaps in just the vignettes of adolescent experience, however, they are particularly attuned to the features of the surroundings that circumscribe these identifiable activities. In the first-named novel the setting, richly mined for metaphorical checkpoints on the year's seasonal changes, is urban Trinidad, a world of streets and houses, buses and strangers. In contrast, *Green Days* explores the world of the peasant and village. It evokes a fecund, slower paced milieu which, until the rather terrifying final episodes, contrasts with the tempo of rapidly emerging adolescence.

The exploration of themes involving relationships with the West Indian natural environment has received considerable elaboration. Whether this relationship is peripheral to other concerns or is seen as a central problem for resolution by West Indian man, as in Walcott's work, these writers have repeatedly turned to the island settings as foci for playing out their literary directions. Perhaps the emphasis on this focus leads inevitably to Dennis Scott's conclusion:

It is time to plant
feet in our earth. The heart's metronome
insists on this arc of islands
as home.[14]

African Connection[15]

Undeniably African references are frequently encountered in West Indian writing. Some kind of cult activity is depicted in novels in both urban and rural settings. Although not a few of these lean heavily on the spectacular, orgiastic aspects of these events, recalling the more ludicrous effects of old jungle movies, some have dealt with the African element in an attempt to examine what possibilities exist in the definition of identity.

A particularly ambitious attempt to portray the cultural collision of Africa and Europe is Lamming's *Season of Adventure* in which the conflict centers in the person of Fola, the middle-class mulatto girl.[16] Kenneth Ramchand has called this book "the most significant of the West Indian novels invoking Africa."[17] There are compelling arguments for this judgment. Lamming is not content to use ritual as a device either to demonstrate a cursory familiarity with the occult or as a dazzler for the reader searching for bits of local color. Rather, the question is very directly posed as to what are the existential considerations for a people divided between a remembered and still vital, if altered and attenuated, African past and a present direction that involves the denial of that heritage. This question is an enormously difficult one and Lamming makes clear that it has no facile resolution.

Derek Walcott, too, has dealt with Africa, to the greatest extent in *Dream on Monkey Mountain,* where the invocation of this heritage finds its fullest expression in the tribal ceremony toward the end of the play.[18] The "primitive" quality of this scene is pronounced, a feature which as a dramatic device is more acceptable in a play than in a novel. Moreover, the play is a dream, a series of images, which means that the scene need not be evaluated in terms of its ethnographic accuracy.

Another of Walcott's plays, *Ione,* is the only piece of West Indian writing known to me which includes African social patterns.[19] The two families, headed by patriarchs and descended from a common male ancestor, are portrayed as lineages in opposition. Despite these forays into African survival and memory, the key issue for Walcott seems to be how to incorporate the African and European, as expressed in the following:

how choose
Between this Africa and the English tongue I love?
Betray them both, or give back what they give?

How can I face such slaughter and be cool?
How can I turn from Africa and live?[20]

For one writer, the Barbadian poet and historian Edward Brathwaite, the question of identity, at least at one level, is not such a vexed issue. No single body of work in West Indian literature goes further toward exploring and resolving the African heritage and presence as does Brathwaite's trilogy, *Rights of Passage, Masks,* and *Islands.*[21] In the first of these volumes of poetry, which deals with slavery and its legacy, Brathwaite concludes with the rhetorical question:

Should you
shatter the door
and walk
in the morning
fully aware
of the future
to come?[22]

Although his answer is direct—"There is no turning back"—it is not simply arrived at, for a conception of the future requires an understanding of the African experience, past and present. Thus, in *Masks* the author must remove himself in time and space to reacquaint himself with his cultural antecedents. It is only after this journey that he can return to confront the contradictions of a West Indian existence in *Islands.* For Brathwaite, then, the invocation of Africa is not just a stylistic trick, or even an anthropological search for retentions, but a means to deal with the existential problems posed in his society. The environments of Brathwaite's concern are not the landscapes and seascapes of the islands but the inner visions, products of culture and history.

Literature and History

Apart from some examination of recent historical events dealing with nationalism and regional political issues, West Indian writing has rarely taken the historical tradition of the islands seriously in its purview. Perhaps this may reflect a general acceptance (albeit loud public denial) of Naipaul's contention that the West Indies has no historical tradition worthy of serious consideration.[23] Nevertheless, there is a marked absence of interest in themes that center on slavery and the trade, resistance, rebellion, and the effects of European power struggles in the area on social life in the islands.

One historically important area that occasionally surfaces in literature is that of the stereotypic depictions of black people, slave and free, which have in the past so influenced the interpretations of history and images in literary sources. Brathwaite, for example, takes the figure of Tom, the slave Uncle Tom, and expands on a role that has been the source of much malign expression.[24] Brathwaite's Tom is not just a bowing, servile darky, but he has a range of personality characteristics; he is a psychologically assaulted, but whole individual, however mocked by his history.

Stereotypic figures are also presented in Walcott's *Ti Jean and His Brothers,* in which appear three black figures, frequently encountered in literary and other accounts.[25] Gros Jean is the buck nigger, strong-backed, but weak in the head, whose witlessness and reliance on brute strength are his final undoing. Mi Jean is the prototypical Afro-Saxon, the sycophant who is the exemplification of imitation being the sincerest form of flattery. His comeuppance occurs only after he realizes, too late, that the colonizer is not about to admit the imitator into the inner circle. That leaves Ti Jean, a figure who appears rather less frequently in those accounts describing the "character and social manners of the negro," and only then during periods of turmoil and rebellion when the planters' paranoia surfaces in print. Ti Jean is the realist, unresponsive to the destructive flattery of the master, the realist who understands that the only way to change the system is to destroy it. That he is the hero and ultimate victor in the play, defeating the plantation owner/devil, is a measure of Walcott's recreative hope, only rarely achieved in the West Indian reality.

In a quite different direction, a most significant novel dealing with the literary interpretation of actual historical events is V. S. Reid's *New Day.*[26] The action of the novel spans the period in Jamaican history from the Morant Bay Rebellion in 1865 to the "new day" of the constitutional revisions of 1944 which promised a new political order. As the story is told through the eyes of an old man who was a participant in the 1865 rebellion and a witness to the 1944 events, it provides a view of a people who are the inheritors of their own unique history. It is in this effort that the book's significance lies, for Reid lends a heroic quality to these people and events that is entirely absent from the history lessons most Jamaicans learned at school. Although in *New Day* Reid has opened up a new direction for others intent upon mining historical sources, none has followed his lead. It may be that the enterprise must await the day when these writers attain a more complete understanding of this history.

Color and Class

The issues of color and class that presently divide West Indians and frustrate attempts to develop a sense of community did not receive extensive treatment in literature until recently. The disinclination in the past to confront these social issues directly is best exemplified in the contrast between the poetry written a generation ago and that contained in some recent collections.[27] With the exception of some iconoclastic writers like E. M. Roach and Martin Carter, the poetry of the 1950s and before did not touch on the themes of conflict and struggle.

These issues *were* the subject, however, of some novels, especially those of Roger Mais. His milieu is the city, Kingston, and the yard culture of the poor urban dweller. In two novels, *The Hills Were Joyful Together* and *Brother Man,* Mais portrays the reality of what it is like to be poor and black in the city, the one locale in the island where the material opulence of the wealthy is continually on display.[28] Mais depicts this existence not as a nether world, as some have suggested, but as a functioning community, constrained by and confronting a situation where wealth and skin color are the only marks of status.

Another writer who characterizes the poor is Orlando Patterson, whose first novel, *The Children of Sisyphus,* also focuses on the urban poverty scene of Kingston.[29] Patterson's writing has occasionally been criticized and unfavorably compared with that of Mais. If it is lacking, it is only a matter of style, not of sociological accuracy, a characteristic that Patterson strives for, sometimes at the expense of readability.

If the characters in Mais' and Patterson's urban shanties have in most cases come to some kind of terms with the harshness of their environments and the constraints that limit their chances, then the protagonists in novels of the colored middle class appear to be continually searching for *persona.* There is a strong hint that survival for these people, Naipaul's mimic men,[30] lies in the assumption of some guise that masks the conditions of inequality in the society and blinds them to the aimlessness of their own civil servant existence. In *Nor Any Country,* Paul Breville explains to his brother his escape to schizophrenia: "They think I'm mad, . . . All right. I encourage them to think so. I behave as if I am. Deliberately. . . . This is the only world I can inhabit now, where they can only laugh and tolerate. I can never fail or disappoint now. Nobody expects anything of me. Not even myself."[31]

These novels convey the notion that the colored middle class is in a cultural limbo—denied full membership as Englishmen, a status that would be commensurate with their education and training, and unable or unwilling to respond to the vitality of the urban and rural folk culture that surrounds them. Even when a return to these roots is attempted, as in the instance of Jerry Stover in Andrew Salkey's novel, *The Late Emancipation of Jerry Stover,* the experiment frequently culminates in disaster.[32]

In this discussion, one more work deserves mention because it deals directly with the issue of race and the pathological consequences it can engender in a setting where color and privilege have for so long been interrelated. John Stewart's *Last Cool Days,* set in his native Trinidad, confronts the subject of racial awareness with a starkness unusual in West Indian literature, a directness that belies the author's long residence in the United States.[33] Perhaps like Trumper in *In the Castle of My Skin,* the West Indian writer must leave the islands "to know what it mean to fin' race,"[34] to comprehend an identity that is every bit as profound a reality in his homeland.

The Uses of Language

As indicated earlier, the mere production of literature in the language of the colonizer is in itself a political act in societies so markedly colonial as the West Indian. In the West Indies, creative literature has been written in English; the problems of creating an indigenous written art form in the foreign language of the colonizer, which are problems common to African and Asian writers, are not paramount for the West Indian artist. But the specific use of language, the decision whether to use dialect and Creole in the effort to deal with themes and to create a distinctive, even nationalistic literature, is most certainly at issue here.[35]

Some works have employed Creole speech extensively. Walcott and Garth St. Omer, both St. Lucians, have produced works rich in the use of patois, the Creole of that island.[36] The difficulty of such an effort appealing to any but a very select readership is evident in the development of St. Omer's novella, *Syrop,* which was originally written with dialogue in patois but was later published with translation into roughly equivalent English dialect.[37] Another earlier use is in Reid's *New Day,* where the narration by the old man, John Campbell, is almost entirely in dialect, a device used with great effect, particularly in descriptions of the Jamaican landscape.[38]

Others have used dialect sparingly, most often in dialogue to catch the "flavor" of verbal exchange in the island setting. Often enough, however, some of this use of dialect is for humorous effect, to present a particular character as ludicrous. Employed in this fashion, the use of dialect differs little at times from the linguistic atrocities attributed to blacks in travelers' accounts written during and just following the slavery period.

Recently, the use of dialect has taken a decidedly different turn, particularly in works of poetry. This change was signaled in the 1971 special literature issue of *Savacou,*[39] the organ of the Caribbean Artists' Movement. The outcry which greeted the publication of dialect poetry in that issue is indicative of the embarrassment some felt in confronting the artistic use of "bad talk," "bad English," or "broken English." It is also indicative of a larger issue, the one of particularistic as opposed to universalistic criteria for the critical evaluation of literature.[40] Without going into this issue at great length, there appears to be no reason why at one point in time much West Indian writing, published and read primarily outside the islands, did not take a universalistic bent. Given the current political ferment in the area, however, the direction toward particularistic concerns and themes, especially in poetry, is both understandable and necessary.

HISTORY

Mazrui notes that a controversy concerning the writing of history in East Africa focuses on three levels: methodology, content, and application.[41] The West Indian historian has somewhat different problems, and this difference relates to some basic contrasts between the two regions. One of the principal questions in Africa, as Mazrui indicates, concerns the validity of oral tradition as source material, or, put another way, whether nonliterate traditions can be said to have histories at all. Such a problem is not so compelling for the West Indian historian. Although an examination of oral sources might aid the historian—and the issue of time dealt with in terms other than past, present, and future may prove just as troublesome in the West Indies as it has for African historians—the basic problems seem to be at Mazrui's level of application.

Mazrui raises the issue of the commitment of scholarship; specifically, he questions whether the study of history is to be directed toward an accretive or a corrective enterprise.[42] This distinction speaks directly to the most important problem for West Indian historians, namely, the correction of historical interpretations that have been heavily Eurocentric in their conceptions. The problem is not just one of counterbalancing some distorted data selection, but is also one of deriving new orientations with which to approach the data. This observation is not new, for West Indians from J. J. Thomas through C.L.R. James and Eric Williams pointed out these necessities before the advent of the current grup of historians. Nonetheless, this task must be accomplished if West Indians are to make history serve a new and heightened self-image.

The following sections, one concerned with events in the Eastern Caribbean, specifically St. Lucia, and the other with a series of situations in Jamaica, demonstrate two points. The first section is an examination of how to proceed in the reinterpretation of historical events and figures. The second involves a people's sense of their own history through the presentation of themes in the popular realm, themes that have to do with popular notions of historical postures which nations or peoples assume or with relationships between nations or population segments within a nation. The second section examines a popular theme through which Jamaican society has been interpreted and contrasts it with the "official" portrait of that society.

Victor Hughes and the Brigands' War

In the last decade of the eighteenth century, the tremors that spread from the Haitian Revolution and the French Revolution touched nearly all of the islands of the Lesser Antilles in the form of violent confrontations. The last bitter struggle of the French and English for control of the area and the glimpse of release from servitude by an awakened black population combined to fashion the most turbulent period of the three centuries since European exploration had begun in the Caribbean.

During this time, a series of developments led to what has been termed the "Brigands' War," an especially bloody set of engagements between forces composed of British militia opposed by an army made up of a few French revolutionaries and large numbers of black and mulatto freedmen and ex-slaves. Adolph Roberts, in a relatively dispassionate discussion, notes that the confusion prevalent in the Antilles following the French Revolution so weakened the French position that by early 1794 the British, often in consort with French Royalists, were in control of most of the Eastern Caribbean.[43] By the latter part of that year, however, many of these same islands were controlled or under siege by a new force in the region. Under the direction of Victor Hughes, a mulatto born in France, the revolutionary forces first took Guadeloupe, and from that base Hughes sent missions to many of the other islands to enlist blacks and incite slave rebellions. The strategy worked in St. Lucia, St. Vincent, and Grenada, all of which fell into Hughes' hands. Matters remained thus for two years until the islands again returned to the immensely superior forces of the British; Hughes retained only Guadeloupe. The fighting did not end with these defeats, for the black armies continued to wage guerrilla campaigns against the British and in so doing controlled large portions of the interiors of some of the islands.

Let us now turn to a discussion of how these events are interpreted and how the character and singular accomplishments of Victor Hughes and his associates are assessed in the histories of this era.

For many writers of West Indian history, the events in the islands were mere adjuncts to the European history of that period.[44] Consequently, the events described above are most often dealt with in terms of French-British oppositions or, within the French sphere, in Royalist-Republican terms. The inaccuracies resulting from such an orientation are pointed up in Burns' description of the Brigands as comprising "whites of extreme revolutionary views, and escaped slaves."[45] In fact, these armies were mostly black and were composed of men legally free under the Republican regime. The incorrect identification of these forces is not as serious an error as the inability to recognize the importance of these struggles for people who realized that their newly found freedom would exist only as long as they could defend their territories against superior forces. Roberts reports, for example, the following situation in Guadeloupe upon the restitution of slavery and the trade: "A great many [Negroes] committed suicide rather than return to bondage. Four hundred former slaves locked themselves up in a fort, and when they became convinced that they would not be exempted from the abhorred decree they touched off the gunpowder magazine. All were killed."[46] Such accounts ought to provide some clue as to the degree of the blacks' commitment to maintaining a political situation that would insure their continued freedom.

In their treatment of Hughes, the historians certainly cannot be accused of ignoring the man. Indeed, they seem to take special relish in applying the most florid adjectives whenever his name appears. Brian Edwards found it difficult to deal with Hughes in any but the most scurrilous terms, stating that "his name has since become proverbial for every species of outrage and cruelty . . . " and that he was "savage, remorseless, and bloody" and an "inexorable tyrant."[47] Burns saw him as "an audacious and bloodthirsty revolutionary leader,"[48] and in local histories of the period in St. Lucia Hughes is described as "a ruffian" and is characterized by his "violence and greed."[49] Alec Waugh, the popularizer of West Indian history, provides us with the most colorful account of Hughes' character and bloody proclivities:

> Of less than medium height, with a corpulent torso that he encased in clothes that were too tight for it, with thick, stocky legs and a plebian, sensual mouth, pitted by smallpox, abrupt in manner, jerky, with a Southern accent, Victor Hughes rarely looked anyone in the face, but when he did, his small grey eyes inspired either terror or repulsion.[50]

Other revolutionary leaders, associates of Hughes, who occupy prominent positions in the struggles of the ex-slave populations, come off little better in the hands of the historians. For example, Julian Fedon, Hughes' lieutenant in Grenada, is variously characterized as a "skillful but barbarous leader" and "as ruthless and brutal as Hughes himself."[51]

The problems created by this kind of writing and interpretation of West Indian history are almost self-evident. These problems are not relegated to difficulties in orientation (which are recognized by some of these writers, although limited to such designations as "Anglophile" versus "Francophile"), or to the tendency to ornament descriptions of certain personalities. Rather, they are of a more profound nature, for in explaining the conflicts of the time in terms of their significance for what was happening in Europe, these writers have failed to take account of the largest category of people directly involved and the ones for whom these events were most significant. Moreover, the view of this history provided in these accounts prevails in the islands today, and it is this interpretation of their histories that islanders see symbolically represented throughout the West Indies. For an example let us now turn, within the general context of the preceding historical discussion, to a local situation, a particular event, and the manner in which it is represented symbolically.

In St. Lucia, the period preceding the revolutionary era is described as one of "peaceful colonisation," and it is noted that "great advances were made."[52] These "advances" were, of course, accomplished through the expansion of plantation agriculture employing a slave labor force. This golden era of peace and prosperity came to an end following the conclusion of the American Revolution and the subsequent resumption of full-scale hostilities between the British and French in the Eastern Caribbean. The instability produced by these conflicts enabled others to seek their own solutions to the question of who would control their destinies. That all residents of the colony did not share in the prosperity of that time is evidenced in the following account from Breen. In about 1784, "the island had been infested by the Maroon Negroes, who taking advantage of the defenceless situation of the planters, had committed the most wanton depredation on different estates, and even cruelly murdered some of the inhabitants."[53] These insurgents were brought under control during a brief period of French rule in the island, but the impetus for internal revolt did not abate and was renewed less than a decade later.

In 1793, after a visit from an emissary of the new French Republican regime, the following situation ensued: "The work of the estates was discontinued, the plantations were deserted, and nothing prevailed but anarchy and terror, in the midst of which the Negroes under arms were discussing the 'rights of man'."[54] The abolition of slavery was decreed on February 4, 1794, and the self-interest of the vast majority of St. Lucians was served. The emancipation was shortlived, however, as a British force recaptured the island two months later and set the stage for the entry of Victor Hughes.

Although the British captured the fortress on Morne Fortune over-
looking Castries Harbor, they failed to pacify much of St. Lucia. The
ex-slaves-turned-liberators moved their arena of operations to the
interior of the island where they continued to harass the British troops
for a year. By this time, in early 1795, Hughes, in Guadeloupe, had
received sufficient goods and troops from France to make new incursions into the Southern Caribbean. In St. Lucia the garrison, weakened by disease and the effects of repeated battles with the black insurgents, capitulated without much struggle, and the island was once
again in the hands of the blacks.

In the months that followed, this controlling army fiercely repulsed
all British attempts to recapture the island. Moreover, military operations were pursued to the point that the whole island was pacified and
subsequently served as a base for launching revolutionary forays into
other islands of the Antilles. Expeditions embarked from St. Lucia for
St. Vincent, Grenada, and Martinique to join with revolutionary
forces in those islands in their common cause of liberation. The British
could hardly tolerate these military losses for long, and in 1796 an
invasion fleet with 12,000 men moved on St. Lucia, which had been
out of British hands for more than a year. Again they moved toward
the symbol of military control of the island, the fortress on Morne
Fortune above Castries. Converging on the promentory, they were
engaged by the revolutionary army which had liberated the island.
In the ensuing struggle, both sides battled fiercely for the fortress;
the blacks, outnumbered more than five to one, resisted the superior
force for a month. When the British army finally captured the hill and
forced the defenders to surrender, it did not mark the end of resistance,
for some of the blacks again took to the interior where they fought a
guerrilla campaign for over a year. The storming of the Morne did,
however, signal the end of a period of freedom for St. Lucian blacks,
a condition they would not achieve again for over forty years. Today
many remnants and edifices mark the many struggles for control of
the Morne Fortune and, ultimately, control of the island. Some bear
plaques and some are noted in guidebooks, while others are merely
piles of debris, the importance of which has gone unremarked. An
exception is a column erected in 1932 to commemorate the event of the
capture of the hill described above. An inscription on the stone reads:

On the 24th May, 1796, the 27th. Regt. stormed and captured
Morne Fortune. As a mark of the Regiment's gallent conduct Sir

Ralph Abercrombie ordered the French garrison to lay down their arms to the 27th. Regt. and directed that the King's colour of the 27th. Regt. be hoisted at the fort for 1 hour prior to the hoisting of the Union Flag.

The continued recognition of this event in the form of an annual ceremony attended by members of the St. Lucia Police Force is symbolic of the kind of irony that has become a part of the blacks' popular expression of their histories. This kind of self-mockery ought not to escape a people engaged in the reinterpretation of their own history. Perhaps it is best summed up in the words of a St. Lucian who has written: "Today we have a monument to mark this reintroducton of slavery in St. Lucia. Black officials pay tribute to it. It may perhaps be a demonstration of the native irony of our people. On the other hand it can be looked upon as an insult to Black people."[55]

Jamaica, The Persistence of an Image

A particular image of Jamaican society and the relationships it has engendered among its sectors has prevailed for well over a century. This image grew directly out of the tandem institutions of plantation agriculture and African slavery. Since emancipation in 1838, it has been held up to mirror a society which, through official channels, has sought to foster a public model of progress in the achievement of egalitarian ideals and interracial harmony. The counterversion that has occupied a continual place in the minds of most Jamaicans, and that has repeatedly been invoked in the numerous popular movements of self-liberation and expression, is at considerable variance from that of the racial paradise.

Briefly stated, Jamaican society is portrayed as rigidly divided between exploiter and exploited, between oppressor and oppressed, opposed categories that correspond with the racial opposition between white and black in the society.[56] Thus, the position blacks in Jamaica have occupied through time is directly analogous to that defined during slavery. This image has often been characterized in Biblical terms: the island is seen as a Babylon for the blacks. Most political movements have emphasized the image and have claimed to seek its resolution.[57] The proposed solutions have ranged from that of socialist revolution to an apocalyptic cleansing to "evolution not revolution." Nonetheless, the image has remained, capitalized upon by politicians seeking votes and employed by large numbers of Jamaicans in interpreting their society and its history. The brief portraits that follow examine examples of this persistence, how the image has been reinforced, and how people have acted upon it.

1831: The "Baptist War."[58] In 1831, the island, after more than two centuries of slavery and associated acts of resistance, erupted in what became the largest rebellion during the pre-emancipation era. Despite the fact that these events marked the culmination of the nineteenth-century trend toward the acceleration of resistance and rebellion, and that the intention of the 1831 action was to involve all of the slaves of the island, there was initially little violence except the burning of several estates in the western parishes. The response of the authorities operating through the militia was immediate and overwhelming. During the next fortnight, the retribution heaped upon slaves through outright killing and subsequent executions left over 500 dead.

In examining the underlying factors leading to this rebellion, writers have stressed the importance of the Baptist missionary movement and its activities among the slaves which involved discussions of human rights and the emancipation debates in England.[59] The division in the society is expressed in more than ecclesiastical terms, however, for as Patterson notes, the slaves in their response to the missionizing influence had Africanized the Baptist faith that was being offered them.[60] It was this syncretic process that gave rise to the religious movement known as "Native Baptists." This development represents more than just a curiosity for students of acculturative processes, for, as Patterson suggests, "Among those of the non-white population who developed a genuine interest in Christianity, religion became inseparably linked with social status *and political action.*"[61] [My emphasis.] Thus, the "Baptist War" was actually a struggle that was underlined by the most fundamental structural, racial, and cultural divisions in the society.

1865: Morant Bay. The series of events leading to the Morant Bay Rebellion in 1865 have been the subject of much debate and printed controversy, much of which revolves around the governor of the period, John Eyre. This is unfortunate, for a discussion focusing on the character and deeds of an individual tends to obscure an understanding of how these events reflect the relationships and recurrent actions that have long characterized Jamaican society.

In the quarter century following emancipation and the end of the apprenticeship period in 1838, the society and economy of Jamaica underwent some profound, if impermanent, changes. The decline in sugar production and the abandonment of estates were complemented by a dramatic rise in the number of independent smallholders and the production of foodstuffs for subsistence and local markets. The abundant indications of the growth of a resourceful, independent peasantry constituted an ominous sign for the oligarchic element that had held the reins of economic and political power in the island during much of its colonial history.[62]

The prosperity depicted here, that of smallholders released from bondage and managing through initiative and hard work, is not the kind of prosperity that the historical accounts of the area have portrayed. Moreover, in view of the continual decline of sugar and the abandonment of estates, it was not the kind of prosperity the Jamaican government was to allow to continue. By the early 1860s, the rising prosperity of the peasantry had been reversed; the government had levied taxes with a view to driving labor back to the plantations and had succeeded in creating a desperate situation for many Jamaicans. The government's wretched treatment of the smallholders was noted by E. B. Underhill who sounded a warning after a visit to the island in 1860. He mentioned particularly the heavy taxation, absence of justice, and denial of political rights as conditions making life unbearable for the peasantry.[63]

With this situation as a backdrop, the rebellion at Morant Bay took place in October 1865. After a confrontation between police and residents of the parish concerning the release of prisoners, violence broke out and a number of people, including some policemen, magistrates, and the *Custos* or local administrator, were killed. Retribution by the government under orders of Governor John Eyre was devastating. The number of dead after a two-week siege is unknown, but over 400 were executed with or without trial and more than 1,000 houses and properties were destroyed in the parish of St. Thomas in the East.[64]

Two aspects of the event, the actions leading up to it and its aftermath, particularly concern us here. First, the conditions that confronted the peasantry were made known to those who had the power and the responsibility to act on their behalf. Their impossible situation was regarded as totally inconsiderable by that sector of the society charged with maintaining the public good.⁶⁵ Second, a small incident, confined to a single parish, was dealt with as if it were an all-out attack on the foundations of the society; the governor's action, with subsequent acquiescence by most of the Jamaican establishment, was intended to demonstrate where the locus of power lay.

*Marcus Garvey in Jamaica.*⁶⁶ Despite the persistence of an official version which has repeatedly suggested progress and growth in Jamaican society, the relationships between population segments during the immediate postslavery period underwent very little change until Marcus Garvey appeared in the public life of the island. The Jamaica of 1915 is described in dismal terms by Brown: "Although seventy-eight years have passed since the total abolition of slavery, however, the condition of laborers in Jamaica remains practically the same as it was then." He characterizes the laborer's position as "still an economic slave."⁶⁷

This is the society into which Garvey was born and grew to young manhood, one in which the lot of most people of similar origins was fundamentally unchanged, despite the introduction of "stable government" following the Morant Bay massacres in 1865. Two brief periods of Garvey's career when he was resident on the island are examined here, and his reception and treatment by the custodians of power in the society in each instance are contrasted. The two periods are from 1914 to 1916, when Garvey was active in pan-African efforts in Jamaica before departing for the United States, and from 1927 to 1934, after his deportation from the United States.

The first period was a time of intense effort and creativity for Garvey, during which he founded and widely publicized the aims of the United Negro Improvement Association. This activity followed Garvey's odyssey which had brought him into contact first with black workers throughout the Caribbean and next with continental and African advocates of the pan-African ideal in London. His zeal and dedication to the task of forming an international association for the expression of African solidarity and the uplift of black peoples elicited curiously divided responses in his native island. He reported some cooperation from influential white officialdom and clergy and disdain from the Jamaican colored middle class for whom any hint of an African connection was anathema. His decision to quit Jamaica for the United States was not the result of abject failure of his efforts, but rather stemmed from his realization of the importance of directing such a movement from a central, powerful nation like the United States, which had the largest black population in the Western Hemisphere.[68]

The second period was marked by a somewhat different response to Garvey as an individual and to his pan-African efforts. In 1927, he had returned to Jamaica, no longer a bright, if untried, young man initiating an ideal, but the persecuted leader of the largest black mass movement in history, branded by the establishment press and government of the United States as a dangerous (if only because demented) figure. His reputation as a danger to the established order followed him to Jamaica and gave his opposition an excuse to frustrate his efforts over the next seven years.[69] This time, however, it was the Jamaican colonial establishment which continually attempted to hamstring Garvey's operations. The colored sector of the population may still have been queasy about an identification with blackness or Africa, but Garvey's essential problem was that he *was* a threat. By then, through word and accomplishment he represented a decided contradiction to the underlying assumptions on which Jamaican society was based.

Labor Unrest and the Modern Political Era. The labor riots that occurred in the West Indies in the late 1930s had more direct political effect in Jamaica than elsewhere.[70] The 1938 riots again provoked a massive display of force by the colonial government, even as they demonstrated once again the correctness of all those reports of successive Royal commissions which had cautiously suggested that all was not well on the Jamaican labor scene. At this juncture, however, the stage was set for the emergence of a new political force: the urbanite, middle-class labor leader and/or lawyer who, representative of a growing city-based collectivity and supported at the polls by an expanded electorate, came to power throughout the islands. As an immediate consequence of the 1938 disturbances, two men, through their personalities and political organizations, came to dominate Jamaica's electoral politics over the next quarter century.

The institution of a universal adult franchise in 1944 set the stage for the rise of Alexander Bustamante and Norman Manley to power in Jamaican electoral politics.[71] Bustamante, in particular, employed some of the same tactics of mass appeal that others had before him, some of whom had arrived too early to capitalize on the new expanded electorate and others who had chosen other avenues. But the two leaders and their political parties formed the movement of the time;

they shared mass support of the electorate; and they were the vanguard of the organized labor movement. The promise for changing the society was there in their rhetoric and their presence. Yet, twenty-five years after the riots both men had grown old. Whatever dreams they had had they had compromised, and the promises for societal transformation had faded. The "new day" many had envisioned had not become a reality.

A preoccupation with personalities can frequently impede the writing of history and the analysis of political developments, particularly when these personalities are still living or their memories remain fresh. The examination of Jamaican progress in the years following the 1938 riots and the institution of universal suffrage provides a case in point of this kind of obscurant analysis. Lewis, in drawing comparisons between personalities, suggests that Garvey would have had the same fortune with an expanded electorate as Bustamante, but that "the development of modern Jamaica might have been fundamentally different," presumably in the direction of a fundamental transformation of the society.[72] Manley's biographer, on the other hand, indicates the singular achievements of his subject and lays the blame for Jamaica's and the West Indies' retarded political maturity on the pettiness of others.[73] Both of these approaches are misplaced.

Lately, the standard for studies of recent political and social change has risen with the publication of a series of monographs by social scientists resident in and committed to the area. In the case of Jamaica, this trend is exemplified by Trevor Munroe's analysis of the island's political life in the modern era.[74] Proceeding from a picture of the structural situation at the time of the riots and the elections of 1944, Munroe charts events since that time without extensive reference to the character and personal idiosyncrasies of Bustamante and Manley. Rather than demonstrate the importance of their personalities, Munroe concentrates on the nature and interests of those sectors of the society that they came to represent. In this regard, Munroe is able to account for the paucity of structural change generated by these two principal figures and the political battles they waged. His conclusion concerning the role the middle and working classes would have had to play in any societal transformation during this period again illustrates the facile nature of analyses focused on personalities.[75]

The Jamaican Present. The question remains whether Jamaican society has been transformed in the period since World War II. Certainly, much has happened internally and in the larger world that impinges on the life of the island with even greater insistence. But what evidence exists for the alteration of those basic divisions in Jamaican society, repeatedly indicated in the historical events depicted above? To what extent is the image of Jamaican society sketched at the outset still a valid one, and does it remain useful in informing the behavior of the majority of Jamaicans?

A striking example of how patterns of inequality have persisted to the present in Jamaica is evidenced in the following excerpt from a 1962 report on the Jamaican economy to the prime minister. After detailing some "remarkable" characteristics of the previous ten-year period of economic growth, the writer states:

This proud trend is only marred by the undeniable increase in inequality in the island, despite the efforts of the government. The income in agriculture has hardly increased—the production of food seems to have actually declined. The problems of the small farmer are especially acute, though the extensive and costly Farm Development and Settlement Schemes were directed precisely at the relief of this sector. In the urban scene, too, the share of wages has diminished, while total company profits have increased. Within the wage sector, the discrepancy between the earnings of the skilled workers in the organized trades and the rest have also shown striking increase. While unemployment has been reduced, it remains a grave problem. This increase in inequality might explain, at least partially, the less than complete economic psychological impact of the magnificent economic record of the Government of Jamaica.[76]

The preceding account could not be a better example of tongue-in-cheek irony if it were so intended. Its obvious message is that the negative aspects of the economic picture most directly affect the well-being of the overwhelming majority of the population, rural smallholders, and the urban unskilled. Thus, despite the modern growth of the Jamaican economy, the same sectors of the labor force that have contributed work out of proportion to their rewards in the past remain outside the benefits accruing from this remarkable growth. What is more, it is precisely in the area of the traditional basis of the economy, the sugar industry, where modernization is phasing out workers who for generations have maintained and have depended upon the plantation.[77] There is ample indication that the industry, itself symbolic of the divisions in the society, remains incapable of self-examination, still demanding special privilege in the economy, and still unresponsive to assertions of workers' rights.[78]

Today, then, much in the structure of Jamaican society represents a continuation of basic, long-standing schisms. The emergence of the Rastafarians as exemplifying a spiritual mirror to catch the reflection of this society and the widespread appeal of the cultural aspects of this movement are indicative of the continued currency of the image. The startling fact is that the seriousness of the situation has not mitigated the manipulation of images by contemporary politicians, a situation reminiscent of that which followed the 1938 unrest.[79] These politicians recognize that these trends in Jamaican self-recognition are serious, but whether they will formulate programs commensurate with the gravity of the situation remains an unanswered question.

Nonetheless, there are now a few realities that the Jamaican power elites can ill afford to ignore. The image of the society depicted in Rastafarian dogma and implicit in the actions of Jamaicans for over a century now seems to have much greater popular support than in the recent past.[80] Moreover, many young, educated Jamaicans espouse this characterization, and all the more firmly as a result of the repressive actions of recent governments. Finally, it is an image which informs political action; it has done so in the past and, unless important changes are effected, it will do so in the future.

CONCLUSION: SYMBOLS AND IDENTITY

The discussion of literature in this essay surveys a few directions West Indian writers have already charted and suggests others that have only been minimally explored. While it is difficult to predict the future course of creative endeavor, two related trends may eventually alter the relationship between the artist and the West Indian public. First, younger intellectuals and artists are now remaining in the islands or are returning after brief periods abroad rather than maintaining an expatriate existence as so many did in the past. Whether this trend will continue obviously depends partly on the growth of a local readership.

Closely linked with this trend is the second, the enthusiasm of younger writers for poetry and their use of the language of the masses. This trend is an important one, for poetry lends itself, much more than prose, to performance; thus, the artist can be assured a wider audience and the influence that the written word has historically had in West Indian society.

In sum, West Indian writers have often sought to define an identity for their people, not so much in a patriotic or historical sense as in an attempt to explore (1) the relationship of the individual to the natural environment, (2) racial identity, and (3) an acceptance, if less than exhaltation, of indigenous cultural forms. Mazrui has noted the tendency of African writers to move beyond the patriotic themes evoked during nationalistic struggles to dealing with "postnational" issues.[81] Whereas writers of the earlier period emphasized the African/European contrasts in an effort to celebrate indigenous forms, the more recent trend is self-critical and focuses on topics such as postcolonial political corruption. In contrast, much of West Indian literature has never had to under go this transition, for it has contained an element of self-criticism from its inception. This literature expresses great awareness of the subtleties and complexities of the social patterns of the islands. As such, it has underscored the absurdities of color and class distinctions, along with their distructive ramifications, with as much alacrity as it has condemned the role of the European colonizer as an historical and social malignancy.

The discussion of the events of the late eighteenth century in the Eastern Caribbean suggests the possibilities that historical information can be reinterpreted to serve West Indian self-interest. Reinterpretation of the historical data is needed not only to better serve propagandistic interests of nationalistic movements, but also for its scholarly value. The earlier accounts, bound by Euro-centric interpretation, are inimical to regional self-pride, and in addition are frequently inaccurate or misinformed. Application of a West Indian perspective can help correct erroneous misconceptions and can contribute to a fuller historical understanding of the region.

The question with which the writer of Jamaican history—and perhaps of all West Indian history as well—must concern himself is whether the popular image of Jamaican social life is correct. This is not to say that it may be verifiable by historical evidence on every count but rather whether the popular image is a view which, taken into consideration, might more fully inform the historian. Can it be that black

Jamaicans have had a better informed view of social and political realities than have some of the scholars who have sought to interpret the historical evidence?

This view is also related to nationalistic symbols. If Paul Bogle has been elevated to the status of national hero on the basis that he was simply an individual who opposed an inept and cruel governor, Edward John Eyre, then the symbol is ephemeral, amounting to little more than recognition of an interesting historical event over which must ado was made in England.

If, on the other hand, Bogle is seen as symbolic of the oppression of black people and the event of Morant Bay as epitomizing the profound historical divisions in Jamaican society, then the symbol of the national hero has a decidedly different character. If Jamaicans come to view their history in those terms, the results may be a strengthened national identity and an informed revolutionary nationalism as well.

Mazrui writes of five processes fundamental to nation-building: cultural fusion, economic interpenetration, social integration, conflict resolution, and shared national experience.[82] Since this essay on West Indian history and literature has not specifically addressed economic and political issues, the processes of economic interpenetration and conflict resolution are of little concern here. The other three processes are more pertinent to our discussion, however. The creation of literature and the interpretation of historical experience are both directly concerned with these issues; they may contribute to and inform action designed toward these processes as ends.

One of these processes may bear a somewhat different relationship to the work of writers and historians. The achievement of social integration, the "process by which gaps between the elite and the masses, the town and the countryside, the privileged and the underprivileged, are gradually narrowed,"[83] may not be positively related to the efforts described above. With regard to the discussion of historical events in Jamaica, the direction in which some historical interpretation may influence this process seems questionable. A tendency—whether in literature or the writing of history—to throw into sharper focus the divisions of the society may, at least in the short run, exacerbate the conflict and the gaps between collectivities who see their interests as opposed.

Writers of literature and history can help a people to achieve cultural fusion and positive self-definition. Specifically, in the West Indian situation, they can help the people to see themselves as more than mere adjuncts to the history of other nations and to realize that their cultural tradition is not stunted and derivative. In turn, these achievements can lead to the kind of collective introspection from which a heightened sense of peoplehood can emerge. While the question of whether history is shaped through the actions of the masses or through the thoughts of the intellectuals is moot, it seems that if the West Indian renewal Walcott envisions is possible, the contribution of writers and historians toward cultural fusion and positive self-definition must be sustained and continually experimental.

NOTES

1. This essay is largely part of my continuing study of matters of identity among black people in the Caribbean and in Great Britain. Any insights that may be found here are attributable to conversations with many people, most importantly John Stewart in Illinois, George Odlum and Fergus Lawrence in St. Lucia, and John La Rose in London; persisting blind spots are my responsibility. The use of the terms *West Indies* and *West Indian* refers to that part of the Caribbean archipelago that was under the recent colonial domination of Great Britain.

2. Derek Walcott, "The Caribbean: Culture or Mimicry?" *Journal of Interamerican Studies and World Affairs* 16 (1974):13.

3. A full background to the issues and problems of the contemporary West Indies may be found in the introductory chapters of two excellent general works on the region. See Gordon K. Lewis, *The Growth of the Modern West Indies* (London: MacGibbon and Kee, 1968), pp. 15-68; and David Lowenthal, *West Indian Societies* (London: Oxford University Press, 1972), pp. 1-75.

4. Lewis, *The Growth,* p. 18.

5. Ali A. Mazrui, *Cultural Engineering and Nation-Building in East Africa* (Evanston, Ill.: Northwestern University Press, 1972).

6. Mazrui, *Cultural Engineering,* p. xv.

7. Ibid., p. 23.

8. Derek Walcott, "Tales of the Islands, Chapter X," in *In a Green Night* (London: Jonathan Cape, 1962), p. 30.

9. Gerald Moore, *The Chosen Tongue* (London: Longmans, 1969), pp. 20-26.

10. See Walcott, "Return to D'Ennery, Rain," in *In a Green Night,* pp. 33-34; idem, "Homecoming: Anse La Raye," in *The Gulf* (London: Jonathan Cape, 1969), pp. 50-51; idem, *Another Life* (New York: Farrar, Straus, and Giroux, 1973), pp. 32-38.

11. The three plays mentioned are collected in a volume, *Dream on Monkey Mountain and Other Plays* (New York: Farrar, Straus, and Giroux, 1970).

12. George Lamming, *In the Castle of My Skin* (London: Michael Joseph, 1953).

13. Michael Anthony, *The Year in San Fernando* (London: Andre Deutsch, 1965) and idem, *Green Days by the River* (London: Andre Deutsch, 1967).

14. Dennis Scott, "Homecoming," in *Uncle Time* (Pittsburgh: University of Pittsburgh Press, 1973), p. 8.

15. In a recent publication, Edward Brathwaite pursues the topic of Africa in Caribbean writing in much greater depth. The interested reader is advised to consult his "The African Presence in Caribbean Literature," *Daedelus* 103, no. 2 (1974):73-109.

16. Lamming, *Season of Adventure* (London: Michael Joseph, 1960).

17. Kenneth Ramchand, *The West Indian Novel and Its Background* (London: Faber and Faber, 1970), p. 149. As noted above, a thematic approach necessarily results in some distortion of the purposes of a writer, a suggestion that seems most justified with respect to the work of Lamming. Because his writing is so many-faceted, and because he is working with ideas at different levels of reality and consciousness, his work is often misrepresented by critics. A contrast, however, is the fine insight into his art given in an interview with George Kent. See Kent, "A Conversation with George Lamming," *Black World* 22, no. 5 (1973):4-15, 88-97.

18. Walcott, *Monkey Mountain*, pp. 308-320.

19. Walcott, *Ione* (Mona, Jamaica: Extra-mural Department, University College of the West Indies, 1953).

20. Walcott, "A Far Cry from Africa," in *In a Green Night*, p. 18.

21. Brathwaite, *Rights of Passage* (London: Oxford University Press, 1967); idem, *Masks* (London: Oxford University Press, 1968); and idem, *Islands* (London: Oxford University Press, 1969).

22. Brathwaite, "Epilogue," in *Rights of Passage*, p. 86.

23. See V. S. Naipaul, *The Middle Passage* (London: Andre Deutsch, 1962) and idem, *The Overcrowded Barracoon* (London: Andre Deutsch, 1972).

24. Brathwaite, "All God's Chillun," in *Rights of Passage*, pp. 16-20.

25. Walcott, in *Monkey Mountain*, pp. 81-166.

26. V. S. Reid, *New Day* (New York: Knopf, 1949).

27. For examples of recent trends in poetry, see Andrew Salkey, ed., *Breaklight* (Garden City, N.Y.: Anchor/Doubleday, 1973) and *Savacou*, no. 3/4 (1970/1971).

28. Roger Mais, *The Hills Were Joyful Together* (London: Jonathan Cape, 1953), and idem, *Brother Man* (London: Jonathan Cape, 1954). These two are now collected along with a third novel in *Three Novels* (London: Jonathan Cape, 1966).

29. Orlando Patterson, *The Children of Sisyphus* (London: New Authors, 1964).

30. V. S. Naipaul, *The Mimic Men* (London: Andre Deutsch, 1967).

31. Garth St. Omer, *Nor Any Country* (London: Faber and Faber, 1969), pp. 104-105.

32. Andrew Salkey, *The Late Emancipation of Jerry Stover* (London: Hutchinson, 1968).

33. John Stewart, *Last Cool Days* (London: Andre Deutsch, 1970).

34. Lamming, *In the Castle*, p. 295.

35. For discussions of the use of language in West Indian writing, see Moore, *The Chosen Tongue*, pp. xviii-xx, and Ramchand, *West Indian Novel*, pp. 77-114.

36. There is a problem of readership here because lexically patois is of mostly French derivation. For treatments of the language, see Mervin Alleyne, "Language and Society in St. Lucia," *Caribbean Studies* 1 (1961):1-10, and Douglas Midgett, "Bilingualism and Linguistic Change in St. Lucia," *Anthropological Linguistics* 1$2 (1970):158-170.

37. St. Omer, *Syrop*, in *Introduction 2: Stories by New Writers* (London: Faber and Faber, 1964). For another example of the alterations the writer must make to accom-

modate his work to a larger audience, compare Walcott's *The Sea at Dauphin,* collected in *Monkey Mountain,* with an earlier version (Mona, Jamaica: Extra-mural Department, University College of the West Indies, 1958).

38. Reid, *New Day.*

39. *Savacou,* no. 3/4 (1970/1971).

40. The particularistic-universalistic controversy is characteristic of black American literature as well. This is not surprising considering that literature is used as a vehicle for self-assertion and for the definition of community. Interestingly, metropolitan critics in both the United States and Great Britain are perfectly happy with black writers who employ universalistic themes as long as they stick to parochial settings in black America and the islands. The paradox of the writer seems to be that, to achieve critical acclaim, the topics he chooses and his approach to them must not confuse the critic, and at the same time he must not become overly ambitious and overextend to areas with which he is not familiar. Understandably, many writers in both areas have chosen to ignore the critics altogether, and the result has been a growing indigenous literary criticism. Examples are Ramchand, *West Indian Novel;* Wilfred Carty, *Black Images* (New York: Teachers College Press, 1970); Louis James, ed., *The Islands in Between* (London: Oxford University Press, 1968); John La Rose, ed., *New Beacon Reviews Collection One* (London: New Beacon Books, 1968); Sylvia Wynter, "One Love—Rhetoric or Reality?—Aspects of Afro-Jamaicanism," *Caribbean Studies* 12 (1972):64-97; and a number of articles by Gordon Rohlehr.

41. Mazrui, *Cultural Engineering,* pp. 3-22.

42. Ibid., pp. 14-16.

43. W. Adolph Roberts, *The French in the West Indies* (New York: Bobbs Merrill, 1942), pp. 223-232.

44. See Eric Williams, *British Historians and the West Indies* (New York: Scribner's, 1966), especially Chapter 5.

45. Sir Alan Burns, *History of the British West Indies* (London: Allen & Unwin, 1954), p. 542. Under the subheading "The War in the Lesser Antilles," Burns repeatedly characterizes the opposing forces in terms of "British" and "French."

46. Roberts, *The French,* p. 229.

47. Brian Edwards, *The History, Civil and Commercial of the British Colonies in the West Indies,* 2 vols. (London: John Stockdale, 1807), vol. 2, 470-474.

48. Burns, *West Indies,* p. 567.

49. B. H. Easter, *St. Lucia and the French Revolution* (Castries: The Voice Publishing Co.l, 1965), pp. 10, 11.

50. Alec Waugh, *A Family of Islands* (New York: Doubleday, 1964), p. 205.

51. Burns, *West Indies,* p. 568; Waugh, *Family of Islands,* p. 211.

52. Rev. Charles Jesse, *Outlines of St. Lucia's History* (Castries: St. Lucia Archaeological and Historical Society, 1964), p. 24.

53. Henry H. Breen, *St. Lucia: Historical, Statistical and Descriptive* (London: Cass, 1970), p. 74. (Original printing, 1844.)

54. Ibid., p. 78.

55. Hilford Deterville, "The Liberation of Black St. Lucians," *The Crusader* (Castries), May 24, 1970, p. 11.

56. Sociologically, Jamaica is not a two-category racial system. This consideration, however, is beside the point of the characterization elaborated here since all that has been written of color-class continua and "social color" frequently glosses the fact that in Jamaica most black people are poor and most poor people are black.

57. This Biblical imagery appears not only in the characterization of Jamaican society by Rastafarians or by vote-seeking politicians but in the popular realm as well. In *New Day*, V. S. Reid depicts George William Gordon exhorting a congregation with lines from the 137th Psalm, the "Rivers of Babylon" Psalm (p. 27).

58. This section is compiled primarily from accounts by Orlando Patterson, *The Sociology of Slavery* (London: MacGibbon and Kee, 1967), pp. 272-282; Mary Reckord, "The Jamaican Slave Rebellion of 1831," in R. Frucht, ed., *Black Society in the New World* (New York: Random House, 1971), pp. 50-66; and Philip Curtin, *Two Jamaicas* (Cambridge, Mass.: Harvard University Press, 1955), pp. 82-89.

59. Curtin, *Two Jamaicas,* pp. 83-84.

60. Patterson, *Sociology of Slavery,* pp. 211-212.

61. Ibid., p. 213.

62. Eric Williams, *British Historians,* pp. 87-88.

63. Quoted in ibid., pp. 102-105.

64. The events of Morant Bay are variously reported in a number of sources, including Williams, *British Historians,* pp. 117-126; Curtin, *Two Jamaicas,* pp. 195-197; and Douglas Hall, *Free Jamaica 1838-1865* (New Haven: Yale University Press, 1959), pp. 245-248.

65. An example of indifference at the highest level is the "Queen's Advice," quoted in Hall, *Free Jamaica,* pp. 244-245.

66. Garvey's career, his writings, and his political philosophy have been the subject of numerous studies. The interested reader is particularly urged to consult Amy Jacques-Garvey, *Garvey and Garveyism* (London: Collier-Macmillan, 1970) and John Henrik Clarke, *Marcus Garvey and the Vision of Africa* (New York: Vintage, 1974). Much of the material in this section is drawn from these sources.

67. E. Ethelred Brown, "Labor Conditions in Jamaica Prior to 1917," *Journal of Negro History* 4 (1919):351.

68. Clarke, *Marcus Garvey,* pp. 49-70.

69. Ibid., pp. 259-264, 276-283.

70. K.W.J. Post, "The Politics of Protest in Jamaica, 1938: Some Problems of Analysis and Conceptualization," *Social and Economic Studies* 18 (1969):375.

71. For more elaboration of this period and the politics and political organizations of Bustamante and Manley, see Post, "Politics of Protest"; Trevor Munroe, *The Politics of Constitutional Decolonization* (Mona, Jamaica: Institute of Social and Economic Research, University of the West Indies, 1972); and Rex Nettleford, ed., *Manley and the New Jamaica* (New York: Africana Publishing Corp., 1971).

72. Lewis, *The Growth,* pp. 177-178. The suggestion that Garvey may have had the political success of Bustamante confuses tactics with programs. I have already indicated that Garvey's problems in Jamaica after 1927 resulted from the implications of his proposed programs for profound changes in that society. It is therefore questionable how much success he might have been able to achieve at a later time.

73. Nettleford, *Manley and Jamaica,* pp. lxxxii-xciv.
74. Munroe, *Constitutional Decolonization.*
75. Ibid., p. 190.
76. Thomas Balogh, *The Economics of Poverty* (New York: Macmillan, 1966), pp. 293-294.
77. See, for example, the account of "Mitchell Town" in L. Alan Eyre, *Geographic Aspects of Population Dynamics in Jamaica* (Boca Raton, Fla.: Florida Atlantic University Press, 1972), pp. 101-119.
78. An examination of the "Symposium on Sugar and Change in the Caribbean" is instructive in this regard. See *New World Quarterly* 5 (1969):32-57.
79. Electioneering in the 1972 campaign provides a current example. See W. Richard Jacobs, "Appeals by Jamaican Political Parties: A Study of Newspaper Advertisements in the 1972 Jamaican General Election Campaign," *Caribbean Studies* 13 (1973):19-50.
80. A rather dramatic example is the success of Michael Manley's 1972 election campaign. The use of Rasta-tinged rhetoric, the identification with the "sufferers," and the employment of reggae music and other cultural aspects particularly associated with Kingston's urban poor cast Manley's campaign in sharp contrast to that of his opponent. See also Rex Nettleford, *Mirror, Mirror: Identity, Race and Protest in Jamaica* (Kingston: W. Collins and Sangster, 1970), pp. 39-111.
81. Mazrui, *Cultural Engineering,* pp. 36-37.
82. Ibid., pp. 277-293.
83. Ibid., p. 277.

BIBLIOGRAPHY

Alleyne, Mervin. 1961. "Language and Society in St. Lucia," *Caribbean Studies* 1:1-10.
Anthony, Michael. 1965. *The Year in San Fernando.* London: Andre Deutsch.
_____. 1967. *Green Days by the River.* London: Andre Deutsch.
Balogh, Thomas. 1966. *The Economics of Poverty.* New York: Macmillan.
Brathwaite, Edward. 1967. *Rights of Passage.* London: Oxford University Press.
_____. 1968. *Masks.* London: Oxford University Press.
_____. 1969. *Islands.* London: Oxford University Press.
_____. 1974. "The African Presence in Caribbean Literature," *Daedelus* 103, no. 2: 73-109.
Breen, Henry H. 1970. *St. Lucia: Historical, Statistical and Descriptive.* London: Cass. (Original edition, 1844.)
Brown, E. Ethelred. 1919. "Labor Conditions in Jamaica Prior to 1917," *Journal of Negro History* 4:349-360.
Burns, Sir Alan. 1954. *History of the British West Indies.* London: Allen & Unwin.
Carty, Wilfred. 1970. *Black Images.* New York: Teachers College Press.
Clarke, John Henrik. 1974. *Marcus Garvey and the Vision of Africa.* New York: Vintage.
Curtin, Philip. 1955. *Two Jamaicas.* Cambridge, Mass.: Harvard University Press.
Deterville, Hilford. 1970. "The Liberation of Black St. Lucians," *The Crusader,* May 24.
Easter, B. H. 1965. *St. Lucia and the French Revolution.* Castries: The Voice Publishing Co.

Edwards, Brian. 1807. *The History, Civil and Commercial of the British Colonies in the West Indies*. Vol. 2. London: John Stockdale.

Eyre, L. Alan. 1972. *Geographic Aspects of Population Dynamics in Jamaica*. Boca Raton, Fla.: Florida Atlantic University Press.

Hall, Douglas. 1959. *Free Jamaica 1838-1865*. New Haven: Yale University Press.

Jacobs, W. Richard. 1973. "Appeals by Jamaican Political Parties: A Study of Newspaper Advertisements in the 1972 Jamaican General Election Campaign," *Caribbean Studies* 13:19-50.

Jacques-Garvey, Amy. 1970. *Garvey and Garveyism*. London: Collier-Macmillan.

James, Louis (ed.). 1968. *The Islands in Between*. London: Oxford University Press.

Jesse, Rev. Charles. 1964. *Outlines of St. Lucia's History*. Castries: St. Lucia Archaeological and Historical Society.

Kent, George. 1973. "A Conversation with George Lamming," *Black World* 22, no. 5: 4-15, 88-97.

Lamming, George. 1953. *In the Castle of My Skin*. London: Michael Joseph.

_____.1960. *Season of Adventure*. London: Michael Joseph.

La Rose, John (ed.). 1968. *New Beacon Reviews Collection One*. London: New Beacon Books.

Lewis, Gordon K. 1968. *The Growth of the Modern West Indies*. London: MacGibbon and Kee.

Lowenthal, David. 1972. *West Indian Societies*. London: Oxford University Press.

Mais. Roger. 1953. *The Hills Were Joyful Together*. London: Jonathan Cape.

_____. 1954. *Brother Man*. London: Jonathan Cape.

_____. 1966. *Three Novels*. London: Jonathan Cape.

Mazrui, Ali A. 1972. *Cultural Engineering and Nation-Building in East Africa*. Evanston, Ill.: Northwestern University Press.

Midgett, Douglas. 1970. "Bilingualism and Linguistic Change in St. Lucia," *Anthropological Linguistics* 12:158-170.

Moore, Gerald. 1969. *The Chosen Tongue*. London: Longmans.

Munroe, Trevor. 1972. *The Politics of Constitutional Decolonization*. Mona, Jamaica: Institute of Social and Economic Research, University of the West Indies.

Naipaul, V. S. 1962. *The Middle Passage*. London: Andre Deutsch.

_____. 1967. *The Mimic Men*. London: Andre Deutsch.

_____. 1972. *The Overcrowded Barracoon*. London: Andre Deutsch.

Nettleford, Rex. 1970. *Mirror, Mirror: Identity, Race and Protest in Jamaica*. Kingston: W. Collins and Sangster.

Nettleford, Rex (ed.). 1971. *Manley and the New Jamaica*. New York: Africana Publishing Corp.

New World Quarterly. 1969. "Symposium on Sugar and Change in the Caribbean," vol. 5:32-57.

Patterson, Orlando. 1964. *The Children of Sisyphus*. London: New Authors.

_____. 1967. *The Sociology of Slavery*. London: MacGibbon and Kee.

Post, K.W.J. 1969. "The Politics of Protest in Jamaica, 1938: Some Problems of Analysis and Conceptualization," *Social and Economic Studies* 18:374-390.

Ramchand, Kenneth. 1970. *The West Indian Novel and Its Background*. London: Faber and Faber.

Reckord, Mary. 1971. "The Jamaican Slave Rebellion of 1831," in R. Frucht, ed., *Black Society in the New World*. New York: Random House.
Reid, V. S. 1949. *New Day*. New York: Knopf.
Roberts, W. Adolph. 1942. *The French in the West Indies*. New York: Bobbs Merrill.
St. Omer, Garth. 1964. "Syrop," in *Introduction 2: Stories by New Writers*. London: Faber and Faber.
_____. 1969. *Nor Any Country*. London: Faber and Faber.
Salkey, Andrew. 1968. *The Late Emancipation of Jerry Stover*. London: Hutchinson.
Salkey, Andrew (ed.). 1973. *Breaklight*. Garden City, N.Y.: Anchor/Doubleday.
Savacou. 1970/1971. Special issue, no. 3/4.
Scott, Dennis. 1973. *Uncle Time*. Pittsburgh: University of Pittsburgh Press.
Stewart, John. 1970. *Last Cool Days*. London: Andre Deutsch.
Walcott, Derek. 1953. *Ione*. Mona, Jamaica: Extra-mural Department, University College of the West Indies.
_____. 1958. *The Sea at Dauphin*. Mona, Jamaica: Extra-mural Department, University College of the West Indies.
_____. 1962. *In a Green Night*. London: Jonathan Cape.
_____. 1969. *The Gulf*. London: Jonathan Cape.
_____. 1970. *Dream on Monkey Mountain and Other Plays*. New York: Farrar, Straus, and Giroux.
_____. 1973. *Another Life*. New York: Farrar, Straus, and Giroux.
_____. 1974. "The Caribbean: Culture or Mimicry?" *Journal of Interamerican Studies and World Affairs* 16:3-13.
Waugh, Alec. 1964. *A Family of Islands*. New York: Doubleday.
Williams, Eric. 1966. *British Historians and the West Indies*. New York: Scribner's.
Wynter, Sylvia. 1972. "One Love—Rhetoric or Reality?—Aspects of Afro-Jamaicanism," *Caribbean Studies* 12:64-97.

Norman E. Whitten, Jr.

9

RITUAL ENACTMENT OF SEX ROLES IN THE PACIFIC LOWLANDS OF ECUADOR-COLOMBIA*

Probably every Euro-American scholar who has worked in a black or Afro-American community in Latin America or the Caribbean has experienced what he regarded as exotic and prosaic rituals. The exotic has all too often been classed as "sacred" and the prosaic as "mundane." Prosaic ritual has received relatively less attention than the exotic, and even where exotic ritual has been found to be secular, many investigators have groped for evidence of past cults. The literature on Afro-American ritual life is full of the results of searches for syncretism, retention, and reinterpretation of "exotic" African forms, but it is deficient in a portrayal of the *range* of ritual life in contemporary settings. Furthermore, the anthropological search for exotic, distinctive ritual features of ethnic units in complex societies often obscures the importance of all ritual behavior in the lives of the participants.

This essay is a deliberate attempt to merge the analysis of exotic and prosaic, distinctive and nondistinctive ritual with a discussion of social structure. The focus is one structural feature—sex roles.[1] Other features such as consanguinity, affinity, group formation, network maintenance, rank, stratification, and mobility are discussed in Whitten (1974).

In order to merge the study of social and ritual forms in Afro-American systems of adaptation, still more clarification is needed. Ulf Hannerz (1970:314) recently summarized the failure of anthropology to discuss sex roles at all in Afro-American cultures:

*From *Ethnology,* Vol. 13, No. 2. Copyright © 1974 by *Ethnology.* Reprinted by permission of *Ethnology.*

Most of what has been said about the sex roles of New World black people can find its place in one of three perspectives [represented by the work of Melville Herskovits, e.g. 1941, 1943; E. Franklin Frazier, e.g. 1932, 1934, 1939, 1942, 1949; and Raymond T. Smith, e.g. 1956, 1963] . . . this means that the studies only marginally involve the discussion of sex roles *per se,* as they are first of all studies of the family or household as an institution.

The institutional set of activities discussed as "family and household" has also been considerably garbled until recently because many scholars have consistently failed to distinguish between appropriate domains of activity. González (1970:223-232) recently clarified the approach to these domains.

I suggest that we reserve the term "household" for the cooperative group which maintains and participates in a given *residential* structure, even though the contribution of any one individual may be only part time. . .

"Family" seems most usefully defined in terms of kinship networks; that is, in terms of the kinds of kinship bonds among the different individuals considered to be members of the unit.[2]

The concepts "household" and "kinship network" must be clearly distinguished; it cannot be automatically and unquestionably assumed that they belong to the same domain of activity. With an understanding of sex roles as a component of social structure related to household, kinship, and other domains, it will be possible to devise techniques for assembling data that will lead to a productive set of concepts about any particular Afro-American, or any other, style of life. This essay illustrates an approach that allows for considerable synthesis of materials from various domains, and that also serves to document the breadth and complexity of one particular Afro-American sex role system as viewed through several ritual settings.

The area discussed includes the lowland rainforest of the Pacific littoral which extends from Buenaventura in west-central Colombia to Esmeraldas, in northern Ecuador.[3] The activity patterns are manifested by black people who constitute the lower class in any town.[4] This area has over half a million black people who make up 90 percent or more of the population. They share a set of activities, institutions, and beliefs that are quite apparent in both secular and sacred ritual contexts. Variations in sex role enactment in some of the ritual contexts are described, and the relationship of such an enactment to household, kinship, community, and intercommunity continuity is suggested. The structure that emerges from an analysis of contextually patterned complementary and contrastive role relationships is referred to here as "Afro-Hispanic culture." This essay outlines three secular contexts of sex role enactment, briefly discusses some aspects of the Afro-Hispanic world view in relationship to daily life, presents three sacred ritual contexts, and finally indicates the relationship of ritual enactment to social structural continuity.

SECULAR CONTEXTS OF SEX ROLE ENACTMENT

The Cantina Context

The setting is a small room in which two to eight men gather, day or night, to drink *aguardiente* (rum) and engage in ritual exchanges of songs, riddles, *décimas,* and stories. They tell exaggerated tales of politics, travel, and sexual exploits, and relate events involving demons, phantom ships, spirits, and souls of the deceased. Children may sit on the outer steps listening, and other men and women usually loiter nearby, also listening to the stylized conversations within.

Music does not dominate this setting. When it is played, it is almost always either a Mexican *ranchero,* or a ballad from the highlands of Ecuador (in Ecuador) or in a style associated with an inland area of Colombia (in Colombia). The musical aspect signals national or international identification, but the nonmusical *content* expressed is on the whole characteristic of Afro-Hispanic culture. It consists of traits that are generally not found in the interior of Colombia or Ecuador; when present, they are in different forms and have quite different meanings.

In the *cuentos,* or stylized stories, one man relates a tale known to the others, but always with his own elaboration. The speaker endeavors to establish a deep emotional tone through onomatopoeia; he imitates animals, demons, spirits, and human sounds of agony and ecstasy. Three themes dominate: extensive travel, great bouts of interpersonal combat, and amazing feats of sexual intercourse. In all cases, elaborate intrigue characterizes the plot. Political discussions are greatly stylized and never fall to the level of local events; rather, the upper reaches of national and foreign governments are elaborately described. Fear of the unknown is also communicated in this secular ritual setting, and always the means for combating the manifestations which the unknown may take at a particular time are explained. It is in this setting that one may learn all there is to know about the fearful creatures known as *visiones* (ghosts and spirits), *brujas* (witch-ghouls), and *brujos* (diviner-sorcerers). In all cases the means of overcoming the fear creatures—through direct male physical force, proper diagnosis by men, or male trickery—is stressed. Male strength, wit, and planning over female, spirit, and supermale adversaries pervade all the stories.

In the *décima,* men recite memorized poems, competing for accuracy with others who may know the poem, while in the *adivinanzas* (riddles) individuals again express competitively their self-assertion, trying to present a riddle that cannot be answered by anyone in the setting, or by answering someone else's riddle. There are enough modes of expression through the *décimas, cuentos,* boasts of successful encounters with powerful adversaries or sexual exploits, and stories of inside knowledge of foreign governments, so that each individual finds some mode of self assertion of his male attributes.

"Truth" has no place in the cantina context. Men pass on information of an emotional tone and potential social complexity, but they do not give accurate information on economic, political, or social events. The context, it seems, asserts the primacy of the male individual in the competitive dyad: man against man, man against spirit, man against any system.

The Saloon Context

The saloon context takes place at night. It depends upon music, without which none of the ritual behavior described below occurs. The music is national, featuring hot coastal music such as *cumbia, gaita, merecumbea,* or *guaracha,* interspersed with slower *boleros, valsas,* and *rancheros.* (For another description of this context, see Whitten, 1968.) Men dominate women in the setting and use women to help solidify male-male dyads, forming chains of cooperative male associations on which any person depends for aid in work-a-day life. The idiom of kinship usually expresses such a male dyadic chain.

Groups of men actually working together sit and drink together. From time to time, one member of the group asks a woman to dance and takes her to another man in his work group, offering him the dance requested of the woman. Men not working together sit apart, or stand outside, and periodically invite a woman to dance with another man. The recipient is then obligated to close the exchange by ritual return of an acceptable token, or, as the donor prefers, to reciprocate in some way at a later date.

A man who wishes to initiate sexual relations with a woman should approach the woman as she arrives at the saloon. He moves rapidly toward her, walking in time to the music, swinging his arms with palms facing straight back, and smiling broadly. This signals his intention not only to the woman, but to all others within viewing distance. He asks her to dance with him and makes his proposition during the dance. She may refuse to dance or to spend the night with him; by saying nothing she consents. Not uncommonly, sexual unions, publically signaled in this manner in a saloon, continue and often result in marriage.

Two important social adjustments relating to sex roles are enacted in the saloon context: (1) the solidifying of male social relationships (dyads and networks) through prestation of alcohol and the ritual giving and lending of dance partners, and (2) actual male-initiated household rearrangement as men begin to establish a new sexual partnership. In the saloon context, ritualized male activity signals continuity in male cooperation and in the practical prerogative of men to move from one sex partner to another. Both male-male dyad and male-female dyads are expressed as cooperative, but the latter are male initiated.

The Currulao Context

The secular *currulao* or marimba dance *(baile marimba)* is performed every Saturday night on hinterland rivers and in the all-black *barrios* of large towns, and more sporadically in the smaller, less segregated towns. It provides a context in which males express assertiveness, while women express female dominance; neither the male nor female sex roles dominates the other, although a symbolic arena of competition pervades all aspects of ritual activity.

The *currulao* takes place in a special house—*casa de la marimba*—which contains the marimba, two large base drums *(bombos),* and two conical single-headed drums *(cununos).* For an understanding of the interplay between expressive roles, see Figure 1.

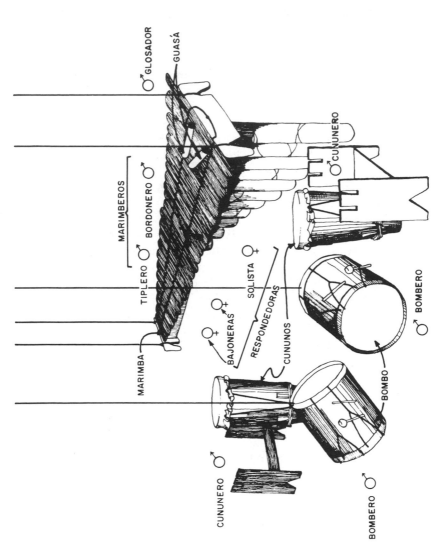

Instruments for the *Currulao* with the Musicians and Their Positions Indicated.

Two *marimberos* play the marimba—the *bordonero* who plays the melody, and the *tiplero* who plays a harmony. Two *bomberos* and *cununeros* accompany the marimba. A *glosador* sings the improvised verses while facing three female chorus singers. The three singers have two roles: one *solista,* who is the lead chorus maker, and two *bajoneras,* who harmonize with her and maintain the chorus which the *solista* begins. Two primary triads are at work in the development of marimba music. The first is formed by the *bordonero* with lead *bombero* and *glosador,* the second by the *solista* with the lead *cununero* and *bajoneras.* The *tiplero* and other two drummers take their cues from the interplay between the two triads. The two primary triads are in continuous antagonism to each other, the antagonism expressing sex role competition over initiation of an action sequence.

The *bordonero* sets the melody and the lead *bombero* joins him; they rehearse most of an afternoon prior to a dance, with various *cununeros,* alter *bomberos,* and *tipleros* fitting their parts to the dominant melody and rhythm. In the towns where formal permission is necessary to hold the *currulao,* women make the arrangements. In the evening the male members of the marimba band begin to play. Men and women arrive, the men taking seats and the women greeting one another, talking loudly, and ignoring the men. Some women go through a few dance steps with one another. When the *respondedoras* arrive, they move into the circle of drums, shake the tube-shakers *(guasas)* which they have brought with them, and sing a chorus of a favorite tune while the drummers and *marimberos* strengthen their beats and become more redundant. More women dance with women.

Next the *glosador* enters, standing next to the *bordonero.* When the women start singing, the *glosador* looks at them, listens, and then enters with a long falsetto *grito,* or call. He breaks in on the chorus being sung by the *respondedoras,* calling them to sing and to listen to him. Next he moves to a verse, which the *respondedoras* answer with a set chorus. At this time the two antagonistic triads within the marimba dance form.

Women dancers move toward men, asking them to dance. They may break their own pair and each invite a man, or the two women dancing together may move toward one man and both dance with him. A man who wishes to dance signals by standing erect, handkerchief in right hand hanging gently over his right shoulder. The woman holds her skirt slightly out to one side, swings her handkerchief from side to

side, and in a distinct dance step bearing no resemblance to saloon
dancing, approaches the man. The woman steadily advances, pivots,
and retreats, while the man becomes more excited, leaps into the air,
stamps his feet in time with the *bombo,* shouts, and waves his handkerchief or hat. He may even open his arms as if to grab the woman,
but as she turns to him, he retreats (Whitten and Fuentes, 1966; Whitten, 1968; Friedemann and Morales, 1966-1969).

The ambiance is always tense. It is part of the relationship between
glosador and *solista,* each of whom is the apex of an antagonistic triad
of performers. The *glosador* leads in singing his verses, and the *respondedoras* harmonize with his long notes. The chorus following the
glosador's verse is usually in contradiction to the intent of his verse.
As the *glosador* sings and yodels about going on a trip, leaving a woman, injuring women through his great penis, or becoming the devil,
the women sing back that their own men are being held or that they
are not losing their men, and they allude to the venereal diseases in
other women and how the marimba chases the devil away. The music
and voices get louder and louder. The *respondedoras* and *glosador*
begin to sing their phrases simultaneously, until finally all words dis-
solve into an intricate harmonic structure of yodels, falsettos, and
glissandos up and down the scale. The *respondedoras* inevitably "win"
in their struggle for dominance with the *glosador.* Before the end of
the song, they reassert lyrics over harmonic structure. They loudly
sing the choruses and may even take over some verses. As this hap-
pens, the *glosador* may walk away from the marimba to have a drink
or to dance. The music continues until the women stop singing. However, if they wait too long he may return and trick them by beginning
yet another song, giving the women no rest and exhausting those particular *respondedoras.* There are many other patterns, all of which
symbolize the same male-female struggle for initiation of a conse-
quential set of actions. The *bambuco* pattern sketched here is the most
common pattern.[5]

The *currulao* normally lasts until dawn, but it may go on for two or
three days. It seldom ends until the dances and musicians are too exhausted to continue. By this time the singers have completely lost their
voices. All participants return to their own homes and to their own
spouses. Unlike the saloon context, no rearrangement of sexual partners takes place. When pushed to explain why no one initiates sexual
advances or tries to leave the dance to sleep with a new partner, in-

formants invariably, and forcefully, state that this dance is a *baile de respeto* (a ritual dance, or one involving respectful role relationships). The *currulao* presents a ritual context in which the role conflict between the male rights of self-assertiveness and mobility, and the female rights of household stability and maneuver to hold a particular man, are expressed and portrayed. In the *currulao* context, male and female sex roles are equal and antagonistic as both strive ritually to dominate action sequences; the strife is portrayed in gesture, song texts, dance styles, and the structured tension between *glosador* and *respondedoras*. A competitive, egalitarian, male-female dyad is enacted.

The Living Walk, The Dead Wander

Before moving to sacred contexts, we need some information on the integration of daily life and world view in this Afro-Hispanic culture. A structural relationship exists between the mobility and social responsibility of the living, and the disposition of souls of the deceased. A male youth must achieve a degree of social independence and sexual experience before he is considered ready for marriage; and his sexual relationships with a young woman may obligate him to some extent to her relatives, if she becomes pregnant. Having achieved the status of father, with concomitant independence from his matricentral cell signaled by new responsibility to an affinal group, the soul of the man will tend to wander after his death, both in this world and in other worlds. A woman who bears a child demonstrates a degree of social independence; her position in the mother-child dyad, and the implied position in a potential or real mother-husband dyad, both stress residential permanence, the complement to male mobility.

Let us pursue the relationship of living and dead. It is commonly said that a male must *andar y conocer* (literally "to walk [travel] and to know" [learn]) before he becomes a man. The phrase expresses the positive value placed on traveling and learning to cope with the environment. There is a deeper meaning, too, for in the black idiom *andar* means "to strut." Walking in the manner prescribed for saloon giving, or for making sexual overtures to a woman, or for breaking a characteristic circling pattern during saloon dancing as an act of individual assertion is known as "walking." When a black person in the Pacific littoral is asked what he means when he says *conocer* in the above phrase, he will invariably laugh, raise both hands above his head with elbows bent, fists clenched, thumbs pointing back, and move his arms and upper torso back and forth—the gesture symbolizing sexual intercourse in the wet littoral. Hence, to *andar y conocer* also means to learn the ritual style for symbolizing cooperation and attracting a woman, and to learn the proper styles for sexual intercourse. The appropriate styles of behavior in the saloon context, it will be remembered, relate to the ritual means of signaling male-male dyadic relationships, which ramify into networks of association. The combination of *andar y conocer* is important, for it expresses the man's need to know his way around in the social lattice of male support, as well as to know what he is about in his sexual relationships with his lover or wife.

It is said that the soul, *alma,* of a man who has died must wander. People seem less clear on whether all women must wander, but when asked about a specific woman they invariably say that she, when young, would be found by her mother *andando con cualquiera* "walking with anyone." This phrase applied to a specific woman means that she was having sexual affairs as a young girl. When pressed further and asked if any woman avoids such sexual affairs, the answer is yes—*las virgenes,* the virgins; and the speaker immediately lets us know that they live in *gloria,* heaven, which is part of *el cielo,* the sky (see Figure 2). So it seems that all male and female adult souls do indeed wander, and they must be directed away from the settlement in which they lived. This is done in the *novenario,* one of the wakes for an adult.

The souls of prepubescent girls, of pubescent girls who everyone agrees never had sexual intercourse with a man, and of boys up to an indeterminate age when they become somewhat independent go directly to *gloria* when they die—to live as *angelitos,* little angels, with God, Jesus, the saints, and the virgins. They alone do not wander. Their ascent is symbolized in the *chigualo,* the wake for a dead child.

Saints are also a mobile lot. Women are able to summon them from *gloria* and to make requests of them. Women do this publicly on special saints' days, at which time they sing *arrullos,* spirituals, until the spirit of the saint enters the house where the spirituals are being performed. These same spirituals are sung during the *chigualo* and it would seem that the relationship between the living and the heaven-spirit is the same in both cases. The soul of the dead child ascends as an angel into *gloria* to the accompaniment of *arrullos,* just as the saints descend from *gloria* to help the women to the acompaniment of *arrullos.* Sometimes this latter musical context directed to saints is simply called

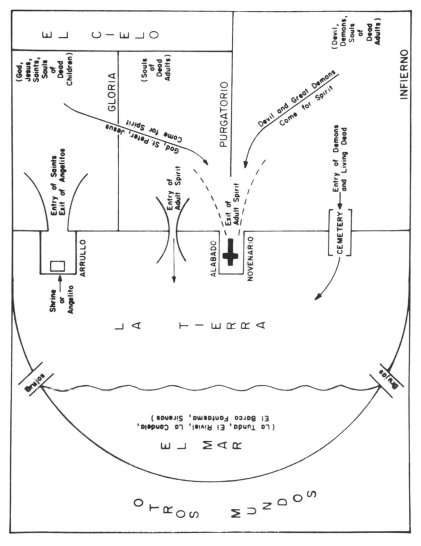

The Afro-Hispanic Universe.

arrullo, and sometimes it is referred to as *velorio.* The diagram in Figure 2 shows a representation of this Afro-Hispanic universe.

We return now to ritual contexts and to a discussion of the *alabedo-novenario,* the *chigualo,* and the *arrullo* to saints.

SACRED RITUAL CONTEXTS OF SEX ROLE ENACTMENT

The Alabado-Novenario Context

The house in which an adult dies is precariously balanced between earth *(la tierra)*, purgatory *(purgatorio)*, and hell *(inferno)*. During the wake following death, called *alabado*, and the second wake, which is held about nine days after burial, called *novenario*, men and women from the local community cooperate in all endeavors with incoming hinterland relatives. They express equality in their roles, which are jointly oriented toward maintaining solidarity of a grouping of kinsmen around the now deceased person, while at the same time rearranging particular kin ties so that no one can trace a relationship through the deceased. (This process is described in Whitten, 1968, 1970a, 1974.) Although much attention is given to kinship in this sacred ritual con-context, affinity and consanguinity are deliberately blurred. For example, a brother of a deceased man may regard the wife of the deceased as his sister during and after the *alabado-novenario*, or formally broken affinal bonds may be recalled in a re-linking of "cousins" to one another. Full cooperation between male and female sex roles is expressed; a cooperative, egalitarian, male-female dyad is enacted as the living solemnly take a position against the dead.

The Chigualo Context

The *chigualo* context takes place following the death of a child. It is not so solemn as the *alabado-novenario*, heaven is open to the setting, and women are the interaction initiators. Most *chigualos* are held in the first two years of life, for infant mortality is very high during this time. Women attend to all matters of washing the child, seeing that it is baptized (if it has not already been baptized), inviting male drummers to play during the night, and arranging with well-known *cantadoras* (women singers) to be on hand for the singing of *arrullos*. Men become linked in *compadrazgo* (ritual kinship) relationships if they are invited by the child's mother to help with the preparations, burial, or expenses involved in the *chigualo*. Kinship terms often later replace the *comadre-compadre* terms used in the *chigualo*. When this occurs, the mother of a dead child becomes the crucial locus in genealogical space for the reckoning of kinship ties.

The actual ritual is signaled by a man beating a rapid rhythm on the *bombo*, which begins immediately at nightfall but may begin at any time when the drummer hangs the drum. Within minutes of hearing this rhythm, people come to see what woman has lost her child; some remain and some leave, the decision reflecting a willingness to be included in the network of stipulated kinsmen radiating, at this time, from the mother of the deceased.

The child is placed at one end of the room, and candles surround the corpse on the table. The mother and her close siblings sit near the corpse, while other women assemble on the sides of the room. They make up a chorus, singing *arrullos* and clapping their hands for rhythm. The drummers (two *cununeros,* one *bombero*) group themselves against the opposite wall, and still other men and women sit at the far end of the room, near the main door. The scene is set for the arrival of the *cantadoras.* The female chorus has been singing since dark, and the ambiance is moderately solemn but amicable. Drummers "obey" the women, and "follow" their leads; men (including the child's father and/or the mother's husband) serve rum and coffee under the women's direction.

The chorus sings songs symbolizing the entry of the *angelito* (dead child) into heaven, and the *bombo* frightens the body- or soul-snatching Tunda apparition away, so that life within the house now opened to the sky is safe for all children, living and dead. The *cantadoras* enter around eleven or twelve at night, take up their positions, and begin to shake maracas and to sing choruses more complex in rhythm and counterpoint than those sung by the general female chorus. Some of these women summon pesonal saints, or saints for all women, such as San Antonio, and petition things for themselves as the chorus steadfastly sings the child's entry into heaven. Sometimes the *cantadoras* will dance. If the corpse is very small, they may even pick it up and dance with it, swinging it to and fro.

After the arrival of the *cantadoras,* the ambiance of the *chigualo* "loosens." Adults come and go, and many take turns on the drums. Young men and women even engage in mild sex play, and children climb over everyone and everything, poking at the dead child and listening to the songs telling of the ascent of its soul into heaven. Within the house there is no danger, for the only avenue open to *el cielo* is to *gloria*—saintly spirits enter through *gloria* at the women's request. The only danger at this time, Tunda, is kept at bay by the male *bombero.* Only if children wander from the house are they in jeopardy, for Tunda could appear before them, leaving them *entundada* (frightened by the apparition) to be henceforth unable to cope with life. So the children stay and sleep in the house of the *chigualo,* within comforting range of the *bombo,* under the doors of heaven opened to them by the women.

Tunda also attacks children without adult escorts who make themselves vulnerable by insulting, or being rude to, someone acting the role of mother. Mothers threaten children with the *entundada* phenomenon, and are regarded by boys as being capable of invoking Tunda to punish them, should the growing youth use his increasing strength, or wit, to challenge female authority. When a boy is ready to challenge his mother, he must also be ready to thwart Tunda.

The *chigualo* continues unabated until dawn, when it abruptly ends. The *cantadoras* go home, and those who have been served rum throughout the night hurriedly put the child in a little coffin *(cajita),* close the lid to the cries of anguish of the mother, and with the drummers still beating, head for the cemetery singing *arrullos* and swinging the coffin.

A cooperative sex role relationship where women initiate interaction, dominate men, and solidify. a network of kinsmen radiating from the matricentric cell (mother-dead child) is portrayed in the *chigualo.*

The Arrullo Context

The setting for a saint's propitiation, sometimes called *velorio* (which means "wake" in standard Spanish but refers to spirit or saint propitiation in this Afro-Hispanic culture), is about the same as for the *chigualo.* The focus is on a shrine, however, rather than a table used for a bier. Drummers and singers arrange themselves more or less as described above. There are usually at least two *bombos* during the *arrullo* to a saint, and there may be even more. The sound of more than one *bombo* most clearly differentiates the music of this event from that of the *chigualo.*

Women in a particular settlement, or *barrio* of an urban area, undertake to organize the *arrullo* for a saint. They must keep the dates for the saints clear, and they must arrange for the *arrullo,* which means paying the male drummers for their performance and renting the drums. They must build the shrine, or pay a man to do it, and, if necessary, hide all preparations from local priests who often regard these *arrullos* as pagan rites to be stamped out. Only women reap the general benefits of saintly aid which may occur after an *arrullo,* but men who wish to petition for luck in fishing must do so during this female-dominated sacred event.

Men attend the ritual to drink rum and *guarapo* (sugar beer) served by the women. The women often have difficulty maintaining the sacred ambiance, as some men may try to turn the *arrullo* into a saloon context. When men begin exchanging drinks, or try to dance, the women may even abandon the house in which the *arrullo* is held and retire without drums to shake maracas, sing, and invite a particular saint to enter the house.

The most significant saint in the Pacific Lowlands culture area is San Antonio, and the majority of songs sung in all *arrullos* (and in the *chigualo*) are directed to him. Although his own special day is June 13, women may use all special days, in one way or another, to invite San Antonio to enter the house and to help them in their pursuit of men or their endeavors to hold onto them. In San Lorenzo, western Ecuador, for example, men say that San Antonio is the *alcahuete de las mujeres,* a pimp. Girls petition him for greater sexual attractiveness vis-à-vis a desirable male, just as older women petition him for the power to hold their particular men. San Antonio is also a broker or "lawyer," (see Price, 1955:181) between the living and the dead, between the living and the spirits, and between spirits. He is the only saint who can work miracles on his own. He serves women in all matters, and fishermen in their exploitation of the marine environment.

Regardless of the particular day on which an *arrullo* is held, the songs to San Antonio tend to be of the longest duration and represent some of the most complicated rhythms (such as the *Bunde*). There are more than 40 of them. Frequently during a song to San Antonio, the *cantadoras* engage in complicated counterpart symbolizing competition between women: one petitions one thing from San Antonio, while another petitions something else. One may be asking where San Antonio is, while a second sings: "he is under my bed." A third woman then responds: "he is having sexual intercourse with me!" After such theme-countertheme textual and musical interplay, the women give shouts and hug one another. By so doing, they seem to symbolize a oneness of general endeavor—attracting and petitioning San Antonio— as well as an individuality of specific purpose.

No particular tension exists in the *arrullo,* except that provoked by men who refuse to acknowledge the importance of saints to the women's stratagems and needs. The saints are not bothered by the men's irreverence, for they are propitiated and petitioned by women, who are the sole legitimate action initiators in this context.

Saints are considered to be vain and to like ceremony. During the Easter and Christmas seasons, a street parade, called *Belén,* occurs, if not blocked by the clergy. Women arrange this parade, and they work closely with men on formal *Belén* logistics. Often as many as 20 *bombos* and 100 or more singers with maracas march or strut in a large town parade. Women set a route for the procession in terms of main streets or major trails leading past the fronts of houses; then, as the procession gets underway, the women lead it to and fro across the backyards of houses, weaving in and out, delighting the saints, and frustrating the men, who are not sure where they will be led next as the women follow their day-to-day backyard visiting routes with the saints.

In the *arrullo* context, women dominate everything, summoning saints into the home from heaven, and leading them through their community visiting routes. They give the saints the variety and ceremony which they are said to enjoy, and they enact both female sexual solidarity and individuality in trapping and holding men. The men in this ceremony are paid for their endeavors, and they are dispensed with if they do not follow the female lead. Only when fishermen wish to petition San Antonio, after he is summoned by women, can a man take an active role in the *arrullo.* When the women stop singing, they tell a particular man to recite a sacred *décima,* called *la loa.* When the sacred petition for good fishing for another year has been made, the women see that all the men pay for the ceremony; they then return to the patterns of behavior sketched above. The *arrullo* context portrays female-female sexual solidarity, and female dominance.

RITUAL ENACTMENT OF SEX ROLES: A SUMMARY

In the Pacific Lowland culture area of Ecuador-Colombia, sex role enactment ranges on a continuum from male to female initiation of interaction. These differences in role activation seem to reflect a continuum from male self-assertiveness to female dominance. In the cantina context, males assert their individual power over women, their mobility, and their ability to trick spirits and the dead. In the saloon context, men express male network solidarity by the exchange of women as tokens, and they also express and enact actual changes of spouses. During the *currulao,* also a secular context, men express their prerogatives of mobility and allude to their relationship to the devil, while the women collectively express their prerogative to hold particular men and seek in turn to resist male innovation in song and dance. In the sacred *alabado-novenario* context, men and women express equality in sex role relationships as a human group against the unwanted dead. In the *chigualo* context, women control interaction patterns and become central to intrahousehold reckoning of responsible kinsmen and contributors while opening the household to spirits of heaven. In the *arrullo* to saints, women assume a dominant intracommunity position, bringing the saints from heaven to the community and manipulating them to female bidding.

Sex Role Variation and Social Structure

The social system of the Pacific Lowlands is described elsewhere (Whitten, 1965, 1968, 1970a, 1970b, 1974; Whitten and Szwed, 1970b). Specific households are embedded in networks radiating from male broker nodes which are strategic to socioeconomic striving. Household maintenance tactics tap a localized kindred. Affinity, attenuated affinity, and consanguinity are all manipulated in traversing genealogical space for any ego central to household maintenance. Within the household, the universal matricentral cell (See, e.g., Fortes, 1949, 1953, 1958, 1969) is maintained by a mother's recruitment strategies for male support. She uses both affinal and consanguineal dyads for such maintenance. The ramifications of these ties extend well beyond the household. Recruited men in the role of husband are the authority figures in the household, when they are actually present (Whitten, 1965:121-143; 1974:153-157), but their responsibilities to the household involve them in constant strategies of male-male network maintenance outside of the household that taps a dispersed kindred. Male mobility—horizontal, spatial, socioeconomic (see Whitten, 1969; 1974)—eventually leads to polygyny, or serial wives. Responsibility to "abandoned" wives for aid in child rearing accrues to the husband-father's matricentral consanguines and affines.

Male self-assertiveness provides continuity in Afro-Hispanic culture through mobility strategies. The female interaction initiative provides stability through household permanence and through maneuvers between households in a residential community which contribute to community permanence. Community and residential permanence, in turn, contribute to male mobility by providing bases for dispersed networks. Suprahousehold and supracommunity networks of recipro-

cating males themselves are necessary for intrahousehold and intracommunity stability in the boom-bust political economy. The respective contextual roles of domain-specific male and female interaction
initiation complement one another; each contributes to social structural
continuity, while allowing considerable organizational variety and
adaptability. Ideally, within this Afro-Hispanic culture, women stabilize the domain of household and community; men stabilize the domain
of kinship and network maintenance. Practically, each domain is
activated by maneuvers in the other domain. The specific role complementarity in the household domain leads to apparent conflict during
actual separation of spouses, but it provides for continuity of the
household by reference to the intrahousehold female prerogative and
the male mobility prerogative.

Together, the various ritual contexts enact the full, impressive,
range of sex role differentiation necessary to household, kinship network, community, and intercommunity maintenance. An analysis of
this enactment in terms of interaction initiators and domain prerogatives allows us to explore sex role portrayal and its relationship to cultural continuity, regardless of whether or not rapid change is taking
place.

NOTES

1. The delineation of sex role variation in the ritual contexts and its significance to
daily lifestyle and social strategy was pointed out to me by my wife, Dorothea S. Whitten, who also commented on an original draft of this manuscript. This essay is a revised
and expanded version of a paper presented at the 70th Annual Meeting of the American
Anthropological Association, November 21, 1971. Conrad Arensberg's incisive comments on this paper during the symposium clarified many issues. He pointed out that
the interaction initiation aspect of the role relationship was the crucial feature in many
of the activities which I described in the original paper. The data and themes sketched
here are more fully discussed in Part II of Whitten (1974).

2. For an elaboration of these ideas, see González (1965, 1969), Goodenough (1970),
and Whitten (1970a, 1970b, 1971, 1974).

3. The Colombian Chocó is specifically excluded from this analysis. Although data
from the Pacific Lowlands (the area south of the San Juan River and west of the Cordillera Occidental) are frequently included with those of the Chocó (the area north of the
San Juan River, including both the coastal strip and the area east of the Serranía de
Baudó but west of the Cordillera Occidental), I think that the differences in the two
areas warrant separate treatment. I do not believe that the analysis presented here will
fit the Chocó, although many of the specific elements are distributed regularly in the
two areas.

4. These contexts find different specific outlets according to four niches (patterned black activity sets) governed by settlement size; the scattered rural dwellings, the settlement with up to 300 people, the town with several hundred to 3,000, and the urbanized town with about 5,000 to 100,000 people. The niches themselves exist in three environmental zones: sea-mangrove edge, mangrove swamp, and rainforest *tierra firma* (see Whitten, 1974). "Lower class" refers to an intracommunity perspective, not to national standing in regard to power over economic resources. Intracommunity mobility patterns involve considerable rearrangement of behavior in specific contexts, and also a concept of ethnic lightening, regardless of actual phenotype. Whitten (1965, 1968, 1969, 1974) discusses the relationship of class and mobility to ethnic identity, and also indicates the kinds of choices people make about attending and/or performing in various contexts according to economic, social, and political variables.

5. Other fairly common styles include the *caderona* (big-hipped woman, who symbolizes the sexually exciting woman, capable of luring men away from their homes in the saloon context). During this dance, couples do a waltz-like step and loosely embrace. The *glosador* sings of his particular sexual episodes, bragging of his ability to "Dry up" women, while the *respondedoras* keep singing "shake it, shake it" (*remeniate caderona, caderona vení meniate, ay vení meniate*) as a torment to the man. The *glosador* also sings of the inherent responsibility for progeny in sexual intercourse, particularly with young girls who have been certified as virgins by midwives, and the women refer to marriage resulting from pregnancy. Other dances are described in Whitten (1974).

REFERENCES CITED

Fortes, Meyer. 1949. *The Web of Kinship Among the Tallensi*. London: Oxford University Press.
_____. 1953. "The Structure of Unilinear Descent Groups." *American Anthropologist* 55:17-41.
_____. 1958. "Introduction. The Developmental Cycle in Domestic Groups." *Cambridge Papers in Social Anthropology*, ed. by Jack Goody, pp. 1-14. Cambridge: Cambridge University Press.
_____. 1969. *Kinship and the Social Order*. Chicago: Aldine.
Frazier, E. Franklin. 1932. *The Negro Family in Chicago*. Chicago: University of Chicago Press.
_____. 1934. "Traditions and Patterns in Negro Family Life in the United States." *Race and Culture Contacts*, ed. by E. B. Reuter, pp. 191-207. New York: McGraw-Hill.
_____. 1939. *The Negro Family in the United States*. Chicago: University of Chicago Press.
_____. 1942. "The Negro Family in Bahia, Brazil." *American Sociological Review* 7:465-478.
_____. 1949. *The Negro in the United States*. New York: Macmillan.
Freilich, Morris (ed.). 1970. *Marginal Natives: Anthropologists at Work*. New York: Harper & Row.
Friedemann, Nina S., and Jorge Morales Gómez. 1966-1969. "Estudios de negros en el Litoral Pacífico Colombiano: Fase I." *Revista Colombiana de Antropología* 14:55-78.

González, Nancie L. (Solien). 1965. "The Consanguineal Household and Matrifocality.'
American Anthropologist 67:1541-1549.
———. 1969. *Black Carib Household Structure: A Study of Migration and Moderni-
zation.* Seattle: University of Washington Press.
———. 1970. "Toward a Definition of Matrifocality." *In Afro-American Anthro-
pology: Contemporary Perspectives,* ed. by Norman E. Whitten, Jr., and John F.
Szwed, pp. 231-244. New York: Free Press.
Goodenough, Ward H. 1970. *Description and Comparison in Cultural Anthropology.*
Chicago: Aldine.
Goody, Jack (ed.). 1958. "The Developmental Cycle in Domestic Groups." *Cambridge
Papers in Social Anthropology,* No. 1. Cambridge: Cambridge University Press.
Hannerz, Ulf. 1970. "What Ghetto Males Are Like: Another Look." *In Afro-American
Anthropology: Contemporary Perspectives,* ed. by Norman E. Whitten, Jr., and
John F. Szwed, pp. 313-344. New York: Free Press.
Herskovits, Melville J. 1941. *The Myth of the Negro Past.* New York: Harper. (Paper-
back edition, 1958. Boston: Beacon.)
———. 1943. "The Negro in Bahia, Brazil: A Problem in Method." *American So-
ciological Review* 8:394-402.
Price, Thomas J., Jr. 1955. Saints and Spirits: A Study of Differential Acculturation in
Colombian Negro Communities. Ph.D. dissertation, Northwestern University.
Reuter, E. B. (ed.). 1934. *Race and Culture Contacts.* New York: McGraw-Hill.
Smith, Raymond T. 1956. *The Negro Family in British Guiana.* London: Routledge
and Kegan Paul.
———. 1963. "Culture and Social Structure in the Caribbean: Some Recent Work on
Family and Kinship Studies." *Comparative Studies in Society and History* 6:24-46.
Whitten, Norman E., Jr. 1965. *Class, Kinship, and Power in an Ecuadorian Town:
The Negroes of San Lorenzo.* Stanford: Stanford University Press.
———. 1968. "Personal Networks and Musical Contexts in the Pacific Lowlands of
Colombia and Ecuador. *Man* 3:50-63.
———. 1969. "Strategies of Adaptive Mobility in the Colombian-Ecuadorian Littoral."
American Anthropologist 71:228-242.
———. 1970a. "Network Analysis and Processes of Adaptation Among Ecuadorian
and Nova Scotian Negroes." *In Marginal Natives: Anthropologists at Work,* ed. by
Morris Freilich, pp. 339-403, 609-612. New York: Harper & Row.
———. 1970b. "Network Analysis in Ecuador and Nova Scotia: Some Critical Remarks." *Canadian Review of Sociology and Anthropology* 7:269-280.
———. 1971. "Review of González, Nancie L. Solien, Black Carib Household Structure." *Social and Economic Studies* 20:101-103.
———. 1974. *Black Frontiersmen: A South American Case.* New York: Halsted (Wiley).
Whitten, Norman E., Jr., and Aurelio Fuentes C. 1966. "¡Baile Marimba! Negro Folk
Music in Northwest Ecuador." *Journal of the Folklore Institute* 3:168-191.
Whitten, Norman E., Jr., and John F. Szwed (eds.). 1970a. *Afro-American Anthropology: Contemporary Perspectives.* New York: Free Press.
———. 1970b. "Introduction." *In Afro-American Anthropology: Contemporary
Perspectives,* ed. by Norman E. Whitten, Jr., and John F. Szwed, pp. 23-60. New
York: Free Press.

Michael Craton

10

PERCEPTIONS OF SLAVERY: A
PRELIMINARY EXCURSION INTO
THE POSSIBILITIES OF ORAL
HISTORY IN RURAL JAMAICA

Ten years ago, Miguel Barnet's brilliant editing of the autobiography of Esteban Montejo, centenarian ex-slave, substantially extended and modified commonly held views of Cuban slavery.[1] Yet, even this exceptional direct testimony shed more light on the culture of Cubans of African descent who combined peasant cultivation with plantation wage labor than on slavery itself. What are the chances therefore that the oral tradition among a creolized and partially modernized population in the anglophone islands can be used to illuminate an institution that ended fifty years earlier than in Cuba? This essay explains briefly the methodology and rationale of a series of some fifty interviews concerning slavery carried out in 1973 in Lluidas Vale, central Jamaica, by a Jamaican graduate student, under the direction of a British historian of the Caribbean region. The conclusions that follow tentatively suggest that such an enterprise has definite value, though it predictably suffers even more from the fading of the traditions and the overlaying of extraneous influences than was the case for the work on Esteban Montejo.

The first problem in any oral history project is to decide whom to interview and then to identify properly each informant. In the West Indian context, particularly in the context of Lluidas Vale, it had to be decided whether the most valuable informants were likely to be old or young, prominent citizens or more modest persons, literate or illiterate, eloquent or less readily encouraged to testify, still involved in plantation life, townsmen, villagers, or pure countrymen. In his masterly *Oral Tradition,* based largely on the problems of African research, Jan Vansina summarizes the qualities of the good informant:

[he should be a person who] still lives the customary life, who
recites traditions without too much hesitation, who understands
their content but is not too brilliant—for if he were, one would
suspect him of introducing distortions—and who is old enough
to have acquired some degree of personal experience of his cultural environment. In short, a good informant is the common
man who has reached a position which enables him to be conversant with traditions.[2]

How well do Vansina's principles apply to the persons questioned in
Lluidas Vale? Certainly, all of the local informants still lived the traditional life, though some had also resided in other parts of Jamaica,
even different countries. For the most part they were deeply rooted in
the surrounding district, not only since birth but for generations on
both sides, as far back as could reliably be traced. In this respect they
were by no means exceptional, for recent surname analysis has suggested a quite remarkable locational stability in the vicinity of Worthy
Park Estate dating back to slavery times.[3] Whether this stability can
be attributed to the presence of the sugar estate itself, only an analysis
of another rural area far from sugar cultivation would show. Certainly,
a high proportion of those interviewed had some direct or indirect
connection with Worthy Park. This finding was not solely a function of the nature of the research, which began with an interest in the
Worthy Park slaves and their descendants. Some of the people interviewed in the earliest phase of the study were among those known to
have been employed by the estate for many years. Subsequent interviews were less selectively chosen, so that overall the subjects were
almost randomly chosen from the district at large. They included independent cultivators and villagers as well as peasants partly employed
by the estate and pure wage-earners. Such is the nature of the district,
however, that few had escaped entirely the ubiquitous influence of the
privately owned sugar plantation that dominates Lluidas Vale and its
surrounding hills (see Map).
    Jamaica no longer has a vigorous tradition of historical storytelling
such as is common in many preliterate cultures, let alone does it have
"schools" to teach classic traditions such as are found in parts of
Africa, Polynesia, and Latin America.[4] Even the sessions for the exchange of folk tales and riddles described by Bates and Trowbridge
(1896), Cundall (1904-1905), Jekyll (1907), and Beckwith (1929)[5] seem

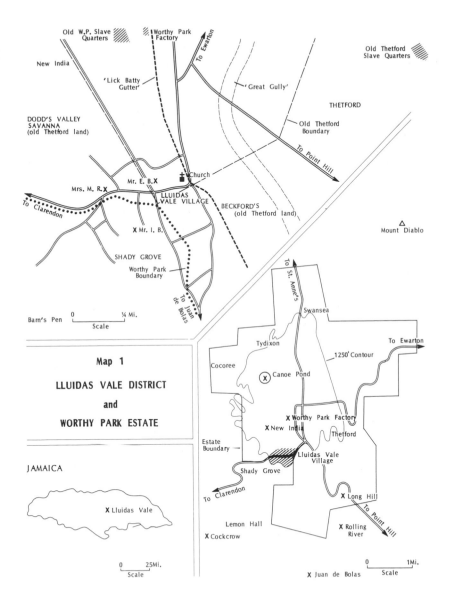

Lluidas Vale District and Worthy Park Estate *Drawn by Gary Brannon.*

to have been killed by radio and the cinema, if not by the system of compulsory education. Many of the middle-aged and older people remember their seniors sitting together on Sundays and holidays to exchange stories, with anecdotes of slavery taking priority on August 1, the holiday celebrating emancipation. A distressing number of them, however, confess ignorance of what was actually talked about. Since 1938 at least, the young have regarded hopes of the future to be more relevant than tales of a "bad old past." Even the rich trove of Jamaican proverbs is seldom any longer drawn on in normal conversation, though fortunately they have been preserved in print by Cundall and Beckwith and as such provide a treasury of native philosophy.[6]

In such a cluttered, modernizing atmosphere it is difficult, but vital, to seek out exceptional people in whom the oral tradition has not died. Next, it is extremely important to establish rapport, so that the tradition flows again with minimal hesitation and conscious distortion (as Vansina advocates)—in much the same way as memory builds on memory to unlock the forgotten, or as dreams are remembered in vivid detail by persons who previously claimed, and believed, they never dreamed.[7] In seeking rapport it was imperative that the actual questioner not be a foreigner, but a Jamaican familiar with the Creole dialect. Moreover, the tape recorder was not used as it was felt to be potentially inhibiting. The questions, though predetermined, were not asked in fixed sequence from a formal questionnaire, with answers recorded on the spot; rather, they were asked informally and written up later. All that was written down at the time of the interview were proper names, genealogical details, and the words of songs.

As a result of these techniques, some of those who at first professed ignorance in due course provided a rich fund of anecdotes. The most notable informant, Mr. I. B., aged 78—who became a respected friend rather than an anthropologist's subject—merely needed to be set in verbal motion and gently directed. He would summon up memory first by concentrated thought and then let it flow in a stream of consciousness, apparently regaining lost inspiration and impetus by wiping his hand over his smooth bald head. One morning he sent word that, under the stimulus of the previous night's discussion, he had dredged up further recollections "in a dream."

Three elderly informants remembered that in the first decade of the twentieth century there was a very old lady living in Lluidas Vale called "Granny Sue" Blair, born a slave around 1816, who possessed a veritable mine of information on slavery days. On this subject she was clearly the recognized local authority, a repository of oral tradition in a preliterate society—a type now almost dead, in a society almost obliterated. Two of the informants had only the vaguest notion of what Granny Sue recounted, but Mr. I. B., who claimed to be related to her, had vivid recollections. As a young boy, I. B. spent many hours with the ex-slave, soaking up details of events, conditions, genealogy, tenures, customs, and lore. An only child, he had more opportunities than most of his contemporaries in Lluidas Vale for education and travel, though by choice he returned to his birthplace long before retirement age. Although he was as poor as most aged countrymen, Mr. I. B. was a greatly respected member of the village community, often consulted on legal and customary matters. Consciously or not, he assumed the mantle of Granny Sue Blair and in 1973 was the nearest equivalent in Lluidas Vale to an historical authority.

Mr. I. B. was literate—his spectacles giving him an almost bookish air—and there seems to be a positive correlation between literacy and the eloquence of oral testimony. Yet, this very eloquence may be suspect, and the testimony of the illiterate poor—cut off from books and even radio and cinema—though simpler, may possess equal or greater validity. In particular, the illiterate are less likely than the literate to confuse "history" with phenomenal events which are read of in books or learned in school and are rarely relevant to everyday life. Mr. I. B. himself, when first asked for local historical mementos, talked chiefly of a "coronation tree" in the Anglican churchyard. With all informants, requests for "old time stories" or "stories of the old people" were much more effective triggers than the quest for formal history. "History" in the popular conception is something dead.

Maturity was one characteristic held in common by the best informants found in the Lluidas Vale district. This was not solely for the reasons cited by Jan Vansina. It is a sad fact, amounting to a rule, that in the West Indies family memories in all classes of society very rarely go back beyond three generations. In most cases people know nothing, not even the names, of their great grandparents. Therefore, under the "three generation rule," in the 1970s it is only possible to reach back the 135 years necessary for direct family links to slavery with persons born in 1910 or earlier. In all younger persons the oral tradition is bound to be less direct. The average age of the best six informants found in Lluidas Vale was 77 years. The oldest of all was Mrs. M. R., over 100 years old, whose father had been born a slave, and whose husband's grandmother had been born in Africa at the turn of the nineteenth century. Bedridden and blind, old Mrs. M. R. still retained memories unique in the district, if not the whole of Jamaica, including, for example, the name of the linen cloth from which many of the slaves' clothes were made, *"haxenbugs."*[8]

The age and family links of the informant are clearly as important to the testimony provided as are the informant's degree of literacy, position in the community, and personal character or characteristics, including color. The researcher should carefully record these before an analysis of the material is attempted. Similarly, the researcher should record the location and lifestyle of each informant, the means of livelihood, and the type of tenure of house and plot. In the case of Lluidas Vale district, these last details were particularly relevant with regard to the dominant presence of Worthy Park Estate, the largest employer and renter for miles around, as can be seen from a brief description of the ten chief informants.

As was true of the great majority of the local countryfolk, all but one of the ten were black rather than brown in color. The three oldest were inhabitants of Lluidas Vale Village (alias Shady Grove), of whom two, the centenarian Mrs. M. R. and Mr. E. B. (an illiterate ex-laborer of 89 whose grandfather was a slave on Thetford Estate) had been closely connected with Worthy Park all their working lives and still lived on rented plots. The third, the Mr. I. B. already mentioned, had never worked for the estate and lived on family "buy land" purchased in 1847.

Of the rather younger informants, Mr. R. B. was an illiterate aged 63, who scraped a marginal existence by combining seasonal wage labor in Worthy Park's fields with the farming of a small plot at Long Hill rented from his occasional employers. Mr. N. B., literate, aged 70, was slightly more independent both in status and attitude, having during his working life combined wage labor on the estate with farming a few acres of "family land."[9] Mrs. D. D., a dark brown lady aged 62, was a literate and highly articulate independent cultivator living on the ruins of the old coffee plantation house at Juan de Bolas, claiming direct descent from its last owner-occupier, who left for England in the 1820s.

Besides these, at least four others provided valuable contrasting testimony. Mr. J. T., literate, aged 56, uniquely combined shopkeeping, the working of a smallholding, and occasional wage labor. Mr. D. G., illiterate, aged 65, was a desperately poor but proudly independent smallholder of Cockcrow, a huddle of huts perched on the Clarendon slope of the local hills, and looking to the ancient decayed estate of Lemon Hall rather than Worthy Park for links with slavery. Mr. C. T., an illiterate aged 53, farming with three other families an enclave of twenty-two acres within Worthy Park land and tracing ancestors outside Lluidas Vale, was as alienated from the surrounding estate as from slavery itself. On the other hand, Mr. W. W., an illiterate field laborer and watchman aged 58, had always been as tied to Worthy Park as any slave. Born in the "barracks" hamlet of New India on the estate itself, he had never left Lluidas Vale. Yet, his antecedents were not chiefly Negro and slave; his grandmother, who died around 1926 at "aged 105," had come to Jamaica from India in 1841.

Once the informants are carefully chosen and clearly identified, the second major problem faced by the oral history researcher is what substantive questions he should ask or lead the informants towards. In the Lluidas Vale project, the questions asked and testimony received fell into four distinct categories, each of which had its pitfalls, scale of credibility, and historical value:

1. Personal antecedents dating back to slavery days
2. Received anecdotes relating to slavery
3. Generalized impressions of slavery
4. Incidental information possibly relevant to slavery, including folklore, folkways, proverbs, riddles, and dialect vocabulary; and facts, attitudes, and anecdotes relating to family, relationships, work, and land tenure.

The decline of the storytelling tradition in Jamaica has one benefit in that the oral researcher is not often faced with the problem of sifting the truth from imaginative fabrications concocted simply for the story's sake. A good rapport also reduces the chances that the researcher is told merely what the informant thinks he or she wishes to hear—a phenomenon notoriously common, for instance, in African oral research. At least half a dozen other well-known research problems remain to be considered, however.

A major pitfall was expected to be obscurantism stemming from a reluctance to resurrect the family past, upon the principle of the Jamaican proverb, "Fowl 'cratch up too much dutty [dirt], him run de risk a findin' him gramma 'keleton'."[10] In fact, such reluctance was rarely apparent. If obscurity resulted from dissociation, it was unconscious and had built up insensibly. Most informants were fascinated, indeed proud, to hear of family links discovered from written records, penetrating the three-generation veil and dating back to slavery days, even Africa. Mr. D. G. and other members of the community of Cockrow, for example, conveyed the sense that a precise knowledge of slave and African ancestors would provide an authenticity denied them by their ignorance and lowly state. Several informants begged for a family tree such as those drawn in detail only for Mr. I. B. and the old white owners of Worthy Park.

Often, however, there was a reluctance to associate with slavery and Africa where no family links were involved, because these were vaguely felt to be part of a grim, even discreditable, past, and therefore not worthy of recall. This reluctance results in part from the common human tendency to remember most readily the sunny, happy days. But it goes deeper. The dominant culture always ignored and devalued the private lives of the slaves, their blackness, and their Africanness; they are still unconsciously depreciated. All students of oral traditions are warned to beware of idealizations of the past. In Jamaica these can take the form of dissociating from slavery and Africa, and preferring European white and Christian cultural norms. One common example is the tendency to refer, even in conversation with other black folks, only to white ancestors, though they represent only a tiny proportion of the genetic mix. Another is the tendency, bred by generations of doctrine in all types of Christian churches, to see no ostensible virtue in African religion, even to deny it persists. *Obi* with only its negative, sinister, and medicinal qualities emphasized is particularly scorned.[11]

Is there not in this tendency to distort (or to perpetuate distortion) some elements of that mythologizing idealization that Malinowski characterized as a society creating a self-justifying "charter"?[12] Indeed, a certain type of informant was found to introduce an element of distortion, consciously or unconsciously, as a form of self-justification or wish fulfillment. Mr. D. R., a handsome man of jet black color but ungrizzled hair which he proudly plastered straight, was the eldest son of the centenarian Mrs. M. R. Himself an elderly man, Mr. D. R. had been for sixty years an unswerving servant and (though illiterate) field headman at Worthy Park, like his father before him. Before the researchers met Mr. D. R., they discovered that a white bookkeeper of the same surname had resided on the estate in the 1780s. Since it was well known that elite workers such as headmen were often colored bastards of plantation whites, it was suggested to one of Worthy Park's present owner-managers that perhaps Mr. D. R., the hereditary headman, was descended from the eighteenth-century bookkeeper. The manager, when he next saw D. R., jokingly remarked on the possibility, finding it humorous because of the headman's unequivocal blackness. D. R., however, was not surprised at the suggestion. "Dat explain," he replied proudly," why me hair so good."

It was subsequently discovered that D. R.'s descent from his bookkeeper namesake was virtually impossible. The bookkeeper had left Worthy Park by 1790, whereas the first laborer of that surname did not appear in the Worthy Park lists before 1846. Nonetheless, when interviewed in 1973, D. R. (who predictably was nominated the most likely informant by Worthy Park's owner-manager) told the researcher, as a matter of fact, that he was descended from "One white 'busha from slavery days.'" Thereafter it was not surprising that D. R. proved to be one of the least reliable of all informants.

D. R. was, however, an explicable, if fairly extreme, type of informant. He was an hereditary servitor, and his position of subordinate authority resulted from slavish fidelity to the plantation ethos. His was the classic "Quashee Personality" in the sense that subscription to dominant norms and stereotyping in return for status led in due course to unquestioning belief in the norms and fulfillment of the stereotype.[13] Some elements of this type of distortion were apparent in most persons living close to Worthy Park. Even those inhabitants of Lluidas Vale who vocally resented the estate's dominance and worked for wages only when they had to did not hesitate to accept the largesse periodically handed out as an act of *noblesse oblige*, or to participate enthusiastically in official estate celebrations such as the Tercentenary of 1970. Praedial larceny was not commonly condemned, and it was regarded as more proper for a person caught redhanded to beg the manager for mercy than to be carried to the police station and the criminal courts. The owner-managers were still regarded as the fount of justice and bounty. The fact that they were white was part of the natural order of things. The persistence of the self-perpetuating stereotype of the Negro—allegedly lazy, larcenous, alternately sullen and manic, craven and childlike—does not need to be stressed.

Elements of distortion were far less common among those who

owed nothing to Worthy Park Estate, such as the proud stoics of Cock-crow. They were without a conscious "society charter," but they were attracted naturally as much to an African past, now almost faded beyond recall, as to the dominant European, white, Christian culture. If the politicians, writers, and teachers continue to encourage negri-tude, in due course the African past may exclusively be called upon to provide the "society charter." Though sufficiently valid, this process will be a somewhat artificial one, relying on education and media dis-semination rather than authentic recall at the local level.

Already the oral researcher has to be extremely careful to distinguish between true oral traditions and those received as educaitonal feedback. No equivalent was found in Lluidas Vale to the ludicrous situation in West Africa, where modern anthropologists found the Ga and Akwapim elders themselves conversant with and heavily reliant upon the research findings of an earlier anthropologist.[14] Nonetheless, there were some obvious cases of feedback and many anecdotes and im-pressions of suspicious provenance. The question of the informant's degree of literacy was important, though not in such simple ways as was at first supposed. Those with a relatively good education would be expected to reinforce their testimony from knowledge received in school or books. Yet, to a heartening degree, most informants dis-tinguished quite clearly between facts on slavery received from books and teachers, and local oral traditions. Their education seemed to give them greater knowledge and greater discrimination as well. On the other hand, it might be presumed that illiterate informants would provide a simpler, yet more authentic, testimony. In fact, much of their testimonies (particularly in the cases of middle-aged illiterates) was not only simple, but also ignorant and riddled with unacknowledged borrowing. To illustrate both the drawbacks and the indirect value of such testimonies, it is useful to quote a summary of all the perceptions of "slavery" detailed by Mr. R. C., a semiliterate smallholder born in outlying Juan de Bolas in 1911:

1. Slaves were under the absolute control of a master. They were given no pay but were *kept.*

2. The masters were all white men. They were called "backra" because they kept the slaves' backs raw with whipping.

3. Slaves ran away when they could, particularly into a local "cock-pit" called Barn's Pen. There their "duppies" [ghosts] could still be

seen—a benign type which loved to gather round fire, appearing either as fireflies or ghostly flames.

4. The name Lluidas was originally Spanish, like the old name for Spanish Town [Santiago de la Vega].[15] St. Ann's Bay was once a Spanish seaport for Lluidas Vale.[16] The old Jamaican coin called a "quattie" was originally Spanish.[17]

5. The slaves were freed by Queen Victoria on August 1.[18] This day was celebrated annually until independence.

6. The Jamaican Creole dialect is basically African.[19]

7. Africa was once a rich country. White men plundered it with the aid of "Black Judases."

Clearly, such testimony has some real value, but in general it was the intelligent elderly with an antiquarian bent like Mr. I. B., or the very elderly preliterate illiterate like Mrs. M. R., who provided the most convincing, consistent, and original details. One partial exception was Mr. R. B. of Long Hill, scarcely older than Mr. R. C. At first, he professed ignorance, having had no schooling; but when encouraged, he "remembered" authentic details unlikely to have been taught in local schools. He reported that the superannuated Worthy Park slaves were still provided for by the masters, but skimpily, and that the mothers of six children were excused from manual work.[20] He also gave the opinion that since slaves were bought and sold, only the fact that the owners had money made them masters. Only when further pressed did Mr. R. B. acknowledge, almost with surprise, that masters were exclusively white and slaves exclusively black.

To a greater or lesser degree, all that is detailed by oral tradition is mythical or at least affected by mythologization. Structural functional anthropologists would, of course, argue that myths are at least as relevant as historical facts.[21] "Whatever neger say," runs an old Jamaican proverb, "if a no so a nearly so."[22] Yet, it is vital to distinguish and separate, where possible, the elements of myth and fact. This proves a daunting task. Oral traditions are affected over generations by the same processes that transmute human memories during a single lifetime. What is thought to be memory becomes, after the first experience, the memory of a memory. Memories and traditions are subtly changed under the influence of changing circumstances, needs, and perceptions in a manner brilliantly described (specifically for individual memories) by Jean Piaget,[23] until what is regarded as fact becomes myth. After an unspecified number of generations, a whole corpus of folklore, folkways, and folk beliefs may persist, though the society and beliefs that originated them are long forgotten. This entire corpus provides wonderful scope for the anthropological, sociological, and historical imagination. Indeed, it has given rise to the concept of iconatrophy, the notion that folk tales enshrine the traces of a forgotten *ur* religion. The basic hypothesis of this concept supports the superstructure both of Sir James Frazer's *Golden Bough* and Robert Graves' *White Goddess*.[24]

Parallels of such processes can easily be found in the West Indies, not only in tracing the syncretic development of *voodoo* and *obi,* but more pervasively. For example, in the Lluidas Vale testimonies much can be made of the persistent belief in duppies, particularly slave duppies. Despite Christianity, the belief in "spirits" among Jamaican countryfolk of all ages is almost as widespread as one would expect it to be in rural West Africa. These Jamaican spirits consist not only of people's ghosts but also such terrific manifestations as the "Merrymaids" [mermaids] and the "Rolling [Roaring] Calf." Often they are associated with specific places—burial sites, rivers, trees, areas of "bush." At least five of the Lluidas Vale informants related the duppies directly to slavery. Besides Mr. R. C., who talked of the runaways' duppies in Barn's Pen, Miss E. R., daughter of the aged Mrs. M. R., mentioned that slave duppies were often seen where gourd trees, and "dragon's blood" croton bushes marked old slave burial grounds. Mr. H. O., an illiterate nonagenarian of Cockcrow, remembered being told as a child not to venture into the bush during holiday celebrations, for the slave dupplies were dancing there and might take him as one of their own. Mr. C. T. of Canoe Pond told of an empty metal cup thrown down by a duppy poltergeist, which was thereafter always kept full of water; and of ghostly whiplashes heard proceeding from Thetford to Cocoree on August 1.

Mr. E. B. was, as in all of his testimony, objective and circumstantial. He recalled that in the days when August 1 was still celebrated, no one would dare walk by the "breeze mill" at Thetford, for singing and drumming were said to be heard there, coming from the site of the old slave quarters. E. B. suggested that the old slaves were not Christians, but heathens, and that the custom of burying kinfolk in the houseyards was African in origin. His slave-born grandfather was buried on the family land at Rolling River, but E. B. had buried his parents in the churchyard, for fear of "spoiling the land"; that is, deterring potential purchasers.

Few of the inhabitants of Lluidas Vale are as dispassionate or perceptive as Mr. E. B. They believe in duppies as unquestioningly as they take part in the nine nights' ritual of the "setup" when someone dies. They also believe that the newborn are not fully human until they have survived nine days.[25] Traces of animistic religion are clearly retained, relating the spirits of the living to those of the dead and the yet-to-be-born, and associating all human spirits with what Christianity teaches is the inanimate world. Some connect these beliefs with slavery days, or even with Africa, but not in any systematic way. Indeed, one of the severest problems for the historian seeking to use oral traditions is that ordinary countryfolk have no awareness of most of the concepts in which sound historians are schooled; notions of historical truth, proportion, development, and morphology are unknown to them. At a basic level, nonliterate cultures rarely have any more sophisticated concept of time than that determined by the seasons of the year, the generations of important persons, or occasional phenomenal events.

In view of such ahistoricity what is the oral researcher to do with the gathered testimonies? Nearly all theorists of oral tradition agree that corroboration is necessary before oral testimonies become valuable historical material. Even M. J. Herskovits, who seized on evidence of African survivals in the West Indies wherever he could trace them, called oral traditions "soft" evidence—valid, but leading only to probabilities, which become certainties only with corroboration from other sources.[26]

Five types of corroboration appear to be available to West Indian, as to all, oral history researchers. That of which Jan Vansina makes most detailed analysis—textual correlation—is, however, of less practical use in the West Indian context. Verbatim testimony was virtually nonexistent in Lluidas Vale. The one partial exception was the "Tenke Massa" song that many informants remembered was sung at the August 1 celebrations as far back as 1880. The following six variants are quoted without comment to suggest the possibility of correlative analysis:

1. (Mrs. M.R., 100)   If you kick me, mi kick yu back;
                       Tenk you Massa.
                       If yu buck mi, mi buck yu back;
                       Tenk yu Massa.

	If yu lick mi, mi lick yu back; Tenk yu Massa.
2. (Mr. C.B., 80)	Massa, you buck me now and me buck you back; Massa, you kick me now and me kick you back; Massa, you beat me now and me beat you back.
3. (Mrs. C. B., 75)	Tenke Massa; Yu love mi, mi love yu; Tenke Massa.
4. (Mrs. A. B., 75)	Howdy Massa; Yu kick mi, mi kick yu back; Tenke Queenie.
5. (Mr. N.B., 70)	King give mi mi freedom; Tenke Massa.[27]
6. (Mrs. M.R., 100)	Driber 'tan mi side, but let mi talk to mi 'busha; Whan 'busha gan, is mi an' yu deyah; Howdy 'busha, tenke Massa.

A less specific correlation can be made between stories of similar content told by different informants. The most common anecdotes of all, related by more than a dozen persons, concerned the August celebrations. These celebrations ostensibly commemorated emancipation, but it is worth noting that they supplanted the traditional "Crop-over" saturnalia of slavery days—a brief interlude of legitimate catharsis involving feasting, singing, dancing, satire, and role reversal, during which a version of the "Tenke Massa" song may well have been sung. Several informants also recalled complex "Set Dances" from the days of their youth, which almost certainly date back to slavery days and even earlier.[28] Another credible common anecdote, recalled by three unrelated old persons, was that slave mothers were driven so hard that they carried their infants on their backs as they worked, slinging their breasts over their shoulders to suckle them.

Unfortunately, there are virtually no precise corroborations possible in Lluidas Vale of the type provided in parts of Africa by phenomenal events such as eclipses and natural disasters. At first hearing, anecdotes about "Charles Price Rats" seemed to provide a precise link with the distant past, since the slaveowning magnate after whom they were named, one of the owners of Worthy Park, died in 1772. Yet the label, applied to any large rat, is common usage throughout Jamaica, and its origin is now obscure.[29] A similar apparent link with the eighteenth century was the phrase "Lick-Batty Gutter," used by several informants to describe the Worthy Park aqueduct and said to refer to the savage driving of the slaves used to build it (in the 1750s). The plausibility of the link is weakened, however, by the concurrence of the obviously spurious etymology of the word "backra," attested to by a similar number of informants.[30]

References to external events dating back beyond present lifetimes were remarkably absent in the Lluidas Vale testimonies. The earliest specific reference was to "Missis Queen's Bogue's War" (the Boer War, 1899-1902) by Mr. E. B., born in 1884. At least this reference provides negative evidence to suggest that Lluidas Vale has until modern times been isolated and introspective. Of the experience of the Middle Passage of the slave trade, said by Stanley Elkins to have been "almost too protracted and stupefying to be called mere 'shock,'"[31] absolutely no trace remained.

For an historian, the most satisfying corroborations are those provided by archaeology and by estate and island records. In 1970, the oral tradition about Thetford's windmill was borne out by some hacking and digging at the traditional site,[32] and in 1973, another local tradition was vindicated over professional skepticism. Mrs. D. D. and her family at Juan de Bolas, an area where coffee had not been grown commercially in living memory, maintained that the ruins of Queenborough's old coffee factory were to be found in the valley below the house. An expedition with cutlasses indeed revealed ruins, but a preliminary exploration of their layout, coupled with the evidence from the island records that Samuel Queenborough had been a sugar producer in 1800, convinced the explorers that this was not a coffee but a sugar factory. More systematic uncovering, measurements, and comparison with plans of authentic coffee factories, however, convinced the explorers that the oral tradition was correct. Further corroboration was provided by island records showing that Juan de Bolas Estate switched to coffee production around 1820.

One way in which oral traditions could actually aid archeology is in identifying the exact sites of the five slave cantonments of Lluidas Vale, all of which have left no superficial traces. In a similar experiment, an aged Worthy Park retainer confidently pointed out boundary markers and lines of the separate estates, but they bore no possible relation to authentic old maps. While this example might not encourage optimism, it should be considered that the identification of ancestral homes and burial places might well be expected to be nearer the consciousness of local blacks than such owner-oriented matters as property demarcation.

Of all the enterprises undertaken in connection with the research in Lluidas Vale, none occasioned as much excitement as the family tree constructed for Mr. I. B., a genealogy at least as extensive and authentic as many of those to be found in *Burke's Peerage.* Three fortunate survivals in the fragmentary marriage and baptismal registers of St. John's Parish provided the key link between Mr. I. B.'s encyclopedic knowledge of his family relations and the family relationships that had been deduced for the entire Worthy Park slave population between 1783 and 1838. As a result, a family tree was provided for Mr. I. B. which included eight generations, dating back some 210 years to a slave called Sarah born at Worthy Park in 1763. Unfortunately, this geneaology has been the only one that has been established with any certainty. The factors responsible are the "three generation rule," the chaos in many Jamaican families, the custom of casually changing names, and the fragmentation of most parish records, rather than any great locational or social mobility.

The final method of corroboration possible is useful, if delicate: the correlation of oral testimony with early written accounts of folk and slave life. Of perhaps 250 different items of specific information about the past garnered from Lluidas Vale, the most exciting concerned small details of daily living not likely to be mentioned in local school history classes or to be read in most modern books. In these cases, such nineteenth-century social commentators as Underhill, Sewell, Phillippo, or even the eighteenth-century writers on slavery, Edwrds, Beckford, Long, Leslie, Sloane,[33] provide ways of correlating oral data with written records. In this category, the following were mentioned by Mr. E. B. and Mrs. M. R. alone: details of food eaten, such as salt herring and shad, corn meal (issued by the masters), and "cunny rabbit" (coney or agouti), as well as the distinctively West African dishes, *fu-fu* and *sham-sham;* clothing issued such as the linen trousers, smocks, and broad felt hats of the men, and the voluminous skirts, petticoats, and head kerchiefs of the women; the huts with their wattle-and-daub walls, grass roofs, earth floors, and hammocks; the double-ended, goatskin-covered *tambu* drum and bamboo flutes used for dancing; the punishments such as the driver's whip, the cat-o-seven-tails ("seven blows in one"), the treadmill at Linstead, and the fierce dogs used to track down runaways; and finally such miscellaneous items as cockfights, the clandestine making of "tin" sugar with wooden hand-mills, digging with hoes, and the importing of building bricks as ballast in the sugar ships. Such details are invaluable and should be gathered before they are finally lost; for even much of the folklore and many of the folkways recorded as common currency by Martha Beckwith as recently as 1919-1924 have already faded from memory.[34]

What findings then can be derived from this preliminary excursion into Lluidas Vale? Briefly, there are eight tentative conclusions:

1. Authentic oral traditions from the era of formal slavery have been almost eradicated. If they are worth preserving, they should be recorded soon.

2. The results of subliminal memory are as valuable as consciously remembered material, but both are likely to represent myths as fact.

3. The most plausible informants are the elderly, the least modernized, and the locationally rooted, but the nature of all testimony depends upon personal attitudes. These depend, in turn, as much upon individual characteristics as upon factual knowledge, eloquence, or even intelligence. Particularly noteworthy are age differences, family and community roles, employment histories, land and house tenures, types of education, and psychological characteristics. In this study, all testimonies were affected by the presence of the nearby sugar estate, which has been in continuous operation for over 300 years. Modern relationships clearly affected views of ancient slavery. Those informants with the most independent character tended to be the most objective, but there was a correlation between, on the one hand, independence and objectivity, and, on the other, the propinquity to and dependence (psychological as well as material) upon the estate.

4. In all oral testimonies, there is a tendency to *meld* the past and to make little historical differentiation between events. In Lluidas Vale, the overwhelming senses were of community and of an historical continuum. Slavery had left hardly more traces than the African past and far fewer than the culture of peasant and plantation society since 1838.

5. Slavery was felt to be something from the "bad old past," productive of cruelty, hardship, and alienation. Yet slavery, as commonly understood, clearly related not solely to the formal institution that

ended in 1838, but also the socioeconomic effects of the plantation system in general.

6. Political awareness and official mythology, as much as modernization, education, and the media, are currently helping to reshape the past. Political parties or ideological groups have almost obliterated the people's consciousness of the past—right or wrong—that overlays and changes memories or feelings genuinely held. Slavery has come to stand generically for the socioeconomic evils of the bad old days, but with a decidedly political slant. Until 1976 the official heroes of Jamaica were not primarily those who resisted and overturned formal slavery, but nineteenth- and early twentieth-century protopolitical figures such as George William Gordon, Paul Bogle, Marcus Garvey, and the modern political leaders Alexander Bustamante and Norman Manley.[35] Significantly, the celebration of Jamaican independence (1962) has now taken the place of the traditional August celebrations—a change that some of the older country people genuinely regret.[36]

7. The young (whose testimony plays little part in this study) are increasingly alienated from the plantation system as well as from the countryside and traditional ways. In contrast, amid the disorienting clamor and clutter of modernity, the elderly, much as their counterparts throughout the world, have retained some traces of nostalgia. In particular, they tend to long for the greater sense of community, the closer family links, and the familiar local culture of the days of their youth. They may even be ambivalent about the days of formal slavery, when, they believe, the social groups were more tightly knit and the old culture was in its purest form.

8. In this atmosphere of contrapuntal mythologization, it is now probably too late for oral testimony to be used either to add much information about formal slavery or to make an accurate judgment on whether the written sources have correctly depicted formal slavery. In the last analysis, the historian is driven back to his own traditional methods.

NOTES

1. Interviews, started in 1963, were first published as *Biografía de un Cimarron* (Havana, 1966); translated as *The Autobiography of a Runaway Slave* (London: Bodley Head, 1968). In 1968, Andrew Salkey obtained an equally remarkable interview with Esteban Montejo, then aged 108; *Havana Journal* (London: Penguin, 1969), 166-185.

2. *Oral Tradition; A Study in Historical Methodology* (London: Penguin, 1973), 192. The book was first published as *De la Tradition Orale; Essai de Methode Historique* in the Annales du Musée Royal de l'Afrique Centrale, 1961, and was first published in English by Routledge and Kegan Paul, 1965.

3. Initially, this related only to a comparison of Worthy Park's Apprentice and first wage laborers of 1834-1846 with the workforce of 1963-1973; but the findings were corroborated by a comparison between these names and names drawn from the district immediately surrounding and from Jamaica as a whole. This research is being separately developed in a paper to be entitled "Sons of Slavery; Changes and Continuities in the Worthy Park Work Force, 1834-1973." Like the research on which the present essay is based, it is to be incorporated in a forthcoming book, *Searching for the Invisible Man; Slaves and Plantation Society in Jamaica,* to be published by Harvard University Press in 1977.

4. Specifically, the Bono-Mansu, Rwanda, Hawaiians, Marquesas, Maoris, Incas, and Aztecs; Vansina, *Oral Tradition,* 31.

5. William C. Bates, "Creole Folk-lore from Jamaica," *Journal of American Folklore* 9:38-42, 121-126; Ada W. Trowbridge, "Negro Customs and Folk-stories of Jamaica," ibid., 279-287; Frank Cundall, "Folk-lore of the Negroes of Jamaica," *Folk-lore* 15:87-94, 206-214, 450-456; 16:68-77; Martha W. Beckwith, *Black Roadways; A Study of Jamaican Folk Life* (Chapel Hill: University of North Carolina Press, 1929), reprinted by Negro Universities Press, 1970.

6. Frank Cundall, *Jamaica Negro Proverbs and Sayings* (Kingston, 1910), reprinted as *Jamaica Proverbs* (Irish Universities Press, 1972); Martha W. Beckwith, *Jamaica Proverbs* (New York, 1925), reprinted by Negro Universities Press, 1970.

7. This phenomenon was noticed, though on the way to dubious conclusions, by J. W. Dunne, *An Experiment with Time* (London: Faber, 1939).

8. Osnaburgh cloth, from Germany, for which there does not seem to be a modern reference in the literature.

9. For the distinction between "family," "buy," and rented land, see Edith Clarke, *My Mother Who Fathered Me; A Study of the Family in Three Selected Communities in Jamaica* (London: George Allen and Unwin, 1957), 33-69.

10. Cundall, *Proverbs,* No. 590.

11. As late as 1929, Martha Beckwith tended towards a description of "Obeah" that was little different from that found in eighteenth-century plantocratic writers; *Black Roadways,* 104-141. Orlando Patterson in *Sociology of Slavery; An Analysis of the Origins, Development and Structure of Negro Slave Society in Jamaica* (London: MacGibbon and Kee, 1967), 185-189, mainly follows Beckwith, attributing the spiritual elements in Jamaican Negro religion to "Myalism," which is clearly of Christian derivation. In comparison, see Edward Brathwaite, *The Development of Creole Society in Jamaica, 1770-1820* (Oxford: Clarendon Press, 1971), 218-220: ". . . in African and Caribbean folk practice, where religion had not been externalized and institutionalized as in Europe, the obeah-man was doctor, philosopher, and priest," ibid., 219.

12. B. Malinowski, *Magic, Science and Religion* (Boston, 1948).

13. The attitude is perhaps encapsulated in the quotation given by Miss L. A., aged 76: "To reap Eternity we must labour full time for the Lord"—applying it as much to the earthly master as to God. For a rather limited view of the Quashee Personality, see Orlando Patterson, *Sociology of Slavery,* 174-181, 285. This description shows many

282   Michael Craton

similarities to that of the American "Sambo" in Stanley M. Elkins, *Slavery; A Problem in American Institutional and Intellectual Life* (Chicago: University of Chicago Press, 1959), 131-132, 192, 227-228. Patterson's Quashee concept is viewed critically both in my *Sinews of Empire; A Short History of British Slavery* (New York: Doubleday, April 1974), Chapter 4, and my recent article, "Searching for the Invisible Man; Some of the Problems of Writing on Slave Society in the British West Indies," *Historical Reflections/Réflexions Historiques,* September 1974. In particular, it is pointed out that the true Quashee (who carried the Akan name for those born on Sundays or possessing certain special qualities) were usually favored, able, well-assimilated slaves—more akin to the traditional American "Uncle Toms."

14. Daniel F. McCall, *Africa in Time Perspective; A Discussion of Historical Reconstruction from Unwritten Sources* (Boston: Boston University Press, 1964), 60.

15. The origin of the name Lluidas is certainly obscure. It first appears around 1670 as "Luidas," without the Welsh-sounding double "l." There is a faint chance it may be Spanish, though a corruption of "Lloyd's" seems more plausible.

16. St. Ann's Bay was the site of the first Jamaican "capital," Sevilla la Nueva (1510-1524), but it was not used as a port for Lluidas Vale sugar until the early twentieth century.

17. There was no such coin. A "quattie" was "three cents" or 1½d., that is, a *quarter* of 6d., a common silver coin of the British period; Beckwith, *Black Roadways,* 49.

18. This clearly applies to "Full Freedom" on August 1, 1838, since Queen Victoria did not become queen until 1837. The first Emancipation Act came into effect on August 1, 1834, in the reign of William IV. See below, note 27.

19. Of course, it is not. Africanisms—vocabulary and constructions—comprise the second largest component of Jamaican Creole, but amount to less than 10 percent; Frederic G. Cassidy, *Jamaica Talk; Three Hundred Years of the English Language in Jamaica* (London: Macmillan for the Institute of Jamaica, 2d ed., 1971), 394-397.

20. This was a fact, following a local act passed in 1787.

21. Vansina, *Oral Tradition,* 12-14.

22. Beckwith, *Proverbs,* No. 865. This editor, however, provides a very dubious explanation, for some reason equating "neger" with "obeah-man."

23. "Throughout our life, we reorganise our memories and ideas of the past, conserving more or less the same material, but adding other elements capable of changing its significance and, above all, of changing our viewpoint." Jean Piaget and Bärbel Inhelder, *Memory and Intelligence* (London, 1973).

24. Sir J. G. Frazer, *The Golden Bough* (New York, 1907-1913); Robert Graves, *The White Goddess* (New York, 1948).

25. During the research period in Lluidas Vale in 1973, a memorable setup occurred, conforming closely to the accounts given in Beckwith, *Black Roadways,* 70-87, and Edith Clarke, *My Mother Who Fathered Me,* 217-227.

26. M. J. Herskovits, "Anthropology and Africa; A Wider Perspective," *Africa* 29 (1959):230. Jan Vansina cites many descants on this theme, mainly relating to African research *(Oral Tradition,* 8-18).

27. It seems strange that only one middle-aged informant should attribute emancipation to the king rather than the queen, except that it is plausible that the "Massa" thanked is actually William IV rather than God or the secular master. While on the topic of songs remembered, one informant, Mr. E. B., recited the chorus of a song he believed was African:

Talala Hey
Talala Hey
Talala Hey-la
Sy-mon Petre ha wan harss fe charm dem!
28. Brathwaite, *Creole Society*, 220-225; Patterson, *Sociology of Slavery*, 231-236.
29. Many countryfolk recall that "Charles Price Rats" were once smoked and eaten. This may refer to the *agouti* or Jamaican coney. Some commentators have speculated that Sir Charles Price introduced the canepiece rat *mus sacchivorus* into Jamaica; others, that the "Charles Price Rat" is the mongoose, introduced into Jamaica long after the time of Sir Charles Price; Michael Craton and James Walvin, *A Jamaican Plantation; The History of Worthy Park, 1670-1970* (London: W. H. Allen; Toronto: University of Toronto Press, 1970), 93.
30. In fact, it is almost certainly from the West African *mbakara,* "he who surrounds, or governs"; Cassidy, *Jamaica Talk,* 155-156. The whole question of local variation in dialect usage, and the ways in which even such excellent books as Cassidy's *Jamaica Talk* can be normative, needs further study. For example, two Lluidas Vale informants testified to the uses of *Bunga-men* for Africans (adj. *bungu*) without any of the disparaging connotation ascribed to the term by Cassidy—as to almost all generic African labels, including the common modern usage "quashy-fool"; *Jamaica Talk,* 157-159.
31. Elkins, *Slavery,* 100.
32. This in turn was corroborated by a close examination of Hekewill's panoramic view of Lluidas Vale in 1793, which disclosed a windmill on Thetford's hillock, almost obscured by trees; London, Public Record Office, C.O. 441/4/4; Craton and Walvin, *A Jamaican Plantation,* 173.
33. Perhaps the best short bibliographies of Jamaican material with a predominantly anthropological and sociological slant are given in Beckwith, *Black Roadways,* 229-233, and Cassidy, *Jamaica Talk,* 407-417.
34. Though there must be some doubt that all the traditions recorded by Miss Beckwith in 1919-1924 actually still existed then. The author had an unfortunate habit of mixing up her own researches with the findings of previous writers. One anecdote at least, the custom of fellow-feelings among Middle Passage "shipmates," is even taken from Bryan Edwards (1793), without a later citation; Beckwith, *Black Roadways,* 54; Bryan Edwards, *History, Civil and Commercial, of the British Colonies in the West Indies,* 3 vols. (London, 1793), II, 95. The expression crops up again in Cassidy (1961), *Jamaica Talk,* 156, 399.
35. One thinks, in contrast, of the public statues in Port-au-Prince: heroes of the revolution against slavery and imperialism such as Toussaint and Christophe, but also a magnificent representation of *Le Marron Inconnu.* Political campaigning in Jamaica provides a treasury of cultural ambivalence. In 1973, for example, Michael Manley campaigned successfully on a combination of radical rhetoric, negritude, and the Judaeo-Christian connotation of his nickname, "Joshua," sensibly playing down the reflected charisma that came from being the son of one of the official heroes of Jamaica. In 1976, Manley's government added to the pantheon of national heroes Samuel Sharpe, leader of the 1831 slave rebellion, and Nanny, the legendary Maroon.
36. "What independence they give we ma'm? You think we got independence?" commented one old lady. Perhaps, however, she was merely echoing a similar skepticism that might have been heard in the old days about the nominal freedom celebrated on August 1.

Bibliography

The references that follow are categorized in accordance with the area, time, and topic of the essays in this volume. These are only selected items; for more extensive references, consult the bibliographies of the individual essays.

JOURNALS

Carribbean Review
Caribbean Studies
Handbook of Latin American Studies
Hispanic American Historical Review
Journal of African History
Journal of Inter-American Studies and World Affairs
Latin American Research Review
Luso-Brazilian Review

AFRICAN BACKGROUNDS
West Africa

SURVEYS

Davidson, Basil. *A History of West Africa* (New York: Anchor, 1966).
Fage, J. D. *Introduction to the History of West Africa* (Cambridge, Mass.: Cambridge University Press, 1970).
Osae, T. A., S. N. Nwabara, and A.T.O. Odunsi. *A Short History of West Africa: A.D. 1000 to the Present* (New York: Hill and Wang, 1974).

Monographic Studies

Akinjogbin, I. A. *Dahomey and Its Neighbours, 1708-1818* (Cambridge, Mass.: Cambridge University Press, 1967).
Alagoa, E. J. *A History of the Niger Delta* (London: Oxford, 1972).

_____. *The Small Brave City-State. A History of the Nembe-Brass in the Niger Delta* (Madison: University of Wisconsin Press, 1972).

Crowder, Michael. *A Short History of Nigeria* (New York: Praeger, 1966).

Dike, K. Onwuka. *Trade and Politics in the Niger Delta* (Oxford: Oxford University Press, 1956).

Fage, J. D. *Ghana: An Historical Interpretation* (Madison: University of Wisconsin Press, 1969.

Feierman, Steven. *The Shambaa Kingdom: A History* (Madison: University of Wisconsin Press, 1973).

Gamble, D. P. *The Wolof of Senegambia* (London: Oxford, 1957).

Herskovits, Melville. *Dahomey, an Ancient West African Kingdom* (New York: J. J. Augustin, 1938).

Ikime, Obaro. *Merchant Prince of the Niger Delta* (New York: Africana, 1969).

Kopytoff, Jean Herskovits. *A Preface to Modern Nigeria: The "Sierra Leonians" in Yoruba, 1830-1890* (Madison: University of Wisconsin Press, 1969).

Newberry, Colin. *The Western Slave Coast and Its Rulers* (Oxford: Oxford University Press, 1961).

Polanyi, Karl. *Dahomey and the Slave Trade* (Seattle: University of Washington Press, 1968).

Ryder, Alan F. C. *Benin and the Europeans, 1485-1897* (Cambridge, Mass.: Cambridge University Press, 1967).

Vansina, Jan. *The Tio Kingdom of the Middle Congo, 1880-1892* (London: Oxford, 1973).

Central and Portuguese Africa

Birmingham, David. *Trade and Conflict in Angola: The Mbundu and Their Neighbours under the Influence of the Portuguese, 1483-1790* (Oxford: Oxford University Press, 1966).

Chilcote, Ronald. *Portuguese Africa* (Englewood Cliffs, N.J.: Prentice-Hall, 1967).

Duffy, James. *Portugal in Africa* (Baltimore: Penguin, 1963).

_____. *Portuguese Africa* (Cambridge, Mass.: Harvard University Press, 1961).

Isaacman, Alan. *Mozambique: The Africanization of an Institution. The Zambesi Prazos 1750-1902* (Madison: University of Wisconsin Press, 1972).

Vansina, Jan. *Kingdoms of the Savanna* (Madison: Wisconsin Press, 1968).

Wills, A. J. *An Introduction to the History of Central Africa* (New York: Oxford University Press, 1973).

The Atlantic Slave Trade

Curtin, Philip. *The Atlantic Slave Trade. A Census* (Madison: Univeristy of Wisconsin Press, 1969).

Duignan, Peter, and Clarence Clendenen. *The United States and the African Slave Trade 1619-1862* (Stanford: Stanford Unviersity Press, 1963).

Studer, Elena F. S. *La trata de negros en el Rio de la Plata durante el siglo xviii* (Buenos Aires, 1958).

Verger, Pierre. *Bahia and the West Coast Trade, 1549-1851* (Ibadan: Ibadan University Press, 1964).

_____. *Flux et reflux de la traite des nègres entre le golfe de Benin et Bahia de Todos os Santos du 17ᵉ et 19ᵉ siècles* (The Hague: Mouton, 1968).

AFRICAN LIFE IN THE AMERICAS BEFORE ABOLITION
General

Cohen, David, and J. P. Greene. *Neither Slave Nor Free* (Baltimore: Johns Hopkins University Press, 1972).

Pescatello, Ann M. *The African in Latin America* (New York: Alfred A. Knopf, Inc., 1975).

Hispanic America

Aguirre Beltrán, Gonzalo. *La población negra de México* (México D.F., 1946).

Aimes, Hubert H. S. *A History of Slavery in Cuba, 1511-1868* (New York, 1907).

Barrett, Ward. *A Mexican Sugar Hacienda* (Minneapolis: University of Minnesota Press, 1970).

Bowser, Frederick P. *The African Slave in Colonial Peru, 1524-1650* (Stanford: Stanford University Press, 1973).

Corwin, Arthur. *Spain and the Abolition of Slavery in Cuba, 1817-1886* (Austin: University of Texas Press, 1967).

Dias-Soler, Luis M. *Historia de la esclavitud en Puerto Rico, 1493-1890* (Rio Piedras: University of Puerto Rico Press, 1965).

King, James F. "Negro Slavery in New Granada" in James F. King, ed. *Essays in Honor of H. E. Bolton* (Berkeley and Los Angeles: University of California Press, 1945).

Klein, Herbert. *Slavery in the Americas: A Comparative Study of Virginia and Cuba* (Chicago: University of Chicago Press, 1967).

Knight, Franklin. *Slave Society in Cuba During the Nineteenth Century* (Madison: University of Wisconsin Press, 1970).

Lockhart, James. *Spanish Peru, 1532-1560* (Madison: University of Wisconsin Press, 1968).

Mellafe, Rolando. *La esclavitud en Hispanoamerica* (Buenos Aires, 1964). Translated as *The History of Negro Slavery in Latin America* (Berkeley and Los Angeles: University of California Press, 1976).

_____. *La introducción de la esclavitud negra en Chile: Trafico y rutas* (Santiago de Chile, 1959).

West, Robert. *Colonial Placer Mining in Colombia* (Baton Rouge: Louisiana State University Press, 1952).

Portuguese America (Brazil)

Bethell, Leslie. *The Abolition of the Brazilian Slave Trade* (Cambridge, Mass.: Cambridge University Press, 1970).

Conrad, Robert. *The Destruction of Brazilian Slavery* (Berkeley and Los Angeles: University of California Press, 1972).

Degler, Carl. *Neither Black Nor White* (New York: Macmillan, 1971).

288 Bibliography

Eisenberg, Peter. *The Sugar Industry of Pernambuco, 1840-1910* (Berkeley and Los Angeles: University of California Press, 1973).
Fernandes, Florestan. *The Negro in Brazilian Society* (New York: Columbia University Press, 1968).
Goulart, Mauricio. *Escravidão africana no Brasil* (São Paulo, 1950).
Pierson, Donald, *Negroes in Brazil* (Carbondale: Southern Illinois University Press, 1968).
Stein, Stanley. *Vassouras. A Brazilian Coffee County 1850-1900* (Cambridge, Mass.: Harvard University Press, 1957).
Toplin, Robert Brent. *The Abolition of Brazilian Slavery* (New York: Atheneum, 1972).
Viotti da Costa, Emilia. *Da Senzala a Colônia* (São Paulo: Corpo e alma do Brasil, Difusão Européia do Livro, 1966).

French America-Caribbean

Elisabeth, Leo. "The French Antilles" in David Cohen and J. P. Greene, eds. *Neither Slave Nor Free* (Baltimore: The Johns Hopkins University Press, 1972), 134-171.
Gisler, Antoine. *L'esclavage aux antilles francaises (17ᵉ-19ᵉ siecle): Contribution au problème de l'esclavage* (Fribourg: Editions Universitaires Fribourg Suisse, 1965).
Hall, Gwendolyn Midlo. *Social Control in Slave Plantation Societies. A Comparison of St. Domingue and Cuba* (Baltimore: Johns Hopkins University Press, 1971).
Herskovits, Melville. *Life in a Haitian Valley* (New York: Alfred A. Knopf, Inc., 1937).
James, C.L.R. *The Black Jacobins* (New York: Random House-Vintage Books, 1963).

British Caribbean

SURVEY
Lowenthal, David. *West Indian Societies* (Oxford: Oxford University Press, 1972).

SPECIFIC STUDIES
Adamson, Alan. *Sugar Without Slaves: The Political Economy of British Guiana, 1838-1904* (New Haven: Yale University Press, 1972).
Bennett, J. Harry. *Bondsmen and Bishops: Slavery and Apprenticeship on the Codrington Plantations of Barbados, 1710-1838* (Berkeley and Los Angeles: University of California Press, 1958).
Craton, Michael. *Sinews of Empire. A Short History of British Slavery* (New York: Doubleday, 1974).
Curtin, Philip. *Two Jamaicas. The Role of Ideas in a Tropical Colony 1830-1865* (New York: Atheneum, 1970).
Gouveia, Elsa. *Slave Society in the British Leeward Islands at the End of the 18th Century* (New Haven: Yale University Press, 1965).
Hall, Douglas. *Five of the Leewards 1834-1878* (Barbados: Caribbean University Press, 1971).
Handler, Jerome S. *A Guide to Source Materials for the Study of Barbados History, 1627-1834* (Carbondale: Southern Illinois University Press, 1971).
_____. *The Unappropriated People: Freedmen in Barbados Slave Society* (Baltimore: Johns Hopkins University Press, 1974).
Herskovits, Melville, and Frances Herskovits. *Trinidad Village* (New York: Alfred A. Knopf, Inc., 1947).

Jayawardena, Chandra. *Conflict and Solidarity in a Guianese Plantation.* (London: Athlone Press, 1967).

Patterson, Orlando. *The Sociology of Slavery: An Analysis . . . in Jamaica* (London: MacGibbin and Kee, 1967).

Sheridan, Richard. *Sugar and Slavery. An Economic History of the British West Indies 1623-1775* (Baltimore: Johns Hopkins University Press, 1974).

Wilson, Peter J. *Crab Antics: Social Anthropology of English-Speaking Negro Societies in the Caribbean* (New Haven: Yale University Press, 1973).

Dutch Caribbean

Buschkens, W.F.L. *The Family System of the Paramaribo Creoles* (The Hague: Martinus Nijoff, 1974).

Hartog, J. *Curaçao: From Colonial Dependence to Autonomy* (Aruba, 1968).

Herskovits, Melville. *Surinam Folklore* (New York: Columbia University Press, 1936).

Hoetink, H. "Surinam and Curaçao" in David Cohen and J. P. Greene, eds. *Neither Slave Nor Free* (Baltimore: Johns Hopkins University Press, 1972), 59-83.

Lier, R. A. J. van. *Samenleving in een grensgebied: een sociaal-historische studie van de maatschappij, in Surinam* (The Hague: Nijoff, 1949).

OTHER GENERAL STUDIES ON THE SLAVE TRADE, SLAVERY, ABOLITION, AND POSTABOLITION

Cruz, Guillermo. *La abolición de la esclavitud en Chile* (Santiago, 1942).

Curtin, Philip. *Africa Remembered: Narratives by West Africans from the Era of the Slave Trade* (Madison: University of Wisconsin Press, 1967).

Davidson, Basil. *Black Mother* (London, 1961).

Davis, David Brion. *Problem of Slavery in Western Culture* (Ithaca: Cornell University Press, 1966).

Deerr, Noel. *The History of Sugar,* 2 vols. (London: Chapman and Hall, 1949-1950).

Hoetink, Harry. *Slavery and Race Relations in America* (New York: Harper, 1973).

Lombardi, John. *The Abolition of Slavery in Venezuela* (Westport, Conn.: Greenwood Press, 1971).

Mörner, Magnus. *Race and Class in Latin America* (New York: Columbia University Press, 1970).

_____. *Race Mixture in the History of Latin America* (Boston: Little Brown & Co., 1967).

Whitten, Norman. *Black Frontiersmen: A South American Case* (New York: Halsted [Wiley], 1974).

_____. *Class, Kinship, and Power in an Ecuadorian Town* (Stanford: Stanford University Press, 1965).

CONTEMPORARY RACE RELATIONS AND MAJOR THEORETICAL WORKS ON THE BLACK EXPERIENCE IN THE AMERICAS

Abrahams, Roger. *Deep Down in the Jungle: Negro Narrative Folklore from the Streets of Philadelphia* (Chicago: Aldine Publishing Company, 1970).

_____. *Deep the Water, Shallow the Shore* (Austin: University of Texas Press, 1974).

_____ (edited with John Szwed). *Discovering Afro-America,* special issue of the *Journal of Asian and African Studies* (Leyden: E. J. Brill, 1975).

Aptheker, Herbert. *American Negro Slave Revolts* (New York: Columbia University Press, 1943).

Bastide, Roger. *Les Ameriques Noires: Les Civilisations Africaines dans le Nouveau Monde* (Paris: Payot, 1967).

_____. *Les Religions Africaines au Bresil* (Paris: PUF, 1961).

Bastien, Rémy. *La familia rural Haitiana* (Mexico, DF: Libra, 1951).

Bernard, Jessie. *Marriage and Family Among Negroes* (Englewood Cliffs, N.J.: Prentice-Hall, 1966).

Blake, Judith. *Family Structure in Jamaica* (New York: Free Press, 1961).

Clarke, Edith. *My Mother Who Fathered Me* (London: Allen and Unwin, 1957/1966).

Craton, Michael. *History of the Bahamas* (Collins, 1962/1967).

_____. *A Jamaica Plantation* (Toronto: University of Toronto Press, 1970).

_____. *Searching for the Invisible Man* (Cambridge, Mass.: Harvard University Press, 1976).

Courlander, Harold. *The Drum and the Hoe: The Life and Lore of the Haitian People.* (Berkeley and Los Angeles: University of California Press, 1960).

Crowley, Daniel. *I Could Talk Old Story Good: Creativity in Bahamian Folkore.* (Berkeley and Los Angeles: University of California Press, 1966).

Engerman, Stanley, and Eugene Genovese. *Race and Slavery in the Western Hemisphere: Quantitative Studies* (Princeton: Princeton University Press, 1974).

Fogel, Robert, and Stanley Engerman. *Time on the Cross* (Boston: Little Brown and Co., 1974).

Frazier, E. Franklin. *The Negro Family in the United States* (Chicago: University of Chicago Press, 1939).

_____. *The Negro in the United States* (New York: Macmillan, 1957.)

Genovese, Eugene. *Roll, Jordan, Roll* (New York: Pantheon, 1974).

_____. *The Slave Economies,* 2 vols. (New York: Wiley, 1973).

Gonzalez, Nancie L. *Migration and Modernization: Adaptive Reorganization in the Black Carib Household* (Seattle: University of Washington Press, 1969).

Henriques, F. M. *Family and Colour in Jamaica* (London: Eyre and Spottiswoode, 1953).

Herskovits, Melville. *The Myth of the Negro Past* (New York: Harper, 1941; Boston: Beacon Press, 1958).

Hoetink, Harry. *Two Variants in Caribbean Race Relations* (London: Oxford University Press, 1967).

Leyburn, James. *The Haitian People* (New Haven: Yale University Press, 1941).

Olien, Michael. *The Negro in Costa Rica: The Role of an Ethnic Minority in a Developing Society* (Winston-Salem: Wake Forest University, 1970).

Smith, M. G. *The Plural Society in the British West Indies* (Berkeley and Los Angeles: University of California Press, 1965).

_____. *West Indian Family Structure* (Seattle: University of Washington Press, 1962).

Smith, Raymond, T. *The Negro Family in British Guiana* (London: Routledge and Kegan Paul, 1956).

Whitten. Norman, and John Szwed, eds. *Afro-American Anthropology* (New York: Free Press, 1970).

Index

292   Index

ABOUT THE EDITOR

Ann M. Pescatello is the senior research associate at the Center for South and Southeast Asia, University of California, Berkeley, and is also the director of the Council on Intercultural and Comparative Studies. Specializing in Spanish and South Asian history, she has written numerous articles for such journals as the *Journal of Asian History*. Her previous books include *The African in Latin America* and *Power and Pawn: The Female in Iberian Families, Cultures, and Societies* (Greenwood Press, 1976).